BACKING INTO THE LIMELIGHT

A Biography of T.E. Lawrence

T.E. Lawrence was hailed as a sensitive genius and denounced as a neurotic fraud. The fiction and the facts of his extraordinary life have been fused into one of the most intriguing and widely publicized stories of the twentieth century. For Michael Yardley, after three years of extensive research that took him to the Middle East, Texas and even to Hollywood, the most interesting thing about Lawrence is not what he was but how he was perceived. In his biography Yardley sets out to peel away the disinformation, distorted memories and pure fantasy from the facts and examines the origin and development of Lawrence as a media hero. He has also managed to uncover new material about Lawrence, including important, previously unpublished letters concerning Lawrence's relationship with the Press and with the American journalist and lecturer Lowell Thomas.

Michael Yardley is a freelance journalist and broadcaster specializing in the subjects of terrorism, weaponry and defence.

HARRAP PAPERBACKS

BACKING INTO THE LIMELIGHT
A BIOGRAPHY OF T.E. LAWRENCE
By Michael Yardley

JOHN BUCHAN
A MEMOIR
By William Buchan

MY CHINA YEARS
By Helen Foster Snow

A NARROW STREET
By Elliot Paul

HOLLYWOOD, ENGLAND
THE BRITISH FILM INDUSTRY IN THE SIXTIES
By Alexander Walker

NATIONAL HEROES
BRITISH CINEMA IN THE SEVENTIES AND EIGHTIES
By Alexander Walker

THE MGM GIRLS
BEHIND THE VELVET CURTAIN
By Peter Harry Brown and Pamela Ann Brown

THE WARNER BROTHERS
By Michael Freedland

BACKING INTO THE LIMELIGHT

A BIOGRAPHY OF T.E. LAWRENCE

Michael Yardley

HARRAP
London

To Tara

First published in Great Britain 1985
by HARRAP LIMITED
19–23 Ludgate Hill, London EC4M 7PD

This edition first published in 1986

ISBN 0 245–54473–9

Designed by Robert Wheeler
Photoset, printed and bound in Great Britain by
Redwood Burn Limited, Trowbridge, Wiltshire

Contents

Illustrations

Maps

Acknowledgments

Had it not been for the constant help and support of my friends and family this book would never have been published. I take this opportunity to offer them my warmest thanks. I would also like to thank all those (and especially the volunteers) who have helped with the typing, research and editing. Similarly, I owe a great debt to all the individuals with specialist knowledge who have consented to being interviewed and who have, in many cases, provided me with vital new documentary material for which I am particularly grateful. Effective journalism, biography or literary criticism is not possible without such gestures. Finally, I would like to thank all those who have been involved in the production and publication of this book.

Quentin Able
Peter Ackroyd
H. B. St John Armitage CBE, OBE
Graham Baird
Rosemary Baker
Dr Caroline Barron
Richard Butterworth
Julia Cave
Robert Cockburn
Douglas Collard OBE
Professor W. R. Cornish
Simon Dally
Jennie Duley
Julian Fergusson
Julian Fox
The late Sir Geoffrey Furlonge KBE, CMG
Martin Gilbert
Colin Graham
Christopher Greenwood
Betty Herbert
David Gwyn Jones
Roland Hammersley DFM
Harold Harris
Roger Horsnell
K. S. Hosain
Christina Hutchins
Peter Jones
Phillip Knightley
Joyce Knowles
The late Pat Knowles
Professor Ariel Lant
Hugh Leach
Rodney Legg
David Loman
Jim Lucas
Jacqui Lyons
Kathy McGrath
Professor David Martin
Tony Martin
Krikor Mazloumian
Edwards H. Metcalf
Jeffrey Meyers
Otto Mikkelsen
Adam Miller
Roy Minton
Suleiman Mousa
The Rt Hon. Anthony Nutting
Nicole Paulissen
Lt Col. Adrian Peck OBE
Walt Pitman
Dr J. B. Post
Mary Rees-Pyves
Sian Rhys
Edward Robinson

Alistair Rosenschein
Pamela Ruff
Lynda Schulman
Simon Scott
Amanda Shaw
Peter Simonis
Christopher Sinclair-Stevenson
Jane Thomas
Viscount Trenchard
David Watkinson
Robert Wheeler
Anne Wilson
John Witherow
John Yardley
Tara Yardley
Vivien Yardley

For permission to quote copyright material, my thanks are due to the following:

The Letters of T. E. Lawrence Trust, The Seven Pillars of Wisdom Trust and Professor A. W. Lawrence, for *The Letters of T. E. Lawrence* (Cape, 1938), *The Seven Pillars of Wisdom* (Cape, 1935; first trade ed.), *T. E. Lawrence by his Friends* (Cape, 1937) and *The Mint* (Cape, 1955); The Letters of T. E. Lawrence Trust and Professor A. W. Lawrence for *The Home Letters of T. E. Lawrence and his Brothers* (Blackwell, 1954), *T. E. Lawrence to his biographer Liddell Hart* (Faber, 1938) and *T. E. Lawrence to his biographer Robert Graves* (Faber, 1938); Messrs Jonathan Cape, Professor A. W. Lawrence and The Letters of T. E. Lawrence Trust, for letters in the restricted collection in the Bodleian, Oxford, T. E. Lawrence's letters to Charlotte Shaw in the British Museum, and any previously unpublished Lawrence letters (© 1985 The Letters of T. E. Lawrence Trust) not covered by the permission of Her Majesty's Stationery Office.

Neither Professor A. W. Lawrence nor the Trustees have given any other assistance in the writing of this book.

Other material quoted is used by kind permission of:

The Trustees of the British Museum (Archive letters relating to Carchemish; Dr Theresa Clay (as literary executor of Richard Meinertzhagen); Phillip Knightley (co-author of *The Secret Lives of Lawrence of Arabia*); John Murray Ltd for *The Independent Arab* by Hubert Young (1933); The Controller of Her Majesty's Stationery Office, for Public Records Office material and other Government documents; Dr Caroline Barron (literary executor of D. G. Hogarth); Times Newspapers Ltd; The Trustees of the Imperial War Museum; The Society of Authors (as agents for the estate of George Bernard Shaw).

Preface

T. E. Lawrence lies buried in a pyramid of half-truths. He died in 1935, having changed his name by deed-poll to T. E. Shaw, but the legend of Lawrence of Arabia lived on. The fiction and the facts of his extraordinary life have fused into one of the most intriguing and widely publicized stories of the twentieth century. The man, the myth and the motive have been examined in minute but not always productive detail. Hero; author; politician: the many aspects of T. E. Lawrence have been the subject of hundreds of newspaper and periodical articles, dozens of biographies (ranging in their approach from naïve sycophancy to open hostility), and a large body of academic work. His life has inspired an internationally successful play (Terence Rattigan's *Ross*) and David Lean's epic but controversial motion picture *Lawrence of Arabia*.

Controversy is a feature of the Lawrence phenomenon. He has been hailed as a sensitive genius drawn into the mayhem of war and the dishonourable world of *Realpolitik* and denounced as a neurotic fraud without any real affection for the Arabs, an imperialist agent whose own machinations and literary obsession led to mental breakdown. The self-appointed guardians of Lawrence's reputation fought, and still fight, to maintain his untarnished image. But the disclosures of, among others, Richard Aldington, Knightley and Simpson, and indeed of Lawrence himself, have meant that the reputation and the man had to be reassessed. However, in spite of the debunkers, the legend has adapted and survived. Fifty years after his death, Lawrence of Arabia is still news.

The enduring fascination of his story is hardly surprising. It has all the ingredients for several best-sellers – romantic and still topical settings, a classic wartime adventure, political intrigue, secret agents, revelations about the famous, mysterious clues, royalty, a personal scandal, conspiracy, human interest, philosophy, and a uniquely talented hero who is constantly trying to beat the system, who renounces high office to follow his chosen path among the humblest of men, and who dies in an accident which has never been fully explained. It is a dynamic story without a finite end. New facts about Lawrence conveniently appear as the Public Records Office declassifies another batch of files, or as an unpublished letter is brought to light. In my own researches I have discovered an unknown diary kept by Lawrence while he was working on RAF rescue boats. It will only, if ever, be published after its current owner's death.

The main problem for any biographer of Lawrence – and there have been over forty – is to peel away the disinformation, distorted memories and pure fantasy from the facts. Lawrence himself said that the best way to hide a truth is with a half-truth. The vast majority of books about Lawrence are frustratingly incomplete or inaccurate. Major questions about his life remain unanswered or tied up in riddles; vital material is still subject to the Official Secrets Act, or withheld by those otherwise entrusted with it. I have tried, whenever possible, to examine source material. This turned out to be a far greater job than anticipated, and has taken me to the Middle East, Texas and even to Hollywood.

My initial interest in Lawrence had been reinforced in 1980 when, as an Army officer, I was posted to Bovington in Dorset, where Lawrence, as T. E. Shaw, had enlisted as a private in the Tank Corps. Every morning I drove past the spot where he fell from his motorbike, fatally injuring himself. Intrigued by local rumours that his death was no accident, I started to read everything I could about him, and was fascinated to find a few elderly people, still living in the area, who had played a part in his life. I visited his cottage, Cloud's Hill, and was invited to tea by Pat and Joyce Knowles, the couple who kept it for the National Trust. I spent spare afternoons at their home opposite the cottage, accepting their hospitality, talking about Lawrence, beginning the notes that were the start of my research.

Pat's father, formerly a sergeant at the camp, had worked as a handyman for Lawrence, and Pat himself became a close friend, a fact borne out by their correspondence. Sadly, Pat died during 1981, but in our conversations and in examining his personal papers (many of them given him by Lawrence), it became obvious that a great deal had been kept secret for reasons which, at least superficially, appeared political. A deeper examination showed that people connected with Lawrence were often unconscious participants in a self-perpetuating conspiracy of secrecy.

A lot of material about Lawrence's life, especially when he was an operational intelligence officer, and about his subsequent involvement in Middle East politics, is lost to history. Records have been mislaid or destroyed, and information has been camouflaged in a mass of professional disinformation. Despite these and many other problems, I was able to find new material, including important unpublished letters concerning Lawrence's relationship with the Press and the American journalist and lecturer Lowell Thomas. In the vaults of the British Museum, I found interesting documents among the Reports and Accounts of the Carchemish dig in Syria, where Lawrence had been sent as an archaeological assistant in 1910, and where his activities in Intelligence may well have started. Similarly, in the Imperial War Museum there was a wealth of material relating to Lawrence's later career in Arabia and in the RAF, as well as evidence of a curious relationship between the Lawrence Trust and *The Sunday Times*. This dated from the 1960s, when the

Insight team wrote a series of revelatory biographical articles about Lawrence's personal life.

During the spring of 1981, while still stationed in Dorset, I was introduced by a friend of the Lawrence family to a gentle Dorset man who had been an eye-witness of Lawrence's fatal accident, and who to date had never come forward. His description of the accident made it clear that those accounts previously published, both officially and unofficially, were incomplete. (Later, when I contacted the person who had introduced me, I was first told that I had never met the witness, and subsequently that his story was not entirely accurate and that he did not want to be involved.)

The new material I had found encouraged me to embark on the project of this book. I visited Syria, Lebanon and Jordan (just as war broke out in the Middle East), and spoke to people who still had memories and information about Lawrence. By reporting on the war, I was able to extend my stay in the area. In Aleppo, Syria, I spoke to Krikor Mazloumian, owner of the Baron Hotel, where Lawrence stayed on his leave from the British Museum archaeological site at Carchemish. At Deraa, a friend found an old man who was an elder of the Shalan clan (who are frequently mentioned in *The Seven Pillars of Wisdom*), still a powerful family in Syria. His memories of Lawrence were second-hand but he stated that some boys of the Shalan are still called 'Aurens' today as a tribute of respect to Lawrence. On the other hand, the guide provided by the Syrian Ministry of Information said that Lawrence had been forgotten and was officially regarded as an 'imperialist spy'. Similarly, representatives of the Palestine Liberation Organisation were hostile and bitter in their opinions of Lawrence.

In Amman, Jordan, during the summer of 1982, I met and interviewed the distinguished Arab historian Suleiman Mousa, author of *T. E. Lawrence – an Arab view*.

In the winter of 1982, my wife and I went to the United States to examine the collections of Lawrence material there. Mr Edwards H. Metcalf, who has one of the most comprehensive Lawrence collections in the world, extended great kindness to us and made some very useful suggestions based on his fifty years of interest in the subject. The Humanities Research Center Archive at the University of Texas in Austin proved to be particularly important, as it contains a vast quantity of items connected with Lawrence, including originals of many letters of which there are only photostatted copies in the Bodleian Library in Oxford. At the Bodleian, unfortunately, scholars are not free to examine the collection. The material is barred until the year 2000, and because of this restriction another Lawrence mystery is effectively perpetuated. The Lawrence Trustees, who control the collection (and many of Lawrence's copyrights), have allowed access to a few 'suitable applicants'. To my knowledge, six people (apart from the Library staff) have been officially allowed access.

In Texas, we also found a wealth of fascinating, long-forgotten press cuttings and magazines which showed that Lawrence's fame in England has always been paralleled in the United States. Presented together, they provide a unique insight, not only into how Lawrence of Arabia was presented to the public, but also into the contemporary methods of the Press.

Suleiman Mousa in Amman had pointed out that the majority of books about T. E. Lawrence have used as their basis Lawrence's own writings, which are then quoted or rejected according to the author's point of view. This is partly explained by the fact that only recently could representative source material about Lawrence be easily obtained. Ironically, as documentary evidence has become available, many witnesses have died, but Richard Aldington, Phillip Knightley and Colin Simpson, Montgomery Hyde and Dr John Mack, have all made important discoveries about Lawrence. Even the best books on Lawrence have sometimes become bogged down in verifying and cross-checking frequently insignificant trivia. Aldington in particular demands a superhuman consistency in his victim. Lawrence was inconsistent – a not uncommon condition in human beings, especially those under extreme mental pressure. Bernard Shaw's wife, Charlotte, once said of him, half jesting, that he was such an 'infernal liar'. Shaw commented some years later that Lawrence was not a liar but 'an actor', a man who played many roles.

It was never my intention to write a conventional biography, though I have tried to answer many of those questions most frequently asked about Lawrence, in addition to many new ones posed by my research. But I have also been concerned not only with Lawrence's reputation but with its nature; not only with the reality but with the media's perception and presentation of it.

The process is everywhere evident today. Newspapers, magazines, radio, television, the cinema – all play their part as a new 'personality' emerges. The public is bombarded with information in which the distinction between fantasy and reality remains blurred. This may be due to deliberate distortion or prejudice, or it may arise from simple confusion on the part of the recipient.

In considering these questions, we are faced with the philosophical issue of the nature of reality. Which is more 'real', the experience of an event in the minds of those it affected at first hand – who may be but few in number – or the description of the event in the contemporary media? The two may be substantially different, but both are only perceptions, and it is evident that the media depiction, which may not be accurate, can still have far-reaching consequences, and becomes an 'event' in itself. I have had first-hand experience, in Eastern Europe and in the Middle East, of how distorted the media version of a serious event may become. The media's portrayal of Lawrence's life has certainly been misleading. By examining the origin and development of Lawrence as a media hero, it may be possible to observe how, and why, such distortions take place.

Particularly important in considering Lawrence's case was the development of 'scientific' propaganda by men like Lord Beaverbrook and John Buchan at their Ministry of Information. This, I believe, is an area which deserves far more attention than it has yet received.

Was Lawrence a true hero, or only a media hero? Today, in the United States and in Great Britain, an individual can become a professional personality – famous only for being famous. Lawrence certainly became famous for being famous, but he continues to be famous, and one of the most intriguing aspects of public interest in his life is that it has endured over such a long period.

There was more to Lawrence than that. His exploits, as they have come down to us, are confused, but they were not entirely fictitious. Indeed, he performed acts of valour which have not been widely reported. A series of recent books (notably *The Illicit Adventure* by H. Winstone) have attempted to prove that the Arab Revolt, and Lawrence's contribution to it, may have been far less historically significant than previously thought. This does not mean that he was not a very brave man. Lawrence himself later conceded that he had only been involved in a sideshow in Arabia during the war, and this partially motivated his attempts to escape his Lawrence of Arabia image. The unconventional route he chose – joining the ranks of the RAF – was doomed to failure; inevitably drawing even more attention to him.

The key to understanding Lawrence both as a man and as a myth lies in understanding the imperial age into which he was born and his reaction to it. His later disillusionment was similar, if more intense, to that suffered by many of the young men who endured the First World War. For me, after three years of research, the most interesting thing about Lawrence is not what he was, but how he was perceived.

Michael Yardley

London
February 1985

Preface

to Paperback Edition

I have made no significant changes to the text of *Backing into the Limelight* for this new edition. I tried originally to write the book in a style which was unpedantic and which gave the reader plenty of information from which to draw his own conclusions. It is not, I believe, the job of the writer to lead the reader by the hand. Too often we are encouraged to write for a passive audience.

This book is intended to be both more and less than a biography. It describes a complex man with many paradoxical traits and the system which moulded him and against which he rebelled. It reveals, I hope, as much about politics and the media as it does about Lawrence the man.

It is amazing that over fifty years after his death, there are still those who believe it in their interests to withhold information about Lawrence and his political involvements. Perhaps it is not so amazing. Perhaps it is in the interests of those who would rule by oligarchy rather than open government.

In the meantime the partially self-created monster which consumed Lawrence is now attacking us all. We have become victims of the modern media machine. No doubt Lawrence would have commented interestingly upon the modern cancer of televised international terrorism.

Lawrence was one of the first people to be subjected to media hype, most notably for his terrorization of the Turks in Arabia, and he was one of the first to use the media methodically for his own political advantage. This process had significant historical consequences and a pathological effect, not least on Lawrence himself.

Lawrence has become an object of obsessive interest. To his 'fans' now, he is a Messianic figure. To his denigrators, a charlatan. Since completing my book I have come into contact with many people who I can only describe as possessed. They are not possessed by Lawrence the man but by their own perception of Lawrence. Lawrence can be all things to all men and women. Herein lies his secret.

Michael Yardley

London, May 1986

PART ONE

1 Childhood

The enigmatic and much publicized figure of T. E. Lawrence, alias LAWRENCE OF ARABIA, has become synonymous with romantic adventure. During the twenties Fleet Street dubbed Lawrence 'The Mystery Man' because of his unorthodox life-style and the cloak of secrecy in which he enshrouded himself. It seems appropriate, therefore, that the Lawrence legend should begin with a family background that was not only melodramatically unconventional but was also a closely guarded secret until twenty years after his death.

The story begins in the middle of the 1880s when an Anglo–Irish squire called Thomas Chapman left wealth, a wife and four daughters to run away with his family's nursemaid, a Miss Lawrence. Chapman adopted his lover's name, and their union, though never sanctioned by a marriage certificate, resulted in five sons. T. E. Lawrence, who would later become famous as Lawrence of Arabia, was the second son. It must have come as a terrible shock to the future hero when he discovered, probably in his teens,[1] that his apparently respectable parents were not married, and that Lawrence was not his father's real name; ironically, it was not even his mother's.

Several writers have suggested that illegitimacy is the key to understanding Lawrence's complex personality. He certainly went to elaborate lengths to conceal it, as might anyone brought up in the late Victorian era. However, Lawrence's attitude towards his illegitimacy was ambivalent, and became more so in later life. He disclosed and even joked about the facts of his birth to his close friends, forthrightly proclaiming his disdain for bourgeois convention, but then involved them in a sometimes bizarre conspiracy to prevent his secret becoming public, while making sure that the world at large was aware of his aristocratic heritage.

The information Lawrence gave to his biographers was vague and misleading, and resulted in a legacy of half-truths and disinformation which continued well beyond his death in 1935. It was not until the publication in 1955 of Richard Aldington's carefully researched but rather spiteful book *Lawrence of Arabia – a biographical enquiry* that the basic facts of Lawrence's background and birth were given wide publicity. Even then, friends of the Lawrence family tried to prevent publication for a variety of reasons, not least because Lawrence's mother was still alive. By persistent detective work,

Aldington pieced together Lawrence's family tree. Since his book, several other biographers have added important details which Aldington may not have published for legal reasons; the story remains by no means complete.

Thomas Robert Tighe Chapman, Lawrence's father, was born in 1846 of a Protestant landowning family of considerable means in Ireland's County Westmeath. The Chapmans had originally come from Leicestershire and, as cousins of Sir Walter Raleigh, had been favoured with a large land grant in County Kerry. The family had subsequently run into financial problems and were forced to sell their estates, but later, through their support of Cromwell in the Irish Rebellion, were again granted land, this time in County Westmeath. There they firmly established themselves, and Benjamin Chapman III became a member of the Irish Parliament and was made the first Chapman baronet in 1782. The house of Chapman continued to prosper through the next several generations. Lawrence's father was the nephew of the fourth baronet and cousin to both the Chapmans who succeeded to the title thereafter. When his older brother died in 1870 Thomas stood in line to succeed his cousin Benjamin Rupert as the seventh baronet. Thomas was linked to another powerful family through his mother, Louise Vansittart, who was related to Henry Vansittart, a member of the Hell Fire Club. Lord Vansittart, secretary to Curzon and inter-war Cassandra, was a further connection.

In 1873 Thomas Chapman married a cousin, Edith Boyd Hamilton. They lived in a substantial house, South Hill, outside the village of Delvin in Westmeath, where he seems to have led the traditional existence of a prosperous country gentleman. By the hazy accounts that survive, the marriage was not a happy one, though the couple had four daughters, the last being born in 1882.

It was to look after these girls that Chapman's estate manager arranged for a young Protestant woman to come from Scotland. Her name was Sarah Junner, though she had previously used the name Maden and, confusingly, was known in the Chapman household as Miss Lawrence. The reason for these several names was that Sarah was illegitimate. The daughter of a Norwegian shipwright journeyman and an English mother, she had been brought up very strictly by an aunt in Scotland whose husband was an Episcopalian minister. The aunt was no doubt relieved when a suitably respectable position was found for the child of sin with whose care she had been entrusted and in whom she had instilled a lifelong sense of guilt.

Sarah was good at her job and attractive – slight, with intense blue eyes (characteristics inherited by her second son). Exactly who initiated the affair between Thomas Chapman and Sarah is open to doubt; T.E. later told Charlotte Shaw, Bernard Shaw's wife who became a friend in the 1920s, that his mother had 'jealously' carried his father from his former life and subsequently kept him 'as her trophy of power'.[2] Whatever the truth, Thomas fell in love with Sarah, and somehow she overcame her strong religious convictions to allow him to set her up as his mistress in Dublin. Here, on 27 December 1885, she gave birth to their first son – Montague Robert, known as Bob – and soon afterwards, as the risk of public disgrace became even greater, Thomas, Sarah and the baby adopted the name Lawrence and left Ireland for Wales, where they were not known and their secret was likely to remain safe. One must at least respect Thomas and Sarah for taking a step which, even a hundred years later, would be considered courageous.

Thomas Chapman's wife Edith has been painted as a 'holy viper', a fanatically religious woman who made her husband's life a misery.[3] Such a description could in fact be applied equally to Sarah. However, the stories about Edith Chapman are not well supported and may have resulted from an attempt to justify her husband's behaviour by those sympathetic to him and his second family. In any event, Thomas Chapman left her and their daughters with most of his wealth, and though it has been reported that he continued to visit Ireland occasionally in order to attend to estate responsibilities, it is unlikely that they ever met again. His daughters, who all remained unmarried during their long lives, followed the career of their half-brother with great interest. Edith never granted her husband a divorce and took on the title of Lady Chapman in 1914 when the sixth Chapman baronet died – Thomas was of course unable to use his title, and his illegitimate sons to inherit it – and when her husband died in 1919 she informed the Home Office of 'Sir Thomas's' death.[4]

Once in Wales, Thomas and Sarah rented a small house in Tremadoc, Caernarvonshire, and it was here that in August 1888 Thomas Edward Lawrence was born. According to his birth certificate, the date was the 15th, but his mother wrote that he had actually been born in the early hours of the 16th.[5] Lawrence usually acknowledged the 16th as his birthday, and this was the date entered on his educational records and apparently celebrated by his family. At school, however, he would show off to classmates by telling them that he shared Napoleon's birthday, 15 August; as one contemporary wrote, 'Thus early was the future taking shape.'[6]

Lawrence's birth in Wales later enabled him to accept an Oxford scholarship reserved for Welsh students, even though he only spent a year of his life there, for in 1889 his parents – always covering their tracks – decided to move on to Kirkcudbright in Scotland.

Lawrence never claimed to have anything but a tenuous connection with Wales, and would gloss over his recent family history when giving information about himself to writers, while at the same time making sure they made reference to his blue-blooded ancestry.

The first book on Lawrence, *With Lawrence in Arabia* (1924) by the American Lowell Thomas, is a highly entertaining and thoroughly unreliable account of Lawrence's exploits in Arabia with a few inaccurate biographical notes thrown in for good measure. From these it is clear that Lawrence gave away as little real personal information as possible, leaving Thomas to elaborate colourfully.

Thus Thomas wrote: 'When we first met in Jerusalem . . . I was unable to draw Lawrence out about his early life', and 'The War had so scattered his family and early associates that I found it difficult to obtain aught but the most meagre information about his boyhood.' 'But in his veins . . . flows Scotch, Welsh, English, and Spanish blood.' Thomas then went on to associate Lawrence with a fictitious Crusader knight, 'Sir Robert Lawrence'.[7]

Although Lawrence denied it, he was the source for much of the book's material, and clearly enjoyed pulling Thomas's leg, inventing several comic escapades. He may well have envisaged that the book would be widely read, but he could not have foreseen its immense success – it went into a hundred printings, and was still available in the 1970s.

Lawrence took more care with his 'licensed' biographers Robert Graves and Basil Liddell Hart, realizing that the books they produced would be the subject of careful scrutiny.

Both these distinguished writers accepted Lawrence's control and censorship of their manuscripts, and allowed him to make extensive alterations. A typical example of this manipulation is a brief genealogical sketch Lawrence wrote for Graves to include in his biography *Lawrence and the Arabs* (published in 1927). It was preceded by a carefully worded explanation for Lawrence's change of name after the Great War and a hint at his illegitimacy:

> A good enough excuse for discarding the name Lawrence was that it never had any proud family traditions for him . . . 'Lawrence' began as a name of convenience like 'Ross' or 'Shaw,' . . . Actually he [Lawrence] is of very mixed blood, none of it Welsh; if I remember rightly it is Irish, Hebridean, Spanish, and Norse . . . His father . . . came from County Meath in Ireland, of Leicestershire stock settled in the time of Sir Walter Raleigh . . .[8]

In Liddell Hart's book, *'T. E. LAWRENCE' in Arabia and After* (published in 1934), as in Graves's, there is again a hint at illegitimacy: 'The friends of his manhood called him 'T.E.', for convenience and to show that they recognised how his adopted surnames – Lawrence, Ross, Shaw, whatever they were – did not belong.'[9] When in 1926, only a year before the publication of Graves's book, David George Hogarth, Lawrence's academic mentor and ex-commanding officer (an accurate though too rigid description of their relationship), asked Lawrence what he would like to be written in a proposed article on him for the *Encyclopaedia Britannica*, Lawrence wrote back in extraordinary fashion, using black ink for information that might be published and red ink for information that was to be kept secret. He expressly forbade him to draw attention to Raleigh.[10] And when another friend, Lionel Curtis, wrote to ask what to include in Lawrence's entry in *Who's Who*, Lawrence replied 'Of course write anything you please', but added that it should not give away his 'original family' nor his 'present address'.[11]

Such contradictions recur throughout Lawrence's life. It was a dilemma he never resolved. He was obviously proud of his distinguished ancestry and wanted it to be known, even if in veiled form; but another more self-critical, introspective aspect of him despised this vanity. Similarly, in a rational mood he would like to believe that his illegitimacy did not matter, but he never seems to have convinced himself, though the rebel in him does seem to have been attracted to the idea of being the bastard son of an aristocrat.

Although illegitimacy would be a burden to all their children, Thomas and Sarah continued to expand their family. Their third son, William – Will to his brothers – was born in late 1889 in Scotland, and for his birth certificate Mr and Mrs Lawrence invented a marriage at St Peter's Church, Dublin. Two years later, the growing family moved again, via the Channel Islands to France, arriving in Normandy in March 1891. Here Bob and Ned, as T.E. was always called at home, attended a local Jesuit school, although they were not of course Catholics, and seem to have been little influenced by the experience. Twice a week the two boys would also attend private gymnastic classes at St Malo in the company of three other English boys. From babyhood Ned was notable as 'a big, strong, active child; constantly on the move';[12] in contrast to his elder brother, who was slower physically and academically.

'Mrs Lawrence' became pregnant again in 1892, and to ensure British nationality for the new baby, went across temporarily to St Helier in the Channel Islands to have her child. On 7 February 1893 Frank Helier Lawrence was born in Jersey,[13] his middle name indicating that his parents were not without a sense of humour. After Frank's birth the family returned to France. The following year they moved yet again, this time permanently back to England. They leased a rural cottage at Langley on the borders of the New Forest, which would remain their home for the next two years. A private governess was hired to teach the boys, with supplementary coaching in Latin from a local schoolmaster.

The Lawrence parents were clearly anxious for their sons to be well educated, and this, together perhaps with a sense of more security in their new identities, may well have been behind their decision to move to Oxford, where a good education could be found at reasonable cost. Finance was an important consideration, for Lawrence's father, following the habits of his class, never took on full-time work and depended on the modest annual income of about £300 from his Irish estate. Sarah, however, was an expert housekeeper, and it is much to her credit that though the family had to live frugally, lack of money never appeared as the handicap it could have been.

Another significant factor in the family's move to Oxford was that Sarah and Thomas had heard Alfred Christopher, Canon of St Aldate's, Oxford, preaching in Ryde in 1885. Christopher was an Evangelist, but unusually sympathetic and flexible, and it seems that Mrs Lawrence had confided in him something of her unusual circumstances. He had reassured the guilt-ridden woman that she was not beyond forgiveness, and to her he was a living example of a virtuous Christian. He was to become an important influence on the family when they moved to Oxford; Thomas Lawrence became a member of St Aldate's church council, and Sarah encouraged her sons to become involved in Canon Christopher's Evangelical movement.

The Lawrences moved to Oxford in 1896 and settled there permanently. They chose a recently built semi-detached house, number 2 Polstead Road, in a quiet middle-class area, and adopted a life-style in keeping with their surroundings. Shortly after they moved in, Ned went to explore the shed at the bottom of the garden and found a pipe which intrigued him. In order to satisfy the need to know, which was to become a feature of his life, he took a hammer and nail and pierced the pipe: water gushed forth and a plumber had to be called in to repair the damage. His brother Bob noted how this curiosity of Ned's developed so that by his teens 'Ned was always the one to mend any object, or find out what was wrong with the electric light, etc.'[14]

Ned, now aged eight, and Bob were enrolled at Oxford High School, which had opened in 1881 to cater for the increasing number of academic and professional families coming into the town. It had quickly developed an enviable reputation for scholarship successes to the university, and Lawrence remained a registered pupil there for the next eleven years until he won a scholarship to Jesus College, Oxford. All the Lawrence boys were educated at the Oxford High School, and in the morning they would cycle to school in single file ranked according to age, each wearing an identical striped blue and white jersey.[15] The age gap between the eldest and youngest was considerable, for the fifth son, Arnold, was not born until 1900. T.E. was particularly fond of Will (later, like Frank, killed in the First World War), but he developed a very special and affectionate relationship with his youngest brother, whom he sometimes called the 'little worm'.[16] (En masse he referred to his brothers as 'the worms'.)

On one occasion, when Lawrence was about fifteen, he took Arnold to the Ashmolean Museum but the small boy became frightened by the statues and asked 'Are they all alive?' After they got back home T.E. carved a face on a rock and gave Arnie a hammer, telling him to smash the face and so prove to himself that it was not alive.[17]

As the boys grew up, it was T.E. who naturally assumed the role as leader. One school friend remembered how 'Out of this prolonged family Lawrence II gradually became distinct by a spareness of body and a pithy energy of speech.'[18] A master at the school noted that he was 'one of few words, self-possessed, purposeful, inscrutable';[19] he was developing into an individualistic and strong-willed boy.

Lawrence did well academically but not outstandingly, and cherished no fond memories of school. He later wrote to Liddell Hart: 'School was usually an irrelevant and time-wasting nuisance, which I hated . . .'[20] His reaction is hardly uncommon, even though his school was a particularly good one. He was oppressed by the regimentation, and developed a particular loathing for organized games; he was upset when his brother Frank became a member of the cricket team.

He was certainly no stranger to corporal punishment, which in adulthood would become an obsession with him. Sarah Lawrence was a strict disciplinarian and it was she rather than her husband who administered beatings on the boys when she thought it necessary. In his brilliantly researched book *A PRINCE OF OUR DISORDER: The Life of T. E. Lawrence*, John Mack relates how Sarah once told Arnold: 'I never had to do it to Bob, once to Frank and frequently to T.E.'[21] The beatings were vigorous and administered to the bare behind of the offender.

Lawrence enjoyed teasing others in a friendly way, but hated to be the recipient of such jibes – a characteristic which he retained throughout his life. A school-friend, E. F. Hall, remembers how Lawrence would wait by the sports field and as each new player arrived, would 'explain to us our merits or deficiencies judged by the Greek standard of physical excellence. I was never certain if this was sheer affectation. . . .'[22] On other occasions, according to Hall, T.E. would silently join a group of boys discussing sports 'contemplating us with that provocative smile of his, till one of us would seize him and close in friendly wrestling. . . .'[23]

Hall continues that it was on one of these occasions that Lawrence broke his leg. However, his mother claimed that this event – which happened at some stage before his sixteenth birthday – occurred when he 'went to the rescue' of a small boy being bullied at school.[24] She suggested that this accident might explain why T.E. did not grow much afterwards, as 'the bones were not strong',[25] a rather unlikely hypothesis for her son's short stature. Lawrence took after her in physical appearance. He had a small but muscular body, unbalanced by a large head, and constantly fidgeting small hands. Despite this, he was handsome, almost pretty, with his mother's extraordinary blue eyes, and a 'curiously nervous smile' and soft voice.[26]

Perhaps Lawrence's smallness explains his fear of being measured against other boys on the playing-field. He would rather prove his worth on his own terms, following the harshest self-inflicted rules. Hall noted Lawrence's 'iron will',[27] 'ruthlessly fast-driven'[28] brain, his generosity and craving to be liked – characteristics also mentioned by other school-friends. Hall also pointed out that Lawrence himself later wrote in *The Seven Pillars of Wisdom* that his craving to be liked was 'so strong and nervous' that it prevented him from ever opening up fully to another human being.[29]

Arnold Lawrence has stated that the root of his brother's emotional problems was their mother's dominance.[30] Mrs Lawrence, although she was very strict, almost sadistic in her puritanism, was also intensely loving and demanding. She lived through her sons, hoping they might atone for her own failings by taking up the Evangelistic principles which she regarded as the only route to salvation. Apart from regular church attendance, there were daily bible readings at home; Lawrence became an officer in the Church Lads Brigade for two years and taught at Sunday school until, so the story goes, he was dismissed for reading a poem by Oscar Wilde to his students.[31] During their short lives Will and Frank remained devout Christians, and Bob was in fact in China doing missionary work when T.E. died in 1935.

When she was dying in an Oxford nursing-home, Mrs Lawrence kept repeating to herself, 'God hates the sin but loves the sinner',[32] an indication of the guilt she had long suffered and of her stern religious principles. She had considerable hopes for Ned in his childhood, describing him as 'a constant worshipper'[33] who was 'constantly reading the Oxford Helps to the Study of the Bible'.[34] For the first nineteen years of his life, Lawrence did apparently accept the religion he was force-fed, yet as soon as the chance arose he began to give up its formal practice. Nevertheless, the Calvinistic Protestantism with which he had been indoctrinated remained a permanent influence, and provides some, though not a complete, explanation for the masochistic self-denial which became a feature of his life. As a teenager, Lawrence would test his stamina by forbidding his body food and rest, and retrospectively Mrs Lawrence appears to have seen her son's self-imposed training as evidence of his divine mission in life.

Lawrence's struggle to break away and become independent of his mother's stifling will is a feature of his teenage years. All children must go through some similar type of conflict, but in Lawrence's case a successful, mature relationship with his mother was never achieved. He wrote to Charlotte Shaw many years later that no trust had ever existed between his mother and himself; 'I always felt she was laying siege to me, and would conquer, if I left a chink unguarded.'[35] And in another letter to her, he wrote that he was afraid of his mother getting 'ever so little inside the circle of my integrity'.[36] As John Mack noted, this phrase is very similar to one Lawrence used later in *The Seven Pillars of Wisdom* when he described an incident in which he was homosexually abused by the Turks, and lost forever 'the citadel of my integrity'.

Throughout his life, T. E. Lawrence remained terrified that his mother was trying to overwhelm him, although paradoxically he also admitted to being excited by her. It is clear from his post-war letters, especially those to Charlotte Shaw, that he could not forgive or respect his father for being defeated by his mother's will. Thomas Lawrence seems to have been a loving and gentle man who left the day-to-day running of the home, and the discipline of his children, to his strong-minded partner. Yet there was much that was positive about the Lawrence home; apart from living in a well-run, comfortable house, the boys had parents who, despite imposing stern religious discipline, were also genuinely loving and supportive, allowing their sons considerable freedom to travel and pursue their own interests.

The father took an active interest in his children's education and passed on to them his own interests. He encouraged the boys to go cycling, and frequently accompanied them. He enjoyed photography, and T.E. claimed that his father taught him to take photographs before his fourth birthday. This is typical exaggeration, and similar to another boast in which Lawrence stated that he was reading newspapers – 'chiefly police news' – at the same age.[37] However, without doubt Lawrence was a gifted and determined child who picked up skills quickly, and the unsubstantiated yarns about his childhood achievements are similar to those which develop around many other heroic figures. The difference in this case is that Lawrence himself began many of them, often half in jest, but since they were taken up by friends, early biographers and his family, an image of Lawrence the youthful superman resulted.

Lawrence evidently felt the need of a forceful father-figure and created an image of Thomas Lawrence that would fit more into his desire. The kindly, rather distant and elderly friend that Lawrence's father was by T.E.'s Oxford days bears no resemblance to the hard-drinking (Mrs Lawrence ensured that Polstead Road was teetotal) and tough sportsman that Lawrence imagined him to have been in Ireland. It was as a sporting figure that Lawrence described his father to both Lowell Thomas and Robert Graves.

The enjoyment of cycling encouraged by his father enabled Lawrence to escape the rigid confines of home and pursue his youthful interests, which led him beyond the narrow, exam-orientated syllabus of school. He was fascinated with the past, and would cycle many miles to visit churches, castles and ancient buildings. Brass-rubbing was a particular hobby, and even in his teens he would not allow convention to hinder his pursuit of it. His school companion on one of these expeditions, T. W. Chaundry, remembers that some pews covered the brasses from which Lawrence wished to take impressions: 'Lawrence, already ruthless, made short work of the obstruction, and I still hear the splintering woodwork and his short laugh, almost sinister to my timorous ears.'[38]

Lawrence's most consistent school chum, C. F. C. 'Scroggs' Beeson, has recorded, 'Many a trespass was committed in Lawrence's company' and that the two boys were once caught in the crypt of St Cross in possession of human bones.[39] Lawrence, ever resourceful, talked their way out of it. Beeson also recalled that Lawrence, unlike most boys of their age, was not interested in the natural sciences and yet 'had an almost involuntary power of assimilating its technical terms and storing them in memory to be used in the fullness of time in correct context'.[40]

Lawrence read extremely widely but his interest focused on history. He enjoyed epic romances and was fascinated by the Crusades. As one might expect of a boy whose interests were essentially connected with castles and knights in armour, he came to identify with one of England's most romanticized monarchs, Richard I. John Mack has pointed out that Lawrence created another conflict here because Richard Cœur de Lion, despite his popular reputation, was capable of abominable atrocities – as Lawrence would have been aware.[41]

A love of books, and not merely their contents, was to remain with Lawrence throughout his life. In 1904, while still at school, he met an undergraduate, Leonard H. Green, who shared this passion. In those days it was forbidden for schoolboys to visit undergraduates in their college rooms, but, as Leonard Green wrote, 'we took a fearful pleasure in disregarding this rule'.[42] It was with Green that Lawrence first discussed a fantasy that reappears over the coming years – to buy or build a deserted country dwelling, in Green's case a windmill, and live an idyllic life printing precious books.[43]

Leonard Green probably brought Lawrence into contact with the writings of a group of romantic poets, later called the Uranians, some of whom were known personally to Green. This group, which included Oscar Wilde's lover, Lord Alfred Douglas, used poetry to describe the love of men for each other – usually it was the love of an older man for a boy. This is not to imply any overtly sexual relationship between Lawrence and his older friend, but the relationship conformed to a pattern typical of Lawrence's life as a young man, in which his intimate acquaintances, if any, were men.

There is very little evidence on the subject of Lawrence's sexual development in adolescence. Mrs Lawrence is known not to have had much time for girls in her house, and very likely she discouraged any youthful liaisons. According to one story, Lawrence was caught at school in the act of mutual masturbation with another boy, and having been nearly expelled, was soundly thrashed by his mother.[44] And Scroggs Beeson noted that Lawrence was not becoming as interested in girls as he was.[45] But to the outside world, to his family, and to a lesser extent himself, Ned Lawrence was a healthy, bright and energetic teenager, even if highly idiosyncratic. E. F. Hall has written: 'Of his powers and his ability we had no doubt, but it is safe to say that none of us then recognised in him a future leader of men. His eccentricity seemed too pronounced.'[46]

Hall is probably correct: Lawrence did not appear superficially 'leaderlike'. But it is equally clear that the young Lawrence recognized and developed his capacity for leadership. He combined the romantic and practical sides of his nature by devising various adventurous expeditions, which included aquatic escapades, usually on the river Cherwell, and all had in common a heroic goal set by Lawrence. In 1919, Lawrence told Richard Meinertzhagen, an intelligence officer he worked with during the war, that he had wanted to be a hero ever since childhood.[47]

At school Lawrence progressed well, and his father, sensing his son's need for privacy and a peaceful place to study, gave him the use of a shed at the bottom of the garden. Lawrence was working towards an Oxford scholarship, and it may be that the birth certificate he was obliged to produce in 1906 in order to enter for a qualifying examination was the means by which he found out about his illegitimacy. Whatever reasons lay behind it, Lawrence went through a serious crisis when he was seventeen and ran away from home. He bicycled to Cornwall and joined up as a soldier in the ranks of the Royal Artillery. Little else is certain. Lawrence mentioned the episode in several letters later in his life, including one to Liddell Hart in which he stated: 'This is hush-hush. I should not have told you. I ran away from home . . . and served for six months.' He went on to make the unusual comment, 'No trouble with discipline, I having [sic] always been easy.' However, even though he could accept, perhaps even like, the security of Army discipline, Lawrence also admitted that his fellow-soldiers 'frightened me with their roughness'.[48]

On other occasions Lawrence claimed to have served anything from 'a while' to 'eight months' in the Artillery. He could not, however, have served for any more than three months because there is no longer gap that cannot be accounted for, and in all probability his father, having established what had happened – perhaps after a letter or telegram from his son – bought T.E. out after only a few weeks.

In June 1906, after losing time at school, Lawrence failed his first attempt at an Oxford scholarship. He had already, on 30 April, been granted permission by the governing body of the Oxford High School to stay on an extra year – probably the result of a request from Lawrence's father following the Army episode. Lawrence changed his principal subject from mathematics to history and was sent by his parents to have supplementary private coaching from an Oxford tutor, L. Cecil Jane. Jane noted that his pupil, although bright, was not a scholar by temperament and had to be coaxed into new areas of study via his own special interests.[49] With Jane's help Lawrence settled down to his work again and made steady progress.

In the summer holiday of 1906, Lawrence and his friend Beeson set off on a cycling tour of the Normandy and Brittany coasts. The trip went well initially but Beeson decided to return home after two weeks – perhaps the boys had had a quarrel. Lawrence stayed on for another fortnight making, as was his habit, extensive notes on all castles and historic buildings he visited. Medieval latrines seemed of particular interest and were frequently described in his letters to his mother, perhaps in a deliberate adolescent attempt to shock her. Similarly, he occasionally signed off his letters 'ta ta', an expression unlikely to go down well in a household where pub was not a nice word. Yet at the same time Lawrence's correspondence with his mother is intensely affectionate. Thus in one of his first letters from France, he ends 'Love. love, love. love. love. love', and though as one follows the correspondence the protestations of love become fewer and fewer and eventually disappear, one senses that Lawrence is constantly trying to earn his mother's approval while also trying to break away from her.[50]

Lawrence and Beeson remained friends after the trip, and in the autumn of 1906 they made use of a major development in Oxford to unearth various small archaeological 'finds'. Lawrence began to take an interest in ancient pottery and used a system which he later was to adopt in Syria, whereby the workmen on the building sites were given cash bonuses for putting aside any articles of interest. To authenticate their discoveries, the two young men spent a great deal of time in the Ashmolean Museum, where Lawrence already knew a young graduate, Leonard Woolley, who was then a junior assistant keeper. His early acquaintance with Woolley can be positively verified as Lawrence mentions him in a letter home from his first cycling tour in August 1906.[51] It was probably Woolley who introduced Lawrence to the distinguished archaeologist and intelligence expert Dr D. G. Hogarth, who was to play a crucial role in Lawrence's life.

Lawrence was also befriended by another, older man at the Museum, E. T. Leeds, the Assistant Keeper. In recalling his first impressions of Lawrence, Leeds remembered his 'quietude'. 'No hammering on the door, no sudden appearance startling out of concentration, but a silent, unassertive presence slipping into one's consciousness, to ask a question, to bring in some new-gathered relic of Oxford's past, or to further towards fulfilment some self-appointed task.'[52]

In January 1907 Lawrence sat and passed a scholarship exam to Jesus

College, Oxford; there was an additional bonus of £40 as part of a special award reserved for students born in Wales. In March, Lawrence also passed another important examination – the first part of his degree, even though he was still at Oxford High School. Later that month Lawrence received a form from school requesting his advice to other students on how to win a scholarship; his reply was published in the school magazine:

> How can one annexe a vacant emolument? is a question often asked by aspiring youngsters in the Fifth, anxious to shape their ends. Leaving Mathematics and Classics to others, it is my duty to discuss History. History, the refuge of the destitute, provides annually many exhaustions. One wants more than history as it is understood in schools. Dates disgust, facts undigested nauseate, encyclopaedic information aggravates. One must write a nice style: to cultivate this a seat in the back desks in the library on Tuesday and Friday afternoons is essential. Then one must be archaeological. In all my vivas antiquities have been the most important topic: in the last, especially, the merits of collection of pottery and brass-rubbings engrossed the attention of the examiners. In books one must admire Bryce's *Holy Roman Empire* and profess a liking for Stubbs' *Constitutional History*. A large stock of epigrams and the usual copy-book maxims are appreciated. Unkind critics laud the advantages of birth in Wales, or any other of the countries that have conquered England. It should be remembered that no person is so ignorant that he cannot increase our stock of knowledge from him?[53]

During the spring of 1907 Lawrence spent two weeks exploring castles in Wales on his bicycle – perhaps deciding that he ought to learn something about Wales to justify his Welsh scholarship. On returning home for his last term at school, and now unburdened by exams, Lawrence had plenty of time to plan another cycling tour of France for that summer. This time he was accompanied by his father and a camera, and again he visited and made notes on castles in Northern France. Mr Lawrence stayed three weeks and then left his son to go on by himself, during which time Lawrence took the opportunity to join up briefly with Scroggs Beeson, who was also cycling in France. Lawrence, ever trying to prove his independence, then cycled on alone, eventually making his way to Jersey where his parents were holidaying. After a brief stay in the Channel Islands, he returned home to begin his studies at the university; he had no intention of being just another undergraduate.

2 Oxford

On Saturday 12 October 1907, T. E. Lawrence officially joined Jesus College, Oxford. In theory he was meant to take up residence in the college, but in fact, apart from the summer term of 1908, he continued to live at Polstead Road where his parents had a small bungalow built for him at the bottom of the garden. It was a sort of bachelor flat, replacing the converted shed that he had used earlier as a place of study. Of all their sons, the Lawrences only afforded T.E. this privilege, and it may well be that they were worried about the recurrence of a crisis similar to the one that led him to enlist in the Artillery. The building, which is still standing today, consists of a study and a bedroom, and gave T.E. the privacy he seemed to crave, for he took little part in the social and conventional sporting life of the college and remained reclusive. It also confirmed his special status. Leonard Green has described the little bungalow as the most silent place he had ever been in. The walls were draped with heavy cloth to cut out outside noise and there were cushions rather than chairs for sitting.[1]

T.E. was not, however, a hermit. He enjoyed visitors, though always on his own conditions and at his convenience – a trend which persisted throughout his life. It was his 'genius of friendship', as the author Henry Williamson was later to term it, that so many people accepted him on these terms. Soon after his arrival at Jesus, Lawrence met and befriended Vyvyan Richards, a third-year student who was half-Welsh and half-American. They shared an interest in books, especially those of William Morris – they cycled together to see the Kelmscott Chaucer at Morris's house at Broad Campden in Gloucestershire – and, as he had done with Green before, Lawrence envisaged setting up a private press. This time materials were actually bought, including oak beams from a demolished house, to put aside for the day when they would build a 'Pre-Raphaelite Hall'. The relationship between Lawrence and Vyvyan Richards was obviously close. Richards wrote later in his biography of Lawrence:

> The rest of my life at Oxford, rather more than a year, was spent in a golden atmosphere of almost daily companionship with this my new exciting friend while he was in Oxford. Nightly, too, I might have said; so often would his little racing bicycle come silently after midnight into the Iffley Road, where I lived in lodgings . . .[2]

Richards goes on to describe how Lawrence would get round college regulations by always being home by midnight – as was the rule – but then would pay 'his calls and went on manifold excursions after midnight',[3] returning home to sleep for a few hours and to take a hot bath. (Lawrence's ability to go without sleep has often been exaggerated, but there is little doubt that his need was considerably less than average.) Richards, who was in awe of his young friend, admitted in the late 1960s that he had fallen in love with Lawrence at first sight.[4]

> He had neither flesh nor carnality of any kind; he just did not understand. He received my affection, my sacrifice, in fact, eventually my total subservience, as though it was his due. He never gave the slightest sign that he understood my motives or fathomed my desire. In return for all I offered him – with admittedly ulterior motives – he gave me the purest affection, love and respect that I have ever received from anyone . . . a love and respect that was spiritual in quality. I realise now that he was sexless – at least that he was unaware of sex.[5]

Richards made some other important observations about Lawrence, notably that although he had few intimate friends, 'it was characteristic throughout his life for him to love to have some private "gallery" for his exploits . . .'[6] 'He wanted your admiration, your impressed wonder, it is true (he said so himself in after years) – but he needed especially someone to share the fun.'[7] He also states that few men have collected about them as many stories as Lawrence and frankly admits that 'the greater proportion could only have come from his own lips'.[8] Richards comments that it was a characteristic of Lawrence never to tell a story against himself as 'his supremacy must never seem to suffer'.[9] A similar urge explained Lawrence's refusal to take part in organized games and hatred of being teased. The unwillingness to be seen publicly to fail, Richards believed, Lawrence took to a pathological level, regarding it as 'an almost sinister side to his sense of power'.[10]

Lawrence's shunning of normal college life to follow his own path gave him a reputation as an eccentric, and his odd image was reinforced by his personal habits – he did not smoke or drink, and ate meat only occasionally. His supervising don, Reginald Lane Poole, a medieval historian whom Lawrence came to admire, remembered that on the infrequent occasions when Lawrence delivered an essay, it was always controversial and probably relied on a romantic passage from the medieval writers Lawrence admired so much. Another of his Oxford tutors, Ernest Barker, noted that Lawrence, although bright, did not wish to become a 'historical' scholar as such; rather the Oxford history school was 'a hurdle to be jumped on the road that led to action'. Similarly, he goes on to suggest that archaeology became for Lawrence a means to adventure.[11]

Barker regarded Lawrence as 'more of the artist than the scholar – but an artist who found greater scope for art in the world of action than in the world of art itself'.[12] He recalled Lawrence's 'daemonic and wilful energy', his insistence on working in his own direction and his apparent need 'to shock,

Lawrence at the Oxford High School 1901, wearing the 'family uniform', a striped jumper. Although he looks younger he is about twelve.

(left to right) *T. E. Lawrence ('Ned') and brothers Bob, Frank and Will.*

Mrs Lawrence aged ninety-seven with her son Dr Robert Lawrence ('Bob').

The Oxford High School 1906. Lawrence is second from left in the back row.

1910: T. E. Lawrence and brothers Frank, Arnold, Bob and Will, left to right.

In camp (1910) with the OUOTC, his University's Officers Training Corps.

D. G. Hogarth

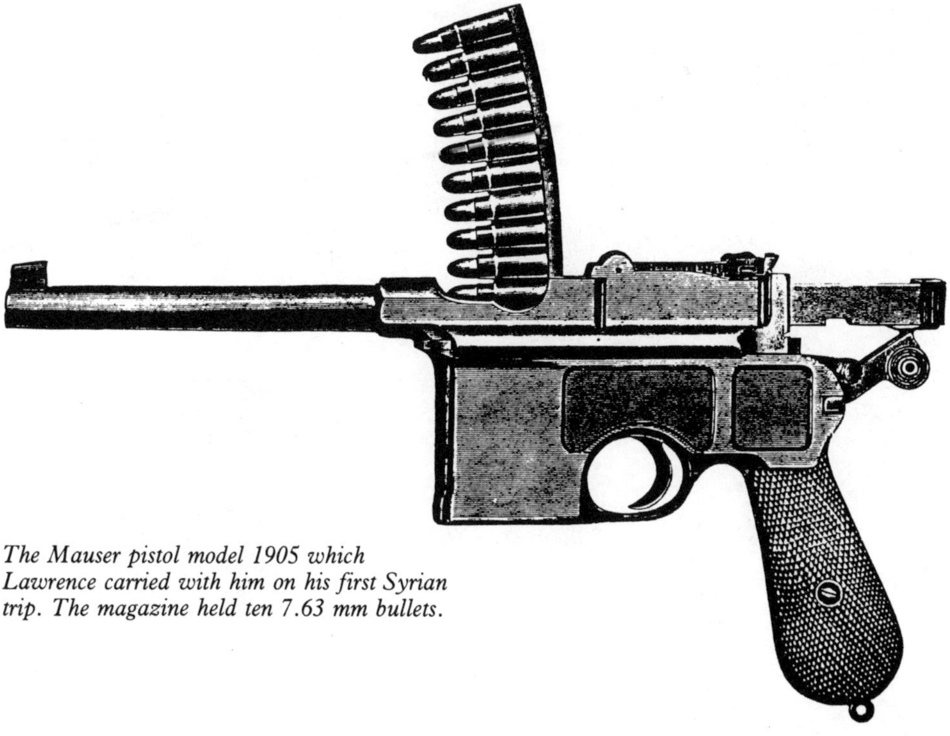

The Mauser pistol model 1905 which Lawrence carried with him on his first Syrian trip. The magazine held ten 7.63 mm bullets.

Group photograph at Carchemish (Lawrence and Woolley front row).

Lawrence and Leonard Woolley on site at Carchemish 1913.

The comfortable living quarters of the British team, which Lawrence described in his letter to E. T. Leeds as their 'great house'.

Dahoum, Abd es Salaam, Gregori and Hamoudi at Carchemish.

Dahoum (left) *in Lawrence's clothes, and vice versa.*

Gertrude Bell.

Leonard Woolley.

Flinders Petrie.

perhaps to wound'.[13] Perhaps typical of this is the incident when Lawrence with a few friends led an underground exploration in a rowing boat of the Trill Mill stream, which runs underneath Oxford, in order to find a Saxon sewer. Amongst the essential equipment, Lawrence took along a .45 revolver and a box of blanks to scare the residents above by firing through the gratings – according to one story, 'as a token against the bourgeoisie'.[14] Another account even claims his mother was a passenger.

One undergraduate who became friends with Lawrence was an American, W. O. Ault, who attended Lane Poole tutorials with him. According to Ault, the crusty don once commented on an essay by Lawrence that it was 'good enough' but the style was that of 'a tuppeny-ha'penny newspaper'.[15] Lawrence taught Ault how to make brass-rubbings, and they cycled together around Oxfordshire, sometimes visiting a local blacksmith who was a practical expert on the manufacture of armour.

With other friends Lawrence frequently cycled to London to visit the Tower Armouries and Wallace Collection. Charles J. ffoulkes, who later became curator of the Tower Armouries, remembers Lawrence attending his lectures in Oxford, after which they would have conversations on the 'style, construction and design of military equipment, on which he had heretical but always practical views'.[16]

Lawrence's passionate enthusiasm for epic literature continued from his schooldays. Malory's *Morte d'Arthur* and Tennyson's popularized account of the Arthurian legends, *Idylls of the King*, were to remain lifelong favourites, and the former together with Homer's *Odyssey* were to be Lawrence's constant companions during the war. He was also particularly fond of medieval French poetry – especially the *chansons de geste*, which later evolved into codes of knightly chivalry.

This interest was used to stimulate wider reading, both by Lane Poole and by D. G. Hogarth, whom Lawrence was introduced to in about 1908. Several biographies of T.E. have suggested that because Lawrence's parents were worried about their second son's future, they asked their religious mentor, Canon Christopher, to introduce Ned to someone who might understand and direct his unusual talents. Christopher then contacted David Margoliouth, the Laudian Professor of Arabic at Oxford, who in turn suggested Dr D. G. Hogarth. This is quite possible, though it seems more likely that Lawrence would have been introduced to Hogarth by his acquaintance and later colleague, Leonard Woolley, who was working at the Ashmolean Museum where Hogarth became Keeper in early 1909. Lawrence later wrote that Hogarth was 'the man to whom I owe everything I have had since I was seventeen'.[17] He was seventeen in 1905, but then Lawrence is rarely accurate on dates.

David Hogarth was an unusually gifted man; a recognized archaeological and Middle Eastern scholar whose lust for adventure had never allowed him to settle into the normal academic routine. In 1897, taking time off from a post as Director of the British School, at Athens, he had acted as a correspondent for *The Times*, covering the Greco-Turkish war. Throughout his life, even into late middle age, he enjoyed travelling in the less stable parts of the Balkans and Middle East, upon which he was a brilliantly perceptive political commentator. In 1909, at the age of forty-seven, he described himself as 'a hunter at hazard' who had fallen into an archaeological career by accident. Several writers have suggested that Hogarth was an intelligence agent in the Middle East before the Great War. (During the Great War he worked overtly as a senior Foreign Office intelligence officer). It is possible that he was but such a modern description is probably too crude. Hogarth was a man deeply committed to the British Imperial ethic who would have thought it perfectly natural, not only to pass on 'intelligence', but to ensure that his travels brought him into areas of potential interest to his friends at the Foreign Office (he had been at school with Sir Edward Grey, the Foreign Secretary 1905–16).

In Woolley and Lawrence Hogarth recognized young men of similar character to his own. Once the apprentice himself – in his memoirs he wrote 'I owe all to Ramsay' (William Martin Ramsay, an archaeologist and traveller in Asia Minor) – Hogarth now became the master. In particular he took Lawrence, seven years younger than Woolley, under his wing and instilled into him his own imperialistic creed, liberal yet paradoxically derisive of democracy. Lawrence began a course of study which ensured that apart from being a competent archaeologist he was well equipped to handle the duties of an intelligence officer when war broke out.

While at Oxford Lawrence continued to read everything he could on the medieval period, but under Hogarth's tutelage he digested the latest works on the art of war, and developed an interest in modern Arabia. One book in particular provided a bridge from his old interests and profoundly affected Lawrence: Doughty's *Arabia Deserta*, a monumental travel epic written in quasi-Elizabethan prose.

At this time Lawrence's world was still one of castles, knights, Crusades, battles, legends and chivalry – a slightly more sophisticated but basically similar version of his life at fifteen. He must have realized that his romantic conceptions did not correspond with reality. The crusading knights' refined code of honour celebrated in literature was frequently ignored in practice. The heroes of medieval poetry would often use the idealized love of a woman who invariably was not their wife as the motivation for acts of valour that otherwise could be seen as murder and adultery; marriage and romantic love were regarded as incompatible. For some of these mythical heroes, chastity of body as well as mind was the ideal.

As a result of his interests, Lawrence decided to make the castles of the Crusaders the subject of his thesis, a new option as part of the final examinations. In the summer of 1908, he therefore went on an extensive three-month cycling tour of France. He took a camera and, travelling alone, went right across the country to the Mediterranean visiting and photographing castles. The trip covered 2,000 miles, and though it was basically uneventful, Lawrence caught a malarial fever after being bitten by mosquitoes, the first of the illnesses that were to plague him in his time abroad. On his return to

England he did, however, mention to Vyvyan Richards, 'Last time I was in France measuring up an old fortress I was arrested as a spy.'[18] This may have been a boast, but it was true that the French in 1908 were busy building enormous fortifications against a possible German invasion, and a tourist taking photographs of nothing but military architecture was likely to arouse suspicion. In the hundreds of photographs, sketch maps and detailed notes that Lawrence made he would have acquired at least some material of value to Military Intelligence.

A month after Lawrence's return to England, he joined the newly formed Rifle Club for Old Boys of Oxford High School. His friend Beeson remembers that he spent many hours practising pistol shooting. Also in October 1908, Lawrence astounded his literary friends at Jesus College by joining the Oxford University Officer Training Corps (OUOTC). Two certificates were then necessary to obtain a special King's commission for use in time of war. They were simply referred to as Certificates 'A' and 'B'; Lawrence had probably studied for the first while an officer in the Church Lads Brigade. Certificate 'B' was only obtainable after a two-year, part-time course in a unit such as the OUOTC. Lawrence remained in the Corps until December 1910, during which time he would have received basic military training in drill, small arms and simple infantry tactics. There were annual camps at Tidworth, held mid-January to mid-March and so not interfering with his summer 'tours'.

Although it has been suggested that Lawrence had little or no military training before becoming an officer in the First World War, this is clearly not the case. He has as much, and possibly more, formal military instruction as an average officer passing out of the Military Academy at Sandhurst today, and was by no means the bookish scholar thrown into action that is sometimes portrayed. In addition, Lawrence had deliberately set out to toughen his will and body from adolescence, and had the advantage of considerable theoretical knowledge from his reading of military history and theory.

Lawrence's practical interest in modern military equipment was evident in the Christmas holiday of 1908, when he and his old friend Beeson scaled Cumnor Hurst in a heavy snowstorm and Lawrence used his new compass to direct them back to Oxford. In order to test the reliability of the instrument, he set an absolutely straight course which typically of him involved climbing over, rather than going around, any obstacle that came their way.

It was in the first half of 1909, when Lawrence was twenty, that there is the only reference to his romantic interest in a woman during his time at college. Janet Laurie, a friend of the Lawrence family since childhood, had come to dinner at Polstead Road, and after dinner Lawrence suddenly asked her to marry him. They had never courted, and being dumbfounded by the proposal, she laughed. It was more from embarrassment but Lawrence, humiliated, did not mention the matter again.[19] After the war he wrote to Charlotte Shaw stating that he would never be the cause of any woman having children, and also telling her that his parents should have followed a similar example.[20]

Early in 1909 Lawrence began to make plans for a summer walking tour of Northern Syria. He wanted to gather more material for his thesis on Crusader castles. He had already formulated a hypothesis that, contrary to established opinion, the Crusaders gave more to Arabic military architecture than they took. It was typical that his theory should be the opposite of the one then in vogue, but also typical – and much to his credit – that he was determined to find evidence to support his ideas despite considerable practical obstacles.

Although Lawrence's fascination with the Crusades and his increasing identification with Hogarth meant that it was only a matter of time before he visited Arabia, it was more than coincidental that Northern Syria was where Hogarth had been travelling in 1908. Ostensibly he had been making a preliminary survey for a British Museum archaeological dig, but the region was also of particular concern to the Foreign Office. Syria, then part of the Ottoman Empire, was of growing strategic importance. Germany befriended Turkey to Britain's cost, and German railway engineers were building a Berlin-to-Baghdad railway which would not only extend Germany's reach dangerously close to Egypt and India, but would provide Britain's main European industrial rival with cheap raw materials and new marketplaces.

Hogarth's probable mission in Syria had been to select a site for excavation in the north of the country which would be suitable cover for observing progress on the construction of the railway, while also being productive enough archaeologically to counter criticism that any new British dig was simply a fake set-up for intelligence-gathering. The site Hogarth recommended finally was Carchemish, some sixty miles north of Aleppo, and precisely the place where the Berlin to Baghdad railway would cross the great Euphrates river. The choice was given plausibility because the site had already been recommended to the British Museum in 1876 and work had been carried out there up to 1881, when the site was abandoned.

Lawrence continued with the preparation for his own Syrian trip. He had some background knowledge. Vyvyan Richards noted that in 1908 Lawrence was taking an interest in Egyptology and attended lectures in Oxford given by the famous archaeologist Flinders Petrie. He found the idea of exploring most attractive, and realized that it would increase his reputation as well as ensuring him a good degree. The very real prospect of danger was, if anything, another good reason to go, and an excellent opportunity to test the martial skills he had developed.

Following an introduction from Hogarth, Lawrence wrote for advice to the veteran explorer Charles Doughty, author of *Arabia Deserta*. On 3 February 1909 Doughty wrote back, suggesting that the idea of a walking tour of northern Syria was at the least imprudent. Lawrence was not put off and with Hogarth's help went ahead with his preparations. Syria, under Turkish control, was a country where any European would draw attention to himself and, without the proper arrangements, would be liable to land in gaol accused of spying. Hogarth accordingly pulled strings on Lawrence's behalf and, via the Principal of Jesus College, Sir John Rhys, obtained from Lord Curzon, the Chancellor of the university, special passes of safe conduct negotiable with the Turkish authorities. These 'iradehs', which were to be collected from the British Embassy in Beirut, were a very special privilege and, as Lawrence later commented to Liddell Hart, 'a piquant passport for a tramp'.[21]

Hogarth also introduced Lawrence to a young ex-Oxford archaeologist, H. Pirie-Gordon, who the previous year had spent five months studying Syrian and Palestinian architecture. Pirie-Gordon was part of Hogarth's circle and as a political intelligence officer later served with Lawrence and Hogarth during and after the war. Lawrence and he got on well when they met in May 1909, and Pirie-Gordon lent Lawrence an annotated map of the region which he had made the year before. (Lawrence, on his return, gave back the map with fresh bloodstains on it, much to Pirie-Gordon's concern.)

Lawrence realized that he would need some rudiments of the Arabic language if he was to get by in the remote parts of Syria, and here he was helped by Professor Margoliouth and a Syrian Protestant clergyman, the Rev. N. Odeh, who had recently retired from a mission in Cairo. By the time he left England in June 1909 he had learnt the basics, but no more, of Arabic.

The story of what took place next has been the subject of fanciful exaggeration by Lawrence, who even when he did something genuinely admirable, seemed to need to embellish his achievement. Almost immediately after the university term ended, Lawrence sailed for Port Said, which he found an unpleasant and overcrowded tourist trap. He had to wait there five days for another boat to take him to Beirut, sailing north up the Palestinian coast past Jaffa, Acre, Tyre and Sidon to arrive at the beautiful harbour at Beirut on 6 July. There he visited the British Consulate, only to find his special papers had not yet arrived, so he stayed at the American School for the next few days. The 'iradehs' still did not arrive but he managed to obtain a less comprehensive letter of safe-conduct and set off with this on the first part of his tour, to Palestine, where he probably thought the protection of the special passes would not be required.

Lawrence travelled light. He had a special suit with lots of pockets, a few toilet articles (he rarely needed to shave), two spare shirts, some socks, a sun helmet, a camera and tripod, plenty of spare film, and a heavy Mauser pistol with adjustable sights. To take a firearm on such a journey was a wise precaution, even though it was technically illegal within the Ottoman Empire. The Mauser, nicknamed the broomhandle, was one of the first successful semi-automatic small arms and a direct predecessor of the submachine gun; although bulky – and expensive – it had far superior fire-power to the Smith and Wesson, Colt or Webley and Scott revolvers that one might have expected Lawrence to carry. He was to be grateful to it. As he was to write to his mother later in the trip, 'I'm rather glad that my perseverance in carrying the Mauser has been rewarded [he had just been shot at and returned fire], it is rather a load but practically unknown out here.'[22]

Lawrence hired a Christian Arab guide and travelled south to Sidon and to the Sea of Galilee, where, commenting on the wilderness around it, he said 'The sooner the Jews farm it all the better.'[23] Then, turning back on himself, he went to Nazareth and Haifa, then north up the Mediterranean coast to Tyre, back past Sidon, and finally returned to Beirut. He had been marching for three weeks, averaging fifteen miles a day (he claimed twenty-two), which was nevertheless an extraordinary achievement over the rough terrain.

On Friday 6 August he set out again from Beirut, having this time picked up his special papers from the Consulate, and went north up the coast towards Jebail, the ancient site of Byblus. There was an American mission here, which put him up for four days, after which he continued his journey north and arrived at Tripoli on the Mediterranean coast. (The Lebanese Tripoli, not Tripoli in Libya.) He then marched north to Latakia, via Homs, and on up to Antioch, now the southernmost tip of Turkey.

En route, Lawrence was, or so he claimed, attacked at Masyad in the coastal hinterland halfway between Tripoli and Antioch. According to one version of the story, a mounted bandit shot at Lawrence from two hundred yards, at which Lawrence shot back with his pistol and grazed the offender's horse. Another, more fanciful version was told by Lawrence to a Christian Arab woman, Miss Akle, who helped him with his Arabic at the American school at Byblus. In this version Lawrence was fired at by a 'cruel looking Turk' and on shooting back, he knocked the gun out of the man's hands and wounded his little finger. The two men then made friends and Lawrence bandaged the wound.[24] However embellished, a genuinely frightening incident had taken place, and afterwards Lawrence, taking advantage of the power of his 'iradehs', arranged for a mounted escort, though he himself continued to travel on foot.

In early September he arrived at the great trading city of Aleppo, which impressed him by its vivacity, and he set off enthusiastically to explore the souk and its twenty miles of subterranean passages. Up to this time he had written home to his mother in detail about what he had seen and done, but after his arrival in Aleppo there is a gap in the correspondence. We know that he travelled north of the city, as Hogarth had done the year before, and even if he did not travel as far as Carchemish he certainly went very close. It is possible that he was making an up-to-date reconnaissance of the area for Hogarth, which would have been particularly important because Hogarth had left Syria in mid-1908 before the 'Young Turk' Revolution and the latter was likely to have brought significant changes in the region, which was intrinsically unstable.

During the second week of September, Lawrence travelled out of Aleppo and was again attacked and again stories of the incident conflict. Lawrence later told Liddell Hart that he was beaten and knocked down by a robber who grabbed his 'revolver'. Awaiting the *coup de grâce*, T.E. claims that he had the presence of mind to snatch at the trigger guard of the gun, which he describes as a 'Webley' now held by his assailant, 'so collapsing the pistol'.[25] Webley pistols have never had such a mechanism, and even in the unlikely event that

Lawrence had changed weapons in Aleppo, the story just does not ring true. Lawrence told Robert Graves a similarly fanciful yarn but this time the robber did not kill him because he was unable to release the safety catch on the pistol, which in this version is described as a 'Colt revolver'.[26]

Some sort of attack, nevertheless, must have taken place, however Lawrence distorted it. On 22 September Lawrence returned to Aleppo and wrote to his parents that he had read an article in a newspaper which said that he had been murdered near a place called Aintab.[27] Three days later he wrote to Sir John Rhys, the principal at Jesus College, apologizing for his absence, the reason for which was that he had been beaten up and had his camera stolen.[28] Professor Jeffrey Meyers, a distinguished expert on Lawrence's life, believes that Lawrence may have been sexually molested during this incident. If this was so – and Meyers makes a powerful case based on Lawrence's own writings – then it might explain why Lawrence was inconsistent in his description of the event.[29]

After Aleppo, Lawrence set off south towards Damascus, a city which he told Liddell Hart he visited on the 26th (though this may not be accurate), and then continued straight back to Beirut and on to Port Said to catch the boat home. Here again fantasy intrudes, for Lawrence claimed that, having lost all his money, he was forced to work on the docks at Port Said to earn a passage home. Given the poor payment for such work, it would have taken him many months to earn enough for his ticket, but whatever the truth, Lawrence acquired a ticket and was back in Oxford by 14 October.

He had collected enough material to write a good thesis, apart from proving himself as a potential intelligence agent. He also brought back several important Hittite seals for the Ashmolean's collection and, on a personal level, a special Syrian purple dye with which to stain vellum bindings, for Lawrence still had his plans to set up a private press.

He was now in his final academic year and worked hard to achieve the brilliant degree that he had been almost immodestly certain of since the middle of 1909. He settled back into the routine of study in his bungalow, where later in the year he was joined by a Persian cat which had appeared on the wall outside and refused to go away. Lawrence thought it 'the most beautiful animal I have ever seen'[30] – though after the war it was often said of Lawrence that he hated animals, and children, which was not true.

Lawrence's thesis on the Crusaders would not exempt him from more conventional examinations and he kept up his private coaching with L. Cecil Jane. He claimed that he left the work on his thesis until the final two weeks of the summer term, which may not be altogether fanciful since Lawrence's thesis is quite short and relies on the photographs which accompany it. It was published in 1936 after Lawrence's death as *Crusader Castles*, and though interesting, it is rather a disappointment when reread today – more a testament to Lawrence's achievement in completing a perilous 1,000-mile journey on foot in Syria than proof of his deliberately controversial hypothesis that Byzantine architecture had not influenced the castles of the Crusaders.

Lawrence, as expected, passed his degree with first-class honours and his tutor, Lane Poole, gave a dinner party for the examiners in celebration of his student's degree. Lawrence planned a fourth year at Oxford to add a B.Litt. to his BA, and during the summer before his return to university went on two further cycling tours of France. The only record of the first journey is a postcard from Beauvais; the second, which began in mid-August, was with his brother Frank in north-east France. The two young men were not always welcome, for Lawrence was not averse to breaking into buildings closed to the public. At Courcy, Frank wrote to his girl-friend Florence: 'Ned & I, evading the 'gardien', went over the rest of the castle by ourselves . . . forcing locks & climbing over doors and up walls . . .'[31] It was also at Courcy Castle that Lawrence brought out a fifty-foot tape measure in order to measure architectural details precisely.

Frank, the boy scout of the family, brought some flint and steel to use for fire-making, a skill that T.E. soon learnt from him, recognizing that it might be useful. Frank returned home on 30 August, to be replaced a little later by Will. Like Frank, Will was an accomplice to T.E.'s exploits and when the latter wanted to make a sketch of the Bayeux tapestry – any sort of reproduction was forbidden – Will 'acted as decoy' while his brother quickly drew the sections that interested him.[32] They cycled to Caen on 4 September, when they split up. Lawrence spent the next month travelling on his own, probably spending some time in Paris before returning to Oxford by mid-October for his degree ceremony.

Here, Hogarth had plans for his *protégé*. He wanted Lawrence to accompany him to Carchemish, where excavations were due to begin in 1911. The new Turkish government has granted permission to the British Museum to reopen the site in the spring of 1910 and Hogarth was to direct operations. By using his influence, he obtained a senior demyship for Lawrence from his own college, Magdalen, which would give Lawrence sufficient financial independence to return to Syria, ostensibly as a member of a British Museum sponsored archaeological dig.

Lawrence duly prepared himself. Among the aids to his archaeological duties, he ordered a special and very expensive, camera from London which had as its most important feature a powerful telephoto lens. This equipment would have been beyond Lawrence's means and must have been bought for him. It would be very suitable for discreetly recording the progress made by the German railway engineers in Syria.

3 Carchemish

The British Museum's official report, 'Carchemish I', begins: 'In the early spring of 1911 . . . the digging party left England composed of D. G. Hogarth, R. C. Thompson and T. E. Lawrence.'[1] In fact Lawrence had left England early in December 1910, having been sent ahead by Hogarth to familiarize himself further with the country. The error in the report may be accidental, but if so, it seems a misleading way to begin a detailed historical and scientific record.

Lawrence had proceeded to Port Said via Naples, Athens (where he visited the Acropolis) and Constantinople, of which he wrote 'as much life as Athens stood for sleep'.[2] From Port Said, he sailed to Beirut, arriving just before Christmas. His plan was to go to the American mission up the coast at Jebail (ancient Byblus), where he had stayed in 1909, to improve his Arabic. He kept up his habit of writing home regularly, and on 31 December 1910 included in a letter to his mother, 'don't show Mr. Hogarth any more letters of mine, please!'[3] Did Lawrence feel ashamed of some useful bragging or had he perhaps committed a more serious indiscretion?

Lawrence's published letters of this period are very human and written in a spirit to console his family, who must have been concerned about him. In one written at Jebail on 24 January 1911, Lawrence talked of his intention to write one day a 'Seven Pillars of Wisdom', implying that it would be a book about the Crusades.* (After the war, Lawrence claimed that he did write such a book but destroyed it.) He also wrote, at length, about starting up another printing scheme with Vyvyan Richards when he returned home.[4]

By 18 February Lawrence was back in Beirut where he had arranged to meet R. Campbell Thompson, the second member of the digging party, who had arrived the day before. Thompson, a slightly eccentric character himself, proved to be a little difficult to locate, as on arriving in Beirut he had disappeared in search of a piano – a piece of equipment which he regarded as essential for the long nights in northern Syria. Lawrence eventually tracked him down and wrote home, with some amusement, that his interesting new col-

*The reference is of course a biblical one, to Proverbs 9:1. This has 'Wisdom has built her house, she has set up her seven pillars'.

league had also brought with him several guns and a few hundred rounds of ammunition.[5]

Hogarth arrived two days later, bringing with him an experienced foreman – Gregori Antoniou, a Cypriot whom he had employed before. Gregori's formidable personality is described in Hogarth's book, *Accidents of an Antiquary's Life*.[6] Hogarth had planned that his party should take the train to Aleppo but the line was blocked by snow, so instead they went by sea to Haifa, finding time to visit the monastery at Mount Carmel, and then proceeded to Damascus via Deraa by rail. This was the first time that Lawrence travelled on the railway which he later took an active part in attacking. They reached Damascus, the capital of modern Syria, on 26 February and after a 24-hour delay because of the bad weather set off for Aleppo.

When they reached Aleppo, the British team took rooms in the Baron Hotel and spent a week buying provisions and animals for transport to their final destination. Hogarth, who liked to travel in comfort, had already brought with him nine sorts of jam and three types of tea. While in Aleppo, they paid their respects at the British Consulate and dined there on most evenings during their short stay.

An official British presence in the city had long been regarded as of particular importance – it began in the reign of Elizabeth I and continued until after the Second World War. In 1911, the Consulate was a vital intelligence centre for monitoring German ambitions in the area, and during his time at Carchemish, Lawrence reported to, and soon befriended, the British Vice-Consul, R. Fontana. He would sometimes borrow money from him when funds from home were late in arriving: Lawrence's letters show that shortage of cash was a recurrent problem throughout his stay at Carchemish. Lawrence also developed a friendship with Fontana's wife Winifred, although at their first meeting she remembers being 'chilled' by 'something uncouth in Lawrence's manner' which contrasted with his 'donnish precision of speech'.[7]

Nevertheless, a friendly relationship developed, based partly on their mutual love of literature. Mrs Fontana would get the latest books for Lawrence, and whenever he was in Aleppo they would have long discussions on recent literary trends. Lawrence, after initial protests, became a regular dinner guest at her dinner parties, where his wit was appreciated by his hostess, if not always by the other guests, who sometimes fell victim to his sarcasm. Mrs Fontana retained fond memories of Lawrence, recalling with many others that he always looked about eighteen. She also noticed – as another woman friend, Clare Sydney Smith, did nearly twenty years later – how well Lawrence got on with her children.

During the British team's week in Aleppo, Hogarth was briefed by Fontana, and on 2 March wrote to F. G. Kenyon, a director of the British Museum:

> It seems certain that the Baghdad railway is going via Jerablus [Carchemish]. Could

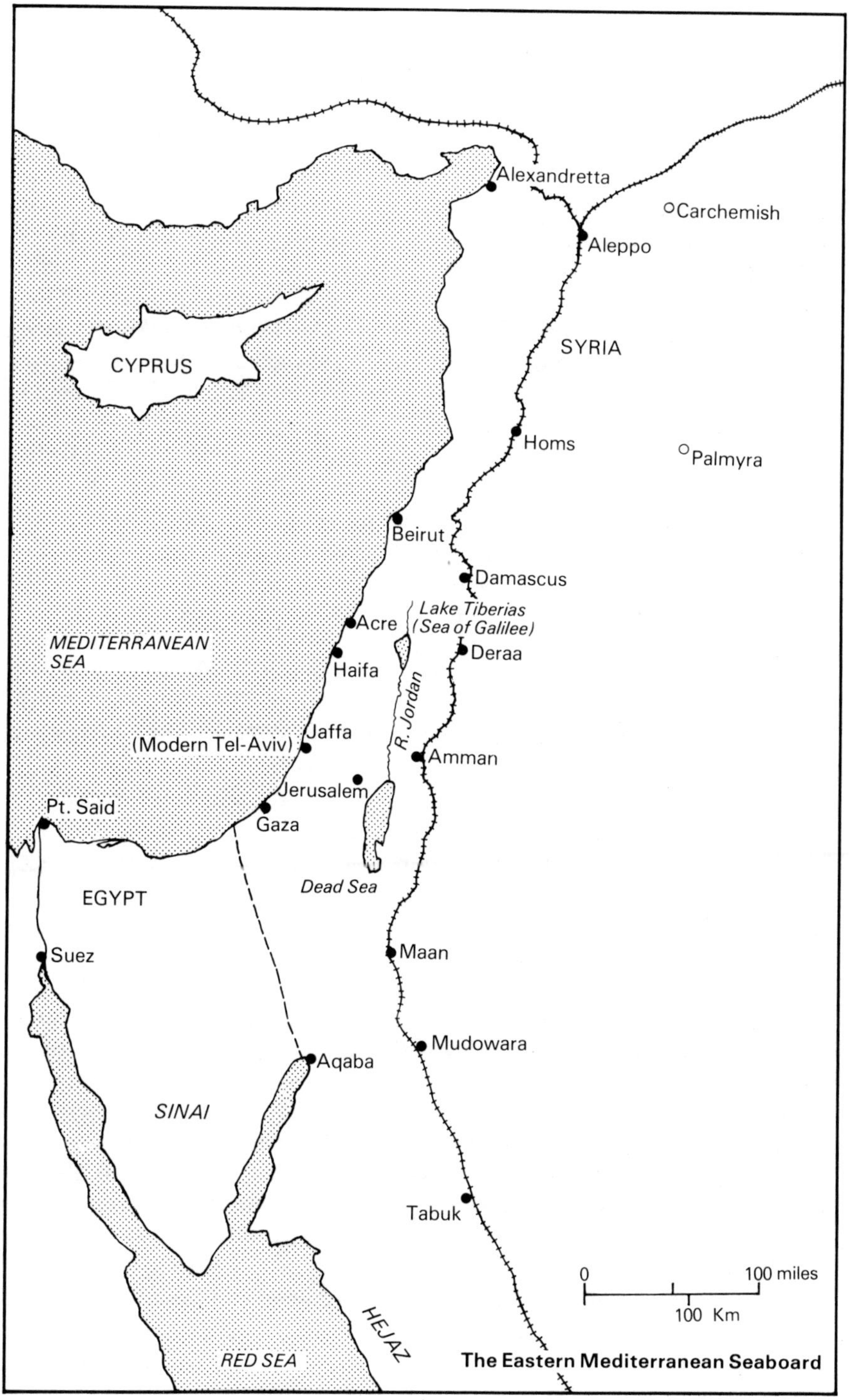

The Eastern Mediterranean Seaboard

> you please inform Sir Edward Grey [the Foreign Secretary] about the latter in view of complications with the railway. If the company gets (as usual) a wide strip (ten kilometres or so) on either side of the line, it will include our site. But your right to excavate it ought to be reserved and it would be easy in any 'pourparlers' Grey *may be* engaged upon to put in a word to this effect. I think you would be wise to see him officially on the subject at once.[8]

A week later Hogarth, Thompson and Lawrence set out for Carchemish with a baggage train consisting of ten pack horses and eleven camels. When they arrived, the only shelter available near the site was a licorice warehouse, and of necessity this became headquarters and residence. Hogarth only stayed long enough to establish the excavations and returned to England in April, leaving Thompson in charge. The new excavations continued until July, and during that period Gertrude Bell, an expert on Mesopotamia and a school-friend of Hogarth's daughter, visited the site.

At first Gertrude Bell was critical of the methods employed by the British archaeologists – she had just visited a 'scientific' German site at Kalaat Shirgat. Lawrence and Thompson, rather insulted, went all out to blind her with their knowledge and, apparently, succeeded. 'Gertie' recorded her first impression of Lawrence in a letter to her step-mother – 'he is going to make a traveller' – her greatest compliment.[9] She was to become a friend and colleague to Lawrence during the war, when she served as a captain in the same exclusive intelligence unit, the Arab Bureau. She would refer to Lawrence as her 'dear boy'.

As well as his special archaeological studies at Carchemish, Lawrence was spending as much time as he could exploring the region and taking photographs whenever possible. On 12 July he wrote home telling his mother that the British Museum were going to send him, care of his Oxford address, a proof set of the prints of the two hundred photographs he had taken, many with his own special camera with the telephoto lens. His instructions to her were clear – she was allowed to look at them herself '*but don't show them to anybody else on any account*' [Lawrence's emphasis] and, further, she was not to mention that she had seen any photographs.[10]

A few days later, Lawrence went to explore the region around the Euphrates but fell seriously ill, probably with typhoid. His sketch diaries of the period mention frequent attacks of fever while he was in Syria, which often led him to collapse. Apparently, he overcame his health problems by sheer willpower. Somehow he got back to the camp at Carchemish and found a senior worker, Hamoudi, still on the site. Hamoudi took Lawrence into his own house, which was much against the local custom in case the patient died, and nursed him back to health. Still unwell, Lawrence returned to England in August 1911.

The first season at Carchemish had been successful and there were plans to continue the project in the autumn. The British Museum, however, did not have sufficient funds and Hogarth, who realized the strategic importance of the site, found an 'anonymous' benefactor to supplement the money put up by the British Museum. The accounts preserved in the files of the Museum show that during the period 1911–14, the British Museum put up £3,859 and the 'anonymous fund', established in 1912, put up £4,999.[11]

On 21 November 1911 a letter was sent from the Foreign Office to Kenyon at the British Museum about Hogarth's excavations:

> . . . His Majesty's Vice-Consul at Aleppo reports that on October 23rd a rumour reached him to the effect that the Baghdad Railway was likely to traverse the precise spot at Jerablus [Carchemish] where Dr. Hogarth has lately been excavating, and that the site itself was threatened with destruction.
>
> He states that in September last [1910] the German consul at Aleppo, Herr Rossler, wrote to him privately protesting against a statement in an anonymous letter, which appeared in *The Times* of August 9th [1910] to the effect that the Baghdad Railway was likely to demolish Carchemish and Tel Ahmar. He mentioned this matter to Meissner Pasha [the regional governor] and explained to him and to the German Consul that it was not possible for him to contradict the statement complained of or to communicate in any way with a newspaper.
>
> His Majesty's Vice-Consul called upon the German Consul and referring to his letter, enquired whether after all there was not some truth in the rumour of which he had previously complained. Mr Rossler replied that he feared that part at least of the site was in danger of being interfered with; but that, so far as he was aware, the danger was not immediate and that nothing was being done at the moment, as the plans were still under consideration in Germany. He said that he was convinced that every care would be exercised not to infringe British rights; and he added a suggestion that it 'might be well for Dr Hogarth (or whoever was concerned) to have a representative on the spot to protect any property from injury by natives or other untoward accident'.
>
> His Majesty's Vice-Consul states that he has no information of Dr Hogarth's plans, but that he heard privately a few days before his despatch from Mr T. E. Lawrence that some members of the party were likely to return to Jerablus to resume operations in the autumn. He also heard vaguely that part of the land in the neighbourhood in question is British property.
>
> He has, however, no information as to what, if any, British interests are threatened. He hopes to start on a tour on the 30th instant, and intends if possible to visit Carchemish.[12]

The letter to *The Times* had been written by Hogarth. It was a technique of press manipulation that he passed on to Lawrence, who after the war made many anonymous contributions to newspapers for political ends.

The Foreign Office foresaw the Berlin-to-Baghdad railway linking up with the new 'Pilgrim' railway in southern Arabia to create a larger and even more threatening network. The 'Pilgrim' railway had also been built for the Turks by German engineers, its construction funded by subscriptions started in 1901 from Muslims throughout the world. Its advertised intention was to link Damascus directly to Mecca and thus facilitate the journey of any Muslims making the sacred trip to Mecca. The local Bedouin tribes had, however, objected to this plan because it robbed them of a major source of income –

plundering the pilgrims' caravans. The Turks had negotiated, paid a levy to some tribal chiefs, and finally stopped the railway at Medina after laying 820 miles of track. The luckless pilgrims were left to make the rest of the journey, from Medina to Mecca, by road.

The Berlin–Baghdad railway had been funded more conventionally. In 1888 a joint German–British company had been granted a concession to build a line from Constantinople to Ankara, but the Germans were then allowed to buy out the majority of the British interest and in 1901 were granted the further concession to extend the line across the Euphrates and on, up into Mesopotamia to Baghdad and eventually to Basra. Such a link from Berlin to the Bosphorus was undoubtedly against British imperial interests and of increasing concern as war with Germany loomed in Europe.

The excavations at Carchemish, the spot where the Berlin–Baghdad line could most easily be disrupted by destroying the bridge being built across the Euphrates, were clearly of political importance. It would be naïve to assume that the British Museum was not aware of this. Yet as late as 1969 an official of the British Museum was able to state that there was absolutely no political purpose in commencing excavations at Carchemish the very same year – 1911 – that the Germans began construction of the Euphrates bridge.[13]

Lawrence did not return to Syria until early February 1912. He spent January in Egypt working with the famous Egyptologist, Flinders Petrie, excavating a tomb some forty miles south of Cairo at Aafar Ammar. The object was for T.E. to learn some of the latest archaeological techniques before rejoining the site at Carchemish. Here he found a mass of problems. Thompson had left to get married in 1911 and Hogarth replaced him as the director of the site with Leonard Woolley. He arrived in late February to be greeted by the news that the local Turkish authorities would not allow excavations to reopen at Carchemish without Hogarth: the original licence from the Department of Antiquities in Constantinople had been issued in Hogarth's name. Woolley had letters of authorization from the British Museum and from Hogarth but when he and Lawrence went to see the Kaimmakam of Birjiik, the local official responsible for the delay, they were told that the matter was closed.

Woolley finally decided that drastic action was necessary: 'Taking my revolver out of its holster I got up and walking to the side of his [the Kaimmakam's] chair put the muzzle against his left ear. "On the contrary", I said, "I shall shoot you here and now unless you give me permission to start work tomorrow."'[14] Needless to say, the Kaimmakam complied, and the Englishmen heard no more of the incident. Woolley recorded using the same technique on other occasions; like Lawrence, he was a most unconventional archaeologist.

Permanent quarters were built for the British residents at the site and completed in May. They were akin to an Oriental-styled Oxford Senior Common Room, and Lawrence wrote to E. T. Leeds: 'We are building a great house, with mosaic floors and beaten copper fittings, Damascus tiles on the walls (including yours!) and much stone carvings.'[15] Lawrence and Woolley added their fine library and even the extravagance of a small Morris tapestry that Lawrence had recently brought out.

In June the dig closed for the summer. Woolley left for Constantinople and Lawrence went to Alexandretta, where he was shipping some pottery back to the Ashmolean in Oxford. He, Woolley and Hogarth all had loyalties to the Ashmolean and tried to acquire pieces for it – causing some consternation to the British Museum. Kenyon at one point wrote to Hogarth: 'I hope Lawrence has not found his employment under the Trustees so unsatisfactory as to make him unwilling to get things for the British Museum as well as for the Ashmolean.'[16] Kenyon was notoriously pompous and one cannot help but suspect that Lawrence had gone out of his way to annoy him.

In July, Lawrence fell seriously ill again but recovered enough to spend August in Jebail before digging began again in September. It continued until mid-November, at which time Lawrence returned to England for six weeks leave. When he returned to Syria in January 1913 he found it snow-bound. By this time Lawrence was, outwardly at least, fully at ease with the Arab and Kurdish workmen on the site; he treated them as equals, unlike most Europeans of his generation. He gently criticized Woolley for his 'Egyptian hauteur' and 'ruling-race fantasies'[17] and encouraged his senior colleague to be less distant from the men. For his part, Lawrence talked to them about their families, told them about himself and learnt the subtleties of their gestures and modes of speech. Although his Arabic remained heavily accented, Lawrence enjoyed the challenge of trying to pass himself off as an Arab, which was just possible if he was not drawn into long conversation.

Lawrence won the respect of the Arab work-force and would be asked to settle their quarrels. There is no doubt of his organizational abilities and enjoyment of his work. He made the dig fun to work in; for example, he initiated a practice whereby if an object was found, the finder should make known his fortune by firing off his revolver, the number of shots corresponding to the importance of the find. (Nearly everyone on the site was armed, and the possession of a gun was a status symbol. In keeping with this tradition, Lawrence frequently demonstrated his own shooting skill to the native workers. Woolley noted Lawrence 'practised constantly'.)[18]

Part of Lawrence's familiarity with Arab ways was due to a boy called Dahoum who worked as a servant at the camp. Dahoum, who was fifteen years old in 1913, had visited Lawrence when he was seriously ill in Hamoudi's house, and Lawrence later supplied him with books – though specifically not the Bible, which Lawrence thought would contaminate him – gave him the rudiments of an education and made him his personal servant. An intimate relationship grew between them, which was not approved of either by Lawrence's European colleagues or by the workers at Carchemish. (Contrary to popular belief, the attitude to homosexuality is not liberal among all Arabs.) Dahoum posed naked while Lawrence made a carving of him in sandstone, which he then prominently displayed on the roof of the house where Lawrence had invited Dahoum to live with him. The two also swapped clothes to photograph each other.

Woolley described Dahoum as 'remarkably handsome' and wrote that Lawrence was 'devoted' to the boy.[19] He also said that Lawrence's homosexual reputation was 'widely spread and firmly believed';[20] he further stated that it was untrue, just another pose.[21] Lawrence knew what was said about him among the workmen, and as with so many things, affected not to care. But whatever the relationship was, Lawrence genuinely loved the boy. Dahoum was to die of typhoid in 1919, and some scholars have suggested that the mysterious 'S.A.' to whom *The Seven Pillars of Wisdom* is dedicated is Dahoum, whose nickname was 'Sheik Achmed'. It seems more likely, however, that the book is dedicated to an idea or spirit rather than an individual.

Woolley lived close to Lawrence for three years at Carchemish, and his impressions of his companion are therefore particularly valid. He noted that Lawrence rarely if ever admitted affection for anyone, though as in the case of Dahoum the affection was there and 'deeply felt'.[22] On the occasions when Lawrence did show signs of sentiment 'he would at once turn them to ridicule' and 'in all matters of emotion' had 'peculiar distrust of himself'.[23] Woolley found Lawrence's façade difficult to penetrate, and while finding him 'unusually gifted and remarkably lovable'[24] realized that he would never get to know him well. Woolley also noticed his inconsistency; for example, despite being 'vitriolic in his abuse'[25] of missionary work, he was on friendly terms with Miss Holmes at the American mission school at Jebail.

Lawrence deliberately flaunted his friendship with Dahoum in much the same way that he delighted to shock by his dress. Woolley described Lawrence's typical appearance at Carchemish: 'he always wore a blazer of French grey trimmed with pink, white shorts held up by a gaudy Arab belt with swinging tassels ... grey stockings, red Arab slippers and no hat; his hair was always very long and in wild disorder.'[26]

Two Americans who visited the site in 1913 recorded their impressions. One, a Mr Williams, wrote:

> Both Woolley and Lawrence are disappointing as archaeologists. I expected to find grey-haired men with a scholarly stoop . . . Lawrence is apparently in his early twenties, a clean-cut blond with peaches-and-cream complexion, which the dry heat of the Euphrates seems powerless to spoil . . . wearing a wide-brimmed panama, a soft white shirt open at the front, an Oxford blazer bearing the Magdalen emblem on the pocket, short white flannel knickers partly obscured by a decoration hanging from the belt, which did not, however, obscure his bare knees, below which he wore heavy grey hose, and red Arab slippers.
>
> But I fancy these two young men are competent to hold down the Carchemish digs. . . . Far better than their years of excavating and their skill in using French, German, ancient and modern Greek, Turkish and Arabic, is their remarkable knowledge of men. I cannot give a correct estimate of their worth as archaeologists, but I do say they know more about handling orientals than any men I have met during my two years in Syria.[27]

The panama hat Mr Williams refers to was sent out by Lawrence's mother, though he rarely wore it. The second American visitor, Luther R. Fowle, was equally taken with what he found:

> Lawrence, also fresh from the works, was stepping lightly across the mounds of earth, clad in what we Americans would call a 'running suit' and wearing at his belt an ornate Arab girdle with its bunch of tassels in front, the mark of an unmarried man. But he was out of sight in a moment, and when we gathered for supper a freshly tubbed young man in his Oxford tennis suit of white flannel bordered with red ribbon but still wearing his Arab girdle, launched into a fascinating story of the excavations; of relations with the Khurds and Arabs about them; of his trips alone among their villages in search of rare rugs and antiquities.[28]

Lawrence's bachelor belt was taken as evidence of homosexuality by the native workmen when they discovered that it did not indicate, as was its purpose, 'I am looking for a wife.' According to Woolley, Lawrence had had his tassels made bigger than anyone else's.[29]

Off the site, Lawrence frequently wore Arab clothing, which was a means of exploring Syria without attracting undue notice. He was also keeping a close eye on the German construction work going on opposite the site. On his return to Carchemish in early 1913, the political situation was increasingly unstable in northern Syria. In February, Lawrence wrote to E. T. Leeds with important intelligence information for D.G.H. (i.e., Hogarth).[30] (The letter was suppressed from the original edition of Lawrence's collected letters, and other letters to Leeds which were included in the volume made no reference to the recipient but were headed cryptically 'To a friend'.) Lawrence had discovered in a conversation with the German railway manager, Herr Contzen, that building operations on part of the line had been 'suspended, at least temporarily' and the Arab workers sent home. He asked Leeds to pass on to Hogarth that he had gone across a wooden railway bridge on foot and 'entered Mesopotamia', where he found the construction of the railway well advanced: 'They are knocking in the iron piers of the permanent thing.'

Lawrence's activities had attracted the Germans' attention to him as a possible spy, but Lawrence, rather than fade away, proceeded to draw further suspicion by having large pipes dragged up a hill that overlooked the bridge construction across the Euphrates. The Germans, thinking that the mad Englishman was building gun emplacements, immediately telegraphed Berlin – or so Lawrence claimed.[31]

More seriously, in the summer of 1913 Lawrence wrote to Hogarth: 'The old government has life in it yet . . . it is beginning to keep watch on where I go at last.'[32] This did not prevent the Turkish authorities from asking Lawrence to undertake some excavations for them at Rakka in Mesopotamia, though perhaps they wanted a chance to confirm their suspicions.

Lawrence's adventures also extended to gun-running for the British Consulate at Aleppo. His friend Fontana was concerned that the Consulate had no firearms to protect itself in the event of a local uprising (at the time the Kurds were particularly restless in the area). Lawrence, together with two naval officers, managed to bring a consignment of rifles up to Aleppo, having smuggled them through the customs at Beirut. Lawrence wrote, with typically indiscreet exaggeration, 'The Consular need of rifles involved myself, the Consul General at Beirut, Flecker [the Vice-Consul at Beirut, a friend of Lawrence and a poet and author], the Admiral of Malta, our Ambassador at Stambul, two captains and two lieutenants.'[33] The letter was suppressed from *The Letters of T. E. Lawrence*, and the gun-running incident edited out of a version which appeared in the *Home Letters*.

In July 1913, Lawrence returned to England, taking Dahoum and Hamoudi with him. They stayed in Lawrence's bungalow at Polstead Road and proved quite an attraction in Oxford. Given the expense of bringing the two Arabs to England, it seems possible that Lawrence had instructions to bring them in order that they could be trained in intelligence skills, facilities for which were not fully available in Syria. This was evidently not an uncommon practice according to a retired diplomat I spoke to who had spent most of his working life in the Middle East.[34]

By August Lawrence was back in Carchemish and he met Woolley the following month. The lives they were leading out there were far from unpleasant. Books arrived regularly from England and the two men amassed an impressive collection. When, late in the year, the librarian from Munich Royal Library came to visit the German engineers next door, he was so impressed by the Englishmen's library that he spent more time with Lawrence and Woolley than he did with his official hosts. Despite the obvious rivalry between the English archaeologists and their German neighbours, relations were not always unfriendly.

Lawrence had also had an Oxford firm send out an outboard motor boat which he used for trips on the Euphrates. It helped, too, in entertaining the frequent visitors to the camp. In September, Lawrence's brother Will came out and wrote home that Ned was 'a great lord in this place'.[35] Lawrence had gone all out favourably to impress his younger brother, who arrived when Lawrence had another visitor staying with him – Hubert Young, then a captain in the Indian Army. Young, who spoke fluent Arabic, was also interested in the progress being made on the railway, and turned up at Carchemish not knowing what to expect. He was surprised to find an apparently quiet young Englishman living by himself (i.e. with no other Englishmen – Woolley was away at the time) who looked about sixteen; in fact Lawrence was twenty-five. Because of more bureaucratic problems with the Turkish authorities, work on the site was suspended, and Young 'never quite fathomed why Lawrence was still at Carchemish when the "digs" were closed down'[36] but accepted his hospitality and enjoyed being shown around the area by a man who was evidently an expert on the region. Lawrence arranged for a local chieftain to give a banquet in Young's honour, much to the latter's amusement.

After several days at Carchemish, the two Englishmen went out in the small boat Lawrence had brought from England. Their excursion on the Euphrates was interrupted by an explosion and Lawrence exclaimed, 'There are some of those blighters dynamiting fish again.'[37] The 'blighters' in question were four Kurds who took violent objection to Lawrence informing them that not only was it against the law to dynamite fish but it was also 'a shameful thing to do'[38] and would they therefore accompany him to the police station. One of the Kurds drew a knife, while the others began to throw stones at Lawrence, one of which hit him in the ribs. This only made Lawrence more angry, and he and Young went to the local Turkish gendarmerie demanding that immediate action be taken, and then waited outside to make sure it was.

When no policeman appeared, Lawrence went back in, warned the lackadaisical Turkish inspector: 'Take care, my friend. . . . You know that I had your predecessor removed for incompetence, and I shall certainly complain of you to your headquarters if you neglect your duty.'[39] This had the desired effect and the Turk asked Lawrence what should be done with the offenders when caught. 'I should flog them', was Lawrence's reply.[40]

Young was impressed by this strange and forceful young archaeologist, who was obviously very bright and, despite his diminutive appearance, had a powerful personality and physical courage – a fuller extent of which Young would have a chance to observe at first hand when they worked together during the war.

Lawrence's pleasant life at Carchemish was not destined to last much longer. War with Germany was ever more certain, and a clash with the Ottoman Empire would almost inevitably ensue. Britain's strained relationship with the unstable Turkish regime had already brought the countries near to war in 1906. The Turks had been forced to accept a large British presence in Egypt, nominally under Turkish suzerainty, since 1882. In 1906 a young British explorer, Bramley, who had gained a reputation for his camel journey into the Libyan desert, had been sent by Lord Cromer, then British agent and Consul General of Egypt, to see if the Turks intended to extend the Pilgrim railway in the Hejaz to Aqaba, thus threatening British interests east of Suez in the area known as the Sinai Peninsula. Bramley was stopped by the Turks, which provoked an international incident. Lord Cromer, supported by the jingoistic mood at home, claimed that the Sinai Peninsula was in fact part of Egypt, and the Sultan was threatened by the presence of a British fleet at Piraeus. Diplomatic exchanges with the Foreign Secretary, Sir Edward Grey, followed and the Sultan was forced to give way. Grey, Hogarth's friend, was commended for his skills but it was not an episode that the Turks would forget. Wilfrid Blunt described it in his diary as 'The beginning of Grey's blunders'[41] and it helped ensure that Turkey would ally herself with Germany and Austria in any future conflict.

In 1911, Kitchener, who was now British Agent in Egypt, set in train a scheme to update the maps of lands between Gaza and Beersheba. More problematical was the much-needed mapping of the lands farther south, extending down to Aqaba, an area in undisputed Turkish control where a British presence would, at best, be politically sensitive.

Negotiations were opened with the Turks, and the militant nationalist government, the Young Turks in the Committee of Union and Progress, rather surprisingly gave permission for a limited survey. Some protection was also given in the form of Turkish 'gendarmes' – who could of course conveniently report back on the British party.

Captain S. F. Newcombe of the Royal Engineers was appointed as the director of the survey, but to give it a plausible cover the whole operation was theoretically conducted under the auspices of a respectable archaeological organization – the Palestine Exploration Fund (which still exists). The Fund's patron was the King, its president the Archbishop of Canterbury, and the executive committee included Hogarth.

It was this survey that in late 1913 Lawrence and Woolley were asked to join. In early January of 1914, Lawrence wrote to his mother en route to Palestine: 'We are obviously only meant as red herrings, to give an archaeological colour to a political job.'[42] Newcombe rode from his camp to meet Lawrence and Woolley at Beersheba on 10 January. He expected to be joined by two 'eminent scientists' and was pleasantly shocked to find two young men, whom he later described as looking twenty-four (Woolley) and eighteen (Lawrence).[43] Interestingly, on the fifteen-mile journey back to the camp south of the town, Newcombe noted that Lawrence could only ride a horse with difficulty – and later he noticed that Lawrence had even more difficulty with a camel.

In the weeks that followed the three young men got on well together, although both Lawrence and Woolley frequently went off on their own. On 24 January, Lawrence wrote amusingly to Leeds describing their limited menu in camp:

> Hors d'oeuvre: The waiter Dahoum brings in on the lid of a petrol box half a dozen squares of Turkish delight. Then
> Soup: Bread soup. Then
> Turkish Delight on Toast. Then until yesterday
> Eggs. Then
> Sweet . . . Turkish Delight.
> Dessert: Turkish Delight.
> Of course bread is ad lib.[44]

Shortly after this was written, Lawrence met a young American, William Yale, who was ostensibly working for the Standard Oil Company (later Esso) surveying the Negeb – a mission which sounds rather similar to the one Lawrence was engaged in. Yale remembers that on their first meeting he 'played me for a sucker'.[45] Lawrence quite correctly had not given away his cover and pretended to be a tourist. According to an interview with John Mack, Yale had been told later by Lawrence that a telegram from London had given orders to investigate Yale's presence in the area.[46] During the war Yale was a member of the US State Department and he had a curious habit of turning up in many places where Lawrence was.

In February Lawrence joined Newcombe in Aqaba – Woolley had disappeared into the desert on another mission. Newcombe wanted to map the area around the city but the local Turkish governor objected and appealed to higher authority. Newcombe immediately received orders from Kitchener not to continue without Turkish approval, but this did not stop Lawrence, who accompanied by Dahoum went off for two days visiting Faroum Island, near Aqaba. He had been refused a boat by the Turkish governor but improvised a raft. He was found by the Turkish police, who tried to escort him out of the area, only to be given the slip by Lawrence and Dahoum. They had already worked out a system whereby when Lawrence was being watched, Dahoum – to whom he had taught photography – took the camera and did the work while Lawrence distracted the soldiers.

Having parted with the Turkish escort, Lawrence and Dahoum rode up the Wady Musa and on to Petra. Here Lawrence met two English women, Lady Evelyn Cobbold and a friend, who lent him enough money to buy two railway tickets so that they could make their journey back to Carchemish. Meanwhile, Newcombe had also fallen foul of the Turkish authorities and was escorted to the Egyptian border by an armed guard.

Lawrence and Dahoum were back in Carchemish by 8 March and were shortly joined by Woolley, who had not been in contact with anyone for several weeks and had been causing Lawrence some concern until his eventual reappearance. Digging was again prevented by bureaucratic problems with the Ottoman authorities, as well as a shortage of funds from England, and Hogarth was due with more funds from the anonymous benefactor.

The Sinai operation had been a success and the Turks, realizing that they had been duped, regretted that they had allowed any sort of survey to take place. To ease the tension, Kitchener was keen that Lawrence and Woolley should publish their official archaeological record of the operation as soon as possible. While the digging was delayed, Lawrence had time to begin the paper-work, though by 27 March work on the dig recommenced and Lawrence got back to his old routine.

A few days before this, there was an incident in the German camp opposite that proved serious enough to be reported in *The Times*. Fontana sent a special despatch to the Foreign Office commending Lawrence and Woolley for their bravery in the affair and it brought them to the attention of Sir Edward Grey. He was sufficiently impressed to send a copy of Fontana's despatch to Kenyon at the British Museum:

> Aleppo
> 26th March, 1914
>
> Sir:
> I have the honour to confirm my telegram to Your Excellency No. 4 of the 22nd instant reporting that Mr Woolley and Mr Lawrence, who are excavating on behalf of the British Museum at Carchemish (Jerablus) were deliberately fired on by a Circassian named Zacharia during a shooting affray there between Kurdish

> workmen and the German engineers on the Baghdad railway and their Circassian guards . . .
>
> The affray originated through a Kurd having received less wages than those to which he thought himself entitled. He protested loudly and tried to force his way into the German Bureau, but was ejected by a Circassian who, in the struggle, fired his revolver. The other Kurds near him, to the number of fifteen or twenty, then began to stone the engineers, who took refuge in the Bureau. The Circassians fired on the Kurds who withdrew to the railway embankment, and from there fired their revolvers at the Bureau, the Germans firing from one of the windows. A large crowd of about 250 Kurds and Arabs then collected on the steep Kalaat mound, at a distance of about 100 yards from and above the embankment and Bureau, and to this mound Mr Woolley and Mr Lawrence also hurried as soon as the firing began. It was there that the Englishmen were twice deliberately fired at, from below, by the Circassian Zacharia, at a distance of about 100 paces, a boy standing by Mr Lawrence's side being wounded by the second shot. From the enquiry I made it is evident that no shot was fired from the mound, in spite of the fact that the arrival of a wounded Kurd, believed to be dead, caused the greatest excitement, and the beginning of a rush was made down the hill. Mr Woolley himself pursued and disarmed the foremost man, Mr Lawrence also seizing another, and by superhuman efforts and good humour the Englishmen, aided by their headmen Hadg Wahid, Hamoudi and two others, managed to stop the rush and calm the crowd. Had they failed, the six Germans in the Bureau, which is a mere hut, would undoubtedly have been slaughtered.
>
> It seems that three Kurds were killed and four wounded in the affray, which did not last long. There is some intention, I believe, of paying blood-money to the families of the killed and of the wounded, a wise project which will leave no pretext for vengeance later, as far as individuals are concerned. Mr Woolley and Mr Lawrence have acquired the affection and confidence of their men merely by treating them as men and brothers and they have won a great reputation for integrity, kindliness and learning throughout the Jerablus region. Had it not been so, they could not have held back upwards of 300 Kurds and Arabs eager to rush the German Bureau.
>
> I propose suggesting to the Vali [local Turkish governor] that distinguished Ottoman Decorations conferred upon both Mr Woolley and Mr Lawrence, who saved the situation at Jerablus and who have, besides, rendered such signal services to the Ottoman Museum, would serve to materially demonstrate the well-earned gratitude of the Ottoman Government.[47]

This is an early record of Lawrence's courage, and though written by a friend who had not himself witnessed the affair, there was no doubt that Lawrence and Woolley had acted bravely.

A few days later, on 31 March, Hogarth arrived at Carchemish and spent the next couple of weeks on the site before disappearing again on his travels. Lawrence wrote home just afterwards: 'I don't think that I will ever travel in the West again: one cannot tell, of course, but this part out here is worth a million of the rest.'[48]

In May, Captain Newcombe and a sub-lieutenant, Grieg, visited Lawrence and Woolley at Carchemish. Newcombe needed information on a new road that the Germans had built across the Taurus mountains to supply the construction of their railway, and Lawrence and Woolley set out on his behalf. According to Woolley, Lawrence and he had the good fortune to run across a disgruntled Italian who had been working for the Germans and was willing to hand over a set of blueprints to get his own back on his old employers.[49] The drawings were exactly the information that Newcombe required, and Lawrence and Woolley returned to Carchemish.

They were now under increasing pressure from Kitchener and the Egyptian War Office to present and publish an account of their archaeological discoveries during the Sinai survey in order to appease mounting Turkish anger. It was necessary for them to return to England to do the work and in June they left Carchemish, Lawrence travelling to Damascus 'dressed à l'Arabe'[50] before making the rest of the journey home. Dahoum was given the job of looking after the site in their absence.

Lawrence later wrote: 'Turkey . . . was sore about the Sinai survey, which it felt had been a military game. K[itchener] insisted on the Palestine Exploration Fund bringing it [their report] out PDQ [pretty damn quick] as whitewash. Woolley and I had instructions to get it done instanter.'[51] To this end, Lawrence and Woolley, guided by Hogarth, prepared a suitably obscure academic treatise to justify the activities of the British survey part, which finally emerged as a predictably turgid book, *The Wilderness of Zin*. It was too late to improve strained Anglo-Turkish relations. World events moved so quickly that the book was not printed until December 1914, two months after Turkey had entered the war and following Lawrence's official appointment as an intelligence officer in Egypt. By then, it was safe to include the ironic dedication, 'To Captain S. F. Newcombe, RE, who showed them "the way wherein they must walk, and the work that they must do"'.

As for Carchemish itself, all the British archaeologists who worked there – Hogarth, Campbell Thompson, Woolley and of course Lawrence – were to become active intelligence officers during, and after, the First World War, all four being attached to the same exclusive Foreign Office special intelligence unit, the Arab Bureau. Similarly, the three visitors to Carchemish most prominent in Lawrence's letters, Gertrude Bell, Young and Newcombe, were all to work with Lawrence and Hogarth within or attached to the intelligence services.* The importance of the excavations from the standpoint of their overt purpose of archaeology is debatable. A British Museum expert who has visited the site told me that their scientific contribution was negligible but that they did obtain some nice pieces for the Museum.[52] The finds, from which the Ashmolean also benefited, were certainly not valueless.

*It is also notable that despite opportunities Lawrence appears to have taken no active interest in archaeology after the Great War.

4 The War Begins

From the aspect of biographical research, the most confusing phase of Lawrence's life is his wartime career. There is a mass of conflicting information, and even this is incomplete. There are many months where little or no material can be found. This situation is probably explained by the secret nature of Lawrence's work, although one suspects that his own love of intrigue may have compounded the problem. He was operating in a part of the world which seventy years later remains highly unstable, and although some papers relating to his activities as an intelligence officer have been released through the Public Records Office, it is evident that documents have also been mislaid and in some cases deliberately destroyed, specifically those relating to his involvement with the secret service.

To these already considerable difficulties must be added a political situation which was complicated in the extreme and which involved a bewildering array of agencies and individuals. Moreover, the topography, place and tribal names of the region are not always easy to grasp – a problem made even worse because of the lack of standardization in transliteration from Arabic into English. This situation delighted Lawrence and prompted him to spell Arabic names as the fancy took him, sometimes not even being consistent in the same paragraph.

It is therefore not surprising that recent biographies of Lawrence have tended to skip through the war years, only examining specific episodes. Nevertheless, the war years must be considered in detail because it is in the records of this phase of Lawrence's life that one may establish not only if his fame was deserved, but also see how it evolved.

When Britain entered the First World War on 4 August 1914, Lawrence was in Oxford completing *The Wilderness of Zin*. L. B. Namier, then a student at Balliol, remembers that a day or two after war had been declared Lawrence and he, sharing the martial enthusiasm of their compatriots, went to practise rifle shooting at a disused clay pit in north Oxford.[1] (Namier went on to become a member of the Foreign Office's propaganda department from 1915–17, and from 1918–20 was a political intelligence officer.) Lawrence was eager to get into uniform as soon as possible, a sentiment shared by a whole generation of young Englishmen, few of whom had his special qualifications.

Lawrence's stories of how he first obtained the King's commission conflict.

He told John Buchan that initially, having tried to join up as a regular officer, he had been rejected by the War Office, which he claimed had been swamped by a glut of 'six footers'.[2] To Liddell Hart Lawrence explained that he and Woolley jointly approached Captain Newcombe about a possible job in Intelligence (Newcombe was theoretically an officer of the Royal Engineers) and were put on a waiting list.[3] Impatient of delays, Woolley went off and became a lieutenant in the Royal Artillery – an appointment which did not prevent him from later returning to work with Lawrence who, with Hogarth's help, had meanwhile obtained a job in geographical Intelligence at the War Office.[4] Lawrence had gone to an interview with Colonel Coote Hedley, head of MO4 (Military Operations 4), the geographical division of Military Intelligence, and was immediately taken on to fill a gap in the Colonel's staff. Lawrence told Liddell Hart that Hogarth had arranged the interview and 'pulled the strings', and although Hedley later denied this, it is clear that Hogarth played a major role.[5]

Lawrence was initially taken on in a civilian capacity, and according to legend, the new map-maker was asked one day to present some improved maps of Belgium to General Sir Henry Rawlinson (who had just been appointed to lead an expedition 'to the relief of the Belgium Army'). On seeing the casually dressed young man, the old General boomed, 'I want to talk to an officer', and Colonel Hedley, not wanting to repeat the incident, was forced to get Lawrence a commission as soon as possible, skipping the normal formalities. Lawrence states that he then went along to the Army and Navy Stores in Victoria Street and kitted himself out as a subaltern. He designed his own uniform, which included such idiosyncratic touches as leather tunic buttons to avoid the problems of polishing brass.[6]

Lawrence joined Colonel Hedley's staff at MO4 at the end of September 1914. Earlier that month, he had written 'the War Office won't accept me till the Egyptian W.O. has finished with me'.[7] (The Egyptian War Office was a semi-autonomous department which ran the Anglo-Egyptian Army.) Lawrence was working in Intelligence from the first day of the war, first for the Egyptian War Office on the Sinai project, then, with a brief overlap, for the War Office in Whitehall; simultaneously he was also in touch with the Foreign Office via Hogarth.

Lawrence worked through most of October at the War Office in uniform without being officially commissioned, but on the 26th, just four days before Turkey entered the war, he was gazetted 2nd Lieutenant on the 'special list' – a War Office peg for personnel who had no official regiment. Despite his lowly rank, the new maps officer rapidly became a valued member of Hedley's staff, which had become seriously depleted because many experienced men had been posted overseas.

Lawrence realized that his work would soon take him abroad, a fact made clear by a letter he wrote on 18 September to a Mrs Reider, a teacher from the American Mission School at Jebail who had returned to the United States on holiday.[8] We can see something of Lawrence's plans as he thanks the

American woman for two Colt automatic pistols which she had sent him by request (he only asked for one). The weapons were of a pattern then unobtainable in England, as the first weeks of the war had produced a rush on London gunsmiths. Experienced officers realized that the standard issue .455 Webley revolver of the time, though powerful, was inaccurate, cumbersome and difficult to use, and therefore prudently provided themselves with a better alternative. Similarly, Lawrence – whose enthusiasm for the latest inventions persisted throughout his life – wanted a pistol he could rely on. The Colt was even more modern and effective than his Mauser.

David Garnett, editor of *The Letters of T. E. Lawrence*, included an editorial note to the letter to Mrs Reider which said he had found a related letter, but could not include it, in which Lawrence had remarked that 'a nemesis' might be awaiting him, and that he feared he would 'be served a copy of his own book and told to find his way about the country [Sinai] with its help'.[9]

Garnett was severely restricted in what he might use, and perpetuates more mystery by publishing another contemporary letter, headed 'To a friend' – Sunday [autumn 1914]' (the friend was Leeds at the Ashmolean). Lawrence wrote: 'Though I'm not appointed to anything, yet they can't sack me now, as I know most of their secrets.'[10] Lawrence, a compulsive writer, was sometimes extraordinarily indiscreet in his correspondence, which partly explains the steps taken to prevent the unauthorized publication of his letters. However, the cryptic editorial comments which appear throughout his published letters also serve to confirm Lawrence's mysterious image and create a demand for a less expurgated edition of his correspondence. (A second, revised edition is currently being prepared by the Lawrence Trust.)

When on 30 October 1914 Britain officially declared war against the Ottoman Empire, for Lawrence the 'great game' began in earnest. The declaration was soon followed by a Turkish attempt, encouraged by Germany, to instigate a Jehad or Holy War against the British – a possibility that severely worried the British Government of India, which controlled a large Muslim population. However, for the Muslim world to accept such a grave proclamation the Sherif of Mecca, Hussein – directly descended from the Prophet and officially 'The Keeper of the Holy Places' – would have to endorse the Turkish Sultan's proposal. He did not. To declare a Jehad only against the British Empire would have been absurd: the Germans were the Turks' allies but they, no less than the British, were regarded as infidels by the pious; moreover, there were many Christian officers in the Turkish Army.

Hussein anyway had his own plans and had already been in secret contact with Kitchener, who remained the British Agent and Consul General in Egypt until August 1914. Kitchener had realized war with Germany was inevitable and anticipated that a clash with the Ottoman Empire would follow, though he reasoned it might temporarily be forestalled by diplomacy. In the meantime, he had thought it prudent to investigate, as quietly as possible, the chances of enlisting the help of the subject peoples who had suffered under Turkish repression. The Arabs in particular might prove useful allies, but only if they could be organized and suitable leaders found. There were twenty million Arabs widely dispersed within the Ottoman Empire, many of them integrated into the Turkish Army and Civil Service. The Turks had been forced to accept their large Arab population – smaller minority groups, notably the Armenians and the Bulgars, had been systematically exterminated – but despite their numbers and relatively privileged status, the Arabs were far from secure. The unstable Ottoman regime, increasingly fearful of Arab nationalism, looked upon all Arabs as potential traitors.

The Arabs were not a united racial group. Between the urban populations of Syria and the Bedouin tribesmen of the Hejaz there were (and are still) enormous differences, and even language – the main common factor of the Arab people – varied greatly from region to region. Nor did the Arabs in 1914 have any single obvious spokesman, though some individuals and families had great influence, notably Ibn Raschid based at Hail, Ibn Saud (the founder of Saudi Arabia) in southern Arabia, Al-Idrisi in the Yemen, and the Sherif of Mecca, Hussein, in the Hejaz. It was to be Hussein who with British support initiated the Great Arab Revolt of 1916. During the first half of 1914, the Sherif's second son, Abdullah, made a trip to Cairo and took the opportunity to contact the British secretly as his father's representative. If Hussein rose against the Turks, would His Majesty's government give support? Kitchener made no promises but Abdullah was encouraged to keep in touch with the High Commissioner, Sir Henry McMahon, and with his influential assistant, 'the Oriental Secretary', Ronald Storrs, with whom Abdullah subsequently maintained a secret correspondence.

Abdullah's family – the Hashemites (the current royal house of Jordan) – claimed direct descent from Mohammed through his daughter Fatima. As guardian of the Holy Cities, and thus the overseer of the annual pilgrimage of Muslims from all over the world, the Sherif had the necessary influence to initiate a revolt, at least in his own region, but he needed external backing for it to be effective. Despite his prestige, Hussein's position in the Hejaz was by no means secure. He had been appointed Sherif of Mecca in the last days of the old Turkish regime only after a long struggle. In 1898, Hussein and his immediate family had been brought to Constantinople and kept there under open arrest for over a decade. This confinement, typical of the seesaw of Ottoman politics, had been due to intriguing by Hussein's political enemies and a long-running argument with the contemporary Sherif of Mecca – his uncle – who distrusted his nephew's ambitions. Hussein had used this setback to good advantage by making new allies in the capital, and at the same time had ensured that his sons benefited from a modern education.

Through shrewd lobbying, he was eventually appointed Sherif of Mecca in the turbulent summer of 1908, but the Young Turks of the Committee of Union and Progress were in the process of taking over the Turkish government in a bloodless and, at the time, popular revolution. Their popularity was short-lived, for it soon became clear that their rule was as autocratic as their predecessors'.

The Young Turks began to implement a pro-Turkish policy in direct opposition to Arab, and other minority, aspirations. Even before they came to power, the Young Turks had sought to block Hussein's appointment as Sherif of Mecca, and afterwards they tried to interfere with his local autonomy. Nevertheless, through necessity, he developed a working relationship with the new Ottoman government; his sons gained useful experience serving as officers in the reorganized Turkish Army; his second son, Abdullah, and his third son, Feisal, were both active within the Turkish Parliament. In 1911 Hussein helped the Turks crush an uprising by Al-Idrisi in the Yemen – for which he was denounced by Arab nationalists, who thought, not unjustly, that he had been bought by the Turks who paid him an allowance as Sherif of Mecca: Hussein was always dependent on outside financial support to maintain his ever vulnerable position in the Hejaz.

Ideally, Hussein and his sons wanted an independent kingdom of their own, an ambition encouraged by increasing political repression throughout the Ottoman Empire. The Turks had a reputation for eliminating adversaries, however prestigious, which strengthened Hussein's desire to rule his own kingdom. However, this did not mean that Arab nationalism and Hussein's plans were synonymous. The Sherif, although he had influence, was far from universally popular, nor was he the only pretender to the throne of an independent Arab kingdom, and it was not without difficulty that he exerted a degree of control over the fiercely independent tribes in the Hejaz. Many of these recognized no secular leader above their chiefs – kingship was a foreign concept. Similarly, the ideals of nationalism meant little to illiterate nomads, whose way of life had remained essentially the same for five hundred years. Cities, especially those in Syria, were the intellectual hotbeds of Arab nationalism: in Damascus, Aleppo, Baghdad, Cairo and also Paris, the ultra-secret societies swore in new members and awaited their opportunity.

Some informed European intellectuals were also sympathetic, among them Lawrence. Having witnessed the corruption and inefficiency of Turkish rule in Syria, which led him to despise the Ottoman Empire, he dreamed of, and later planned, an 'independent' Arab state which would come under the benevolent administration of the British Commonwealth, perhaps even becoming 'the first brown dominion'.[11] To the Arab nationalists this would appear to be exchanging the old oppressor for a new one, but as Europe became engulfed in crisis, both the nationalists and Hussein recognized that a unique opportunity had arisen to further their respective causes.

The declaration of war against Turkey and the possibility of a Jehad changed Kitchener's necessarily cautious initial response to Hussein's plans for an anti-Turk uprising. Hussein was sent a message by the Foreign Office through his son Abdullah at the beginning of November 1914:

> Lord Kitchener's Salaams to Sherif Abdullah . . . If the Arab nation assist England in this war that has been forced upon us by Turkey, England will guarantee that no internal intervention takes place in Arabia, and will give Arabs every assistance against external aggression.

> It may be that an Arab of true race will assume the Khalifate at Mecca or Medina and so good may come by the help of God out of all the evil that is now occurring. . . . If the Emir of Mecca is willing to assist Great Britain in this conflict, Great Britain is willing, recognising and respecting the sacred and unique office of the Emir Hussein . . . to guarantee the independence, rights and privileges of the Sherifiate against all external foreign aggression, in particular that of the Ottomans. Till now we have defended Islam in the person of the Turks; henceforward it shall be in that of noble Arabs.[12]

Hussein, although delighted to receive this news, was not yet ready to rise openly against the Turks, and instead bided his time and sounded out his neighbours. None of this did much to allay the fears of the British Government of India, who not fully aware of the secret negotiations with Hussein, felt it necessary to proclaim:

> In view of the outbreak of war between Great Britain and Turkey . . . His Excellency the Viceroy is authorised by His Majesty's Government to make the following public announcement in regard to the Holy Places in Arabia, including the Holy Shrines of Mesopotamia, and the Port of Jeddah, in order that there may be no misunderstanding on the part of His Majesty's most loyal Moslem subjects as to the attitude of His Majesty's Government in this war, in which no question of religious character is involved.
>
> These Holy Places and Jeddah will be immune from attack or molestation by the British Naval and Military forces, so long as there is no interference with pilgrims from India to the Holy Places and Shrines in question.
>
> At the request of His Majesty's Government, the Governments of France and Russia have given similar assurances.[13]

It was, however, difficult for the Government of India to keep full control of events in the Red Sea. In early November, the cruiser HMS *Minerva* had shelled Aqaba, a port within Hussein's domain where many pilgrims to Medina and Mecca alighted. The reason for the incident had been the presence of a small Turkish and German force there, which the captain of *Minerva* hoped he might induce to surrender. The ship left when she could not attain this aim but the Germans used the unsuccessful attack for propaganda, provoking an immediate response by the Foreign Office to the High Commissioner in Cairo. The statement was also published by Reuters:

> His Majesty's Government have no intention of undertaking any military or naval operations in Arabia, or against its ports, unless such a course becomes necessary for the protection of Arab interests against Turkish or other aggression, or in support of any attempts by the Arabs to free themselves from Turkish rule.[14]

By the end of 1914, frequent requests were being made by the Egyptian High Command to London for intelligence officers, in particular specialists who knew the region and spoke Arabic. Lawrence was an obvious choice. On 3 December, he wrote to W. J. Crace, the Secretary of the Palestine

Exploration Fund who was responsible for publishing *The Wilderness of Zin*, that he was just about to leave England with Woolley and Newcombe to take up new residence at 'General Headquarters, British Army Occupations, Cairo'. He also told Crace not to bother sending out the proofs of the book as 'the Censor would never pass them. Much better Egypt shouldn't know.'[15] One can only imagine what complications Lawrence envisaged: 'Egypt' can hardly refer to the Egyptian War Office, who had pressed for the production of the book in the first place.

Lawrence, along with Woolley, Newcombe (who had been recalled from France), Aubrey Herbert MP, George Lloyd MP (later Lord Lloyd, who became High Commissioner of Egypt from 1925 to 1929) and one Captain Hay, were posted to reinforce intelligence staff at GHQ Cairo.

On 20 December Lawrence sent a letter to Hogarth[16] (who was still in England helping to complete the manuscript of *The Wilderness of Zin*), and explained that he had been sent to Egypt not so much to reinforce an existing military Intelligence Department (as he had expected) but to help start a new one under the DMI (Director of Military Intelligence), Colonel Clayton, a hard-working and talented officer who was also in charge of political Intelligence in Egypt and had further responsibilities for Intelligence in the Sudan. Lawrence noted that Pirie-Gordon, the archaeologist and 'kinsman' of Hogarth's who had lent him an annotated map of Syria for the first walking tour in 1909, was also in Egypt, in the uniform of the RNR (Royal Navy Reserve). (Hogarth was soon to appear in a similar outfit with the rank of lieutenant commander.) By 1919, Pirie-Gordon had gone through another metamorphosis to become a lieutenant colonel in the Army.

By January 1915, Lawrence was on the threshold of what he expected to be a glorious new adventure, combining the best aspects of the life he had enjoyed so much at Carchemish with considerably more power. In another letter to Hogarth, dated 2 February 1915, he stated his contempt for the average Egyptian officer, who was 'pathetically ignorant of across the border', and went on to describe his own and his friends' work within the small intelligence unit:

> Woolley sits all day doing précis, & writing windy concealers of truth for the press . . . Newcombe runs a gang of the most offensive spies, & talks to the General. I am map officer & write geographical reports, trying to persuade 'em [GHQ] that Syria is not peopled entirely by Turks . . . Aubrey Herbert unearths futile conspiracies.[17]

In these early days working in Cairo, Lawrence was a colleague of Philip Graves, the half-brother of his first official biographer, Robert Graves. Philip Graves had been *The Times* correspondent in Constantinople before the war and joined Cairo Intelligence shortly before Lawrence. He was an expert on the Turkish Army, and Lawrence and he worked together on the *Turkish Army Handbook*, a constantly updated catalogue of the make-up and dispositions of the Turkish armed forces. Lawrence is sometimes credited with being solely responsible for the handbook but it was in fact the brainchild of Philip Graves. Lawrence assisted him in gaining information for the guide, which involved them in the interrogation of incoming Turkish prisoners of war. (Graves was later fiercely critical of Lawrence's *Seven Pillars of Wisdom.*)

On 18 March 1915, Lawrence had the luxury of an 'uncensored' letter to Hogarth, and briefed him on the latest (and highly classified) situation in the Middle Eastern theatre.[18] Lawrence wrote that the Turks had only 50,000 'disaffected' troops in Syria, though 200,000 in the Dardanelles, 200,000 in the Caucasus and 50,000 in Mesopotamia. He referred to a battle between Ibn Raschid and Ibn Saud, in which Captain Shakespeare, a courageous and well-known British agent, had been killed. Shakespeare was Britain's link with Ibn Saud and his death had far-reaching consequences for British foreign policy. Lawrence also noted that the Sherif of Mecca was near to declaring an Arab revolt against the Turks, and that British troops who had been defending the Suez Canal were now being sent to reinforce Indian troops in Mesopotamia.

The second half of the letter was devoted to Lawrence's proposal for occupying Alexandretta, which he pointed out was 'the key of the whole place [Near East] . . . It's going to be the head of the Baghdad line [Berlin–Baghdad railway] . . . In the hands of France it will provide a sure base for naval attacks on Egypt.' (And France was meant to be an ally!) Lawrence continued:

> If Russia has Alexandretta it's all up with us in the near East. And in any case in the next war the French will probably be under Russia's finger in Syria. Therefore I think it absolutely necessary that we hold Alexandretta . . . we needn't hold anything else, either in Syria or Asia Minor. The High Commissioner is strongly of the same opinion, & General Maxwell also. [six words omitted from published letter.] K [Kitchener] has pressed it on us: Winston seems uncertain, & Someone – not Grey – perhaps Parker in the F.O. is blocking it entirely. I think that perhaps you can get a move on.
>
> K. is behind you in any case. Can you get someone to suggest to Winston that there is a petrol spring on the beach.[19]

Lawrence then described his plan for occupying Alexandretta, and its advantages.

It is an extraordinary letter, and might have had considerable repercussions had the French come to know of it. Lawrence, ostensibly a junior officer, was already considering another war. His tone to Hogarth is also interesting; he addresses him as an equal, more like a brother officer or fellow conspirator than a substitute father, the role usually attributed to him.

Lawrence later claimed that it was he who originated the idea for attacking and occupying Alexandretta. In 1929 he wrote to Liddell Hart, 'I am unrepentant about the Alexandretta scheme which was, from beginning to end, my invention . . . (I was a 2nd Lieut. of 3 months seniority!). Actually K. accepted it, and ordered it, for the Australian and N.Z. forces: and then was met by a French ultimatum'.[20] In fact Kitchener had discussed the occupation of Alexandretta before the war with General Maxwell. However, no doubt the details for such an operation fell within the bounds of Lawrence's department at Cairo, and even if he did not originate the idea, Lawrence used all his connections to push through a plan which he may well have modified. Eventually it was shelved as Lawrence had predicted, because of French opposition.

Lawrence wrote another equally strange letter to Hogarth only four days after sending his proposals for Alexandretta. In this he discussed the implications should an Arab revolt occur, but at this stage he was considering Al-Idrisi, whose revolt Hussein had once crushed, as the potential leader, although he acknowledged the importance of Hussein. The letter is characteristically indiscreet, as again he knew that it would not be censored.

> This week is something else. You know India [i.e. the Government of India] used to be in control of Arabia – and used to do it pretty badly, for they hadn't a man who knew Syria or Turkey, & they used to consider only the Gulf, & the preservation of peace in the Aden Hinterland. So they got tied into horrid knots with the Imam, who is a poisonous blighter at the best. Egypt (which is one Clayton, a very good man) got hold of the Idrisi family, who are the Senussi and Assyr together, as you know: and for some years we had a little agreement together. Then this war started, & India went on the old game of balancing the little powers there. I want to pull them all together, & to roll up Syria by way of the Hedjaz in the name of the Sherif. You know how big his repute is in Syria. This could be done by Idrisi only, so we drew out a beautiful alliance, giving him all he wanted: & India refused to sign. So we cursed them, & I think that Newcombe and myself are going down to Kunfida as his advisers. If Idrisi is anything like as good as we hope we can rush right up to Damascus, & biff the French out of all hope of Syria. It's a big game, and at last one worth playing. Of course India has no idea what we are playing at: if we can only get to Assyr we can do the rest – or have a try at it. So if I write and tell you it's all right, and I'm off, you will know where for. Wouldn't you like to be on it? Though I don't give much for my insurance chances again. If only India will let us go. Won't the French be mad if we win though? Don't talk of it yet.[21]
>
> T.E.L.

The Indian Government were trying to block any plans to support Arab independence, supported by the Indian Foreign Office which believed that the Turks were not only more reliable than the Arabs but also that the Ottoman Empire provided an important buffer against Russian agitation in India – a view held by many statesmen in England. Kitchener, conversely, had already noted that an independent state in Palestine would act as a buffer between Egypt and Turkey. Lawrence, Clayton, Hogarth and all supporters of an Arab revolt were fully aware of the potential dangers of Arab nationalism. They, and for that matter the Sherif of Mecca, did not want to see a united Arab Empire, but rather an independent Arab state that would be to Turkey's disadvantage.

Clayton later wrote to the Foreign Office, shortly before the Arab revolt became a reality:

> India seems obsessed with the idea that we mean to form a powerful Arab Kingdom. Such was never the intention and would in any case be impracticable. Whole idea was to retain friendship of Arabs by agreeing to recognise principle of Arab Independence and promising to assist them to establish such forms of administration under British and French guidance as may be found most suitable in the various districts. The various ruling chiefs will naturally remain practically independent and, though the Sherif might become the nominal head of the Arab confederation and thus qualify himself to assume Khalifate, the lack of cohesion which is always quoted is our main safeguard against the establishment of a united Arab Kingdom which might be a threat against British Interests.
>
> There is little doubt that our negotiations to date have gone far to defeating Turko-German propaganda among the Arabs, which, if successful would have grave results.[22]

Throughout the war the Government of India mistrusted these intentions and deliberately obstructed the Hashemite Arab revolt. Inter-departmental feuding between the India Office and the British Foreign Office developed into open war. In Cairo on 18 April 1915, Lawrence wrote to Leeds at the Ashmolean complaining that the Government of India refused to hand over their authority in the region to Egypt and preferred to leave it 'in the hands of a juggins in Delhi, whose efforts are to maintain the Aden Hinterland – a cesspit – in its status quo. Pouf.'[23] Whatever the attitude of the Indian Government, Lawrence pressed on towards his ambition of a successful Arab revolt, which of course entailed contacting and making use of Arab nationalists.

It was during this period that Second Lieutenant Lawrence became known for driving ostentatiously large motorcycles and for his scruffy appearance – part of a general refusal to comply with the established rules of conduct for young officers. He 'forgot' to polish his buttons, 'forgot' to put on his belt, 'forgot' to put on his hat, 'forgot' to salute – all still heinous offences in the British Army. He loved digs at authority and hated pomposity – although he was quite capable of being pompous himself.

Colonel Joyce, Lawrence's immediate superior during the Arabian campaign, remembers of their first meeting 'the intense desire on my behalf to tell him to get his hair cut, and that his uniform and buttons sadly needed the attention of his batman'.[24] (Lawrence described short hair as an 'imitative vice'.) On another occasion, after a meeting with Lawrence, Ronald Storrs had to send his house servant running into the street carrying the Sam Browne belt which his young guest had forgotten.[25]

Lawrence's disregard for authority could also be put to more practical use. Ernest Dowson recalled one occasion when the 'Government press' in Cairo was in desperate need of a spare part for a printing machine. The exact piece needed was available only in an 'enemy' company's warehouse, which was locked. The director of the press, which printed important documents for the Government and the Army, had appealed to GHQ, who said that it was impossible to open the premises without permission from London. Lawrence heard of the problem, and arranged a break-in, appearing the next day with the vital part: 'No explanations were volunteered: no questions asked.'[26]

Officially, Lawrence was still only Map Officer at GHQ Cairo, and according to Dowson, then the director of the Survey of Egypt, Lawrence visited the office about 'two or three times' a week. The Survey was 'an ordinary civil department of the Egyptian Government, built up primarily to carry out the cadastral, topographical and geological survey of Egypt'[27] – but it was linked to MO4 during the war. Lawrence quickly became the 'effective link between the Military Intelligence Service and in due course the Arab Bureau on the one side and the Survey of Egypt on the other.'[28]

Dowson made several important observations on Lawrence's character. He was well aware of Lawrence's gifts, especially his 'rare capacity' to look at problems objectively 'and in the process to get inside the skin of the participants'. He noted his ability 'to get his own way quietly', but also noted how he inexcusably ridiculed people who were not 'pompous', 'inefficient' or 'pretentious', especially when they were a threat to him. 'Many men of sense and ability were repelled by the impudence, freakishness and frivolity he trailed so provocatively.' Dowson has also commented on the Lawrence of Arabia image: 'Many sober and fair-minded men regarded his intrusions of Bedawi robes, accoutrements and bare feet into conventional gatherings as histrionic displays' and the same individuals thus regarded Lawrence as fundamentally 'a posturing stage player'.[29] Nevertheless, Lawrence accomplished important work in Dowson's department and there is little doubt of his skill as a geographical intelligence officer.

Accurate maps were of considerable political as well as military significance. By April 1915, the Allies were already looking forward to an 'imperial carve-up' of the Ottoman Empire. Britain, France and Russia had all made their bids. Italy was brought into the war, suitably bribed by the terms of the Treaty of London (signed on 26 April 1915), which included the following clauses:

Article 8 – Italy will receive complete sovereignty of the Dodecanese Islands [a group of islands off the north-east coast of Asia Minor] which she occupies at the moment.

Article 9 – France, Great Britain and Russia recognise in principle Italy's interest in the maintainance of the political balance of power in the Mediterranean and her rights to receive, in the case of total division or partial division of Turkey-in-Asia, an equal share with them in the Mediterranean basin . . .

Article 10 – Italy will receive in Libya the right and privileges at present belonging to the Sultan . . .

Article 12 – Italy associates herself with the declaration made by France, Great Britain and Russia, leaving Arabia and the sacred Moslem places under the authority of an independent Moslem power.

Article 13 – In the event of the enlargement of the French and English colonial possessions in Africa at the expense of Germany, France and Great Britain recognise in principle Italy's right to demand for herself certain compensations in the sense of an extension of her possessions in Eritrea, Somaliland, Libya, and the colonial districts contiguous to the colonies of France and England.

Article 14 – England undertakes to facilitate the immediate realisation of a loan by Italy on the London market, on advantageous terms, for a sum of less than £50,000,000.[30]

This Treaty, like the infamous Sykes-Picot agreement which followed it, was embarrassingly made public by the Bolsheviks after the revolution of 1917, and used as propaganda against the secret diplomacy of capitalism.

In the same month in which the Treaty of London was signed, there was a partial restructuring of Military Intelligence in Cairo and Lawrence's department assumed responsibility for Intelligence to the newly arrived 'Mediterranean Expeditionary Force' – destined for the disaster Gallipoli. Lloyd and Herbert were temporarily attached to 'Med-Ex'; Woolley was doing other work co-ordinating Intelligence in Port Said; and Newcombe and Lawrence were left 'to hold the fort'. Lawrence was beginning to run a small network of agents (taking some over from Newcombe) as his duties and inclinations broadened from mere geographical Intelligence. Debriefing prisoners, agents and would-be agents became a routine job.

To this end, Lawrence interviewed a nineteen-year-old Christian refugee from Palestine, Charles Boutagy, whose brother had been secretary to the British Vice-Consul at Haifa. Colonel Gilbert Clayton, Lawrence's boss at GHQ, had already offered Boutagy a job as a translator but now Lawrence, nominally a second lieutenant, offered him a more interesting proposition. Boutagy was interviewed by *The Sunday Times* in the late 1960s and told how Lawrence had proposed that he should return to Haifa as a British spy.[31] Boutagy thought this imprudent; as he was of military age, he would in all likelihood be arrested by the Turks as a deserter, and forced to serve in the Turkish Army. This was the very reason he had left Haifa in the first place. Instead, Boutagy proposed his father, who still lived in Haifa.

Elaborate plans were made in which Charles Boutagy (designated 'agent 91') would act as contact and be dropped off at Haifa by a Russian cruiser – no British ship was willing to undertake 'the drop'. The plan was that Boutagy would be transported near Haifa, then row to the beach, meet his father, collect the latest information, and return. However, the mission turned into a fiasco and Boutagy's father was arrested by the Turks for spying. Luckily, he was acquitted, a fact which Charles Boutagy put down to his father being a freemason. This is quite probable as freemasonry was very powerful throughout the Ottoman Empire. The Young Turk revolution of 1908 was inspired by freemasonry. Francis Yeats-Brown, the author of *Bengal Lancer* and later a friend of Lawrence, put down his survival after being caught behind Turkish lines in the war, to the fact that he was a mason: the Turkish police sergeant who arrested him was also a member of the brotherhood and, having exchanged handshakes, spared Yeats-Brown from summary execution.[32]

Charles Boutagy returned to Port Said and ended up working for Woolley. As 'Agent 91', he continued his career acting as an informer on neutral ships.

There is documentary evidence that Lawrence tried to recruit other agents. He wrote to A. B. Watt, a British businessman in Cyprus, asking him if he knew the area of Alexandretta (as Lawrence knew he did). When Watt responded favourably, Lawrence wrote back with details of his terms of employment as an intelligence agent, explaining what his pay would be and reassuring him (and his wife) that the work would not be dangerous![33] Watt was not taken on because the plan to take Alexandretta was scrapped.

Just before first writing to Watt, Lawrence had been informed of his brother Frank's death; within six months his younger brother Will, an observer in the RFC, was also killed in action. Their deaths may have persuaded Lawrence to move out from the safety of his job in Cairo. David Garnett wrote: 'The death of Will . . . was a great shock . . . In a letter I cannot quote . . . he expressed a feeling that it was not right for him to go on living safely in Cairo, and a dread of what returning to Oxford would be like.'[34]

Lawrence had a deep affection for his brother Will. When he heard of Will's death, he was not alone. Hogarth had arrived in Cairo, as a lieutenant commander in the RNVR, on 26 July.

There is a sudden paucity of information about Lawrence's duties in the second half of 1915: in his published letters there is a gap from August 1915 to the end of March 1916. His duties were becoming far more widespread—Lawrence and Hogarth were involved, from the intelligence aspect, in the evacuation of Gallipoli which occurred after the abortive Allied attack on the Dardanelles. At least the evacuation was successful. It took place on the night of 18–19 December 1915 without a single casualty.

5 Cairo and Kut

By the beginning of 1916, the Sherif of Mecca and his sons, encouraged by British promises, were making final preparations for a revolt against the Turks. Britain was pledged to recognize and give material support to a new independent Arab kingdom, which would include parts of Syria and Lebanon. Inconsistently, France, and later Russia, were involved in drawing up the Sykes–Picot Treaty. Under the terms of this complex agreement which assumed an Allied victory, Britain would get direct control of Mesopotamia* and special 'economic and political priority' in the area which includes modern Jordan, but also extends east, parallel to Mosul, and south past Kuwait. Palestine would theoretically be 'international', although Haifa and Acre would be British ports, thus ensuring British control.

France would get absolute control of Lebanon and western Syria (including the whole coastline), parts of northern Turkey and a protectorate over the Syrian interior where it was conceded there would be some sort of local administration as well, though it would be utterly subservient to France because of French control of all Syrian ports. France had an interest in Syria and Lebanon which extended back to the Crusades. Before the Republic, French monarchs had been given the title of 'Protector of Oriental Christians' by the Pope, and had always jealously guarded their interests in the region.

The secret Sykes–Picot Treaty, and the equally secret Hussein–McMahon correspondence in which British promises to the Sherif are set out, clearly conflict. The Bolsheviks were certainly aware of the implications of the conflict when they published the text of Sykes–Picot in *Izvestia* in late 1917. Ronald Storrs later gave as an implausible excuse for the subsequent Anglo-French-Arab misunderstanding that it was partially due to his own translator's colourful prose, and the Sherif of Mecca's classical but imprecise Arabic.[1]

At the beginning of 1916, Lawrence, nominally a second lieutenant, was already involved in the secret communications with Hussein, actually helping to draft some of McMahon's letters; it is probable, but not certain, that he also knew of Sykes–Picot.

*With the exception of the Mosul Oil Fields, which went to France. After the war, Clemenceau agreed with Lloyd George that he would be willing to hand over the control of the Mosul to Britain if HMG accepted an extended French presence in Syria, and also gave France a percentage of the oil revenue from the Mosul.

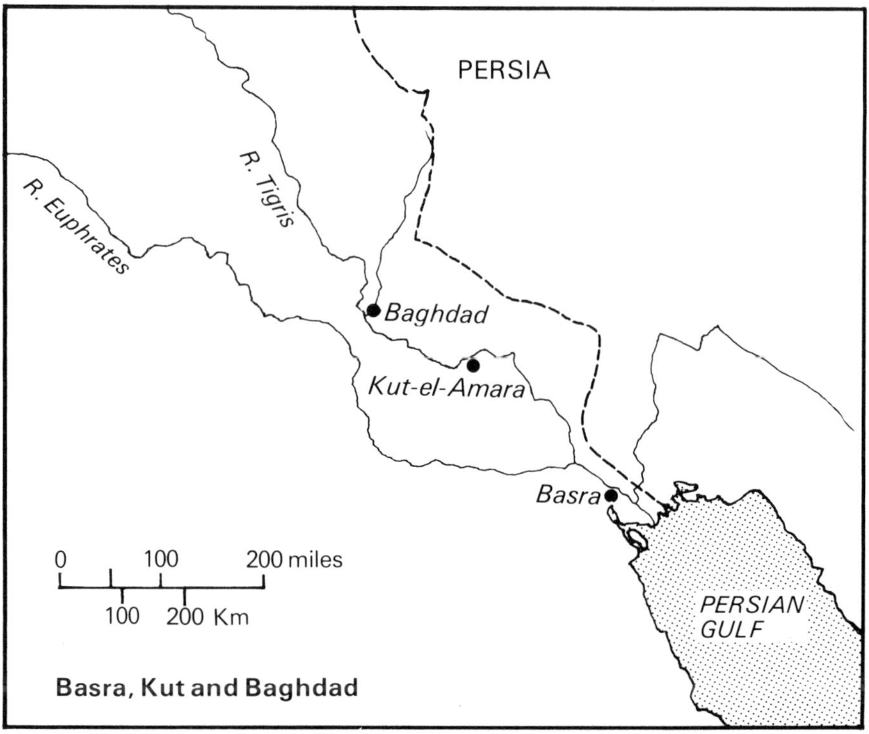

Basra, Kut and Baghdad

In January, Lawrence wrote two perceptive reports on the consequences of an Arab revolt in the Hejaz in which he not only suggested that Hussein was the best leader available, but further advocated the dynamiting of the rail links to Medina – a task he was later to undertake personally. The second of these reports, entitled the 'politics of Mecca', so impressed the High Commissioner that he sent a copy to the Foreign Secretary in London with the note:

> The Memorandum while revealing nothing definitely new, appears to be a clear and able statement of the position of Sherif Hussein and of the attitude which he has adopted in his relations with the various states of the Arabian Peninsula.[2]

The report itself, first publicized in part by Knightley and Simpson, is here produced in full:

> The Politics of Mecca
>
> Sherif Hussein is not working in the British Interests, except in so far as they further the particular dreams and hopes of the political party to which he belongs. His aim is the establishment of a Khalifate (not the only one) for himself, and independence for people speaking Arabic from their present irritating subjection to people speaking Turkish. His aims are thus in definite opposition to the Pan-Islamic party [the Arab Nationalists], who are his strong obstacle, and to the Young Turk party, who are however less dangerous to his schemes; his activity seems beneficial to us, because it marches with our immediate aims, the break up of the

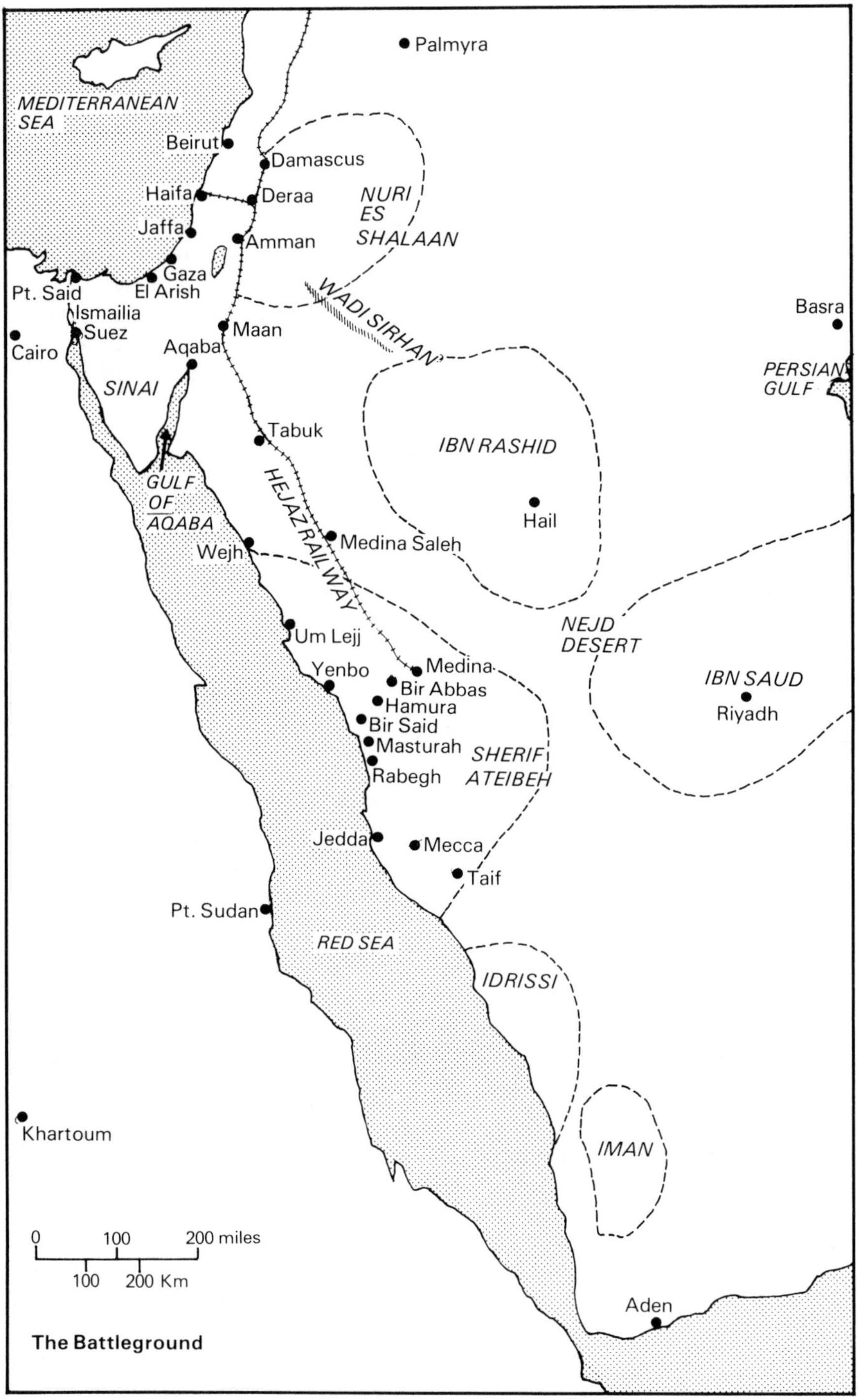

The Battleground

> Islamic 'bloc' and the defeat and disruption of the Ottoman Empire, and because the states he would set up to succeed the Turks would be as harmless to ourselves as Turkey was before she became a tool in German hands. The Arabs are even less stable than the Turks. If properly handled they would remain in a state of political mosaic, a tissue of small jealous principalities, incapable of cohesion and yet always ready to combine against an outside force. The alternative to this seems to be the control and colonisation by a European power other than ourselves, which would inevitably come into conflict with the interests we already possess in the Near East.
>
> Sherif Hussein's activities have already been of use to us. He has held in the Imam from attacking ADEN, he has quieted the Mullah in Somaliland, he has divided the counsels of Ibn Rashid. He has refused to preach a Jehad, or to allow the legal Jehad to be declared; he has countered, and is still countering, Turkish influence in the Hejaz; has prevented the raising of volunteers; and has forbidden the placarding of anti-British news in the public places of MECCA; all this obviously with a mind some day to taking the place of the Turkish Government in the Hejaz himself. If we can only arrange that this political change shall be a violent one, we will have abolished the threat of Islam, by dividing it against itself, in its very heart. There will then be a Khalifa in Turkey and a Khalifa in Arabia, in theological warfare, and Islam will be as little formidable as the Papacy when Popes lived in Avignon.[3]

These are hardly the words of a future saviour of the Arab people: rather they are the cold but brilliant calculations of a young man totally committed to furthering the interests of the British Empire. Lawrence later wrote in 'Seven Pillars' that 'I risked the fraud, on my conviction that Arab help was necessary to our cheap and speedy victory in the East, and that better we win and break our word than lose.'[4]

In February 1916, Hussein at last informed the High Commissioner in Cairo that the moment for an uprising had finally arrived. McMahon replied: 'His Majesty's Government give their approval . . . supplies will be immediately deposited at Port Sudan . . . waiting to hear from you officially of beginning of movement . . .'[5] Realizing his moment had nearly arrived, Lawrence pressed on with his intelligence duties, making as many new contacts as possible and adding to his already formidable knowledge of Arab and Syrian politics. In March, he interviewed Dr 'Abd al-Rahman Shahbander, a prominent Syrian nationalist who had been imprisoned by the Turks in Damascus (he was assassinated in 1940). Shahbander had recently escaped and made his way to Cairo, where he inevitably came into contact with British Intelligence, and Lawrence. He was favourably impressed by the depth of Lawrence's understanding of the nationalist movement, and was surprised by his intimate knowledge of the Arab secret societies:

> This man is different from the rest of the Englishmen whom we have seen so far, that he listens attentively to the political organisation of the Arabs and . . . his questions show a depth in the subject which is not present except with one who has in it a pleasure and a passion.[6]

Lawrence was not yet an officially listed member of the newly formed Arab

Bureau, although he acted as Military Intelligence's liaison officer to the Bureau from its inception. The Arab Bureau had been set up on 1 January 1916 by Lawrence's intelligence chief, Clayton. Hogarth came out from England in March to act as 'director' of the new unit and Lawrence knew all the other officers well, most as personal friends, although he was not officially transferred to the staff until October.

The Bureau was set up as a 'Tiny Intelligence for War Staff for Foreign Affairs', outside the military administration, as a 'duly accorded branch of the Foreign Office'. It was made clear that 'temporary naval or military rank held by officials of the Bureau is in no way indicative of their political status or duties'. Its formation was a direct result of political and propaganda needs, rather than for the purpose of tactical Intelligence.[7]

Although its functions and authority have never been clearly understood, they are clarified in a series of Foreign Office memoranda which have now come to light. In one note, the High Commissioner McMahon wrote to Grey, the Foreign Secretary:

> It [the Bureau] is badly wanted not only to build up knowledge of a little known country and people which must henceforth grow into greater prominence and importance, but to counteract propaganda which, now and hereafter, threaten to injure our position in the Eastern world.[8]

Clayton wrote to Sir Mark Sykes in London (the co-author of the Sykes–Picot agreement):

> . . . it [the Bureau] should, I think, be nominally under the control of the Foreign Office but only so far as it will be under the control of the High Commissioner. It should be in close touch with the Director of the Intelligence Division, Admiralty, and with M.O.6. [underlined in original] at the War Office. A London representative of the Bureau should ensure this.[9]

The Secretary of State for India wrote to the Foreign Secretary:

> It will of course be pointed out to him [an Indian Political Officer – possibly Cox] that the Bureau of Cairo is the central organ through which His Majesty's Government will lay down principles and policy in respect of Arab propaganda in the East, and the central staff in Mesopotamia must there work in strict conformity with the indications received from the Bureau.[10]

The last passage is indicative of the tension between the Foreign Office and the Government of India regarding the formation of the Bureau, which took over many of the Indian Government's responsibilities in Arabia. Thus the Indian Foreign Office sent a terse note to the Foreign Office in London:

> You are I think aware that Captain Lawrence was recently deputed here [to Mesopotamia] temporarily from Egypt in connection with certain projects of which the Arab Bureau was one. From conversations held with him it would appear that the fact that the conduct of it has been retained in hands of Director Military Intelligence has given us a somewhat erroneous impression of the objects and status

> of the Bureau which we regarded as mainly a war measure. In view of modified aspects in which institution is presented to us by Lawrence, I propose that Miss Gertrude Bell [who had made herself particularly popular with the Anglo-Indians] and not Major Blaker should act as corresponding officer for Mesopotamia.[11]

This communication is marked for circulation to MI6 – established 1909 – and an unknown party in Whitehall, possibly an official of MI6, has commented 'very satisfactory' in reference to Gertrude Bell's appointment.

Mesopotamia, as well as the Hejaz, was thought to be a particularly suitable area for anti-Turk subversion, and guided by Hogarth, Lawrence had been working on plans for harnessing Arab nationalism. He was ordered by the War Office to go to Basra to help set up a political intelligence base.

McMahon wrote a note to introduce him to Sir Percy Cox, Chief Political Officer in Mesopotamia, which was within the 'sphere of influence' of the Indian Government. The letter is now part of an American collection and is published here for the first time:

> My dear Cox,
>
> I send these few lines to introduce Captain [Lawrence had been given a 'temporary' promotion] Lawrence who is starting today for Mesopotamia under orders from the W.O. to give his services in regard to Arab matters.
>
> He is one of the best of our very able intelligence staff here and has a thorough knowledge of the Arab question in all its bearings.
>
> I feel sure that you will find him of great use. We are sorry to lose so valuable a man from our staff here.
>
> I hope things are going well on your side. We are anxiously awaiting news of Townshend's relief but have heard nothing for ages.
>
> All is going well here. Please forgive haste . . .[12]

The last lines of McMahon's letter refer to the Anglo-Indian expeditionary force commanded by General Sir Charles Townshend which had run into severe difficulties after an unsuccessful advance on Baghdad. During 1915, an Anglo-Indian army, with support from the Royal Indian Marine, had advanced from Basra on the Persian Gulf towards Baghdad. Townshend had not been in favour of moving so far but the British Commander-in-Chief, Sir John Nixon, had insisted. The operation went well until Townshend's 'Invincibles' approached the outskirts of Baghdad where, already fatigued, they were met by crack Turkish troops, and forced to retreat to the small town of Kut-el-Amara. The Turks, commanded by Khalil Pasha and advised by Field Marshal von der Goltz (a senior German officer personally responsible for reorganizing much of the Turkish Army), fought back hard. Townshend and a force of 10,000 men were besieged at Kut-el-Amara and another Anglo-Indian Expeditionary Force was sent to rescue them but could not break through. The Turks retained the advantage throughout the bitter fighting during the winter of 1915–16. As there was no apparent way of ending the siege by military action, a less conventional idea was mooted: perhaps the Turks could be bribed. Kitchener, who had taken up the post of Secretary of

State for War, approved this extraordinary proposal, and one million pounds was made available to try and buy the freedom (on parole) of Townshend's trapped army.

Sir Percy Cox, in his official capacity as Chief Political Officer of the Government of India, washed his hands of the whole affair, but his opposition, and that of many senior officers, was overridden. Townshend made initial but unproductive contact with Khalil Pasha, and Kitchener decided that officers were required with 'special qualifications for such work'. The experts selected to carry out this most delicate task were T. E. Lawrence, who was about to leave for Mesopotamia anyway, and Captain Aubrey Herbert MP, one of the officers who had been sent out to reinforce Cairo GHQ Intelligence with Lawrence, Woolley and Newcombe in the autumn of 1914.

There is some evidence that Colonel Clayton was not altogether happy about Lawrence, one of his key men, being sent to Mesopotamia. He telegraphed to the Director of Military Intelligence in London: 'I hope he [Lawrence] will not be retained at Basra longer than necessary.'[13]

Lawrence left Cairo on 22 March, and on the 28th the CIGS (Chief of the Imperial General Staff), Sir William Robertson, sent the following telegram (first published in part by Knightley and Simpson) to 'The General Officer Commanding Force D' (Force D was the Army sent to rescue Townshend, and was deployed close to the Turkish lines around Kut):

> From Chief to Intrusive Cairo. 29.3.16.
>
> Clear the line. 14895. Cipher. Most secret and for yourself personally. Captain Lawrence is due at BASRA [six days by steamer from Kut] about the 30th March from Egypt to consult with you and if possible purchase one of the Turkish leaders of the Mesopotamian Army such as Khalil or Negib, so as to facilitate relief for TOWNSHEND. You are authorised to expend for this purpose any sum not exceeding one million pounds. As no suitable native was immediately available Lawrence proceeds alone, but perhaps a suitable go-between can be found in BASRA. Subsequently and independently High Commissioner, Egypt, has suggested to Foreign Office utility [of] negotiating with Arab element in Turkish Army with a view to detaching them from Turks and making them side with Arab movement. Masri, Dr. Shahbander and another Arab officer will probably be sent to MESOPOTAMIA for this purpose, but may arrive too late to affect Townshend's position. If opportunity offers you should co-ordinate and make fullest use of two efforts. High Commissioner, Egypt, will have informed Masri, or will inform him through you of the political promises he is authorised to make to the Arab elements in Turkish Army. India has been asked to release following Turkish prisoners and send them to Basra to act with MASRI and Lawrence – Cavalry Lieutenant Meludpad Effendi, Infantry Lieutenant Ahmed Hamdi and Tahia Katus Hamid, Artillery Lieutenant Sayid.
>
> Addressed G.O.C. Force D. Repeated to Intrusive [Codename of the Arab Bureau] Cairo.[14]

When Lawrence landed in Basra, he was met by Gertrude Bell and R. C. Campbell-Thompson. 'Gertie' had arrived in Basra only three weeks previously and was also working as an intelligence officer for the War Office and the Arab Bureau. Her status and duties were as muddled as those of Lawrence. Letters preserved in Foreign Office files show she had been briefing Lawrence on the political situation in Mesopotamia for some time. Campbell-Thompson, Lawrence's old digging companion from Carchemish, was well established in Basra as GSO2 Intelligence to Force D – a very small world. Bell and Thompson prepared the ground for Lawrence's special mission but could do little to allay the hostility of the Anglo-Indian commanders to London's distasteful 'political' solution to the siege of Kut. Lawrence and Herbert were eventually received somewhat more cordially by the Turks (they crossed into their lines blindfolded under a white flag).

When he first arrived in Mesopotamia, Lawrence had been taken aside by two Indian Army generals and told his mission was dishonourable. Dishonourable or not, Lawrence and Herbert proceeded as ordered, but the Turks could not be bought, even for a million pounds in gold, and the British officers got nothing but coffee and polite sarcasm from Khalil Pasha, who pointed out that he had lost 10,000 men himself over the siege; Lawrence upped the offer to two million – still no sale. Khalil would accept nothing but unconditional surrender.

Lawrence and Herbert did manage to obtain the release from Kut of a thousand wounded in exchange for fit Turkish prisoners, but in all else they failed. On 29 April, the Commander of Force D sent a despatch to London which he had received from Townshend:

> my guns have been destroyed and am destroying most of my munitions. Officers have been sent to Khalil to say I am prepared to surrender . . . I am unable to hold out anymore and must have some food here.[15]

Lawrence and Herbert returned to Force D and stayed to witness the surrender. Of the 12,000 soldiers taken prisoners by the Turks, 5,000 died in or en route to prison camps; a further 26,000 'had been killed in the bungling attempts to relieve Kut'. Townshend was taken to Constantinople and remained for the rest of the war in reasonable comfort.

Lawrence undeservedly gained the lasting enmity of the Indian Army for his activities at Kut, and especially for his subsequent report on the blunders that led up to it. His analysis was frankly critical of the whole campaign.

While in Basra, Lawrence – who had been behaving rather flamboyantly – met another old acquaintance, Hubert Young, who hardly recognized the shy young academic he had met before the war at Carchemish. Young noted that Lawrence had changed:

> [Lawrence] seemed to me thoroughly spoilt, and posing in a way that was quite unlike what I remembered of him at Carchemish. It was then that I first noticed his anti-regular soldier complex, and, perhaps not unnaturally, resented it hotly.[16]

The animosity was not mutual, as eighteen months later Lawrence, by then deeply involved in the Arab Revolt, suggested Young as a suitable replacement should he be killed in action.

When Lawrence's Kut mission had failed, he started work on his original project which was equally distasteful to the Anglo-Indians – the fermentation of an Arab Revolt in Mesopotamia, the plans for which he had been formulating before he left Cairo. The extent of the misunderstanding of such a project is well illustrated by a communication the Indian Foreign Office received from the Intelligence Department of the Anglo-Indian Army at Kut in November 1915 – just a few weeks before Townshend and his men were trapped:

> The formation of an autonomous state in Iraq [Mesopotamia] appears to be impossible and unnecessary. Here in Iraq there is no sign of the slightest ambition of the kind among the people, who expect and seem quite ready to accept our administration. Other ideas grow in the course of years as they have in India, but we are of the opinion that from the point of view of Iraq it is highly inexpedient and unnecessary to put into the hands of the backward people of the country what seems to us the visionary and premature notions of the creation of an Arab State, notions which will only tend to make endless difficulties for Great Britain here and serve no present purpose but to stimulate a small section of ambitious men to turn their activities to a direction from which it is highly desirable to keep them for many years to come. Moreover, so far as we know, there is no person who could be called upon to assume the high position of Ruler of an Independent Arab State.[17]

Four months after this was written, following the ignominious surrender of Townshend's army, T. E. Lawrence received secret orders from Cairo instructing him to implement immediately the plans for a popular rising in Mesopotamia against the Turks. The nucleus of the rebellion would be the group of nationalist leaders the Arab Bureau had collected and were now shipping en masse as a mission to Basra. Lawrence's orders were to meet them and facilitate their actions. Clayton sent these orders:

> As regards actually what you can do both now and when the Mission comes, I have no doubt that we or the War Office will be able to give you fuller instructions, but broadly speaking as far as I can see it will be a matter of seeing how far such Military Co-operations as the Mission can put at our disposal can be made use of and (when their proposals have received the approval of G.O.C.) to do all you can to get the Arab and our own forces to co-operate.[18]

Lawrence was given further instructions from Clayton which involved the expenditure of large sums of money, an indication of his authority, and he was told that if the senior staff in Mesopotamia did not co-operate 'don't hesitate to wire us' as 'we feel sufficiently assured of War Office co-operation to say that we can overcome any difficulties of a minor nature . . . that you can possibly meet with.' But now Lawrence found that a revolt in Mesopotamia was not a realistic proposition. He wrote to Clayton:

> I have been looking up pan-Arab party at Basra. It is about 12 strong. Formerly consisted of Sayed Taleb and some jackals.

> The other Basra people are either from NEJD interested in Central Arabia only and to be classed with Arabia politically or peasants who are interested in date palms or Persians. There is not Arab sentiment and for us the place is negligible . . . BAGHDAD stands on a different footing and should not be entered until policy has been determined on.[19]

It was clear that Lawrence was wasting his time. There was little sympathy for an anti-Turk uprising in Mesopotamia, and Lawrence was ordered to return to Egypt where his talents could be put to better use.

6 Intelligence Analyst

In May 1916, Lawrence returned to Cairo. On his way back, he wrote a report, cataloguing the mismanagement which had led to the tragedy at Kut. It was so strong that it had to be 'bowdlerised' before being shown to the commander of the Egyptian Expeditionary Force, Sir Archibald Murray. Both Gallipoli and Kut were, he maintained, the result of muddled leadership and poor planning.

Fed up with his involvement in Mesopotamia, Lawrence was now eager to get back to work on his favourite project – an Arab revolt in the Hejaz. In England Asquith's government was not anxious to commit British troops to any more sideshows, preferring to save them to restock the charnel house in Europe. Lawrence and the other advocates within GHQ Cairo Intelligence and the Arab Bureau of an Arab revolt did not regard this as a real setback; possibly it was an advantage. They had always planned that an Arab revolt should involve a minimum of British personnel. Moreover, Sherif Hussein, who was about to declare himself, was concerned at the prospect of Christian troops becoming involved in the Hejaz (he was to change his mind later); for the present he wanted only gold and guns.

Several writers have pointed out that Hussein would not have been a particularly popular leader outside the immediate area of Mecca and that this is probably exactly why the British picked him. British interests were best served by a limited and controllable revolt against the Turks, not a Jehad against all infidels or any other sort of Pan-Islamic revival.

On 23 May 1915, McMahon received a telegram:

> Sharif's son Abdallah urgently requires Storrs to come to Arabian coast to meet him. Movement [revolt] will begin as soon as Faisal arrives at Mecca.[1]

On 28 May, Storrs, with Hogarth and Cornwallis (another member of the Arab Bureau) and with £10,000 in gold, went by ship to meet Abdullah but were unable to make contact at the arranged rendezvous. They were sent on to a series of obscure destinations along the Red Sea coast in search of the elusive Arab commander. On 5 June, they at last made useful contact with Zeid, Abdullah's youngest brother, at Samina, and were given the vital information from Abdullah that the revolt would start 'on Saturday next'. They were also told that another £70,000 and considerable munitions were required, including machine guns and mountain guns (the British never gave the Arabs all the heavy weapons they needed, fearing that one day they might be turned against their own defensive positions).

Storrs, meanwhile, had received an anxious telegram from Cairo. The Indian Government, fully aware of the imminence of the revolt, wanted to know whether the pilgrimage to Mecca would be affected; if so, it would cause widespread discontent among Indian Moslems. Storrs finished his negotiations with Zeid, agreeing to the £70,000 and the weapons. Zeid wanted an assurance that the British would intervene if the Turks attempted to advance on the Hejaz from Syria; Storrs states he did not give it. He returned to his boat, telegraphed a report to Cairo, and with Hogarth arrived back in Egypt to be greeted by the news of Kitchener's death.

The revolt went ahead on schedule. The old Sherif literally fired the first shot of the rebellion, walking to his balcony in Mecca, rifle in hand, and taking aim at a nearby Turkish barracks. A few days later, on 13 June, the Turks in Mecca had all surrendered; on the 16th, they gave up in Jeddah, prompted by the bombardment of their positions by H.M.S. *Fox* which had been despatched to give limited assistance. Medina, supplied by the Hejaz railway, held out though besieged, rather inefficiently, by the Sherif's troops. German radio announced on 27 June:

> We are in a position to deny absolutely that there has been any rebellion in the Hejaz at all.[2]

Six days later came the statement:

> A rapid end has been made of the local disturbance in the Turkish province of the Hejaz, which has been grossly exaggerated by the English. On the 27th June the Turkish troops destroyed a camp of about 3,600 Bedouins, about two hours south of MEDINA. 700 Bedouins were killed, and 50 inhabitants of Medina guilty of special crimes have been punished. Order in the province of Hejaz has thus been restored. The small number of participants in the rebellion proves how insignificant the whole affair (so puffed in English and French press) has been.[3]

Despite the claims of the German propagandists, the revolt progressed reasonably well but Medina remained an obstacle too large for the Sherif's force to overcome. Lawrence was not unduly concerned and wrote:

> The Sherif in July betrayed that he was getting anxious about the position of Medina. The carriage of supplies has broken down, his forces are short of food, and are deserting him to the Turks, who can feed them. So long as this does not go too far there would be no harm in the Sherif suffering a mild check. He will be more modest and accommodating if he realises more closely that he is dependent on our help for success.[4]

In a separate report to the Foreign Office, Lawrence noted with satisfaction that the Turks had meanwhile made a similar mistake to the one made by Britain early in the war when Aqaba had been shelled.

The dissemination in Persia of the news of the Turkish bombardment of the mosque of Hussein, while it may not lead so peace-loving a nation to armed intervention against Turkey, will at least ensure a benevolent neutrality towards us, and will more than outweigh the efforts of German agents to turn latent Shi'ite fanaticism against the allies.[5]

The Government of India were now thoroughly worried that both the Arab Bureau and the Arab Revolt were getting out of hand; they knew nothing of Hussein's setbacks or Lawrence's plans and pleaded, unsuccessfully, to the Secretary of State.

After experience of the past few months, we think procedure would be simplified and better co-ordination secured if, so far as India, Mesopotamia, and Aden are concerned, functions of Arab Bureau were combined to original scope contemplated, viz. collection and distribution of Arab Intelligence, and suggestion of propaganda to be used or not as we think best. To make Arab Bureau mouthpiece of policy and principles of His Majesty's Government in regard to Arab questions appears to us after our experience unsuitable. We never know the authority behind their communications, and we should prefer to receive important orders of this kind either from yourself or from High Commissioner, Cairo, who would indicate previous approval of His Majesty's Government.[6]

On the first day of July 1916, Lawrence wrote to his mother:

. . . the revolt of the Sherif of Mecca I hope interested you. It has taken a year and a half to do, but now is going very well. It is so good to have helped a bit in making a new nation – and I hate the Turks so much that to see their own people turning on them is very grateful.[7]

During the summer of 1916, there is a notable gap in Lawrence's correspondence. He found his more mundane duties at GHQ Cairo Intelligence unrewarding and planned to join his friends in the Arab Bureau permanently, thus maintaining closer contact with the revolt. While at GHQ, he had found ways to keep involved in Arab politics. It was Lawrence who suggested producing an 'Arab Bulletin' for the Arab Bureau – a secret intelligence newsheet to be circulated among officers and diplomats with official interest in the Arabian campaign. The proposal was accepted and Lawrence wrote for, and sometimes edited, the Bulletin, which became the official mouthpiece for Bureau policy.

During July, Lawrence helped Storrs produce a set of commemorative stamps of the Sherif of Mecca (T.E. sent a set home for 'the little worm', his youngest brother Arnie). The stamps were produced partly because the Revolt seemed to be stagnating, and also because it was hoped that publicizing its 'success' worldwide might encourage outside support. Lawrence proposed using different-flavour glues to differentiate the values in the dark!

It was partly due to lack of real British support and co-operation that the Revolt was losing momentum. Lawrence wrote, 'The Arab Revolt became discredited.'[8] The animosity between the Foreign Office and the Government of India evolved into open hostility. The Military Intelligence Department at GHQ Cairo had been taken over by Colonel Thomas Holditch, a man who, unlike the former Chief, Gilbert Clayton, had no enthusiasm for the Revolt (and no involvement with the Arab Bureau) – a feeling passed down to him by his own lack-lustre CO, Sir Archibald Murray. It was mainly due to Sir Archibald's cautious and unimaginative command of the Egyptian Expeditionary Force that Britain had failed to take the initiative in the Middle East theatre.

Lawrence set out to make himself deliberately unpopular in Cairo GHQ, in the hope that this might facilitate his posting to the Arab Bureau. In October, he asked for leave to accompany Storrs on a special mission to the Hejaz; this was granted, probably on Hogarth's intervention. Storrs explained the purpose of his trip in a sarcastic parody of a 'typical' Hussein telegram: 'Please come as soon as possible and bring with you the same amount as you brought for me the first time.'[9]

Here at last was the opportunity Lawrence had been waiting for – to visit the leaders of the Revolt which seemed to be slowing down and only needed his 'direction'. He wrote in *Seven Pillars*:

> I had believed these misfortunes of the Revolt to be due mainly to faulty leadership, or rather to the lack of leadership, Arab and English. So I went down to Arabia to see and consider its great men.[10]

Storrs and Lawrence left Suez for Jeddah on H.M.S. *Lama* on 13 October.

If this account of his mission seems slightly inflated, Storrs was obviously not aware at once of his young 'super cerebral' companion's importance. He refers to his diary of the trip in his book of memoirs, *Orientations*, and comments: 'Extracts . . . containing his name, occur with what must now seem a ludicrous infrequency and inadequacy.'[11]

Nevertheless, Storrs found Lawrence a congenial travelling companion. Both men shared an interest in classical literature. They left Suez on H.M.S. *Lama* on 13 October and landed at Jeddah three days later. They were met by Colonel C. E. Wilson of the Sudan Service, who had been appointed British Representative at Jeddah, which was the port for Mecca and as close to the spiritual centre of the revolt as a non-Moslem could get. A reliable and competent officer of the old school, he was the trusted adviser and friend of Sir Reginald Wingate, the Sirdar of the Sudan, who was in theory the man in charge of military operations in the Hejaz.

Wilson had been appointed because the Foreign Office wanted someone permanently in Jeddah to keep in close touch with the Sherif and ensure that a degree of control was exerted over the civil population by acting as adviser on policing and other matters. The British wanted to make sure that Jeddah, a town much frequented by pilgrims en route to Mecca, presented itself favourably to the Moslem world, especially India.

Had Wilson been appointed as 'Governor', the Arabs would have become suspicious about HMG's imperialistic intentions. On the other hand, the appointment of a 'consul' would have encouraged allied and neutral countries to follow suit and brought all manner of unwanted foreigners into a British 'show'. Hence the choice of 'Representative', an unassuming title from the diplomatic lexicon. Storrs had given Wilson his own agent-cum-secretary, Husain Ruhl – codename 'the Persian Mystic' – the man Storrs was later to use as a partial scapegoat for the confusion between Sherif Hussein and HMG over the Sykes–Picot agreement.

When he met the new arrivals at Jeddah, Wilson was 'in a rather defiant mood: uncertain whom he represented and from whom he was to take orders'.[12] This was understandable considering the number of agencies and departments involved: the Foreign Office, the Arab Bureau (which though linked to the Foreign Office was, of course, influenced by Clayton and Hogarth), the War Office, the High Commissioner of Egypt, the Sirdar of the Sudan (Wingate), the India Office, etc, etc.

At least on this visit, Storrs found Abdullah without difficulty. Storrs, Lawrence and Wilson travelled to his camp on the outskirts of Jeddah. Abdullah greeted them cordially but was perturbed by HMG's final decision to send no British troops to the Hejaz (opinions on this matter were always changing within the Hashemite family). Moreover, a flight of aeroplanes, which had been promised and already despatched to Rabegh (the coastal town which protected the approach to Mecca), was being withdrawn on the same day that sightings of Turkish planes had been reported. To make matters even worse, £10,000 in gold, which Abdullah desperately needed to keep his forces together, had not yet materialized. Abdullah accepted Storrs's and Wilson's excuses stoically. When he insisted on briefing Storrs on the military situation, Storrs explained that this was not his field, but Abdullah replied firmly: 'Pardon me: it was your letter and your messages that began this thing with us, and you know it from the beginning, and from before the beginning.'[13]

Following his conversation with Storrs, Abdullah picked up the newly installed telephone and relayed the gloomy situation to his father in Mecca. That evening, Storrs and Wilson dined with Colonel Brémond, the officer in charge of the French mission at Jeddah, a man soon to become an enemy of T. E. Lawrence. His attempts to bring Allied regulars, and French troops in particular, to the Hejaz would if successful have given France the lever in the area she desired. The next day, 17 October, Storrs found that the visible Arab forces, trying to parody unfamiliar European methods, were disastrously inefficient. Lawrence insisted that the solution was to provide a small corps of 'advisors' and not to bring in aliens en masse into the lands of the Bedouins, thus creating all sorts of undesirable repercussions.

When Storrs introduced Lawrence to Abdullah, the Arab was impressed by the young captain's knowledge (he is quoted as saying, 'Is this man God, to know everything?')[14] and Lawrence eased his mind about the effectiveness of Turkish aeroplanes, remarking 'that very few Turkish aeroplanes last more than four or five days'.[15] Storrs successfully prompted Abdullah to help Lawrence to visit his brother Feisal, who was camped inland from Rabegh at Bir Abbes. Abdullah provided letters of introduction and Lawrence left for

Rabegh (half-way between Jeddah and Yenbo) on 18 October, with a sympathetic Arab companion. Before leaving, he sent a telegram to the Arab Bureau:

> For Clayton: Meeting today: Wilson, Storrs, Sharif Abdallah, Aziz al-Masri, myself. Nobody knew real situation Rabugh so much time wasted. Aziz al-Masri going Rabugh with me tomorrow.
>
> Sharif Abdallah apparently wanted foreign force at Rabugh as rallying point if combined attack on Medina ended badly. Aziz al-Masri hopes to prevent any decisive risk now and thinks English Brigade neither necessary nor prudent. He says only way to bring sense and continuity into operation is to have English staff at Rabugh dealing direct with Sharif Ali and Sharif Faisal without referring detail to Sharif of Mecca of whom they are all respectfully afraid. Unfortunately withdrawal of aeroplanes coincided with appearance of Turkish machines but Aziz al-Masri attaches little weight to them personally. He is cheerful and speaks well of Sharif's troops.[16]

This telegram shows clearly the real purpose of Lawrence's mission. He had been sent to assess the strengths, weaknesses and disposition of the Sherifian armies, and plan how British aid might most effectively be given. At Rabegh Lawrence met Ali, the Sherif's eldest son, and Zeid, his youngest. Ali commanded the 500 Sherifian troops at Rabegh and provided Lawrence with a camel and guide to visit Feisal at Bir Abbas.

Lawrence arrived at Feisal's camp on 23 October; he wrote in the *Seven Pillars*, with the advantage of hindsight: 'I felt at first glance that this was the man I had come to Arabia to seek – the leader who would bring the Arab Revolt to full glory.'[17]

In a contemporary report to Clayton, he gave more details:

> Sidi [Lord] Feisal – is tall, graceful, vigorous, almost regal in appearance. Aged thirty-one. Very quick and restless in movement. Far more imposing personally than any of his brothers, knows it and trades on it. Is as clear skinned as a pure Circassian, with dark hair, vivid black eyes set a little sloping in his face, a strong nose, short chin. Looks like a European, and very like the monument of Richard I at Fontevraud . . . Obviously very clever, perhaps not over scrupulous.[18]

The comparison to Richard I is an important clue to Lawrence's view of Feisal. An imposing figure, not large of build but with a magnetic, slightly nervous presence, Feisal spoke some English (unlike his brothers) and, according to Lawrence's romanticized account, at once asked his English visitor, 'And do you like our place here in Wadi Safra?' Lawrence replied, 'Well, but it is far from Damascus.'[19]

Feisal was in command of some 7,000 men; Abdullah had another 4,000 at Jeddah and Ali 5,000 at Rabegh. The Turks had 10,000 men in Medina, 2,500 protecting the Hejaz railway, and 1,200 in Wejh. Feisal had recently retreated from an abortive attack on Medina to 'rest'. He had been discouraged by Turkish artillery, and his men frightened by flying machines. On 24 October,

Lawrence made a thorough inspection of Feisal's camp and was impressed by the toughness of the individual soldiers ('seldom were men harder'), but saw that they lacked co-ordination. He predicted that one serious defeat would scatter them back to their own tribes.

Lawrence and Feisal parted on excellent terms and Lawrence was given an escort to take him to Yenbo, where he was picked up by a British cruiser and taken back to Jeddah. At Jeddah, he met and impressed Admiral Wemyss, and they travelled together to Khartoum to meet Sir Reginald Wingate, the Sirdar of the Sudan. Wingate wrote: 'Lawrence strikes me as a man who has thoroughly grasped the situation.'[20] Lawrence put forward his ideas to Wingate, that no large contingent of European troops should be posted to Arabia, and apparently Wingate was in broad agreement as he telegraphed to the Foreign Secretary that Lawrence was quite right to be concerned about landing Christian troops in Arabia. Within a month, however, Colonel Brémond had persuaded the Sirdar that the landing of an Allied force was essential. When Lawrence returned to Arabia a month later as Liaison Officer to Feisal, Wingate telegraphed to London with a quite different opinion from his first: 'I have no doubt that L [Lawrence] has done all this in perfectly good faith, but he appears to me to be a visionary and his amateur soldiering had evidently given him an exaggerated idea of the soundness of his views on purely military matters.'[21]

This sudden change of opinion is partly explained by the negative first impression that Lawrence had made on Colonel Wilson. When Wingate first met Lawrence he had no idea of Wilson's views on the sometimes provocative captain from the intelligence branch at GHQ, which were that Lawrence wanted kicking and kicking hard at that, then he would improve. At present, I look upon him as a bumptious young ass who spoils his undoubted knowledge of Syrian Arabs etc. by making himself out to be the only authority on war, engineering, manning H.M's ships and everything else. He put every single person's back up I've met.'[22] Wilson was an excellent but conventional officer, and it was inevitable that he should not take kindly to a 28-year-old captain forcing opinions on him. One can assume that when they first met, Lawrence had not saluted, had his pockets unbuttoned and had probably forgotten his hat.

After his visit to Wingate in Khartoum, Lawrence returned to Cairo, where he immediately presented his findings to the senior staff at GHQ. Rabegh, the Hejaz port, immediately threatened by a Turkish advance, was of vital strategic importance, defending as it did a principal approach to Mecca, which was the centre of the Arab Revolt. If the Turks took Rabegh, they would be able to mount an effective attack in Mecca and crush the revolt. The Egyptian High Command had become reluctantly convinced that the protection of Rabegh could only be undertaken by trained Allied troops, and not by Bedouin irregulars. Yet they had no wish to commit their troops to a sideshow, especially as Christian armies would not be welcome in the Hejaz and might even destroy the spirit of revolt, but they saw no more palatable alternative which would both save Mecca and, more to the point, confine the large number of Turkish soldiers conveniently occupied fighting Arabs in Arabia.

For the French, Colonel Brémond had cleverly proposed that he could provide trained Moslem soldiers for the defence of Rabegh, thus avoiding religious problems. This would have been a brilliant political stroke, for it would have given France a foothold in the area. Lawrence produced an alternative plan. Local tribes, he maintained, 'might defend Rabegh for months if lent advice and guns, but that they would certainly scatter to their tents again as soon as they heard of the landing of foreigners in force.'[23] Foreigners included French Moroccans.

This was just the news that the Egyptian High Command and the War Office wanted to hear and, although plans to send Allied reinforcements to the Holy Hejaz were not yet officially shelved, Lawrence was sent back to Arabia as liaison officer to Feisal. From being a thorn in GHQ's side, Lawrence became a thoroughly good fellow, which ironically helped him achieve his ambition of being transferred to the Arab Bureau – thus officially becoming a Foreign Office representative. This special political status would give him much more freedom for initiative than the regular officers posted to the Hejaz.

In *The Seven Pillars of Wisdom*, Lawrence wrote that he had gone down to the Hejaz with Storrs in order to assess the strengths and weaknesses of Hussein and his sons. This is how he summed up the result of his mission:

> The first, the Sherif of Mecca, we knew to be aged. I found Abdulla too clever, Ali too clean, Zeid too cool.
>
> Then I rode up-country to Feisal, and found in him the leader with the necessary fire, and yet with reason to give effect to our science. His tribesmen seemed sufficient instrument, and his hills to provide natural advantage. So I returned pleased and confident to Egypt, and told my chiefs how Mecca was defended not by the obstacle of Rabegh, but by the flank-threat of Feisal in Jebel Subh . . .[24]

According to Lawrence his superiors 'were astonished' at the favourable news, 'promised help, and meanwhile sent me back, much against my will, into Arabia'.[25]

So it was, Ronald Storrs wrote, that 'Lawrence of Carchemish, of Cairo – of any place for a little while – became permanently Lawrence of Arabia.'[26]

7 Field Officer

The next phase in Lawrence's career – the time he spent attached to Feisal's forces as an adviser – has been the subject of the greatest controversy. Lawrence has been branded by some of his more recent biographers as a posing romantic fraud, a lying, bitter and twisted little man. Is it realistic to maintain that Lawrence could have completely fooled so many of his commanders and friends, experienced and perceptive men like Allenby, Clayton, Storrs, Hogarth and Feisal? Did Lawrence cheat his way to a CB, a DSO, a Croix de Guerre, and more than one recommendation for the VC? It is most unlikely. And yet Lawrence, despite his unquestioned courage, did lie, and was inconsistent in his writings. He produced half a dozen subtly conflicting accounts of what happened in Arabia. There were deliberate distortions of history, sometimes for a political motive, sometimes in order to dramatize a real event for the sake of literature, and sometimes for reasons connected with his personal traumas.

As a trained historian himself, Lawrence had a contemptuous attitude towards his own subject, knowing well how to manipulate its process. It was the impressions that historical characters left behind, and not the literal truth of their achievements, which mattered in the perception of historical events. Lawrence would have well understood the so-called Marxist analysis of history, where the truth becomes subservient to an ideological goal. Ernest Dowson noted, 'It is idle to pretend he is not ambitious. He was vastly so'.[1] The question still remains. For what?

To piece together the facts of the Arab Revolt, and Lawrence's participation in it, from Lawrence's writings alone is impossible. When he wrote *The Seven Pillars of Wisdom*, Lawrence was, as he always admitted, self-consciously trying to produce a work of literature, and not a history text-book. In its original 1922 form as preserved in the Bodleian Library, there is a great deal of useful material that is left out of later editions, partly on Bernard Shaw's advice when he acted as Lawrence's editor. It is a pity that the original book is not available to the public, as it is far more readable and informative than the book Lawrence finally allowed to be printed. The whole of Chapter One was deleted from the first published editions; it included the important observation 'This isolated picture throwing the main light upon myself is unfair to my British colleagues.'[2]

Apart from the various versions of *Seven Pillars*, there is other material written by Lawrence which, if not entirely reliable, is at least contemporary to the events it describes. There are several volumes of letters, though a great deal of this correspondence has still not been released by the Lawrence Trust. Scholars are at least free to examine the wartime reports which Lawrence reworked into articles for the *Arab Bulletin*. In addition, many interesting official documents have found their way into the Public Records Office, the British Museum, university libraries, and private collections. Lawrence wrote for newspapers as an anonymous correspondent on Middle Eastern affairs, and contributed a series of leading articles. His journalism is necessarily far less introspective (and gave much more praise of Feisal) than his later literary efforts.

In considering Lawrence's writing, one must recognize that, both during and immediately after the First World War, he went through severe personal crises of such intensity that, from the biographical aspect, one is almost looking at two separate individuals. Lawrence had been driven to write *The Seven Pillars of Wisdom*, not just because of his ambition to create a titanic masterpiece of English prose, but also as a result of the real suffering and his own nagging sense of guilt caused by his involvement in the Arab Revolt. The writing of *The Seven Pillars* became not only a therapeutic necessity but an obsessive compulsion.

Because Lawrence often worked in Arabia without other Englishmen present, biographers have been forced to some extent to use the uncorroborated information provided by their subject's own pen. This book endeavours to point out some of the major inconsistencies in Lawrence's writing in the following chapters, but even material which is factually inaccurate can be historically relevant. The process of transforming Lawrence into a media hero can also be said to have changed the mass perception of history. Similarly, even some historians have minimized the importance of the Arab Revolt in the overall strategy of the First World War; the legend of Lawrence of Arabia could never have been created if T. E. Lawrence had not been involved in the Revolt. Immediately after the war, he acted as a respected and influential Whitehall expert on Arabia, and his reputation, whether deserved or not, played a major role in negotiations over the future of the Middle East.

Lawrence arrived back in Yenbo (one of three major Hejaz ports held by the Allies – the other two being Rabegh and Jeddah) in early December. A small British base had been established there, and an enthusiastic Captain Garland of the Royal Engineers was teaching the Bedouins the rudiments of explosive demolition, periodically disappearing up-country to combine practical demonstrations with sport for himself. Lawrence wrote of him: 'Garland would shovel a handful of detonators into his pocket, with a string of primers, fuse, and fusees, and jump gaily on his camel for a week's ride to the Hejaz Railway.'[3]

Yet he felt compelled to belittle Garland when Liddell Hart asked him

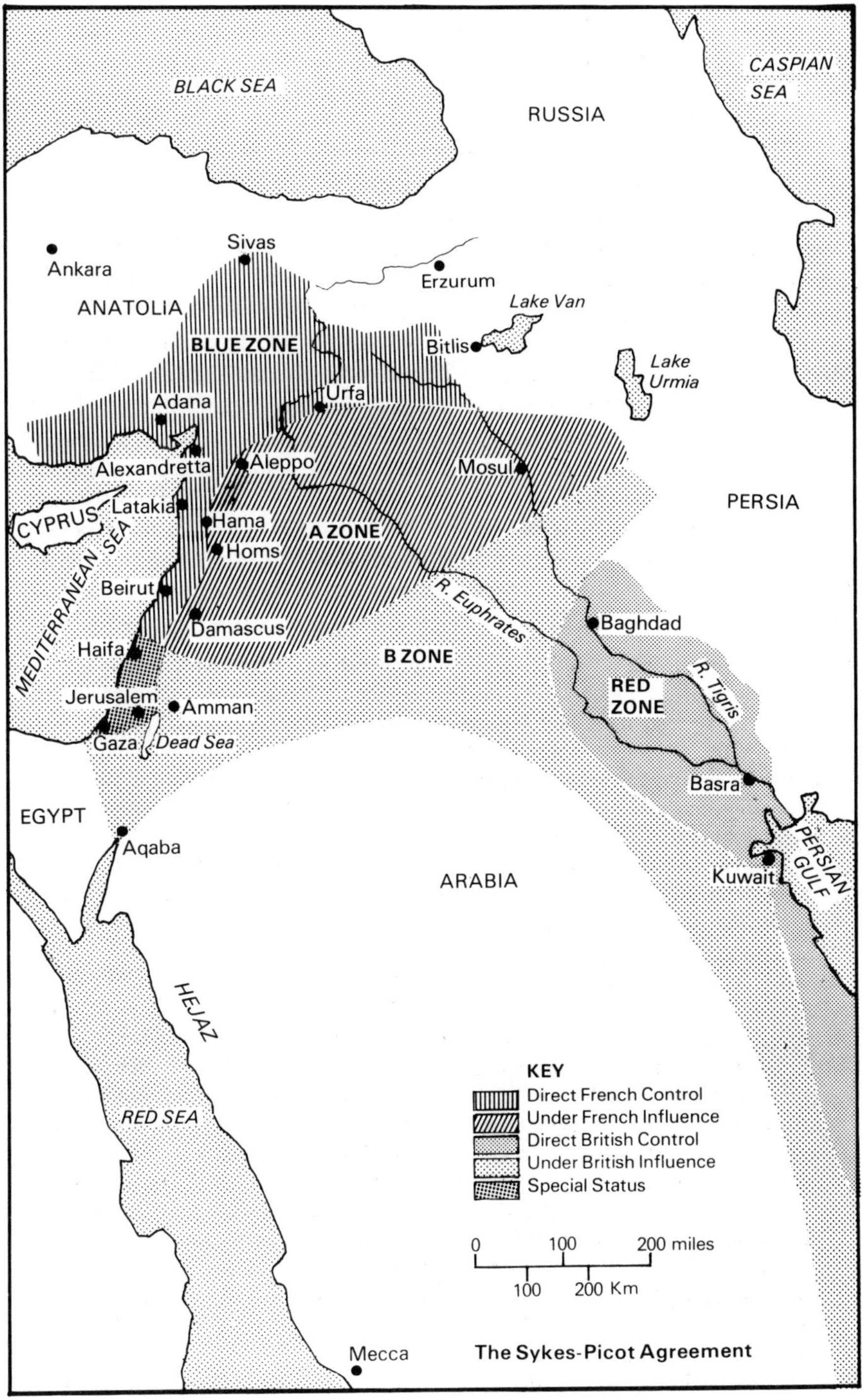

The Sykes-Picot Agreement

if any other officers had been at Yenbo in December. Lawrence's comment to Liddell Hart was: 'Garland was a sick man, an ex-Sergeant . . . apt to stand on his dignity at the wrong comment. Not the type for the job'.[4]

Two other British officers had arrived at Rabegh (fifty miles south of Yenbo) who would also play an important role in the Revolt – Colonel Joyce (nominally Lawrence's immediate superior) and Davenport. They had brought with them a few Anglo-Egyptian troops, and a flight of aeroplanes. Despite this limited British assistance, things were not going well for the Sherifian forces, which had suffered a series of defeats. The Turks had been able to break through to the coast and prevent Feisal and Abdullah's forces from combining to make an effective assault on the Turkish stronghold of Medina. Feisal had left the safety of Yenbo to join his men in the field; Ali, his brother, was stuck in Rabegh; Abdullah was engaged in a limited blockade of Medina. Zeid, who was under Feisal's command, had been surprised by a Turkish advance, had failed to hold his ground, and allowed the Turks to occupy Manra and Bir Said unopposed – much to Feisal's annoyance. Lawrence rode out of Wadi Yenbo to meet Feisal and assess these unfortunate developments. In a despatch to Cairo Intelligence, he described the scene on his arrival:

> There were hundreds of watch-fires burning, with Arabs round them making coffee, or eating, or just sleeping, as well as they could in the confusion of camels. I have never seen so many camels together, and the mess was indescribable, as they were tied up, or crouched here and there all over the camping ground, and more were ever coming up, and the old ones were leaping up to join them, and patrols were going out, and convoys being unloaded, and some dozens of Egyptian mules were bucking all over the middle of the picture.
>
> We shouldered our way through all this din, and made our camels kneel down opposite Sherif Feisal, who was seated on a carpet in the Wadi bed, reading reports and writing orders by the light of a lamp. The night was quite windless. With him was Sherif Sharraf, Kaimmankam of the Imaret and of Taif, his second in command, and Mulud ibn Mukhlus, his Mosul A.D.C. He received me very cordially, and apologised for the accommodation, which was not improved a minute later, when the hay bales of a baggage camel behind Feisal's head became untied, and he, the lamp, Sharraf and myself were temporarily overwhelmed in an avalanche of hay. I sat down with him, and listened to the news, and petitions and complaints and difficulties being brought in and settled before him. The position was, that the Turks, after clearing Zeid out of Wadi Safra, had come forward very fast to Wasta and Bir Said, and were threatening to advance rapidly on Yambo or Nakhl Mubarrek, either to destroy Feisal, or to cut off his sea base. Feisal's spy system was breaking down, and most wild and contradictory reports were coming in from one side and from another, about the strength of the Turks, and their movements. In the absence of news, he had moved suddenly down here, to watch the Yambo roads, with about 2,000 camel-men, and 2,000 infantry, and had got in an hour before I came.
>
> We sat on the rug talking till 4.30 a.m. It got very cold and the damp of the Wadi rose up through the carpet and soaked our cloaks, and a white mist collected slowly

> over the whole camp, which gradually became quiet as the men and the camels all went to sleep, and the fires burnt out. Immediately north of us, rising out of the mist and quite clear in the moonlight, was the eastern end of Jebel Rudhwa, which looks even more steep and rugged close by than it does from the sea. At about 4.30 Feisal decided that we should go to sleep, so we ate half-a-dozen dates, and stretched out on the very wet carpet on which we had been sitting. The Bishah men [slaves] came up and spread their cloaks over him as soon as he had dropped asleep.[5]

Feisal, in unexpectedly high spirits, had put down many of his problems to false rumours, and made a great effort to keep up his army's dwindling morale. In the camp Lawrence, in his shabby khaki tunic, was sometimes assumed to be from the Syrian forces. Because of this Lawrence claims in *Seven Pillars*: 'Suddenly Feisal asked me if I would wear Arab clothes like his own . . . the tribesmen would then understand how to take me.' He adds that, being dressed as a Sheik, he would be able 'to slip in and out of Feisal's tent without making a sensation'.[6] And so, Lawrence was 'fitted . . . out in splendid white silk and gold embroidered wedding garments' (these had been given to Feisal by his great-aunt – an obvious hint at her great-nephew's bachelor status). Shortly afterwards, Lawrence wrote home asking his mother to send a silk head cloth embroidered with silver ducks, 'last used I believe as a tablecloth', which he had bought in Aleppo before the war, and now wanted to complete the effect of his unique outfit. Spectacularly dressed, Lawrence left camp to consider the defences of Yenbo. Critics who condemn his posing in Arab dress should note the comments of Hubert Young, who later joined him and was present with Lawrence at an audience with Feisal in early 1918. Lawrence was dressed unusually in khaki 'of which Feisal did not at all approve'.[7] This is not to imply that Lawrence was not a show-off, but his elaborate costume at least had some justification and was not merely a pose.

Soon after Lawrence's first visit to Feisal, the Turks attempted another attack. During the engagement, warriors of the Juheina tribe, Feisal's left wing, had disappeared from the field. Thinking that they had deserted, Feisal withdrew with his army to Yenbo. Later they claimed they only left the field as, tired after fighting all day, they had rushed back to camp to have a cup of coffee. Lawrence realized the situation was critical, and pessimistically took several photographs as souvenirs of what he feared might be the 'last act' of the Revolt.

The defence of Yenbo became an immediate necessity, and was aided by the arrival of several British warships whose reassuring large grey mass dominated the harbour. The Turks soon made an attempt to assault the port, but were met by an eerie silence, and a wall of brilliant arc-light from the searchlights on board the British ships. For the Turks this came as an unexpected shock. Realizing they could be easily picked off by Arab snipers and the heavy naval guns, they retreated, convinced that Yenbo was held by a superior force. This timely victory showed the demoralized Sherifian forces that the Turks were not invincible. Keen to follow up the success, Lawrence, together with Colonel Wilson who had joined him, urged Feisal to grab the initiative and march on Wejh, another port 200 miles south up the coast, and a better base for Feisal than Yenbo. Such an action, Lawrence wrote, 'appeared not merely the convincing means of securing a siege of Medina, but an urgent necessity if a Turkish advance on Mecca was to be prevented'.[8]

The trump card throughout the Hejaz campaign was British naval superiority in the Red Sea; the Turks by contrast had their railway, which was far more vulnerable. If Wejh could be taken, then the Hejaz Railway, the Turkish lifeline in the Hejaz, could be effectively attacked. The strategy of the operation was that while Feisal moved north, Zeid would put up a diversionary resistance to convince the Turks that Yenbo and its surrounds were still heavily defended. Ali would put on a similar performance at Rabegh. Simultaneously, Abdullah, if he agreed, would act as a decoy by attacking the section of the Hejaz Railway north of Medina, and thus distract more Turkish troops. Feisal had to move before hearing from Abdullah. It was a dangerous operation involving

> a flank march of about 200 miles parallel to the Turkish Communications, by an inferior fighting force, leaving its base (Yambo) entirely undefended, and evacuating its only possible defensive position (Wadi Yambo) in the face of an enemy force of nearly divisional strength in Wadi Safra, not thirty miles away across easy country. The manoeuvre was only made possible at all by the absolute command of the sea and the ungrudging co-operation in transport of ammunition and supplies afforded to Feisal by the SNO [Senior Naval Officer] Red Sea Patrol.[9]

At the beginning of January, the operation was put into effect. First, Lawrence, as yet with little combat experience, set forth with a party of Arabs to the south-east. Their mission, similar to Zeid's, was to disrupt the Turks and convince them of a non-existent threat. He wrote home: 'I was up country hopping about on a camel.'[10] Lawrence made brief contact with several Turkish outposts, and then returned to Nakhl Mubarek (Feisal's camp-site just outside Yenbo) to join in the pageant of Feisal's march north. Lawrence was characteristically poetic in his despatch, describing the scene almost as if it was a fashion parade.

> The order of march was rather splendid and barbaric. Feisal in front, in white; Sharaf on his right in red headcloth and henna dyed tunic and cloak; myself on his left in white and red; behind us three banners of purple silk, with gold spikes; behind them three drummers playing a march, and behind them again a wild bouncing mass of 1,200 camels of the bodyguard, all packed as closely as they could move, the men in every variety of coloured clothes, and the camels nearly as brilliant in their trappings, and the whole crowd singing at the tops of their voices a war song in honour of Feisal and his family. It looked like a river of camels, for we filled the Wadi to the tops of its banks, and poured along in a quarter of a mile stream.[11]

Nevertheless, Feisal's army, however romantic, could only muster a permanent nucleus of 1,200 Ageyl camelmen (who acted as his bodyguards), augmented by volunteers from sympathetic tribes. A mixture of English gold, the spirit of adventure, and the prospect of getting rid of and simultaneously robbing the Turks, kept Feisal's (and his brother's) armies together; whenever a tribe became fed up, they had leave to return home. It was this constantly changing force, and the incentives needed to hold it together, which taxed Feisal's diplomatic skill and Lawrence's patience.

Feisal had been moved out of Yenbo to a temporary position fifteen miles inland where he awaited confirmation of Abdullah's co-operation. Lawrence rode back to Yenbo to confirm the details of naval support, and then went up to the coast by sea to Um Lejj. Ali had in the meantime made a mock advance out of Rabegh, while British planes bombed Turkish positions in the area. By now Abdullah had given his consent, and when he moved north, parallel to Feisal, he encountered and destroyed a Turkish battalion, capturing £20,000 in gold. The combined effect of these concerted actions was to throw the Turks into confusion.

By 10 January, a week after leaving Yenbo, Feisal's forces had concentrated at Um Lejj, a small port about half-way to Wejh, and their agreed rendezvous with the British Navy and fresh supplies. Before Lawrence joined Feisal at Um Lejj he developed a personality clash with another British officer, a Lieutenant Vickery, Newcombe's assistant, highly competent but without Newcombe's flexibility and sense of humour. He not only spoke excellent Arabic but also had extensive experience of desert warfare in the Sudan. Jealous of his own position, Lawrence went out of his way to make a fool of his potential rival, thus increasing their mutual animosity. With Lawrence riding beside him again, Feisal proceeded to Wejh. When they arrived there several days behind schedule, they found that the Navy had already taken the port, using its guns and a small force of Arab regulars commanded by Vickery.

Lawrence was furious. Twenty men had been killed, which he regarded as quite unnecessary. 'Vickery, who had directed the battle, was satisfied, but I could not share his satisfaction. To me an unnecessary action, or shot, or casualty, was not only waste but sin.'[12] Despite his irritation, this was an important victory, both for the Revolt and for Lawrence himself, who now returned to Cairo on a week's leave, able to demonstrate what could be done without Allied troops as long as some co-operation was forthcoming. The Turks were forced (or fooled) into concentrating their efforts to protect their communications, and the threat to Mecca was eliminated. Clayton, Storrs and Hogarth were delighted; so was GHQ.

There was more good news in Cairo. The British had captured Jaafar Pasha, a highly skilled, slightly obese Mesopotamian Arab who had been a senior commander in the Turkish Army. He had been brought to Cairo, where he unsuccessfully tried to escape from detention by the traditional method of knotting sheets together to form a rope. He was a well-known officer and an honourable man, and when he heard of the execution of many of his friends by the Turks, he gave up trying to escape and offered his services to Feisal. Jaafar's abilities as a field officer might well be the deciding force in welding the Sherifian mob into an army. Feisal's father, Sherif Hussein, disliked all Mesopotamians but Feisal knew Jaafar's reputation, and engaged him against his father's wishes. Sudden changes of allegiance were typical of Arab politics and war.

Colonel Brémond, on leave from the French Mission at Jeddah, congratulated Lawrence on the successful capture of Wejh, and suggested it could open the way for an Allied assault on Aqaba, the only important Red Sea port which was still controlled by Turkey. Lawrence was firmly against such an idea. Frontal assault would be a very risky operation, and besides, he had no wish to see French troops occupying this strategic port so close to Suez or any other Red Sea port. Realizing that Brémond was intent on proposing the operation to Feisal direct, Lawrence rushed to Suez and sailed the same night. Ten days later, when the Frenchman arrived and presented Feisal with machine guns and instructors, these were gratefully received, but when it came to Aqaba, Feisal explained that he would be unable to lend his support or sanction to such an operation. His main goal was Medina. Lawrence had won; he had his own plans for Aqaba, and followed up this political victory by returning to Cairo to make sure his views on an Allied assault on Aqaba were made quite clear to General Murray, the commander of the Egyptian Expeditionary Force, who gratefully accepted any excuse not to commit his troops to the 'Arabian Show'.

Wejh, the new Sherifian base, was a busy place, but Feisal was having problems keeping his force disciplined. Some of his trusted Ageyl bodyguards mutinied, and Feisal had the constant problem of holding the Bedouin tribes together as a fighting force – often they were antagonistic towards each other because of centuries of feuding. Meanwhile, useful supplies and personnel began to arrive from Egypt. Captain Goslett, a dapper City of London banker, co-ordinated supply operations in the port, remaining always impeccably dressed and equally efficient. Two Rolls-Royce armoured cars arrived complete with crews – more would follow – and these proved to be a decisive advantage in a war where mobility was paramount. Newcombe, Garland and Hornby were doing excellent work against the Hejaz Railway, using Wejh as their base. It was these officers, rather than Lawrence, who first started to blow up the Hejaz line – but it was a hobby which he soon took up with enthusiasm.

Secure in Wejh, Feisal entertained as many tribal chiefs as possible, eloquently persuading them to swear their allegiance to the Revolt (and to him), a ritual which was usually encouraged by gifts of cash from Feisal's British-stocked coffers. Favourable contact was also made with Nuri Shalan of the Ruwalla, the 'Fox' of the desert and still at that time accepting Turkish gold for his nominal allegiance.* His co-operation, or more precisely his lack of opposition, opened up a route towards the Wadi Sirhan and thus enabled Feisal's messengers to reach the lands of Auda Abu Tayi – an old rogue and formidable warrior who was chief of the fiercest of all the Bedouin tribes, the Abu Tayi Howeitat. A month later, as will be recounted, Lawrence also had the opportunity of meeting Auda, an encounter he eagerly anticipated. Auda was respected throughout Arabia. His reputation in single combat was second to none – it was said he had killed 70 men in hand-to-hand fighting. An alliance with Auda's tribe would be enormously beneficial to Feisal's campaign.

In early March, Lawrence received an urgent message from Clayton. Cairo Intelligence had intercepted a Turkish communication ordering the immediate evacuation of Medina. Lawrence was to do his best (which meant, in practice, that he was to persuade Feisal) to see that either Medina was captured, or the retreating Turkish Army destroyed. Abdullah, who was closest to Medina, had not been in direct communication with Feisal for some time, so Lawrence arranged to go himself with a small escort to Abdullah's camp.

In *The Seven Pillars of Wisdom* Lawrence describes a strange and gruesome event which he claims occurred on the way. Apparently, his companions were not all they might have been and argued incessantly. Lawrence was ill with dysentery – a frequent problem for him – when his pain was suddenly interrupted by a shot. One of the escort, Hamed, a Moor, had killed another man, Salem, an Ageyl, in a heated confrontation. The three other Ageyl present demanded blood. According to Lawrence, he had immediately to sentence and execute the Moor himself, rather than risk a blood feud between the Moors and Ageyls in Feisal's army. This simply does not ring true. Lawrence's action would have started a blood feud anyway – against himself – but it does make a dramatic if grisly story:

> It must be formal execution, and at last, desperately, I told Hamed that he must die for punishment, and laid the burden of his killing on myself.[13]

What is even stranger is the almost loving detail with which Lawrence described how he shot the Moor:

> I . . . gave him a few moments' delay which he spent crying on the ground. Then I made him rise and shot him through the chest. He fell down on the weeds shrieking, with the blood coming out in spurts over his clothes, and jerked about

*In 1982, during a visit to Syria, my companion interviewed an elder of the Shalan clan, still a powerful family in Syria, who told him that some boys in the family are named 'Aurens' because of Lawrence's later association with their family. The old man had great respect for Lawrence who had been his father's friend, and believed that he was an innocent who had fallen victim to politics. His comments were evidence that Lawrence was genuinely respected in the region and that his influence has not altogether disappeared.

> till he rolled nearly to where I was. I fired again, but was shaking so that I only broke his wrist. He went on calling out, less loudly, now lying on his back with his feet towards me, and I leant forward and shot him for the last time in the thick of his neck under the jaw. His body shivered a little . . .[14]

It was hardly a humane killing. Lawrence was a crack shot and could hit a matchbox at thirty paces with a pistol. If the incident really took place, why did he not shoot the man in the back of the neck or the brain first? To shoot him in the chest was foolish, and was not certain to result in an instantaneous kill. Lawrence's account is suspect. Thomas O'Donnell points out that Lawrence devoted more space to considering the misery of his own dysentery than to his deliberate destruction of a human life. In *T. E. Lawrence – An Arab View*, Suleiman Mousa wrote that Lawrence 'could easily have arrested the man [Hamed] and handed him over to Emir Abdullah at Wadi, to be dealt with as he saw fit', and went on to note how often Lawrence described the romanticized minutiae of death. Whether or not describing these hideous incidents gave him pleasure, Lawrence was certainly obsessed with death. In the spring of 1915 he sent his mother some pictures he had taken of the Turkish dead. His brother Frank, serving in the trenches in France, heard of this and wrote back: 'Has Ned sent any explanation of those photos of the dead men? I cannot imagine what he did it for.'[15] (Frank himself was to be dead by the end of the year.)

The story of Hamed is one of the many post-war attempts by Lawrence to degrade himself. The contemporary issue of the *Arab Bulletin*, which meticulously describes the journey to Abdullah's camp, makes not the slightest mention of an argument building up among the escort.

The issue is not a simple one, and to label Lawrence a sadist may be to misjudge his character. The *Seven Pillars* is deliberately written in such a way as to arouse both admiration and disgust. Alec Kirkbride, an officer who served with Lawrence and watched him in action, wrote to Basil Liddell Hart: 'T.E.L. had a horror of bloodshed and it is because of that he tends to pile on the agony in the passages of 'Seven Pillars of Wisdom' dealing with death and wounds – not because he liked to see others suffer.'[16] This was an opinion shared by several other friends of Lawrence. But Lawrence did seem to need to suffer himself. He wrote to W. F. Stirling that he did not want readers to 'enjoy' the *Seven Pillars* and that within its pages he sought to 'condemn' himself.[17]

In March 1917, Lawrence had reached Abdullah's camp where, according to the *Seven Pillars*, he fell ill for ten days. While recovering from dysentery and a fever, he claims to have rethought the whole strategy of the war, and devotes a chapter to it in the *Seven Pillars*. Ignoring Clayton's orders, he suddenly becomes aware that the actual capture of Medina would be foolish, as would engaging and destroying the Turkish force there. Better that they remain stuck, their lines of supply under constant but not total attack. Such a strategy would leave 12,000 Turkish troops stranded in Medina, impotent to cause harm to the Revolt, but simultaneously draining Turkey's dwindling

Lawrence with D. G. Hogarth (centre *and Alan Dawnay*.

British ships offloading at Yenbo.

Feisal.

Hussein.

Ronald Storrs.

Lawrence: The Metamorphoses.

Lawrence's photograph of Feisal setting out from Wejh with his Ageyl bodyguard, 3 January 1917.

Feisal and his 'army' approaching Yenbo. These pictures were probably taken by Lawrence, and illustrate the relatively small scale of operations.

A tulip mine explodes on the Hejaz line.

Lawrence instructing a mortar class.

'Sheik Lawrence and his hired assassins' – as captioned by Lawrence.

Auda the desert warrior who had killed more than seventy men in single combat (not including Turks!)

Lawrence's picture of Lt Colonel S. F. Newcombe and his camel, March 1917.

Lawrence (right) *and Arab leaders.*

Allenby in Jerusalem.

Allied troops arrive in Damascus.

Feisal's headquarters in Damascus. Note the improvised gallows – a reminder to potential malefactors.

Arab forces on their way to Damascus.

Lawrence arrives in Damascus by Rolls-Royce.

resources because of the necessity of supplying the stranded army. The strategic victory would lie in convincing the Turks that it was worth continuing to supply the besieged garrison – not in creating a Turkish Kut. This chapter again is suspect. Even if Lawrence's new strategy was sound, he was most unlikely to have suddenly seen the light in the middle of an intense bout of dysentery. It is more likely that his ideas developed over some months, and were crystallized into ten nights of pain at Abdullah's camp in order to increase the dramatic effect:

> About ten days I lay in that tent, suffering a bodily weakness which made my animal self crawl away and hide till the shame was passed. As usual in such circumstances my mind cleared, my senses became more acute, and I began at last to think consecutively of the Arab Revolt, as an accustomed duty to rest upon against the pain.[18]

Lawrence recovered and with his 'new' plan – which involved constant harassment rather than destruction of the railway – asked Abdullah for help. Abdullah was apparently apathetic, so Lawrence, on his own initiative, persuaded Sherif Shakir to accompany him on an experimental operation against the railway. He established himself at the Turkish station at Aba el Naam and described the attack in a despatch to Cairo:

> March 29th . . . Shakir arrived at 5 p.m., but brought only 300 men, two machine guns, one mountain gun, and one mountain howitzer. The lack of infantry made the scheme of taking the station in rear impossible, since it would have left the guns without support; so we changed ideas, and decided on an artillery action only. We sent a dynamite party to the north of the station, to cut rails and telegraph at dawn. I started at 8 p.m. with a company of Ateibah and a machine-gun, to lay a mine and cut the wire between Abu-el Naam and Istabl Antar. Mohammed el-Gadhi guided us very well, and we reached the line at 11.15 p.m., in a place where there was cover for the machine-gun in a group of bushes and a sandy valley bed about four feet deep, 500 yards west of the rails. I laid a mine, and cut the wire, and at 1 a.m. started back for the main body with a few Ageyl, but did not get in till 5 a.m., through various accidents, and was not able to go forward to the artillery position till 6.30 a.m. I found the guns just ready, and we shelled the station till 10 a.m., when Shakir found that the Ateibah infantry had no water, and we retired to W. Gussed without molestation. Girbis [waterskins] are mostly unobtainable in the eastern Hejaz, which makes it difficult for an Arab force of more than a dozen men to remain in action for half a day.
>
> The results of the bombardment were to throw the upper storeys of the large stone buildings into the ground-floors, which were reported to contain stores and water-cisterns. We could not demolish the ground-floors. The water-tank (metal) was pierced and knocked out of shape, and three shells exploded in the pumping room and brought down much of the wall. We demolished the well-house, over the well, burned the tents and the wood-pile and obtained a hit on the first wagon of the train in the station. This set it on fire, and the flames spread to the remaining six wagons, which must have contained inflammable stores, since they burned furiously. The locomotive was behind the northern building, and got steam up, and went off (reversed) towards Medina. When it passed over the mine it exploded it,

under the front bogies (i.e. too late). It was, however, derailed, and I hoped to see the machine-gun come into action against it, but it turned out that the gunners had left their positions to join us in our attack on the station, and so the seven men on the engine were able to 'jack' it on the line again in about half an hour (only the front wheels were derailed) and it went off towards Istanbl Antar, at foot-pace, clanking horribly.

The north end of the station now surrendered, and about 200 of the garrison of the north end rushed in driblets for the hills (J. Unseila) and took cover there. I examined the prisoners (twenty-four in number, Syrians, of 130th Regt.), and also the brake-van of the train. The box-body had been lined with matchboard, at an interval of about four inches, and packed near the floor with cement (loop-holed) and above the shingle, but it was burning hotly, and the Turks were too close for me to obtain accurate details.

We fired altogether fifty rounds (shrapnel) from 2,200 and 900 yards and about ten belts of machine-gun ammunition. Deserters reported about thirty dead (I saw nine only) and forty-two wounded. We captured the pedigree mare of Ali Nasir (the Egyptian 'Bab-Arab' in Medina) and a couple of camels from the well-house, and destroyed many rails. Our casualties were one man wounded. Had there been enough Arab infantry to occupy J. Unseila, which commanded the trenches at 400 yards (plunging fire), I think we could have taken the entire garrison. The Ateibah were not asked to do very much, and I do not think would have done it if asked. The Juheinah and the gunners behaved very well, and I think that the attack – as an experiment – justified itself. It had the effect, in the next three days, of persuading the Turks to evacuate every outpost and blockhouse on the line, and concentrate the garrison in the various railway stations. This action facilitated the work of the dynamite parties.[19]

It took Lawrence over forty-eight hours to get back to Abdullah's camp, only to set out again at once to make a second attack on the railway, encouraged by the first success. These were Lawrence's first attempts at offensive patrolling, and provided him with valuable field and demolition experience. He has sometimes been credited with this invention of guerrilla warfare, but this is not so. His operations against the railway were not novel theoretically; rather, they were not in vogue. The fashionable theory of war at the time might simplistically be presented as a combination of von Clausewitz's principle of focusing all resources on the main front, with the more recent idea of attempting the complete annihilation of the enemy – total war, or 'murder war', as Lawrence accurately termed it.

Neither of these principles was applicable to the situation in Arabia. Where was the main front? Arguably, it was at Medina, but the Arabs could not attack and capture Medina without outside help, and Lawrence was convinced that they did not need to. As for annihilation, this was not the Arab way of making war; they fought for enjoyment and for booty, but rarely for the total destruction of their foe. That would be like destroying the chess pieces after winning the game. The hit-and-run tactics which Lawrence developed had been used for centuries before the First World War, but since the Second World War they have become routine for 'freedom fighters', guerrillas and terrorists throughout the world, who have recognized the essential vulnerability of large states, with their extended, cumbersome and inefficient command structures in both Army and Government. During the Second World War, *The Seven Pillars of Wisdom* was to be sent by the British to some Resistance commanders as a text book on irregular warfare.

8 An Irregular War

Back in Wejh, in April 1917, Lawrence finally came face to face with Auda, the desert warrior and leader of the Abu Tayi tribe. He had long been intrigued by Auda's romantic image as the toughest of the Hejaz chieftains, and had planned to use both the man and his reputation as weapons against the Turks. He wrote a long despatch home to describe their first meeting:

> The head man of the Abu Tayi is, of course, the inimitable Auda. He must be nearly fifty now (he admits forty) and his black beard is tinged with white, but he is still tall and straight, loosely built, spare and powerful, and as active as a much younger man. His lined and haggard face is pure Bedouin: broad low forehead, high sharp hooked nose, brown green eyes, slanting outward, large mouth (now unfortunately toothless, for his false teeth were Turkish, and his patriotism made him sacrifice them with a hammer, the day he swore allegiance to Feisal in Wejh), pointed beard and moustache, with the lower jaw shaven clean . . . Auda is the essence of the Abu Tayi. His hospitality is sweeping (inconvenient except to very hungry souls) his generosity has reduced him to poverty, and devoured the profits of a hundred successful raids. He has married twenty-eight times, has been wounded thirteen times, and in battle has seen all his tribesmen hurt, and most of his relations killed. He has only reported his 'kill' since 1900, and they now stand at seventy-five Arabs; Turks are not counted when they are dead. Under his handling the Toweihah [Abu Tayi] have become the finest fighting force in Western Arabia.[1]

With Auda's support and Nuri Shalan's co-operation, an advance on Maan (and Aqaba) now became a realistic prospect. Auda and Nuri Shalan controlled the route and offered Feisal's forces safe conduct and, in Auda's case, material assistance in exchange for the promise of plunder and a quantity of gold sovereigns on account. Auda's adherence provided excellent propaganda for Feisal as other tribal chiefs recognized his increasing might and came to Wejh. Even the majority of the tribes that did not offer their fighting services were still sympathetic, since the Turks were universally distrusted, but as Feisal's army grew, so did the tensions within it. Rather than attempt the impossible – to weld hostile tribes into a single force in one camp – Feisal relied instead on the constant nucleus of his Ageyl bodyguard, and then added other tribes, like regiments, commanded by their hereditary leader, depending on the area his forces were operating in. Thus his army was constantly changing but it had the advantage of mobility.

The British were still pressing for the capture of Medina, and Lawrence saw that he could do little to dissuade his senior officers, Joyce and Newcombe, from making a major attack on the Hejaz railway. They believed that the Turks could be forced to surrender. Lawrence wanted to attempt something more audacious – an attack on Aqaba from the rear. Feisal had previously blocked the plan, but he agreed to it after the arrival of Auda. Lawrence dangled the carrot of glory and limitless wealth, obtainable only in Aqaba, in front of the old war-horse, who instantly became his enthusiastic ally in persuading Feisal, and was no doubt convinced by Lawrence that the idea was his in the first place.

Many books (including Lawrence's own) give the impression that Lawrence became a Bedouin commander himself. Suleiman Mousa pointed out that Lawrence was rarely, if ever, officially 'in command' of anyone except British soldiers and his own bodyguard. He was an adviser, a very influential one, but on all major operations he was involved in against the Turks using Sherifian troops or Bedouin, there was always an appointed Arab commander at least nominally in charge.

This particularly applied to the operation on Aqaba, which Lawrence claims he led directly. He did not, whatever impression the *Seven Pillars*, subsequent biographies, or the film *Lawrence of Arabia* may give. He wrote in the preface to Book IV of *Seven Pillars:*

> Nasir, Auda, and I set off together on the long ride. Hitherto Feisal had been the public leader: but his remaining in Wejh threw the ungrateful load of this northern expedition upon myself. I accepted it and its dishonest implication as our only means of victory.[2]

On 9 May, Lawrence, Auda, Nasir, the exiled Sherif of Medina, and about forty Ageyli camel men set out on the mission which was to make Lawrence's career. With them, they carried few supplies but £20,000 from Feisal's privy purse. 'The desert route to Akaba was so long and so difficult that we could take neither guns [artillery] nor machine-guns, nor stores nor regular soldiers.'[3] Lawrence had taken quite a risk; he had no orders to make an assault against Aqaba. He circumvented his immediate commander, Colonel Joyce, and wrote directly to Clayton in Cairo, saying that he was taking the initiative on his own responsibility: 'So I decided to go my own way, with or without orders. I wrote a letter full of apologies to Clayton, telling him that my intentions were of the best: and went.'[4]

As Lawrence marched off towards the north, a political storm was brewing over the genuine nature of French intentions in Syria. Hussein had heard rumours, and needed to be reassured. He knew that Georges Picot had been in contact in Cairo with Syrian nationalists whom France wanted to befriend in order to facilitate her plans for a French Syria. The Sherif was concerned, and asked Wingate what he should do. Wingate immediately contacted Cairo, who suggested that Sykes and Picot might themselves go down to the Hejaz to see Hussein. Sykes went to Jeddah, met the Sherif and convinced him that all was well; this was followed by a visit the next day, 20 May, by Sykes and Picot together. Hussein was temporarily satisfied by their promises. Five months later, he discovered the existence of the Sykes–Picot Treaty, after which he would require rather more persuading.

Lawrence, Auda and Nasir were, meanwhile, proceeding on their long trek, into which Lawrence inserts a contrasting comic but not insignificant episode in *Seven Pillars*. Two Ageyli boys came to his attention for their misbehaviour; one had set fire to their captain's tent. They asked to be punished together, and when Lawrence agreed to this the innocent one, Daud, kissed him on his hand. Lawrence wrote of 'Eastern boy and boy affection' (that is, homosexual) and, finding them amusing, took them on as his own personal servants.

Lawrence and Auda crossed the Hejaz railway at Wadi Diraa, and stopped to blow up the rails at their crossing-place. They were ten days out from Wejh. Lack of water was becoming a major concern, especially when they had to march two hundred miles across the desert. In the *Seven Pillars* Lawrence described the famous incident when a riderless camel was brought to his attention. Gasim, 'a worthless man', had fallen off, and as nobody wanted to go back for him, Lawrence wearily turned his camel around and went to the rescue, saving Gasim from certain death. Auda thought he had been a fool to bother. The incident was magnified even more and transposed as part of the final assault on Aqaba in the film *Lawrence of Arabia*.

The rest of the journey was uneventful, except for a brief skirmish with a hostile Bedouin tribe, before Lawrence and Auda reached the security of Auda's own base camp on the edge of the Wadi Sirhan. While Auda was raising his tribesmen for the attack on Aqaba, Lawrence, for reasons which have never been satisfactorily explained, left camp on 4 June to commence a deep reconnaissance patrol into occupied Syria. He stated that during the two weeks in which he was absent, he went as far as Damascus and was able to have secret meetings with Syrian Nationalists in the suburbs of the city. Suleiman Mousa, the Arab historian, has rejected these claims, but it is possible that they have genuine substance related to Lawrence's role as a secret service agent. Wingate certainly believed in the value of the mission. He wrote to Colonel Wilson on 15 July 1917:

> Lawrence's exploits in the Syrian Hinterland were really splendid and I hope you will have an opportunity of putting in a word that will help him to get the V.C., which in my opinion he has so thoroughly earned. Clayton and G.H.Q. are now digesting the information he has collected with a view to working out a scheme of co-operation from Sinai, Baghdad and the Hijaz. There are at any rate the makings of a useful diversion against the railway line north of Maan.[5]

Lawrence did not get his VC, probably because no British officer witnessed his accomplishment. During his absence, Auda had collected a considerable fighting force of several hundred men, both from his own tribe and from others in the area. Three days after Lawrence returned he set off again on a preliminary attack on the railway to the north, an operation designed to distract the Turks from the possibility of an attack on Aqaba. One hundred tribesmen, Lawrence, and Auda's nephew Zaal struck at the railway between Amman and Deraa, and then returned to the main body. The Turks were obviously anxious about further surprise attacks coming from the desert because Auda, as he advanced to meet Lawrence, found many wells had been dynamited, albeit ineffectively. To ensure that this did not compromise the advance on Aqaba, Auda sent forward an advance party to protect the vital wells at Aba el Lissan, an alternative objective. This spearhead engaged a small Turkish force and alerted the Turkish battalion in the area. When Lawrence and Auda arrived they had to fight a battle, but fortunately they had the advantage of high ground. Auda imprudently decided to storm the well-defended Turkish positions in a mad camel charge. The sight of this broke the discipline of the Turkish regulars. Lawrence described how, in the excitement of the charge, his own racing camel 'out-distanced' the others and brought him to the head of the assault 'when suddenly my camel tripped and went down emptily upon her face, as though pole-axed'.[6] Lawrence claimed that he had accidentally shot the animal in the brain during the final stages of the charge – just possible in the excitement of the moment.

Auda was extremely pleased with himself; his mount had been shot away beneath him and he had bullet-holes all over his clothes, scabbard and pistol-holder. Lawrence describes how the leader of the Abu Tayi put down his good fortune to a powerful charm – a miniature Koran worn around his neck, the production of a Glasgow novelty firm. He then proceeds to inflict on his readers another of his bizarre descriptions of the dead. Dazed by fighting, Lawrence wanders over the field of battle that evening:

> The dead men looked wonderfully beautiful. The night was shining gently down, softening them into new ivory. Turks were white skinned on their clothed parts, much whiter than the Arabs; and these soldiers had been very young. Close round them lapped the dark wormwood, now heavy with dew, in which the ends of the moonbeams sparkled like sea-spray. The corpses seemed flung so pitifully on the ground, huddled anyhow in low heaps. Surely if straightened they would be comfortable at last. So I put them all in order, one by one, very wearied myself, and longing to be of these quiet ones, not of the restless, noisy, aching mob up the valley, quarrelling under plunder, boasting of their speed and strength to endure God knew how many toils and pains of this sort; with death, whether we won or lost, waiting to end the history.[7]

There were three hundred Turkish dead to every two Arabs, Lawrence reported. The battle served to warn the Turkish posts between Aba el Lissan and Aqaba. Auda sent messengers with terms of surrender to the remaining Turkish outposts on the approach to the port, and these were accepted in the cases where the Turks had not already abandoned their positions and retreated to Aqaba. The final approach to Aqaba, and its capture, was uneventful. Initially the Turks, only a few hundred strong, refused to negotiate a surrender.

When they realized that no help was coming, they had little choice but to accept their fate and hope that they would be treated reasonably. On 6 July 1917, after a circular journey of some 800 miles from Wejh, Auda, Lawrence and Nasir entered Aqaba. Their strategy had worked because they had kept the element of surprise. Their victory was a genuinely astonishing achievement, despite the relatively small number of men involved on both sides. It effectively ended the Hejaz war, gave Feisal complete domination of the area, and allowed Britain's navy the use of every important Red Sea port.

Once Aqaba was captured, the question arose of what was to be done with it. Auda's force, their Turkish prisoners and the townspeople had hardly any food left; Auda's men were butchering their riding camels for meat. Auda's force was held together by the most fragile bonds, and if they did not get quickly rewarded they would disperse into the desert, and the victory would be lost. There were no means of communication to Feisal or the British, and a message had to be sent. Lawrence elected to go himself, and thus also to be the first to announce victory. He would travel the hundred and fifty miles across Sinai, direct to Suez. Remarkably, he made the journey, with eight of Auda's tribesmen, in two days, but they arrived on the wrong side of the Suez Canal and could not find a boat. Shatt, formerly a British post, had been abandoned because of a plague.

Lawrence eventually found a telephone and called the Department of Inland Water Transport, who informed him that no transport was available until the next day, when he would be picked up and put into quarantine. Lawrence became irate until, according to *Seven Pillars*, a friendly military telephone operator interceded in a North of England accent, 'It's no bluidy good, sir, talking to them fookin water boogers.' This juxtaposition of drama and farce is characteristic of *Seven Pillars*, and sometimes the reader is dazed by its death drama-joke-death drama-joke structure.

At last Lawrence was able to contact someone he knew at Suez HQ and a launch was immediately despatched, against regulations, to pick him up. From Suez, he left by train for Ismailia, the connecting station for Cairo, attracting some unwelcome attention from military police because of his Arab dress. Always unco-operative and sarcastic with petty officialdom, he was interviewed by a suspicious officer, but arrived at Ismailia without being arrested, and was in time to witness the simultaneous arrival of his old acquaintance, Admiral Wemyss. The Admiral had with him 'a very large and superior general'[8] who turned out to be Allenby, newly sent out to replace General Murray as commander of the Egyptian Expeditionary Force. This was fortuitous (it seems a little too fortuitous) for Lawrence.

Having arranged the despatch of food to Aqaba, and the removal of the Turkish prisoners held there, he proceeded on to Cairo, and arrived, still dressed as an Arab, at Clayton's Arab Bureau office in the Savoy Hotel. He soon found himself called to an interview with Allenby. He dug out his old uniform, and went to meet The Bull – Allenby's nickname. The General was not quite sure what to make of the strange, scorched and scruffy little man who presented himself. Lawrence asked for more weapons, and £200,000 in gold, to which Allenby replied, 'Well, I will do for you what I can.'[9] Lawrence wrote later that he saw himself being sized up: 'Allenby could not make out how much was genuine performer and how much charlatan.'[10]

The capture of Aqaba provided Feisal with a new headquarters, to be built up into a safe base, from which to attack the Hejaz railway. In mid-July, Lawrence's immediate task after leaving Cairo was to go to Jeddah and explain to Hussein, whom surprisingly he had not yet met in person, the necessity of Feisal coming under Allenby's command for the final push into Syria. Their first meeting went well and the Sherif accepted the proposal. The transfer of Feisal's forces to Allenby also received the approval of Wingate, who was still officially Commander of Military Operations in the Hejaz. Lawrence took the opportunity of his visit to Hussein to discuss the Sherif's meeting with Georges Picot. His report to the Foreign Office reflects his own francophobia:

> He [The Sherif] is extremely pleased to have trapped M. Picot into the admission that France will be satisfied in Syria with the position that Britain desires in Iraq. That, he says, means a temporary occupation of the country for strategical and political reasons (with probably an annual grant to the Sherif in compensation and recognition) . . . In conclusion the Sherif remarked on the shortness and informality of conversations, the absence of written documents, and the fact that the only change in the situation caused by the meeting was the French renunciation of the ideas of annexation, permanent occupation or suzerainty of any port of Syria.[11]

In the interests of objectivity it is perhaps worth noting a comment in a secret undated Foreign Office wartime memo regarding Hussein and British commitments to him:

> The position is complicated by the King's habit of ignoring or refusing to take note of conditions laid down by us to which he objects, and then carry on as if the question had been settled between us according to his own desires.[12]

Lawrence's next mission was a very sensitive one at Aqaba. British Intelligence had intercepted a secret communication between Auda and the Turks indicating that Auda was fed up at being left alone, without much food or satisfactory reward. Lawrence managed to patch up the misunderstanding, but realized how fragile alliances of the desert must be. He was now uniquely qualified to commit to paper the fruit of his experiences as liaison and negotiating officer with the Arabs, and this he did in a long and detailed despatch in the *Arab Bulletin*, dated 20 August 1917, which proves conclusively that he was a brilliant actor playing a dangerous game. In the event of his death – which was clearly a possibility at any time – his knowledge of how to deal with the Arab tribes would have been lost.

He expressed the advice he gave 'in commandment form', for greater clarity, and made it clear that it was 'meant to apply only to Bedouin; townspeople or Syrians require totally different treatment', adding: 'Handling Hejez Arabs is an art, not a science, with exceptions and no obvious rules.'

There were 27 articles in this remarkable document, some of them of considerable length, and there is shown here quite a modest selection:

1 Go easy for the first few weeks. A bad start is difficult to atone for, and the Arabs form their judgement on externals that we ignore. When you have reached the inner circle in a tribe, you can do as you please with yourself and them.

2. Learn all you can about your Ashraf and Bedu. Get to know their families, clans and tribes, friends and enemies, wells, hills and roads. Do all this by listening and by indirect inquiry. Do not ask questions . . .

3 In matters of business deal only with the commander of the army, column, or party in which you serve. Never give orders to anyone at all, and reserve your directions or advice for the C.O. However great the temptation (for efficiency's sake) of dealing direct with his underlings. Your place is advisory, and your advice is due to the commander alone. Let him see that this is your conception of your duty, and that his is to be the sole executive of your joint plans.

4. Win and keep the confidence of your leader. Strengthen his prestige at your expense before others when you can. Never refuse or quash schemes he has put forward: but ensure that they are put forward in the first instance privately by you. Always approve them, after praise modify them insensibly, causing the suggestions to come from you, until they are in accord with your own opinion. When you attain this point, hold him to it, keep a tight grip of his ideas, and push him forward as firmly as possible, and secretly so that no one but himself (and he not too clearly) is aware of your pressure.

5 Remain in touch with your leader as constantly and unobtrusively as you can. Live with him, that at meal times and at audiences you may be naturally with him in his tent. Formal visits to give advice are not so good as the constant dropping of ideas in casual talk. When stranger sheikhs come in for the first time to swear allegiance and offer service, clear out of the tent. If their first impression is of foreigners in the confidence of the Sherif, it will do the Arab cause much harm.

8 . . . Sherifs are above all blood-feuds and local rivalries, and form the only principle of unity among the Arabs. Let your name therefore be coupled always with the Sherif's, and share his attitude towards the tribes. When the moment comes for action put yourself publicly under his orders. The Bedu will then follow suit.

11 The foreigner and Christian is not a popular person in Arabia. However friendly and informal the treatment of yourself may be, remember always that your foundations are very sandy ones . . .

12 Cling tight to your sense of humour. You will need it every day. A dry irony is the most useful type, and repartee of a personal and not too broad character will double your influence with the chiefs . . .

13 Never lay hands upon an Arab . . . the less you lose your temper the greater your advantage. Also then you will not go mad yourself.

17 Wear an Arab headcloth when with a tribe. Bedu have a malignant prejudice against the hat, and believe that our persistence in wearing it (due probably to British obstinacy of dictation) is founded on some immoral or irreligious principle.

18 Disguise is not advisable. Except in special areas, let it be clearly known that

you are a British officer and a Christian. At the same time, if you can wear Arab kit when with the tribes, you will acquire their trust and intimacy to a degree impossible in uniform. It is, however, dangerous and difficult. They make no special allowances for you when you dress like them . . .

19 If you wear Arab things, wear the best . . .

20 . . . The strain of living and thinking in a foreign and half-understood language, the savage food, strange clothes, and stranger ways, with the complete loss of privacy and quiet, and the impossibility of ever relaxing your watchful imitation of the others for months on end, provide such an added stress to the ordinary difficulties of dealing with the Bedu, the climate, and the Turks, that this road should not be chosen without serious thought.

21 . . . With the Bedu, Islam is so all-pervading an element that there is little religiosity, little fervour, and no regard for externals. Do not think from their conduct that they are careless . . . Their religion is as much a part of nature to them as is sleep or food.

22 Do not try to trade on what you know of fighting. The Hejaz confounds ordinary tactics. Learn the Bedu principles of war as thoroughly and as quickly as you can . . . A sheikh from one tribe cannot give orders to men from another; a Sherif is necessary to command a mixed tribal force. If there is plunder in prospect, and the odds are at all equal, you will win. Do not waste Bedu attacking trenches (they will not stand casualties) or in trying to defend a position, for they cannot sit still without slacking . . .

25 In spite of ordinary Arab example, avoid too free talk about women. It is as difficult a subject as religion, and their standards are so unlike our own that remark, harmless in English, may appear as unrestrained to them, as some of their statements would look to us, if translated literally.[13]

A senior former member of British special forces has recently told the writer that he found these notes 'invaluable' when he worked in Arabia, and suggested to his younger officers that they should study them too.

From Aqaba, on 12 August, Lawrence wrote home his impressions of the Sherifian family: he genuinely liked Feisal, and his younger brother Zeid, but Abdullah he called 'an intriguer' (Abdullah did not like Lawrence either, a fact which he made clear in his memoirs); Ali was 'a religious fanatic'. Having made these comments, he then wrote of the Arabs in general: 'I do hope we play them fair'[14] – one of the first indications of a guilt which eventually engulfed him.

Major Lawrence (he had been promoted and awarded decorations after Aqaba) now made frequent visits to GHO and the Arab Bureau in Cairo – the visits usually lasted five days. He felt insecure when he was not close to Feisal in case the latter made an impulsive decision in his absence.

Aqaba was filling up with new personnel and equipment. Eight armoured cars and two Rolls-Royce tenders arrived. After they had been unloaded, the only way they could be moved out of Aqaba was by blasting a corridor in the rocky terrain which surrounded the port. S. C. Rolls, one of the drivers who had arrived with the cars, who wrote a book called *Steel Chariots in the Desert*, described how the British soldiers were surprised by Lawrence's first visit.

Busy marking out rocks for blasting, Rolls noticed some Arabs riding towards him:

> 'Yalla! Imshi! Clear off!' I shouted to the first of the Arabs, who was making his camel kneel . . . Looking now, for the first time, full into his eyes, I had a shock. They were steel grey eyes, and his face was red, not coffee-coloured like the faces of the other Arabs. Instead of the piercing scowl there was laughter in those eyes. As he came close I heard a soft, melodious voice, which sounded girlish in those grim surroundings, say 'Is your captain with you?' He spoke in the cultivated Oxford manner. I dropped my cigarette in sheer astonishment . . .
>
> He placed his hand for a moment on my shoulder, 'My name is Lawrence', said he, 'I have come to join you'.[15]

Lawrence used the armoured cars extensively to assist in his ambushes on Turkish trains, and was a very popular commander with the other ranks: 'Lawrence's orders were directions, and he cared nothing about saluting, except that he preferred to dispense with it. Instead of an order, he usually seemed to raise a question ... giving the impression, a true one, that he wanted to have one's opinion of what was best, before he decided on the course to follow.'[16] One of Lawrence's NCOs, Sergeant Brook (who appears in *Seven Pillars* as Stokes, the machine gun instructor) has similarly positive memories: 'It was evident the whole time that he had the devotion of every man under him.' Brook notes how on one occasion when they were under fire, Lawrence 'with complete disregard of flying bullets', 'strolled over to see how we were faring: his bearing made us feel that the whole thing was a picnic.'[17]

9 The Strain Shows

Lawrence wrote home from Aqaba on 5 September 1917 that he was off on another train-wrecking expedition lasting about three weeks, and on 24 September he wrote home again having blown up two locomotives on his trip up country. In the first letter he said that he had been given the CB, Military Division, instead of the VC, adding, 'All these letters & things are so many nuisances afterwards, & I'll never wear or use any of them. Please don't, either. My address is simply T.E.L., no titles please.'[1] He also asked in this letter for the address of Janet Laurie, a girl to whom he had once suddenly proposed marriage – one of the rare references to a young woman in a Lawrence letter.

In a letter of 24 September, he asked his mother to send out an Arab cloak he had bought in Aleppo, of a type and quality unavailable in the wartime Hejaz. He ended the letter: 'Do you know I have not written a private letter to anyone but you for over a year? It is a wonderful thing to have kept so free of everything. Here I am at thirty with no label and no profession – and perfectly quiet. I'm more grateful to Father than I can say.'[2]

It is perhaps worth pointing out that he had written other private letters during the year and that he was just twenty-nine and not thirty. The gratitude to his father was for the settlement of a private income of £250 a year, the proceeds of the sale of some property in Ireland. As for being 'perfectly quiet', this was certainly an exaggeration. The regular raiding parties were taking their toll, and he fell victim to battle fatigue. For nearly a year, he had been driving himself beyond the limits of normal human endurance. On 24 September he also wrote to Leeds at the Ashmolean:

> I'm not going to last out this game much longer: nerves going and temper wearing thin . . . I hope when the nightmare ends I will wake up and become alive again. This killing and killing of Turks is horrible. When you charge in at the finish and find them all over the place in bits, and still alive many of them, and know that you have done hundreds in the same way and must do hundreds more if you can . . .[3]

A few days later Lawrence was off on yet another train-wrecking mission, this time testing a new form of automatic mine. Lawrence's report on this operation, currently in the Public Records Office, is remarkable not for its contents, but because of the way it was written. It starts in ink on the first page, then a different colour ink for the next page, and finally reverts to pencil. His handwriting is erratic and messy, as if he was writing under great stress.

In October 1917, Hogarth wrote to his wife from Cairo about Lawrence's growing fame:

> He is going out of reach again for a spell and they [the Lawrence family] must not expect letters from him; but whenever I have news of him I'll let them know the facts whether through you or direct.
>
> But the intervals will be long. Tell his mother he has now five decorations including the C.B. [Companion of the Bath] (to qualify for which he had to be promoted major) and despises and ignores the lot. Says he does not mind what they give him . . . his reputation has become overpowering.[4]

At this time, Allenby's army was advancing through Palestine, and after a brief delay captured Beersheeba. On orders from Allenby, Lawrence was asked to assist this operation by destroying the rail link between Deraa and Damascus. His mission was to blow up the large bridge at Yarmuk, thus disrupting the Turkish lines of communication in the area. Lawrence failed: his small force was detected by the Turks and had to fight its way out. To try to make up for this setback, Lawrence destroyed other bridges in the area, but he could not avoid the inescapable conclusion that he had let down both himself and Allenby – Lawrence demanded an inhuman and unobtainable perfection in himself. Hogarth realized the dangers his young friend was undertaking, and on 11 November wrote again to his wife: 'I only hope and trust T.E.L. will get back safe. He is out and up against it. If he comes through it is a V.C. – if not, well, I don't like to think about it.'[5]

Lawrence did not get a VC. Nevertheless, he continued to take part in a series of very dangerous operations in the same area. On 14 November, he was at Azrak camped in an old ruined fort, and from there he rode towards Deraa on another special mission for Allenby. Lawrence was to make a reconnaissance in the vicinity of Deraa – the town which acted as a railway junction between Amman and Damascus. This would be a dangerous undercover operation, well behind enemy lines. T.E. successfully examined the area around Deraa, and then decided that he would have to enter the town in order to complete his mission.

The story of what happened next has been told many times and there are so many versions that the exact truth is inextricably entangled in a web of half-truths. Perhaps the best place to start is with Lawrence's official report to Intelligence GHQ Cairo, the original copy of which is now preserved in the Humanities Research Center in Austin, Texas.

> I went into Deraa disguised to spy out the defences, was caught and identified by Hajim Bey, the Governor, by virtue of Abd el Kadir's description of me. (I learnt all about his treachery from Hajim's conversation, and from my guards.) Hajim was an ardent pederast and took a fancy to me. So he kept me underground until night, and then tried to have me. I was unwilling and prevailed after some

> difficulty. Hajim sent me to the hospital, and I escaped before dawn, being not as hurt as he thought. He was so ashamed of the muddle he had made that he hushed the whole thing up and never reported my capture and escape. I got back to Azrak very annoyed with Abd el Kadir, and rode down to Aqaba.[6]

In later accounts, Lawrence was to embroider this terse outline. According to the 1935 edition of *The Seven Pillars of Wisdom*, he was wandering through Deraa when he was approached by a Turkish sergeant and told, 'The Bey wants you.' Eventually, Lawrence was brought before the Bey, who made sexual advances towards him, which T.E. repelled, and then: '[the Bey] began to fawn on me, saying how white and fresh I was.' Lawrence rejected him again, the Bey clapped and two sentries emerged and pinioned Lawrence, who still managed to knee the Governor in the groin. Once he had recovered from the pain, the Bey beat Lawrence, and then bit him and kissed him. Then he drew one of his men's bayonets 'and pulled up a fold of flesh over my ribs'. Lawrence described in explicit detail how the blood flowed down his side, and how the Bey 'dabbed it over my stomach with his fingertips'. Not being able to bear the pain, Lawrence spoke, and the Bey replied ambiguously: 'You must understand that I know:* and it will be easier if you do as I wish.' Lawrence continued to resist and the Bey, looking at his damaged plaything, 'half whispered to the corporal to take me out and teach me everything'. Lawrence was removed from the Bey's bedchamber, kicked to the stairs and ended up pinioned to the guardroom bench.

He realized he was to be whipped and described his flagellation and the instrument of his torture:

> a whip of the Circassian sort, a thong of supple black hide, rounded, and tapering from the thickness of a thumb at the grip (which was wrapped in silver) down to a hard point finer than a pencil . . . After the corporal ceased, the men took me up very deliberately, giving me so many, and then an interval, during which they would squabble for the next turn, ease themselves and play unspeakably with me.

These last words have a sinister ambiguity. Lawrence goes on to describe the cut each stroke of the whip made: 'At last when I was completely broken they seemed satisfied.' He fell in a heap on the floor, the corporal kicked him: 'I remember smiling idly at him, for a delicious warmth, probably sexual, was swelling through me.' Lawrence was taken back to the Bey, 'but he now rejected me in haste, as a thing too torn and bloody for his bed'.[7]

This whole account in *Seven Pillars* conflicts with what Lawrence later told his friends. Richard Meinertzhagen, an intelligence officer with Allenby, met Lawrence after the war at the Paris Peace Conference. They had known each other in Arabia, and Lawrence, in low spirits, needed to confide in someone. He confessed to Meinertzhagen his two most guilty secrets – his illegitimacy and the true account of what happened at Deraa. Meinertzhagen entered in his

*Two possible interpretations of this statement are: 1) he knew Lawrence was a British soldier, or 2) he knew Lawrence was homosexual.

diary for 20 July 1919 that Lawrence had not written the truth of Deraa, and told him that he had done this 'because it was too degrading', and 'had penetrated his innermost nature'. Meinertzhagen also noted that Lawrence 'lived in constant fear that the true facts would be known'. These were that he had been seized, stripped and bound; then sodomized by the Governor of Deraa, followed by similar treatment by the Governor's servants.... After this he had been flogged.'[8]

To Mrs George Bernard Shaw, Lawrence also wrote of Deraa:

> About that night. I shouldn't tell you, because decent men don't talk about such things. I wanted to put it plain in the book and wrestled for days with my self respect . . . which wouldn't, hasn't let me. For fear of being hurt, or rather to earn five minutes' respite from a pain which drove me mad, I gave away the only possession we are born into life with – our bodily integrity. It's an unforgivable matter, an irrevocable position: and it's that which has made me forswear decent living, & the exercise of my not-contemptible wits and talents.[9]

In the account of the incident which appears in the early Bodleian Library version of *Seven Pillars*, Lawrence wrote that the practice of homosexual domination prevalent in the Turkish Army made military life a 'living death' to normal men, particularly because of the 'revolting forms of sexual disease' they inevitably contracted. These phrases appear also in the more widely published text but they are taken out of the Deraa chapter and placed elsewhere. In both versions Lawrence notes that in some batches of Turkish prisoners up to 50 per cent were infected with syphilis. Representatives of *The Sunday Times* have examined the Bey of Deraa's diaries and state that within them the Bey complains of having at least once contracted gonorrhoea (although his diaries only mention heterosexual encounters). A consultant venereologist and a professor of medicine have confirmed that a man with gonorrhoea would have an 80 per cent probability of passing his disease on in a homosexual encounter, and 50 per cent in the case of syphilis. The endemic venereal disease among Turkish soldiers would mean that if Lawrence had been the victim of a multiple homosexual rape, he would in all likelihood have been infected. Could this be the reason he wrote to Charlotte Shaw that he would have to 'forswear decent living'? Another explanation may be that Lawrence was suffering not from the disease itself, but from venereal phobia, a condition common before the advent of antibiotics.

Several biographers have convincingly shown that the Deraa incident is suspect in time and place, and Desmond Stewart suggests it never happened but hides another related event. The story has many flaws, the most obvious being Lawrence's claim that even when stripped naked, he was not recognized as a blue-eyed European. (After the war he wrote to Liddell Hart that 'no easterner could ever have taken me for an Arab, for a moment.')[10]

Equally implausible are Lawrence's apparently easy escape and sudden return to health. When he returned to camp the outward signs of the severe beating had conveniently vanished and he passed off a story about tricking his way out of Deraa to the general amusement of his companions.

Stewart also noted Lawrence's wartime bond of friendship with a handsome young Arab, Sherif Ali ibn al-Hussein, the Arab commander at Yarmuk when Lawrence failed in his mission to blow the bridge. Lawrence had specifically asked Feisal for Ali, and Stewart suggests that Lawrence and Ali might have been lovers.

Professor Jeffrey Meyers was the first to draw attention to another unusual incident which appears about twenty pages further on from Deraa in the original 'Oxford' edition of *Seven Pillars*. It never appeared in any generally published version. Lawrence describes another homosexual incident, this time between an Arab and a British soldier. Both are teenagers, caught *in flagrante delicto*. The Arab boy is whipped by his elders but his sentence is lessened by Lawrence's intervention. After telling the young British soldier involved that he must be reported, Lawrence explains to his NCO that the boy was not being condemned for moral reasons. Lawrence states his own 'convictions' and 'impulses' were not 'strong enough' to put himself up as a judge of character; rather the boy would have to be punished simply because he had been caught openly with an Arab. To avoid a court martial the young soldier's comrades take matters into their own hands and whip him, giving the poor victim ten extra strokes because he was English! Lawrence decides to forget about the whole incident, and says he was pleased that never again did he hear of another case of any Briton having a sexual relationship with an Arab, which was a good thing 'for reasons other than the sanitary'.[11]

There exists in the Imperial War Museum a carbon copy of a draft contract between *The Sunday Times* and Professor Lawrence.[12] *The Sunday Times* required Professor Arnold Lawrence to give a copyright permission for a book being prepared after a series of articles by the *Insight* team – the articles made public the sworn statements of a man called John Bruce, who is now known to have been employed by Lawrence to beat him after the war. Part of Clause 7b requires 'that no indication be given [in the proposed book] that a British soldier was involved in the sodomy episode described in a cancelled chapter of Seven Pillars, or of the whereabouts in the unpublished text that chapter may be found.' Meyers was also refused permission to quote this passage. It is curious that anyone should be anxious that this episode should not be revealed fifty years after the event.

Summing up the evidence and related matters, it would seem that the Deraa incident did not take place as Lawrence described. It appears typical of his deliberate efforts to degrade himself, and may have been written either to justify his homosexuality to himself, or as a self-inflicted penance for his part in lying to himself and to the Arabs – perhaps both. One cannot blame Lawrence for lying, one can only sympathize with him in the agony he obviously suffered.

10 Convention

Whatever did or did not take place in the Bey's bedchamber, the Deraa incident provided *The Seven Pillars of Wisdom* with its central dramatic pivot. Lawrence was back in the base camp at Azraq by 22 November 1917 in a state of mental and physical exhaustion, and from there he returned to the greater security of Aqaba. By a bitter coincidence, as he left Azraq, the French Government officially announced that they had awarded him a Croix de Guerre. The original citation, not without a political implication, had been drawn up by Lawrence's old rival Colonel Brémond:

> Le Président du Conseil, Ministre de la Guerre, cite à l'ordre de l'Armée:
> LAWRENCE, Thomas Edouard, Major à l'Etat-Major du Haute-Commissaire du Gouvernement Brittanique en Egypte pour le motif suivant:
> Officier supérieur de la plus haute valeur. Par son action personelle a su grouper autour de lui contingents bédouins à la tête desquels il a accompli ses opérations de la plus grande audace, avec le succès le plus complet, sans eau et sans ravitaillement, compromettant les communications des troupes turques du Hedjaz.
>
> Paris, le 23 Novembre 1917
> Signé: *L. Mordacq.*[1]

Characteristically Lawrence wrote home to complain of the award:

> The French government has stuck another medal on to me: a croix de guerre this time. I wish they would not bother, but they never consult one before doing these things. At least I have never accepted one, and will never wear one or allow one to be conferred on me openly. One cannot do more, for these notices are published in the Press first thing, and to counter-announce that one refused it would create more publicity than the award itself.[2]

Events in Russia during 1917 were to have serious and immediate implications for the Arab Revolt. After the revolution in November the Bolsheviks immediately withdrew support from Russia's former allies. As part of their propaganda to discredit the capitalist system, they published the texts of some of the most sensitive secret treaties to which their Tsarist predecessors had been signatories. The details of the Sykes–Picot agreement appeared in *Izvestia* and were subsequently translated into Arabic and republished by the Turks. Sherif Hussein was understandably concerned by the apparent duplicity of the British Government. This public announcement of the concessions which the British had made to the French led to a mild panic, both in Whitehall and in Cairo. The problem was eventually solved by the most dishonest diplomacy, when the gullible Sherif accepted a British explanation that Sykes–Picot was in fact only a draft of an agreement which had never been fully ratified, and which the Turks were using as a psychological weapon to disrupt Anglo–Arab relations. The inconsistencies between translation and retranslation created enough uncertainty for the British to convince Hussein that he had not been conned, and the matter was allowed to rest temporarily until the day of reckoning when British and Arab forces arrived in Damascus.

When did Lawrence become aware of the existence of the Sykes–Picot agreement? His own writings are drastically contradictory. During the latter part of 1917, he was beginning to feel guilty for his part in misleading the Arabs, and his attitude towards their cause seemed to undergo a change. Moreover, an announcement had just been made in England which would profoundly alter the future of the Middle East. The Balfour Declaration stated:

> His Majesty's Government view with favour the establishment in Palestine of a national home for the Jewish people and will use their best endeavours to facilitate the achievement of this project, it being clearly understood that nothing shall be done which may prejudice the civil or religious rights of existing non-Jewish communities in Palestine, or the rights and political status enjoyed by the Jews in any other country.

Lawrence had always been in favour of Jewish immigration in Palestine, believing that Jewish and Arab interests were not mutually exclusive and could be combined with Britain's, to the detriment of France. He took on the role of convincing Feisal and his father that Jewish settlement in Palestine was to their benefit, and wrote later to Clayton: 'For the Jews, when I see Feisal next I'll talk to him and the Arab attitude shall be sympathetic, for the duration of the war at least.'[3] Lawrence allowed himself to be used; the British Government had already deceived the Arabs over Syria, and were now doing exactly the same thing with Palestine. Prompted by a proposal of Hogarth's, Lawrence thought a Zionist offer to finance the new Arab state might be exchanged for the acceptance of Jewish colonization of Palestine.

When Lawrence returned to Aqaba on 26 November, he found orders from Allenby asking him to come at once to Gaza. The Commander of the Egyptian Expeditionary Force was anxious to be briefed on the latest situation in the Hejaz, but also, as a gesture of confidence, wanted to extend to Lawrence the honour of being present at the historic entry into Jerusalem. Allenby's advance in Palestine, after a difficult start, had been progressing well, and on 9 December he entered Jerusalem with suitable, but not overly martial, pomp and ceremony. Lawrence borrowed normal British Staff uniform for the occasion after a hurried search for suitable donors. The British arrival in Jerusalem was carefully preplanned because of the potential repercussions of occupying a city sacred to so many religions around the world. The War Cabinet had ordered that Jerusalem was to be taken without a fight. General Allenby walked into the city at the Jaffa gate, having dismounted from his horse. This action had been prompted by a jibe at the Kaiser, who had once ridden into the Holy City.

While in Palestine Lawrence met Richard Meinertzhagen, Allenby's Chief of Intelligence. Meinertzhagen records this, his first meeting with Lawrence, in his diary for the evening of 9 December.

> As I was working in my tent last night – about 10 p.m. – in walked an Arab boy dressed in spotless white, white headress with golden circlet; for a moment I thought the boy was somebody's pleasure-boy but it soon dawned on me that he must be Lawrence whom I knew to be in the camp. I just stared in silence at the very beautiful apparition which I suppose was what was intended. He then said in a soft voice 'I am Lawrence, Dalmeny sent me over to see you'. I said 'Boy or Girl?' He smiled and blushed, saying 'Boy'.[4]

The question reveals something of the questioner. Lawrence sat down on Meinertzhagen's bed and together they discussed the Arab 'side-show' – a term Meinertzhagen noted his visitor did not like at all. Meinertzhagen, who became a fervent Zionist, states rather too forcefully that Lawrence's effort in Arabia was 'not having the slightest influence on Allenby's main campaign'. He also recalls how vehemently Lawrence opposed regular British soldiers encroaching 'on his political sphere', namely Arabia. The two men sat talking till past midnight and, despite 'bombastic exaggerations', Meinertzhagen liked Lawrence and noted his charm and impish sense of humour: 'He is ambitious and makes preposterous claims whilst acting like a demure little schoolgirl.' Meinertzhagen was surprised that Lawrence made no mention of his colleagues in Arabia, in particular Dawnay and Newcombe: 'he never mentioned any by name; he wished me to believe that his was the credit for every success.' Meinertzhagen also mentions Lawrence's loathing of the French, and ends his diary entry:

> I shall look forward to seeing Lawrence again for, in spite of his ambition, he has very great charm and a delightful quiet way of talking. But if he starts any of this impresario nonsense, pretending he is nobody at the moment and expecting hero-worship the next moment, I shall prick his bubble with a pop. One cannot act modesty and advertisement at one and the same time.[5]

Lawrence could! The diary entry is an interesting impression of Lawrence (including a current of suppressed sexuality), but it seems probable that, as was Meinertzhagen's habit, he made amendments with the advantage of hindsight.

During Lawrence's stay in Palestine, Allenby had found time to discuss with him the future of the Arabian War and the final push into Syria. Feisal's troops would have an important role in his operation, and Lawrence would have to co-ordinate it. Allenby encouraged Lawrence, who was evidently depressed. He recognized Lawrence's talent and gave him plenty of room to use his own initiative as the man on the spot. Lawrence responded very favourably to this type of leadership. The paternalistic General was one of the few men who had the power to motivate him, and Lawrence left for Egypt in far better spirits than when he had arrived in Palestine. In Allenby he had found another father figure.

In Cairo, another substitute parent, Hogarth, greeted him and, amused by his protégé's idiosyncracies, wrote home:

> They put him up at the Residency this time and made much of him. He went about happily in a second Lieutenant's tunic and badges somewhere between a Lieutenant and Captain, and no decorations and no belt. When he went to Jerusalem and Allenby he is reported to have borrowed from one person and another a regular staff outfit with proper badges and even decorations. I only hope he appears in the motion pictures on that occasion, because, otherwise, an unknown aspect of him will be lost.[6]

Hogarth's mild concern was warranted, as no ciné film appears to exist of Lawrence dressed in normal Staff uniform, though several stills survive.

Strongly fortified, Aqaba was now a firm base from which to mount regular raids on the Hejaz railway and Lawrence, aware of the price the Turks had put upon his head, continued to take a leading part. To give himself extra protection, he formed a personal bodyguard made up from the toughest tribesmen he could find. He liked to claim that many of them were outlaws, which is not unlikely as there is independent evidence that his mercenaries caused some alarm among the other residents in Aqaba. They can be seen in a photograph in the Imperial War Museum which Lawrence amusingly captioned 'Sheik Lawrence and his hired assassins'.

In January 1918, Lawrence wrote home with the sad news that Newcombe had been captured in Palestine, having been recently transferred back to the regular Army there; the ever-resourceful engineer subsequently made three escape attempts.

During the Arabian campaign, Lawrence only fought one regular battle. It took place at Tafileh on 25 January 1918. The town of Tafileh had been attacked and occupied by Auda and Nasir earlier in the month; they held it with a small force awaiting relief. Lawrence, Jaafar and Zeid left Aqaba with a contingent of regular reinforcements – mainly Arab troops who had deserted from the Turks, or had been taken prisoner and changed sides, like Jaafar. Such a change of allegiance did not have any dishonourable connotations for the Arab soldier, who in many ways was traditionally a mercenary.

The weather was so appalling that all the men and equipment could not reach Tafileh in time. Lawrence went on ahead and witnessed a formidable Turkish counter-attack on the village. The small defending force – some three hundred men to the Turks one thousand – panicked and retreated from the village. Lawrence writes that he tried to encourage his companions, suggesting a better deployment of their limited human resources, and guided by their British adviser's tactical advice, the Arabs fought back and decimated the Turks, killing 400 and taking 250 prisoners. The victory was apparently due to Lawrence's superior knowledge of the science of war.[7]

For his part at Tafileh, he added a DSO to his unworn collection of decorations, and was promoted lieutenant-colonel. Predictably, he wrote home complaining about the new medal, suggesting such 'good stuff' should go 'to someone who would use it'.[8] This exaggerated modesty contrasts with the fact that Lawrence received the medal because of a report he himself had composed for headquarters. In *The Seven Pillars of Wisdom*, he commented:

> It was meanly written for effect, full of quaint similies and mock simplicities; and made them think me a modest amateur, doing his best after the great models . . . Headquarters loved it, and innocently, to crown the jest offered me a decoration on the strength of it. We should have more bright breasts in the Army if each man was able, without witness, to write his own despatch.[9]

During February Lawrence was in Jerusalem and it was there that Ronald Storrs, who had been created Military Governor, introduced him to the American journalist Lowell Thomas and his cameraman Harry Chase. This meeting, and their subsequent reunion in Arabia, was later to have such a profound effect not only on Lawrence's life, but on all perceptions of him and of the Arab Revolt, that some space must be devoted to consideration of how Lowell Thomas, and many other correspondents, arrived in the Middle East at that time.

The Allied governments, particularly Britain, had been very slow to recognize the importance of propaganda. A great deal had been left to the uncoordinated actions of far-sighted individuals. The British Press magnate Northcliffe, owner of *The Times* and the *Daily Mail*, had done his best but had been restricted by ridiculous blanket censorship during the first two years of the war. After the downfall of Asquith's government in December 1916, the new Prime Minister, Lloyd George, was in close touch with Northcliffe. He had a very different attitude to the Press and saw that a specific propaganda department was needed. Colonel John Buchan, the author, was appointed Director of Information, directly responsible to the Prime Minister. The new department combined the Foreign Office's 'News Department', the 'War Propaganda Bureau' and the Home Office's 'Neutral Press Committee'.

America's entry into the war highlighted the propaganda problem. Northcliffe went to the United States in June 1917 as head of the British War Mission, and was appalled to find that the American public were under the impression that the French (then still considered as America's historic ally) were doing all the fighting and suffering all the casualties. Northcliffe initiated a transatlantic propaganda campaign. From England, speakers were sent to the United States, and American journalists were encouraged to visit Britain and the European Front.

Buchan, however, realized that something more comprehensive was needed than his department, and suggested a new Ministry with a man of political power at its head.

Eventually, Lord Beaverbrook, owner of the *Daily Express*, became the head of the Ministry of Information with Buchan as Director of Intelligence. The two men realized that their new Ministry should not only rally British support for the war but also do everything possible to encourage awareness in the United States, especially through the Press.

So it was that John Buchan, in his new and powerful position under Beaverbrook, arranged that Lowell Thomas should visit Allenby's victorious army. Buchan realized that this as yet untold story was the sort of good news that was required both in England and in the United States. As events turned out, Thomas took advantage of the facilities offered to him, but he kept his real scoop until after the end of the war.

It is evident that Lawrence was becoming strained during the spring of 1918. He wrote home from Aqaba on 28 March that his job had become 'too big' for him. The administrative responsibility, together with the strain of combat, was more than even a man of his exceptional abilities could cope with indefinitely. Cairo recognized his importance – and vulnerability – in a necessarily unsubtle manner: they asked him to choose a successor should he be killed. Lawrence suggested Hubert Young, the old acquaintance from Carchemish whom he had briefly met again during his short stay at Basra. In *The Seven Pillars of Wisdom* Lawrence describes Young as 'a regular of exceptional quality, with long and wide experience of war, and perfect fluency in Arabic.'[10] Young wrote of his reunion with Lawrence in Cairo, where he had been summoned under a shroud of mystery:

> It was not until I reported to G.H.Q. at the Savoy Hotel, Cairo, and the door opened to admit the familiar little figure, that I was enlightened. 'They asked me to suggest someone who could take my place in case anything happened to me,' said Lawrence, with his mischievous smile, 'and I told them I thought no one could. As they pressed me, I said I could only think of Gertrude Bell and yourself, and they seemed to think you better for this particular job than she would be. It is quite amusing, and there is plenty of honour and glory to be picked up without any great difficulty.[11]

Young was also impressed by Lawrence's appearance. He has described Lawrence's magnificent robes – Feisal himself could boast no more splendid – and toyed with the idea of obtaining a similar *agal* (headrope) to Lawrence's until he discovered in the Cairo suq it would cost him 'fifty golden guineas'[12] and settled on something less extravagant. In his role as understudy, Young worked with or near Lawrence until the fall of Damascus, and his comments are particularly valuable as he is one of the few European eye-witnesses of Lawrence's train-wrecking escapades:

> Nothing seemed to give him greater pleasure than to squat down less than two hundred yards from the railway-line with an electric exploder tucked away under

> his *aba*, and to watch with complete unconcern the slow approach of a train full of Turkish soldiers . . . As soon as the engine was well over the undiscovered mine, he would jam down the knob of the exploder, retire to his waiting camel and ride away, hotly pursued by the fire of any soldiers who might have escaped from the rear carriages . . . Other British officers did the same kind of thing but not in the same grand manner.[13]

Young noted that 'Lawrence was absolutely without fear' and 'a law until himself' but also that 'he never knew very much about the regular army'.[14] One must conclude from Young's comments, and those of other British soldiers who worked with him, that Lawrence was unquestionably a brave and courageous soldier, even if he sometimes pretended to know more than he did and even if he was a compulsive show-off. Young himself concluded that he could not forgive Lawrence for his hatred of the regular Army, but that he was nevertheless an inspired, if sometimes unrealistic, leader who won the respect of Arab and British soldiers alike because of his 'utter disregard of danger and his readiness to endure not merely discomfort but the worst kinds of hardship'.[15]

11 The Battle for Damascus

During the spring of 1918, Lawrence master-minded a major new offensive against the Hejaz line, and as it became clear, during the early summer, that the Turks were losing the war in the Hejaz and Palestine, concern grew among the Arabs over British and French plans for Syria and the Lebanon. For their part, the British Government, despite Lawrence, were perturbed by Turkish overtures to Feisal. Jemal Pasha, the Turkish commander in Syria, had kept in secret contact with Feisal since the Arab Revolt began, and had made several attempts to offer a separate peace. Feisal had listened to the Turkish offers, kept open the channels of communication, but done little else. As Turkish prospects in both the Hejaz and Palestine became bleaker, nationalist elements within the Ottoman High Command encouraged Jemal Pasha to make his approaches to Feisal even bolder. Lawrence claimed that he was fully aware of all these negotiations (it is not clear whether Feisal realized this), and even used them to British advantage.

On 16 June 1918, the British Government made a declaration of policy, supposedly in response to a petition from seven prominent Syrian nationalists exiled in Cairo. The so-called 'Declaration to the Seven' stated that His Majesty's Government would recognize 'the complete and sovereign independence' of all those 'Territories liberated from Turkish rule by the Arabs themselves'.[1] Feisal and his father saw this as an unequivocal statement that the Sykes–Picot agreement was redundant and had been superseded – a misconception reinforced by Lawrence and other representatives of the British Government. A few weeks earlier, Lawrence had written on an Army notepad (preserved in the British Museum): 'We are calling them to fight for a lie and I can't stand it.'

In preparation for Allenby's forthcoming advance north towards Damascus, Lawrence was constantly on the move between the Hejaz, Egypt and Palestine, his work-load increased by his dual military and political functions. Despite many new responsibilities, he continued personally to undertake daring raids on the Hejaz railway. Several British colleagues noted his refusal to delegate, and the consequent and unnecessary increase of strain on himself.

Militarily, the Hejaz war had become more orthodox as additional trained personnel arrived. Along with human reinforcements came the latest armoured cars and aeroplanes. Lawrence used both to good effect, and later told Liddell Hart that he had flown (as a passenger or observer) 'two thousand hours'[2] during the war – a figure which seems exaggeratedly high. His enthusiasm for aviation was nevertheless genuine.

New equipment arriving in bulk and the fact that victory was in sight did not prevent morale among Feisal's men dropping. Lawrence noted this with concern. As fatigue and dissatisfaction became a serious problem, he had to deal with a rift which was growing between Feisal and his father. German agents were waiting for a chance to exploit these difficulties, and opportunity came in August when Jaafar Pasha, the Mesopotamian officer in charge of Feisal's relatively small contingent of regulars (less than a thousand men), was appointed by Feisal, Commander of the Arab Northern Army. This was merely a new and flattering title for his old job, but German agents somehow persuaded Sherif Hussein that Jaafar had declared himself Commander-in-Chief of the Arab Armies, insinuating that the Mesopotamian was trying to take over absolute control of all Arab forces. Their scheme worked well. Hussein publicly denounced Jaafar, without bothering to find out if the allegations were true, and Feisal, who was already having difficulty coping with the strain of command, broke down and resigned. It has seldom been recorded that Feisal was a naturally nervous man, a fact outwardly reflected in his compulsive chain-smoking. His resignation could not have come at a worse moment for the British. His army was poised, ready to advance northward parallel with Allenby's forces (some elements of Feisal's army had actually started to move). In addition, the loss of Feisal's public support was a great blow to propaganda at a crucial stage in the war.

In a secret report which has never been published, Lawrence noted the spread of demoralization among the Bedouin and pointed out that, as a result of Feisal's resignation, orders were now being given direct to the Arabs instead of through their chiefs. He thought the situation could be held for another four days.[3]

Prompted by Lawrence, Allenby sent a paternalistic message to Feisal (also published here for the first time):

> It has been brought to my notice that you have tendered your resignation to the King of the Hejaz. It is not for me to interfere in a personal question between your revered father and yourself, but I most strongly urge you to withdraw your resignation which at this junction threatens the destruction of Arab hopes. If your Highness resigns at this time all the work that you and your army have arduously performed will be rendered vain at the very moment when the chance of victory seems brightest. You owe it to the Arab cause and to those who so loyally fought with you to disregard every personal influence and complete the great task which you have so well begun.[4]

In the event, Feisal was persuaded to withdraw his resignation. Hussein sent his son a half-apologetic telegram which Lawrence intercepted and decoded, allowing Feisal only to see the first, less hostile half. A degree of equilibrium was restored to his army, but there were lasting ill effects and an adequate degree of discipline was never again restored.

Allenby's advance began on 19 September. Lawrence's role was to co-ordinate the isolation of Deraa, the major rail terminus south of Damascus, in order to prevent any Turkish reinforcements reaching Syria from the south, and generally to disrupt their lines of communication. Alec Kirkbride, who was at the time a young officer in the Royal Engineers, left a vivid account of how Lawrence and he attacked Nasib station (two stops south of Deraa). Kirkbride's task was to destroy a section of the track while Lawrence blew up a large bridge just north of the station buildings.

'Knowing his habit of using unnecessarily large amounts of explosives', Kirkbride wrote, 'I asked him to give me plenty of notice so that I could fire my charges and get my men away to safety before he blew up the bridge'. Predictably, Lawrence's reply to Kirkbride's caution was, 'Oh, all right, all right, don't fuss!' Following this, Kirkbride recalled 'there was a terrific detonation and an arc of bridge flew high into the air and fell all around my people'. Later that evening, Lawrence made a friendly gesture to Kirkbride by inviting him to have coffee in the presence of his bodyguard, 'a great honour, as he did not normally offer to entertain British personnel'.[5]

The Turks were now retreating to Damascus, thoroughly disrupted by a series of raids from both land and air. Lawrence and Auda, with a body of irregulars, caught up with a retreating column of Turks and Germans at a small village called Tafas which a rearguard of Turkish Lancers was defending. There ensued the gruesome episode which has been dubbed 'the massacre of Tafas' and which Lawrence described in *The Seven Pillars of Wisdom*. First his original report:

> The Turkish Commander of the Lancer rear guard in the village . . . ordered that the inhabitants be killed. These included some twenty small children (killed with lances and rifles), and about forty women. I noticed particularly one pregnant woman, who had been forced down on a saw bayonet. Unfortunately Talal, the Sheik of Tafas, who as mentioned had been a tower of strength to us from the beginning, and who was one of the coolest and boldest horsemen I have ever met, was in front with Auda abu Tayi and myself when we saw these sights. He gave a horrible cry, wrapped his headcloth about his face, put spurs to his horse, rocking in the saddle galloped at full speed into the midst of the retiring column, and fell himself and his mare, riddled with machine gun bullets, amongst their lance points.[6]

According to *Seven Pillars*, the Arabs, wild with rage at the death of Talal and his villagers, then flung themselves on the Turks, showing no quarter. Lawrence himself gave implicit orders to take no prisoners. 'The best of you brings me the most Turkish dead', he declared.

A distant section of Bedouin who had not heard this command had captured two hundred and fifty prisoners and brought them in. Meanwhile, dramatic tension built up when a dying but still conscious Arab was found pinned to the ground by a Turkish bayonet. When he was asked who had done this to him he just managed to nod towards the conveniently close batch of prisoners, who were then shot down where they stood. By the fall of night, Lawrence wrote, 'the rich plain was scattered over with dead men and animals. In a madness born of the horror of Tafas we killed and killed, even blowing in the heads of the fallen and of the animals; as though their death and running blood could slake our agony.'[7]

Official records show that a substantial body of Turkish troops was prevented from strengthening the defence of Damascus because of a victory at Tafas. However, as with the flagellation at Deraa, Lawrence's account of what occurred is disputed. A massacre of some kind did without doubt take place against the Turks and Germans, but Suleiman Mousa, the Jordanian historian, has brought forward evidence that the initial massacre by the Turks at Tafas may have been exaggerated by Lawrence in an attempt to justify the subsequent orgy of killing by some members of the Arab forces.

The contemporary press coverage of the Arabian War, in so far as it concerned Lawrence, is a cause of considerable speculation. No picture of or report about him was published in a British newspaper during the war – an omission which has perplexed some researchers and made others suspicious of Lawrence's real accomplishments. In fact there was a definite reason for this lack of enterprise, highlighted in the memoirs of R. D. Blumenfeld, editor of the *Daily Express*. The British Press was strictly censored from 1914, and on 26 September 1918 (by coincidence the day of the massacre at Tafas) the *Daily Express* received the following instructions from the Censorship and Press Committee:

> The Press are earnestly requested not to publish any photograph of Lieut. Colonel T. E. Lawrence, C.B., D.S.O. This officer is not known by sight to the Turks, who have put a price upon his head, and any photograph or personal description of him may endanger his safety.[8]

These instructions were issued because, two days before, a story appeared in the Paris newspaper *L'Echo* about Allenby's advance which made significant mention of Lawrence – the first time his name appeared in the Press in connection with his military activities in Arabia:

> At the side of General Allenby and the French General Priépape [whose role was minimal] it should be added that Colonel Lawrence was playing a major part in this victorious enterprise, utilising his experience of the country and its people and putting his organisational ability at the disposition of the British Commanding Officer. His name will become legendary in Great Britain.[9] [Author's translation.]

The Censorship and Press Committee's instructions were sufficient to kill the story as far as Lawrence was concerned, but it may well be that the restrictions on reporting his activities intrigued Fleet Street and contributed to the coverage he was later given.

In the official account of Allenby's campaign, *The Advance of the Egyptian Expeditionary Force*, produced shortly after the war in Cairo by the Government Press and the Survey of Egypt, there is only brief but laudatory mention of Lawrence, with no hint of his political importance. Readers are simply informed that Turkish reinforcements might have reached Damascus, 'had it not been for the destructive activities of Lieutenant Col. T. E. Lawrence, C.B., and his Arab Camel Corps and armoured cars'. The same account makes reference to Lawrence's most famous role as a train-wrecker, saying that the scheme 'of blowing up trains was evolved, and under the direction of Lieut. Colonel T. E. Lawrence this form of military activity began to rank almost as a national sport'.[10]

The Advance of the Egyptian Expeditionary Force, under the editorship of Lieutenant-Colonel H. Pirie-Gordon, gave a straightforward account of the Arabian War and of the events leading to the capture of Damascus, emphasizing the role of the Arab commanders, but minimizing that of their British advisers.

Lawrence's exact role during the days leading to the occupation of Damascus will never be satisfactorily explained. It may well be that, motivated by guilt, he took it as his personal responsibility to scupper the Sykes–Picot agreement, and to ensure that Feisal became king of an Arab administration in Syria. However, some historians suggest that his actions may have been prompted not so much by sympathy to the Arab people or Feisal, but rather by his own brand of British imperialism, which included a histrionic distrust of the French. This point of view is supported by the Foreign Office records now available in the Public Records Office.

Allenby's force having successfully defeated the Turks in Northern Palestine, the occupation of Deraa and Damascus was only a matter of time. Arab regular and irregular forces had played a comparatively small part in the overall operation; the vast bulk of the work was done by the Australian Mounted Division, commanded by General Sir Harry Chauvel, and the 4th and 5th Indian Cavalry Divisions, commanded by Major-General Sir George Barrow and Major-General H. J. M. Macandrew, respectively. But political restraint was put on all these units. Chauvel's orders were that he should approach Damascus and isolate it, but should not enter the city unless forced to for tactical reasons. It is clear that Chauvel was far from happy with his instructions.

As he led the final advance on the city, the climax of the Arabian campaign took place against an extremely ambiguous political situation. Britain had become entangled in contradictory promises to the French and Arabs (not to mention Balfour's promises to the Zionists), and the Government was looking for a way to circumvent the Sykes–Picot Treaty. If British forces occupied Damascus, there would be no way of avoiding a direct handover to the French. If, however, it could be shown that Arab troops had occupied the capital of Syria, and suffered considerable losses in doing so, then it just might be possible to persuade the French that there was no alternative to accepting the situation. But to make this plausible, it had to appear that there was a race between the Arab and the British with Damascus as the finishing line.

On 27 September, Lawrence asked Alec Kirkbride to join a party riding to Deraa immediately after the Turks had finally retreated from it. The group consisted of Nuri Said, a high-ranking commander in Feisal's army, several other well-known Arab nationalists and half a dozen of Lawrence's personal bodyguards. 'Lawrence joined the force', Kirkbride wrote, 'and remarked, "We must get there before the cavalry".'[11] They did so and hoisted the flag of the Hejaz before the Anglo-Indian cavalry arrived under the command of General Barrow, to whom Lawrence was theoretically attached as a liaison officer.

By 30 September, General Chauvel's units were in the suburbs of Damascus, and some of his troops entered the city before the Arabs in an attempt to prevent the complete breakdown of law and order. Realizing the political implications if Chauvel's troops were acknowledged as the first to enter Damascus, Lawrence secretly left General Barrow's camp at Deraa. Kirkbride saw him rush past in a Rolls-Royce tender:

> I waved, but Lawrence did not look round; he was staring ahead in the fixed way I had noticed a few days before. It was, I told myself, the race to Dera'a all over again with even greater problems at its end.[12]

Just outside Damascus, Lawrence met Nasir, Feisal's cousin, and Nuri Shalan, and sent them into the city to raise the Hashemite flag. However, this had already been done by two opportunist Algerian brothers, Mohamed Said and Abd el Kadir. Moreover, Mohamed Said had, with Nasir's approval, declared himself Civil Governor (Nasir was ill and was in no mood to take responsibility). This did not fit in with Lawrence's plans – he detested the two Algerians, and indeed it was Mohamed Said who, he claimed in the *Seven Pillars*, had originally denounced him to the Turks in Deraa. It seems probable that Said's and Kadir's pro-French sympathies contributed to Lawrence's hatred. When he arrived in Damascus with Auda, he removed Mohamed Said and replaced him with Shukri Pasha. The city remained in chaos, a situation not helped by Sherifian irregulars intent on getting their share of the spoils. Suddenly, all the rivalries which had been partially suppressed returned. 'With his extraordinary habit of wanting to do everything himself, Lawrence took me into the streets to see what was going on', Kirkbride wrote. Lawrence was particularly disturbed by the fact that wounded Turkish prisoners were being murdered in cold blood. Kirkbride recalled:

> We must have looked an ill-assorted couple, he short and in Arab robes with no arms but an ornamental dagger, and myself long and lanky in khaki wearing a large service revolver. When we found anyone butchering Turks he went up and asked them in a gentle voice to stop, while I stood by and brandished my firearm. Occasionally, someone turned nasty and I shot them at once before the trouble could spread . . .[13]

Kirkbride noted, with apparent surprise, that Lawrence 'appeared to be genuinely shocked by the free use which I made of my revolver' and told Kirkbride not to be so 'bloody minded'. It is evidence of his paradoxical nature that, despite a fascination with violence, he actively intervened throughout the war to prevent the wanton destruction of human and animal life.

Lawrence began to restore a degree of control in the city through Shukri, whom he had appointed Governor, but his attitude irritated Chauvel when the General entered the city and was presented, by Lawrence, with a *fait accompli*. In a report first published by Knightley and Simpson, Chauvel wrote:

> Lawrence's excuse for his unceremonious departure from General Barrow was that he thought I would like him to come in at once and find out what the situation was and tell me. He then proceeded to tell me that Shukri was the Governor of Damascus.[14]

Chauvel asked Lawrence to bring forward the former Turkish Governor of the city, but Lawrence replied that he had left the day before 'and that Shukri had been elected by a majority of citizens' – evidently a very quiet election! But Chauvel seems to have taken Lawrence's word for the political desirability of the situation.

Having attained his goal, Lawrence was now tired and disillusioned. Readers of the *Seven Pillars* are subjected to yet another gruesome interlude as the author uses the scene at a Turkish hospital in Damascus to express his wider revulsion:

> I stepped in, to meet a sickening stench: and, as my eyes grew open, a sickening sight. The stone floor was covered with dead bodies, side by side, some in full uniform, some in underclothing, some stark naked. There might be thirty there, and they crept with rats, who had gnawed wet red galleries into them. A few were corpses nearly fresh, perhaps only a day or two old: others must have been there for long. Of some the flesh, going putrid, was yellow and blue and black. Many were already swollen twice or thrice life-width, their fat heads laughing with black mouth across jaws harsh with stubble. Of others the softer parts were fallen in. A few had burst open, and were liquescent with decay.[15]

William Yale of the US State Department, who had met Lawrence in Sinai before the war, also witnessed the scene but blamed Lawrence for misleading readers by failing to point out that the hospital had been sacked by Arab looters. In the final and very brief chapter of the book, Lawrence returned to the hospital and was taken for an Arab by a British Medical Officer who scolded him disgustedly as being responsible for the horrific scene and slapped his face.

On 3 October, Allenby and Feisal arrived in the city. The French had been demanding their 'rights' in Syria and Lebanon, and it became clear that any scheme to keep them out would fail. Allenby was forced to appear surprised that Lawrence had given so much support to the establishment of an Arab administration. Chauvel described the historic meeting of Allenby, Feisal and Lawrence at which Allenby dramatically told Feisal that France was to be the 'protecting power' of Syria, and further, that the Arabs had no claim to Lebanon whatsoever.

> Feisal objected very strongly. He said that he knew nothing of France in the matter; that he was prepared to have British assistance; that he understood from the Advisor whom Allenby had sent him that the Arabs were to have the whole of Syria including the Lebanon but excluding Palestine; that a country without a port was no good to him; and that he declined to have a French Liaison Officer or . . . French guidance in any way.[16]

Allenby then turned to Lawrence and asked him if he had not told Feisal that the French were to have 'the Protectorate' over Syria. Lawrence stated that he had not. When asked, 'But you knew definitely that he, Feisal, was to have nothing to do with the Lebanon?' Lawrence replied, 'No, Sir, I did not.'[17]

Allenby then made it clear that Feisal was a lieutenant-general under his command and, for the moment at least, must accept a French involvement. Feisal left dissatisfied. Lawrence stayed behind. According to Chauvel, Lawrence stated that he could not serve with a French liaison officer and that, as he was due for leave anyway, he would like to take it then. 'Yes! I [should] think you had!' retorted Allenby, and Lawrence left. Chauvel thought that 'the Chief had been a little hard on Lawrence'.[18]

Lawrence's account in the *Seven Pillars* of this meeting is substantially different. He says that when he asked Allenby for leave, it was 'the last (and also I think the first) request I ever made him for myself',[19] but that Allenby was at first reluctant, only giving in after considerable pressure. Had he stayed in Damascus, he wrote, he might have been tempted to power. In reality, he had no choice. His position was compromised when he was used as a scapegoat by Allenby. He had been successful in getting Feisal a foothold in Syria but had been unable to get rid of the French. His mission was over.

The Arabian delegation to the Peace Conference with its advisers, Paris, January 1919. Feisal centre front, Lawrence second from right. Feisal's slave is in the background.

Colonel Lawrence in conventional garb.

Gertrude Bell, Lawrence, Sir Herbert Samuel (right of Lawrence) *and Abdullah* (next to Samuel)

1919

ROYAL OPERA HOUSE,
COVENT GARDEN.

PROPRIETORS - - - THE GRAND OPERA SYNDICATE, LTD.

Commencing Thursday Evening, August 14th, and Nightly at 8.30.
. . Matinees Wednesday, Thursday and Saturday at 2.30. .

PERCY BURTON
(by arrangement with the Grand Opera Syndicate)
presents
AMERICA'S TRIBUTE TO BRITISH VALOUR
IN THE PERSON OF
LOWELL THOMAS
in
His Illustrated Travelogue of the British Campaigns:

With Allenby in Palestine
including
THE CAPTURE OF JERUSALEM
and
THE LIBERATION OF HOLY ARABIA.

The motion pictures used in this travelogue were taken by Mr. Harry A. Chase and Captain Frank Hurley. Still photographs by Mr. Chase. Art work by Miss Augusta A. Heyder. Projection by Mr. Chase.

Business Manager (for Lowell Thomas and Percy Burton) W. T. Cunningham.

With authority from the Secretary of War and the Secretary of the Navy of the United States Government, Mr. Lowell Thomas, accompanied by Colonel W. C. Hayes and a staff of photographers, journeyed over sixty thousand miles gathering material for a series of travelogues. Mr. Lowell Thomas was attached to the Allied forces in Europe, Asia and Africa, and was with them from the Orkney Islands to the forbidden deserts of Holy Arabia, from New York to Jerusalem, from Rome to Khartoum, from Paris to Salonika, and from Cairo to Berlin. He was the first pilgrim to tour the Holy Land by airplane, and the first person to go into the holy land of the Mohammedans with a cinema camera. After the signing of the armistice he was the first to visit Kiel, Hamburg, Berlin and other parts of Germany, and bring back the pictorial story of the German Revolution.

By arrangement with Mr. Percy Burton, Mr. Thomas cancelled a number of his engagements in America in order to appear at Covent Garden Royal Opera House for a limited period, under the auspices of the English-Speaking Union.

His travelogue on Allenby's crusade in Palestine and the liberation of Holy Arabia, is not a tale of Jules Verne, but the story of the reality of the present, surpassing the dreams of the imagination of the past.

(Under the auspices of THE ENGLISH-SPEAKING UNION)

President: Rt. Hon. A.
Hon. President: The AMERICAN
Vice-Presi

Field-Marshal Sir DOUGLAS HAIG, O.M.
Rt. Hon. WINSTON CHURCHILL, M.P.
Earl CURZON of KEDLESTON, O.M.
The ARCHBISHOP of YORK.
Sir ROBERT S. S. BADEN POWELL, K.C.B.
Rt. Hon. Sir ROBERT BORDEN, K.C.M.G.
Viscount BURNHAM.

If this Entertainment has given you pleasure why not advise your friends to see an hear it? If you will kindly address this card and leave it with attendant in th interval or on your way out, it will be stamped and posted immediately.

Nightly at 8.30 sharp. Matinees Tuesday, Wednesday, Thursday & Saturday at 2.30 sharp.

COVENT GARDEN OPERA HOUSE.

Colonel Lawrence and Lowell Thomas in Arabia.

Programme from the first night of Lowell Thomas's show.

(right) *Postcard gimmick to advertise Thomas's travelogue.*

WITH GENERAL ALLENBY at Covent Garden Theatre.

A Remarkable Film Lecture Telling the Strange Story of Colonel Thomas Lawrence, the Leader of the Arab Army

Colonel Thomas Lawrence (on Left) with Mr. Lowell Thomas

Colonel Lawrence is here seen at the entrance to his tent with Mr. Lowell Thomas, the American journalist, who at Covent Garden is telling the story of the Arab campaign

Colonel Thomas Lawrence

When war broke out Thomas Lawrence was a young archæological student engaged in work on ancient Mesopotamian cities. His knowledge of Arabia was first made use of in the map department at Cairo, and finally we find him as leader of the whole Arab Army in its fight from Mecca to Damascus. He wore this Arab style of dress throughout the campaign, and gained the confidence of chiefs and followers alike. A price was set upon his head but Colonel Lawrence won through to Damascus at the head of a devoted army

Copyrighted in the U.S.A. **The Palestine Film Lecture at Covent Garden** Drawn by D. Macpherson

A large number of well-known personalities gathered on the opening night last week to hear Mr. Lowell Thomas's film lecture on the Palestine campaign. The lecturer showed pictures of Arab and other cavalry columns in motion which were quite unfamiliar to the man in the street

Mr. Lowell Thomas's wonderful pictures of the operations in Palestine, at Covent Garden, have revealed to many what a really big cavalry "show" means, and what it entails in the way of general organisation and detail, writes a military correspondent. Few laymen, at any rate in England, ever get the chance of seeing large bodies of cavalry massed for operations of war or of peace. In India, where there is elbow room and space, and where cavalry both on manœuvres and in the almost unending warfare on the N.-W. Frontier get more practice than any other cavalry in the world, we have, upon occasion, seen something of it. Ever since the times of what were called the "Kitchener tests," those of us who have served in India have had a taste of what the handling of large masses of Horse means. But even in India, when we perhaps had the equivalent of a cavalry division on manœuvres, it was a ceremonial parade compared to what this tremendous cavalry operation which Field-Marshal Lord Allenby conducted in Palestine connoted. These pictures, perhaps, brought home to the layman what it meant; they perhaps made him think of what it meant in terms of fodder, in terms of sore backs, and in terms of horse-shoes, quite apart from the little matter of the feeding and watering of both the horse and the man on his back. Good cavalry are supposed to be able to exist on the smell of an oil-rag; they are supposed to be able to fend for themselves if put to it.

Sometimes this thing is politely called "foraging," but people have also another name for it. Fending for yourself is possible when only a comparatively small body is involved; it is a different pair of shoes, however, when something very like a whole cavalry corps is on the warpath, as was the case in Palestine. Allenby started his service with the Inniskillings; he has been a cavalry soldier all his days, and the cavalry spirit has been breathed into him since the time when he first learnt how to "carry swords."

No one but a cavalry leader of such brilliance would have dared to conceive an operation of this magnitude over such country. Allenby, however, knew the quality of the cavalry he had under him—hunting yeomen from the "shires" and the "provinces," Anzacs who were bred in the saddle, Sikhs, Punjabis, Pathans, Gukkars from the Salt Range, natural horsemen, and, above all, horse-masters, every man Jack of them, and he took it on and knew that his Horse would not fail him. The most astounding fact to the cavalry soldier, who happens to know what it all meant, was the low percentage of casualties in horse-flesh—on an all-round reckoning, less than 25 per cent. If the percentage had been 50 per cent, it would still have been a magnificent performance. As Mr. Lowell Thomas rightly adjudged, it is the most astounding cavalry achievement in the whole history of war, ancient or modern.

Early periodical review of Thomas's travelogue.

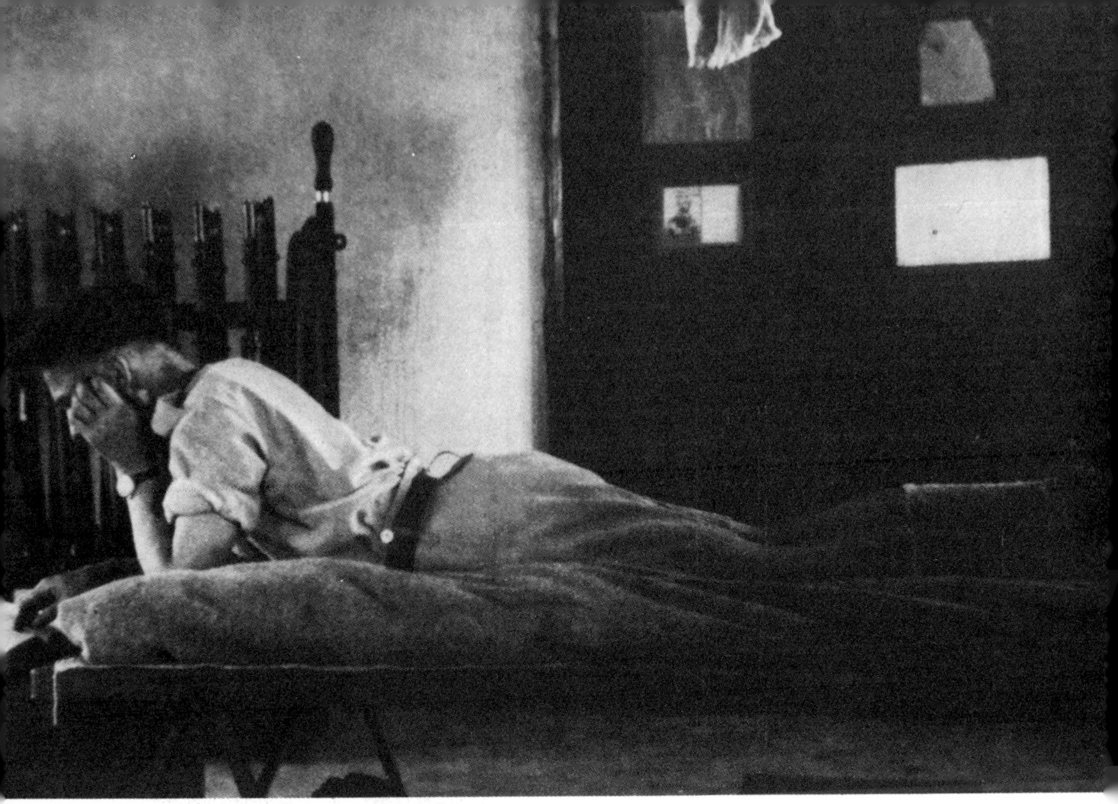

Lawrence at Karachi, 1927.

Sir Hugh Trenchard.

In an uncannily quiet corner of Miranshah.

Lawrence at Miranshah.

EMPIRE NEWS, SUNDAY, DECEMBER 16, 1928.——3

COLONEL LAWRENCE AND TREBITSCH LINCOLN.

Duel to the Death in Progress.

VICTORY FOR THE SPY WOULD SET BRITAIN AND RUSSIA AT WAR!

A secret duel to the death is in progress between Colonel Lawrence of Arabia, and the notorious spy, Trebitsch Lincoln, the traitor. The battle-ground is the wild fastnesses of King Amanullah's country. Victory for Lincoln in this latest treachery would set Britain and Russia at war.

Trebitsch Lincoln.

King Amanullah.

The Queen of Afghanistan.

Revelations by Dr. FRANCIS HAVELOCK.

A RIGOROUS censorship is preventing the real seriousness of the position in Afghanistan from being made clear to readers of newspapers.

It is known that there is a party of revolt against the western system of civilisation, imposed with rash precipitancy upon an ultra-conservative population of hillmen, by the modern and extremely advanced King Amanullah.

It is known also that there has been a clash between intransigeant rebels and the King's loyal forces. There have been executions and deaths. But it has been comfortably thought by the average reader of newspapers in this country that it is only a question of time before the King's forces are triumphant and peace will reign again, at any rate, insofar as peace ever does reign in the turbulent tribes which compose the war-like people of Afghanistan.

There is, however, no justification for this comfortable belief. The real position is full of menace not only to Afghans, not only to the modern King Amanullah and his beautiful young Queen Souriya, who captured all hearts upon her recent visit to London, but to the people of this country because, startling as the tidings may be, should the position develop more seriously war will be the logical conclusion—war between Britain and Russia.

Clash With Russia.

Dr. Francis Havelock, the well-known medical missionary, who has just returned from the wild Afghan hills, tells a story at once dramatic and terrible.

The significance of the doctor's story is in the fact that he is a great friend of the King of Afghanistan, and accompanied him upon part of the great European tour.

Dr. Havelock has lived in India and Afghanistan all his life with the exception of his years at Oxford and London to qualify for his life's work. He is an imperialist of the most liberal type, and most careful not to exaggerate little episodes into "incidents."

According to Dr. Havelock, during the time that the King was away the factions were working against him. The revolt is led by the Mullahs, the priests of Islam, whose fanatical opposition to all things Western is well known.

It was thought at first that the King was sufficiently popular to stamp out the opposition very quickly. That hope has definitely failed. Tribes of hillmen on the Russian frontier and tribes on the Indian frontier are in open revolt.

The censorship has prevented the news from leaking through, but Dr. Havelock states that four serious actions have been fought between the rebels and the King's forces, and there have been at least 6,000 deaths in the fighting. The hospitals are full to their capacity, and are being extended.

British Rifles.

A most disquieting thing is that all the rifles taken from the insurgents are of British pattern.

That indicates clearly that there is a definitely anti-British movement behind the rising. Not that the hillmen are in themselves fanatically [illegible] a quick-fire, it spreads along the hundred of miles of mountain frontier like an evil disease. Before long the tribes in British territory would also join.

To prevent this, big forces have been moved up from the Madras Presidency and Central Provinces. The Peshawar Garrison has been strengthened and mobile columns of artillery and infantry are already on the frontier in readiness.

Russia has made it clear that she will interpret any British intervention as an attempt to re-establish the "Protectorate of Afghanistan"—and will resist the effort!

The position is full of danger. Diplomatic relations have been broken off between Russia and England. It is not possible for two sound statesmen to get together and knock out an agreed plan of action. It is doubtful if there is even a will to peace on the part of the Russian Ministry.

Russia has replied to our precautionary measures by mobilising three divisions and sending them to the Afghan frontier. A brigade of Red Artillery and two squadrons of cavalry,

Colonel Lawrence.

an armoured car section and twenty aeroplanes are also on the Russian side of the frontier.

Should it be necessary for British forces to cross the dividing range and establish a post at the northern entrance to the higher passes above the Khyber then the Russian forces would move south—"To guarantee the sovereignty of Afghanistan."

Such is the position. Kabul has been at times within the last few days practically isolated. Communications by rail are cut and each convoy has to be heavily armed and fight its way through to the southern towns. The hills in the north are in the possession of the rebels.

War Without Warning.

The most dangerous part of the menace is that war could easily descend upon us without the slightest warning. A column moves forward, it meets resistance, fights, and presently finds itself fighting Russian regular forces come to the aid of the resisting Afghans—of whatever political colour.

And we will be fighting on territory not belonging to us and upon which we have no legal right to be.

Dr. Havelock is proceeding to Geneva where he is going to exercise the whole force of his strong personality to get the nations there represented in the League to act together in this danger spot where the low of war is already smouldering.

[illegible]

(Above) *Fiction from the* Empire News.

(Below) *'Seeking peace in Waziristan': the* Daily News, *5 December 1928.*

LAWRENCE OF ARABIA.

SEEKING PEACE IN WAZIRISTAN.

BOMBAY, Tuesday.

Colonel Lawrence has been located in Tochi.

The Peshawar correspondent of the "Times of India" says that under the assumed name of Shaw, Colonel Lawrence is leading an obscure life as an Army clerk at Miranshaw, in a Tochi agency, on the North-West frontier of India.

Colonel Lawrence.

In an interview Colonel Lawrence is reported to have said that he was tired of public life and wanted to lead a quiet obscure existence among the barren hills of Tochi, in Waziristan.

He is busy learning the Pushtu language, and it is inferred that he intends to move into Afghanistan.—Exchange.

LAWRENCE OF ARABIA

Arrest "Ordered" by Afghan Authorities

STARTLING REPORT

A sensational message reached London last night from Allahabad, stating that the Afghan authorities have ordered the arrest of Colonel Lawrence, known widely as Lawrence of Arabia, on the ground that he is believed to be assisting the rebels to cross the frontier. They describe Colonel Lawrence, says the B.U.P., as the arch-spy of the world

(Above) *The Afghans (and the* Daily Herald) *'arrest' Lawrence, 5 January 1929).*

(Right) *Two days later, the* Herald *has second thoughts.*

(Below) *Arrival home: the* Sunday Pictorial, *3 February 1929.*

LAWRENCE OF ARABIA

Afghan Arrest "Order" Unconfirmed

No confirmation was available yesterday at the Afghan Legation in London of the reported Afghan order for the arrest of Colonel Lawrence of Arabia, on the alleged ground that he had assisted Afghan rebels to cross the frontier.

According to a B.U.P., Moscow wire, the official Kabul newspaper, *Amany Afghan*, referring to the story reported in an Indian newspaper that Colonel Lawrence organised and headed the Afghan revolt, considers that the rôle played by Colonel Lawrence has been exaggerated, declaring: "We do not believe in Colonel Lawrence's power and skill. He is only an Englishman."

A strong denial, either that he is Colonel Lawrence, or that he is in any way connected with any State or Government, has been issued by Syed Pir Karam Shah, the Mohammedan, who was mobbed by an infuriated crowd at Lahore on the occasion of the funeral procession of Lala Lajpat Rai.

SUNDAY·PICTORIAL

SALE VASTLY IN EXCESS OF ANY OTHER PICTURE PAPER IN THE WORLD

"Q.Q." BY BRITTEN AUSTIN See page 13

. 725 | Registered at the G.P.O. as a Newspaper. | SUNDAY, FEBRUARY 3, 1929 | Twopence

AWRENCE OF ARABIA HOME FROM INDIA—EXCLUSIVE

Colonel Lawrence, in his uniform as Aircraftsman Shaw, leaving the liner Rajputana in a naval pinnace.

"Aircraftsman Shaw" about to descend to pinnace.

pictures of the arrival at Plymouth yesterday of Colonel T. E. Lawrence, famous ploits among the Arabs during the war. He left Bombay three weeks ago on the liner Rajputana after being transferred from the North-West Frontier Province where he was serving in the Royal Air Force as Aircraftsman Shaw...

was the sequel to persistent rumours, officially denied, that he was acting as a spy in Afghanistan. It has been hinted that he would leave the Rajputana before the liner reached England, and his departure from the ship yesterday was almost unnoticed. The pinnace

The striking similarity between Lawrence and Rudolph Valentino as 'The Sheik'.

12 In Support of Feisal

The Arabian campaign continued for the rest of October after Lawrence left Damascus (on the 4th). As it became clear who the victors would be, tribes who had previously remained uncommitted rose up against the Turks, hoping to get a share of the loot. British and Arab regulars continued fighting with sporadic, if enthusiastic, support from local irregulars until an armistice was signed with Turkey on 31 October. Following the fall of Damascus, Feisal's representatives rushed to Beirut and raised the Hashemite flag – a clear statement of intent which was absolutely unacceptable to France, and had almost certainly been suggested by Lawrence before he left.

Allenby at first gave his approval to the Hashemite presence in Lebanon, but revoked it to prevent a major confrontation with the French. The Hashemite flag was unceremoniously taken down by British soldiers – an act which further damaged Britain's increasingly strained relations with Feisal and Feisal's own prestige among his followers.

Two years of hard fighting and political intrigue had drained Lawrence's emotional and physical resources, but he could not afford to take the rest he so badly needed. He had to get back to England as quickly as possible to enter the debate over the future of the Middle East. In Cairo, he discussed the Anglo-Arab and Anglo-French situations with Wingate, who had replaced McMahon as High Commissioner of Egypt. Wingate had no wish to see the French in Syria or the Lebanon and he was in constant communication with Allenby, who was equally keen that the fruits of his labour did not fall into French hands. Lawrence was gathering powerful allies.

Before Lawrence left for England Allenby gave him the acting rank of full colonel. Lawrence told Liddell Hart that this was a favour he had requested in order that he could travel home in a private rail compartment and avoid the bureaucratic delays which might have hindered a less senior officer – an unlikely but not impossible explanation for his promotion.[1] This homeward journey provided the setting for one of Lawrence's favourite stories. At some stage of the trip he claims he left his train to take a short walk along the station platform, and because a scruffy raincoat concealed his uniform was stopped by a British major. Not realizing that the diminutive and rather dishevelled officer before him was a full colonel, the major demanded a salute, and was humiliated by Lawrence for his audacity.

In Rome, Lawrence stopped briefly to speak to the French diplomat Georges Picot. Within a month Picot would be installed in Beirut, provocatively titled as French High Commissioner in Syria and Armenia. The Frenchman spoke to Lawrence frankly, clearly stating his Government's intentions to assign their advisers to Feisal at once, in accordance with the terms of the agreement negotiated with Sir Mark Sykes. His candour did little to cure Lawrence's francophobia, and he rushed back to London even more determined to smash Sykes–Picot and prevent a French take-over of Syria. So intent was he on this course, and so paranoid about French intentions, that his actions permanently damaged any hope Feisal might have had of coming to reasonable terms with France.

Lawrence was later to tell his biographers that he arrived back in England dramatically on 11 November, the day on which Germany officially surrendered. In fact he was in London by 24 October, and within a few days he was called before the Eastern Committee of the War Cabinet, who sought his opinion as a distinguished expert on Arabian affairs. He was not yet a public figure, although several members of the Committee had already heard of his exploits through mutual friends.

The members of the Eastern Committee included Lord Curzon, the elder statesman of British foreign policy who acted as Chairman; Edwin Montagu, the Secretary of State for India; Mark Sykes, Georges Picot's counterpart; and Lord Robert Cecil, the Assistant Secretary for Foreign Affairs. Also present were senior military and naval commanders and representatives of their respective intelligence services.

Lawrence, dressed in full staff uniform, presented his new plan for the future of Syria and Mesopotamia. He unrealistically, but eloquently, proposed that the Sykes–Picot agreement might be replaced by one of his own formulations, which in several ways was equally flawed but far more favourable to Britain's imperial interests – interests which Lawrence saw as intimately linked with those of the Hashemite family. He proposed that the French might well be palmed off with Beirut and the Lebanon – but not with Syria, where Feisal would rule independently, though under unofficial British protection. Mesopotamia, the real prize, would be put under more direct British control in two zones, Lower Mesopotamia and Upper Mesopotamia, with Feisal's brothers, Abdullah and Zeid, as the respective Heads of State. Britain already had the advantage over France that their troops occupied both Syria and Mesopotamia.

Lawrence offered another important incentive for adopting his plan. Unlike many Arab leaders, Feisal would be willing to support Jewish-Zionist aspirations in Palestine in line with Balfour's declaration of 1917 as long as that country remained under British control. However, Lawrence explained, in return for concessions on Jewish-Zionist immigration to Palestine, the Zionists would have to underwrite and act as financial advisers to Feisal's unstable administration in Syria.

The majority of the committee were favourably impressed – although Mark

Sykes and Edwin Montagu were hardly likely to be enthusiastic – and Lawrence was asked to detail his proposals in a written report. Shortly afterwards, Montagu sent a secret telegram to the Indian Foreign Office in Delhi, outlining Lawrence's proposals for splitting up Arabia:

> Foreign Secret.
>
> Colonel Lawrence, now home on leave from Syria, has submitted proposal to H.M.G. for dealing comprehensively with Arab question. He advocates formation of three Councils of Arab States outside Hejaz and its dependencies, viz: (1) Lower Mesopotamia, (2) Upper Mesopotamia and (3) Syria; to be placed respectively under Abdulla, Zeid and Feisal, sons of King Hussain. Hussain himself would remain King of Hejaz and would ultimately be succeeded by his eldest son Ali. He would have no temporal authority in three states above mentioned, and, in fact, no position at all there beyond insertion of his name in Friday prayers in all Mosques as Emir-el-Momenin (commander of the faithful) . . . I recognise that these proposals . . . conflict with recommendations in [India Foreign Office] Baghdad telegram 8745.[2]

Lawrence was in fact making powerful enemies as well as powerful friends. The India Office, who shared the responsibility for Mesopotamia with the Foreign and War Offices, regarded any Hashemite as unsuitable to reign in Mesopotamia, as they had no real connection with the country. The Anglo-Indians thought Ibn Saud a more suitable candidate, but Lawrence had written Saud off and was soon to be proved to be absolutely wrong.

On 3 October, Lawrence had an audience with the King, officially to be invested with his CB (Companion of the Bath) and DSO (Distinguished Service Order). The story of what occurred at the ceremony is part of the Lawrence legend, and is consequently muddled in various subtly differing accounts. Apparently, having arrived at Buckingham Palace, Lawrence politely informed the King that he could not accept the honours because His Majesty's Government had broken pledges to Feisal which Lawrence had given in the King's name. One official noted:

> During the conversation [with the King] Lawrence said that he had pledged his word to Feisal, and that now the British Government were about to let down the Arabs over the Sykes-Picot agreement. He [Lawrence] was an Emir among the Arabs and intended to stick to them through thick and thin if necessary to fight against the French for the recovery of Syria.
>
> Colonel Lawrence said that he did not know that he had been gazetted or what etiquette was in such matters, but he hoped that the King would forgive any want of courtesy on his part in not taking these decorations.[3]

The King later told Ronald Storrs, 'There I was holding the box in my hand.'[4]

While the incident brought some attention to the Arab cause, it harmed Lawrence's reputation for what at the time was considered as bad form in front of the Monarch. Nevertheless, the King was intrigued by Lawrence, and they later met again privately, by which time the King appears to have commissioned a confidential report, including details of Lawrence's unconventional family background. For his part, Lawrence sent the King the rifle, complete with notches, which he had carried in Arabia as a present, and which is now on display at the Imperial War Museum in London. Whatever embarrassment may have been caused by their first meeting, if not forgotten it was at least forgiven.

On Armistice Day, with the approval of the Foreign Office, Lawrence telegraphed Hussein advising him to send Feisal to Paris at once to act as his representative at preliminary peace talks being held in the city.

> I understand that in about fifteen days time, conversations about the question of the Arabs will take place in Paris. A telegraph has been received from General Allenby to the effect that you will wish to have a representative at these conversations. If this is so, I trust you will send Feisal, as he has gained a personal reputation in Europe through his splendid victories, and this will make his success easier. If you agree to this, you should wire him to prepare to leave Syria at once for about one month, and you should ask General Allenby for a ship to take him to France. In the meantime you should telegraph the Governments of Great Britain, France, America and Italy the fact that your son is proceeding as your representative to Paris.[5]

Feisal was far from happy about leaving Beirut for Europe when his own position was so precarious. He was interviewed and given a preliminary brief by a representative of the British Foreign Office who reported that without the benefit of Lawrence's counsel, Feisal was in a 'nervous condition' and 'overweighted by a sense of responsibility'.

> He fully realises the weakness of his Government and is anxious about leaving it when so much needs to be done . . . he again raised the question of British Advisors and begged that something might be done to strengthen government and inspire public confidence during his absence . . . He is frankly frightened about his mission and complained firstly that he had been given no time to prepare himself and secondly that he had received no instructions as to what he was expected to do . . . He feels his position somewhat acutely since he is going as the representative of his Father whom he knows not to be very popular in Syria, and without any mandate from his people.[6]

Feisal went on to suggest that there should be an immediate election for the Head of State in Syria, which he believed he could win if given suitable support from Britain.

Despite his forebodings he agreed to go to Paris. A British cruiser, H.M.S. *Gloucester*, would pick Feisal up on 22 November and drop him off in Marseilles, where he would be met by Lawrence. However, the French – who foolishly had not been fully consulted – were not willing to accept Feisal as an official representative for anyone, and the French Ambassador in Cairo telegraphed Hussein:

> The Emir Feisal would be received in France with the welcome due to the son of a friendly allied sovereign, but this government was astonished that they have not previously been informed about the visit. It is impossible to consider the Emir as

charged with a mission to the French Government of which the latter had not been informed.[7]

The French Government's pique is understandable. An Arab VIP aboard a British cruiser was about to land in their country, and neither the British nor Hussein had bothered to inquire their opinion. Cambon, the Minister for Foreign Affairs, appointed Lawrence's old rival Colonel Brémond to meet Feisal, and told him:

> With Lawrence you must be precise and show him he is on the wrong tack. If he comes as a British Colonel, in an English uniform, we will welcome him as such. But we will not accept him as an Arab, and if he comes so disguised, then he does not have anything to do with us . . .[8]

Meanwhile in London the Eastern Committee had considered their tactics for dealing with the French, who were evidently intent on sticking to Sykes–Picot to the letter. Curzon, who described Sykes–Picot as 'this deplorable agreement', was looking for a way out, and thought that the solution lay in selectively prompting the fashionable idea of self-determination – where it was to Britain's interests. For instance, if any problem arose in Syria or Palestine with 'the French, the Arabs or anybody else', Britain should press for self-determination, 'knowing in the bottom of our hearts that we are more likely to benefit from it than anybody else'.[9] Lawrence on the other hand was surprisingly cautious in his own attitude to self-determination, which he thought in many ways 'a foolish idea' and only to be given consideration in the case of peoples who had been allies during the war. He also told the committee that there would be no problem 'in reconciling Zionists and the Arabs in Palestine and Syria, provided the administration in Palestine remained in British hands'.[10]

Lawrence realized that Feisal would not become King of Syria without an appropriate propaganda campaign, and built up contacts in Fleet Street through Hogarth, Lord Winterton and Geoffrey Dawson, Editor of *The Times*. On 26 November 1918, the first three anonymous articles appeared in *The Times*, under the heading 'THE ARAB CAMPAIGN, LAND AND SEA OPERATIONS, BRITISH NAVY'S HELP', and stating that the series was by 'a correspondent who was in close touch with the Arabs throughout their campaign against the Turks after the revolt of the Sherif of Mecca'. The three articles – the last two titled 'The Arab Epic' – were all written by Lawrence in the first person as blatant propaganda for Feisal. Feisal was presented as the most romantic hero-commander of the war, and Lawrence remained an anonymous spectator, attributing to Feisal and/or other Arabs a great deal with which he later credited himself in *The Seven Pillars of Wisdom*. Lawrence later claimed that he was also writing for other papers as an anonymous correspondent, and there is some evidence for this, particularly in the latter half of 1919.

On the day that the first article in *The Times* appeared Lawrence, dressed as an Arab, greeted Feisal as he stepped off H.M.S. *Gloucester* at Marseilles. They proceeded to Lyon, where they met Colonel Brémond who was to act as official guide. In his memoirs, Brémond commented dryly on Lawrence: He never left Feisal; he wore his strange white dress, and it must be said that it did not have a very striking effect . . .[11]

Brémond took Feisal aside and explained that Lawrence's presence was not appropriate to the official trip which had been planned. Feisal passed this message on to Lawrence, who did not openly protest and left willingly, though not without reinforcing his warnings to Feisal of France's real intentions. His departure had nothing to do with a sudden discovery that a suspicious party of French diplomats were going to London to discuss Syria in his absence, as suggested by David Garnett without a shred of evidence.[12]

Feisal was now taken on a VIP tour of France, without the benefit of Lawrence's counsel, and was eventually permitted to go to Paris, where he had a brief meeting with the French President, Poincaré. On 9 December, the Arab delegation left for Boulogne, where a British ship, and Lawrence, were waiting to take them across the Channel. As Feisal and Brémond approached the ship, Lawrence (still dressed as an Arab and looking, according to Brémond, 'like a Catholic choirboy'[13]), came down the gangway to greet them and sarcastically remarked to the French colonel that the British Government would be delighted if he accompanied 'our Arab friend' to England. Brémond curtly declined.

Lawrence had carefully planned that Feisal's visit to England should be more productive than his stay in France. The day after he arrived, Feisal (who was staying in the Carlton Hotel) had a secret meeting with Chaim Weizmann to discuss Arab/Zionist co-operation. This was not their first meeting – they had met initially in June 1918 at Aqaba, and Lawrence had met Weizmann as early as January 1918 in Jerusalem.

Prompted by Lawrence, Feisal made a statement to Reuters, in which he stressed the compatibility of Arab and Zionist aspirations and hoped that 'each nation' could work together at the forthcoming Paris Peace Conference to mutual benefit. *The Jewish Chronicle* optimistically wrote that Feisal had reached 'complete understanding' on all issues. Lawrence followed this up by drafting a declaration to be signed by both Feisal and Weizmann. In this highly sensitive statement of intent – unknown at the time even to Feisal's closest friends – it was agreed that Feisal, as representative of the Arabs, would support limited Jewish colonization of Palestine on the understanding that the rights of the Arabs in Palestine would not be affected. Before signing Feisal added a condition; if Britain reneged on her promise of Arab independence (as in fact she did), he '. . . would not be bound by a single word of the agreement'. Lawrence diplomatically translated this phrase to Weizmann as 'If changes are made, I cannot be answerable for failing to carry out this agreement,' a subtle but important change in tone from the original.[14]

For his part, Weizmann left Feisal in no doubt as to the value of Zionist help. Feisal's outgoings in Syria vastly exceeded his income, and without immediate cash support there could be no Arab State. If both parties could reach satisfactory terms, the Zionists would be willing to support Feisal, politically and economically.

Apparently the phrases 'Jewish State' and 'Jewish Government' had also been incorporated into the first draft, but Feisal insisted that these were changed to 'Palestine' and 'Palestine Government'. Acting as the official intermediary of His Majesty's Government, Lawrence did everything in his power to convince both parties that they shared common interests, and in doing so skated over several areas of real, and not easily reconcilable, disagreement. As later events confirm, Lawrence was one of those primarily responsible for the British legacy of confusion in the Middle East. His strategy was to use the dynamic force of Zionism both as a weapon for Britain against the French and as a means of relieving the British Exchequer. He hoped that Feisal's support of Zionist aspirations, already officially if imprecisely backed by Britain in the Balfour Declaration, would ensure British backing for Feisal at the Paris Peace Conference.

It is evident from Foreign Office files in the Public Records Office that support for Feisal's contract with Weizmann was by no means universal. Major J. N. Camp, assistant Political Officer in Jerusalem, came to learn of the arrangement and wrote a graphic memorandum which was forwarded to London from Egypt:

> In my opinion, Dr. Weizmann's agreement with Emir Feisal is not worth the paper it is written on or the energy wasted in the conversation to make it. On the other hand, if it becomes sufficiently known among the Arabs, it will be somewhat of a noose about Feisal's neck, for he will be regarded by the Arab population as a traitor. No greater mistake could be made than to regard Feisal as a representative of Palestinian Arabs (Moslem and Christian natives of Palestine who speak Arabic); he is in favour with them so long as he embodies Arab nationalism and represents their views, but would no longer have any power over them if they thought he had made any sort of agreement with Zionists and meant to abide by it.[15]

It has often been assumed that Lawrence was anti-Zionist. This is quite false; he had many Jewish friends who helped him to arrange introductions for Feisal to suitably powerful backers. He made sure Feisal established as many contacts as possible, and arranged an audience with the King, accompanying Feisal dressed as an Arab. Lawrence's fancy dress caused a few caustic comments among members of the Court, especially after his refusal of decorations. After going to a party at that time, again wearing his costume, he wrote apologetically to a friend excusing his 'lunatic' behaviour and explaining that he could not get out of the habit of dressing like an Arab, especially when confronted by 'British conventions'.[16]

Lawrence did occasionally appear in standard British uniform. At one dinner party, he sat next to the American publisher F. N. Doubleday, who, intrigued by the 'young, small, blond gentleman in khaki', and not aware of Lawrence's reputation – which was gradually spreading through London society – invited him to dine at his hotel, Brown's in Dover Street. Lawrence accepted, but typically arrived a day early, thus missing Rudyard Kipling whom Doubleday had arranged as the other dinner guest. In spite of this, Lawrence became a friend of Doubleday – or 'Effendi', as he was nicknamed by Kipling – and he later became Lawrence's American publisher.

Doubleday did eventually manage to introduce Lawrence to Kipling, and, predictably, the two became friends, sharing the same imperialistic ideals of the Round Table. Kipling suggested to Lawrence (who had already thought of the idea) that a possible alternative to a French mandate in Syria could be an American one – a compromise which Lawrence worked towards at the Paris Peace Conference.

In anticipation of French objection to his presence at the Conference, Lawrence was appointed as a technical adviser to the British delegation. Ten days before the Conference was due to open he accompanied Feisal to Paris.

It had been clear for some time that the French were openly hostile to Feisal, who had not yet been accepted as an official delegate. Initially Clemenceau refused to accept any Arab delegates, but considerable pressure was put on his government by both American and British representatives. Lawrence used all his contacts and personal charm on the relevant politicians and diplomats. He had dinner with Balfour, 'and loaded him full of ammunition'.[17] Philip Kerr, who was an influential friend of Lawrence, did the same with Lloyd George. Eventually the French conceded. Clemenceau agreed that Feisal would be accepted as representative for the Hejaz but not Syria. Lawrence had won the first round.

13 The Peace Conference

The Peace Conference opened officially on 18 January 1919. It was a massive and complex affair, requiring an elaborate organizational structure to cope with the influx of VIPs from all the thirty-two states who had fought against the Central Powers or broken off diplomatic relations with them. The basic purpose was to draw up a peace settlement acceptable to all the Allies, but as well as this it became involved in many other related issues. The fate of Syria and Feisal were hardly the most important items on an agenda which included the economic reconstruction of Europe, yet Feisal's exotic party, stage-managed by Lawrence, attracted a disproportionate amount of attention.

Feisal faced a daunting task in attempting to secure himself on the throne of an independent Syria. Lawrence recognized that this objective could best be achieved by the direct intervention of the United States. President Wilson had claimed that his Fourteen Point Plan would bring a new era of justice to world politics. Point twelve stated that the peoples liberated by the collapse of the Ottoman Empire should have the right of 'absolutely unmolested opportunity for autonomous development'. The British Government, advised by Lawrence, hoped that Wilson would put pressure on France to declare the Sykes–Picot Treaty void.

On 6 February, Feisal, with Lawrence at his side, presented his case for an independent Arab state in Syria to the inner sanctum of the Peace Conference, the Council of Ten, a body made up of the leaders of the ten principal allied Governments. Having read a prepared English translation of Feisal's speech to the Council, Lawrence was asked by President Wilson if, for the benefit of several members who understood only French, he could also read the speech in that language. Lawrence, whose French, unlike his Arabic, was flawless, impressed the Council by an apparently perfect rendition of the original and sat down to applause, adding further to the considerable reputation he was making for himself.

The speech, which outlined Feisal's plans for Arab independence and supported the idea of sending a Commission of Enquiry to Syria 'to find out the wishes of its people', caused an outcry in the French press. Partly because of Lawrence's public relations campaign, Syria had become a *cause célèbre*, and the French, illogically but understandably, felt that having lost so many men in the war, they might at least increase their colonies in the Middle East. One source states Clemenceau told Feisal that if France was not represented in Syria by its flag or by its soldiers, the French nation would consider it a 'national humiliation'. The renowned Marshal Foch, who held similar views, was later dismissed by Lawrence as nothing but a 'frantic pair of moustaches'.[1]

Lawrence usually wore British uniform with an Arab headdress for his official engagements in Paris. An American, Professor James Shotwell, who was at the Conference, had vivid memories of the 'younger successor of Mohamed' and made some interesting notes in his diary on Lawrence's relationship with Feisal. 'The two men were obviously very fond of each other', he wrote. 'I have seldom seen such mutual affection between grown men as in this instance.' He added that the romantic young Englishman was 'the most winning figure, so everyone says, at the whole Peace Conference.'[2]

Lawrence and Feisal became a colourful double act and continued to make efforts at every level to gain support for an independent kingdom in Syria. They attended banquets together and were always the centre of attention because of their costume.

Winston Churchill records that early in 1919 someone said to him 'You ought to meet this wonderful young man. His exploits are an epic.'[3] And so it was that Lawrence was invited to have lunch with Winnie. The hero of the Transvaal and the deliverer of Damascus got on well from the start, and thus began a friendship which was to last until Lawrence's death.

R. V. C. Bodley – who claimed to be a cousin of Gertrude Bell – records an occasion when he persuaded Lawrence to attend a dinner given for Lloyd George. The most interesting part of Bodley's tale is that, during the course of the meal, Lawrence displayed an uncharacteristic interest in a 'beautiful and voluptuous' woman who happened to be sitting next to him. Bodley calls her Valentine de Vacluse (not her real name), a lady with a reputation both for her beauty and her considerable sexual appetite.

According to Bodley, Madame de Vacluse became quite captivated by Lawrence and, forgoing her normal dinner conversation, allowed him to make an impassioned speech to her on the subject of Arabia. Lawrence was flattered by this apparently sincere interest, having for the most part ignored the other guests. He excused himself to discuss the same issues with Lloyd George, and his reception by the Prime Minister, although less exciting, was equally enthusiastic. A delighted Lawrence returned to give his attentions once more to the sensual Madame Vacluse.

At the end of the evening Lawrence parted from the lady and walked home with Bodley, enthusiastically expressing his admiration for the beautiful woman's 'understanding' of the Arab problem. Bodley was sceptical. 'Valentine de Vacluse has never known or spoken to an Arab in her life,' he said. Unperturbed, Lawrence looked forward to a meeting he had arranged with her, and was most incensed when Bodley tried to warn him off, retorting that if Bodley thought he was only interested in her for 'disgusting ideas' he was quite mistaken. The rendezvous took place in Valentine's private apartments, where she tried – unsuccessfully – to seduce Lawrence. The following day

Lawrence met Bodley again. 'You were quite right,' he said. 'Sorry I was peevish about it and I did not thank you for having me meet the PM, but I don't know much about women.'[4]

Not all his encounters with women were quite so traumatic. Gertrude Bell had been staying at his hotel in Paris, the Majestic. She also was an official member of the British delegation. On 16 March she wrote home:

> We had a very delightful lunch today with Lord Robert (Cecil) and T. E. Lawrence – just we four [the fourth being her father]. Lord Robert is I think the salient figure of the Conference and T. E. Lawrence the most picturesque. I spend most of my time with the latter and the former is unfailingly helpful.[5]

She went on to mention that both Allenby and Hogarth were arriving the following Tuesday, 'so that we [the Arab Bureau Lobby] shall be in force'.

Lawrence had a strange and platonic relationship with Gertrude Bell. Details of it remain obscure; they enjoyed each other's company (she more than he) and shared a passionate interest in Arab affairs. However, behind her back, Lawrence was dismissive of 'poor Gertie', perhaps because of her feelings towards him.

Three weeks after Feisal had appeared before the Council of Ten, Chaim Weizmann presented his case for a Jewish homeland to the Allied leaders. A conflict arose between the Zionist and Arab delegations when Feisal stated in a consequent interview with a French newspaper that he was fundamentally opposed to an independent Jewish state. This statement damaged Lawrence's work with Feisal and Weizmann and a hurried meeting was arranged to bring the two sides back together. Advised by Lawrence, Feisal issued new statements of 'common interest', and made the same points in an open letter which was published in the *New York Times* at the beginning of March. Jews and Arabs in the United States watched these events with concerned interest and put pressure on their Government to intervene in Palestine and Syria.

On 20 March, President Wilson endorsed the idea of sending an Allied commission to Syria to ascertain the feelings of the local population. Wickham Steed, who had taken over from Dawson as editor of the London *Times*, invited French journalists to meet English and French Arabists at his Paris apartment to discuss the merits of the proposal. As events turned out, the French refused to send representatives, realizing that, whatever the findings of the Commission, they would be favourable to France. Initially in favour of the Commission, Lawrence came to believe that the wait for its report might unnecessarily delay a settlement.

In *The Letters of T. E. Lawrence*, David Garnett noted a conversation between Feisal and President Wilson's special adviser, Colonel House, Lawrence being 'interpreter'. According to Garnett, Feisal had come to make his position clear to Colonel House before 'going back to Syria in a few days' (in fact, Feisal did not leave France for over two weeks). House asked Feisal what he thought of the Anglo-American Commission of Enquiry and the latter responded favourably, adding that he would be pleased to see either the English or Americans acting as mandatory power in Syria. 'Colonel House said that he was very doubtful if the United States would accept the mandate', and Feisal replied that 'the Arabs would rather die than accept the French mandate'.

Lawrence had the last word; he explained that 'Arabs in Syria wanted an English mandate and the Arabs in the United States wanted an American mandate'.[6] The Commission had by now been appointed, and Lawrence hoped that its American chairman, Dr Henry C. King, President of Oberlin College, Ohio, 'could be induced to report in favour of an American mandate in Syria, after satisfying himself that this was the wish of the inhabitants'. Eventually, the Commission, composed of two Americans, King and Charles R. Crane, and two Englishmen, Sir Henry McMahon, the former High Commissioner of Egypt, and D. G. Hogarth, reported in favour of an American presence – Lawrence and Hogarth had evidently recognized that this might be the only compromise which could be forced upon the French. However, these findings had little effect, as the United States Government did not seem anxious to get involved.

On 7 April 1919 Lawrence received a telegram to inform him that his father was seriously ill with pneumonia after a bout of influenza (the 'flu pandemic having swept across Europe in the winter and spring of 1918–19). Lawrence immediately flew to England, but found his father was already dead. He returned to Paris without delay.

Recently, a diary which Feisal kept during the Peace Conference has come to light.* Feisal wrote in it that the greatest thing about Lawrence was 'his patience, discretion, zeal and his putting the common good before his own personal interest'. After his father had died, Lawrence went to Feisal to explain he would be absent for a few days: 'I am sorry to say that my father has died and I want to go and see my mother for two days.' On being asked when the death had taken place, Lawrence replied:

> A week ago – I received a telegram about his illness, and without permission, left straight away by plane, when I arrived, I found that I was two hours too late. I didn't wait in England for the funeral and family gathering because I realised that you were alone in Paris and that there is a lot of work to be done. I didn't want to leave you, in case something unexpected happened while I was away, and I didn't tell you at the time in case I upset you. I've told you now. I shall be back on Friday.

Feisal was overwhelmed by Lawrence's conduct and wrote: 'Consider such honesty, such faithfulness, qualities of man, which are found in but few individuals.'[7]

A more prolific if less reliable diarist, Richard Meinertzhagen, wrote that he had been seeing 'a good deal of little Lawrence and have got to know him

*It was sold at Sotheby's in London on 28 March 1983 to an anonymous bidder on behalf of an anonymous client for £110,000.

well'. The two lunched together, but Lawrence had been intensely depressed, not over his father's death which Meinertzhagen did not mention, but over the book he was writing:

> [Lawrence] confesses that he has overdone it and is now terrified lest he is found out and deflated. He told me that ever since childhood he has wanted to be a hero, that he was always fighting between rushing into limelight* and hiding in utter darkness but the limelight had always won... He hates himself and is having a great struggle with his conscience. His self-deception filled him with bitterness. Shall he run away and hide, confess his sins and become completely discredited – or carry the myth on into the limelight in the hopes of not being exposed. Poor little man, he's in a ghastly mess and I wish I could help him. But beyond keeping all this to myself, I do not see that I can do much about it. I have strongly advised him to write a straightforward account of his Arabian exploits – I can not call it a campaign – omitting all glorification and embroidery. He says it has all gone too far and that others are pushing him into the limelight. He also excuses himself by saying that none of his exaggerations can be checked or verified – that seems rather ingenuous. He blames Hogarth, Lowell Thomas,† Storrs and many others and complains that people in high places are already beginning to regard him as a little War Hero and that any going back now would be misunderstood. But in reality he only has himself to blame for he has encouraged publicity and runs the risk of discovery as he has so many versions of every little episode.[8]

Meinertzhagen, who could not 'help liking Lawrence', dined with him at the Majestic and even persuaded him 'to drink a little champagne to cheer him up. He usually refused all alcohol.'

What should one make of Meinertzhagen's stories? He did without doubt know Lawrence, and Lawrence did confide in him. Meinertzhagen's 'diary' was not published until 1959 – forty years after the event – and has obviously been selectively and sometimes misleadingly edited. Many of his comments are perceptive, but his errors are compounded by the handicap of a failing memory. It should also be noted that Meinertzhagen was politically motivated; he was an ardent Zionist – a personal convert, like Lawrence, of Dr Weizmann's. (Meinertzhagen was not Jewish, although his name might suggest it. He was of Danish origin.)

On 13 April, Feisal was given an audience with Clemenceau and they came to a compromise. In exchange for Feisal's co-operation, the French would be satisfied with only a limited presence in Syria. Thoroughly disillusioned by his involvement in international diplomacy, Feisal was on the verge of accepting when Lawrence stepped in to stop him, suggesting that he should wait for the findings of the Commission. Clemenceau had been conciliatory, and this outright refusal was foolish diplomacy. Three days later, Feisal left France having achieved nothing for his four months' work and realizing his future in Syria was doubtful. His return to Syria was at least a relief to Allenby, who

*A suspicious line to have been written in April 1919, echoing as it does a much later phrase of Churchill's.

†Lowell Thomas had not even started to publicize Lawrence in April 1919.

was keen that he should make an attempt 'to check the movement towards xenophobia and panarabism' which was sweeping the country and moving across the border to threaten British plans for Mesopotamia.

There was now little to keep Lawrence in Paris. According to both Garnett and Liddell Hart, having obtained permission to fly out with a squadron of British bombers, Lawrence decided to go to Cairo to collect papers and reports which he had left behind at offices of the Arab Bureau. Lawrence may well have found his work on *The Seven Pillars of Wisdom* hindered because he lacked the notes and diaries which he had left behind in Cairo. However, the whole story of his flight to Egypt, and the reasons for which he undertook it, is filled with contradictions.

A flight of fifty British Handley Page bombers was about to leave France on an extended experimental flight to Cairo. One of the squadron commanders, Captain T. Henderson, who had known and piloted Lawrence in Arabia, recalled that he received a telephone call from a British official at the Conference, and been told that he would have a VIP passenger for the trip (he did not know then that it was Lawrence). Henderson suspected that the trip had a political motive.

Lawrence joined the singularly ill-fated flight of aeroplanes (six months later, only half had reached Cairo) and flew first to Italy. On the way, one machine crashed in the south of France – the two pilots and two mechanics were killed. Lawrence's aeroplane also crashed, and in *The Letters of T. E. Lawrence* David Garnett included an account of the flight 'written by one of the pilots' – probably Henderson. Apparently, Lawrence, travelling in 'one of the first machines', crashed in Centocelle in Italy. Both pilots were killed but Lawrence 'escaped with a broken collar-bone, broken ribs and mild concussion'. Lawrence told Liddell Hart that, because of these injuries, he had been 'encased in plaster of Paris'. The anonymous pilot went on to write that Lawrence, 'obviously still a sick man', caught up with the second squadron of British planes when they arrived in Rome and continued his journey. The pilot described Lawrence's mission as 'very hush-hush' and discounted the official excuse that he needed to go to Cairo to collect his kit as 'not the whole story'.[9]

The extensive injuries described by Garnett and Liddell Hart are exaggerated, as Dr John Mack discovered in his researches. He asked Lord Rennell of Rodd (who was working with his father, the British Ambassador in Rome, at the time of the crash) what memories he had of the accident. Lord Rennell's account was lucid, precise and quite definite. On hearing of the accident, he immediately went to the hospital in Rome where Lawrence had been admitted, and found him 'with some not serious injuries'. Lawrence was 'so little injured or shocked that I was able to bring him down in a day or two to stay in the British Embassy'.[10]

Having left Rome, Lawrence's flight proceeded to Cairo via Valona in Albania where the crews were forced to buy food with empty petrol cans; Athens, where Lawrence took Henderson sightseeing; and Crete where, by a remarkable coincidence, Harry St John Philby, British adviser to Ibn Saud, father of Kim Philby, and a great Arabian explorer, arrived in another British bomber as he too wanted to get to Cairo as quickly as possible. St John Philby was arguably Britain's greatest explorer of Arabia; acting as adviser to Ibn Saud, he was himself eventually converted to Islam. He and Lawrence got on well, although their views were absolutely opposed. Philby had warned the Eastern Committee that Ibn Saud, steadfastly loyal to Britain, was a force to be reckoned with, and could evict Hussein from Mecca when he chose (he did exactly that in October 1924). However, at the time British policy was pro-Hashemite and Philby's warnings were ignored.

Philby and Lawrence proceeded to Cairo in the same plane, where, Philby wrote, they 'championed diametrically opposite causes in the hospitable atmosphere of Allenby's home'.[11] Philby, like several other specialists, noted that Lawrence had little knowledge of Arabia proper but was obsessed with Syria.

Somewhere in these exchanges is the clue to the real reason for Lawrence's trip to Cairo. There is a hint in a US memorandum, dated 20 March 1919, which Richard Aldington's researches uncovered. This proposed 'that Captain William Yale accept an invitation tendered to him by Colonel Lawrence to accompany the British Forces on an expedition which they are planning for the month of May against the tribes of Nejd (Ibn Saud's Wahabis)'.[12] Prudently, Yale declined.

There was increasing animosity between on the one hand the British Foreign Office, who supported the pro-Hashemite views of Lawrence and the Arab Bureau, and on the other the India Office, who supported Ibn Saud. Arnold Toynbee describes how it erupted with a bizarre departmental feud:

> In May 1919, they fought each other by proxy in Arabia, on the border between the Najd and the Hijaz at a place called Turaba. In this battle, the India Office's Arab (Abdarrahman ibn Sa'id) defeated the Foreign Office's Arab (King Husayn al-Hashimi); but the Foreign Office then appealed to its ally General Allenby; Allenby threatened to send some Whippet tanks to the Foreign Office Arabs' aid; and the India Office prudently advised its own Arab to retreat.[13]

It seems possible that Lawrence had left Paris for Cairo to act as military adviser to Hussein's forces or as an observer of this battle. Another possibility lies in the recollections of Lord Wavell, who had been working for Allenby in Cairo in the spring of 1919. He recalled that he had been shown a secret Foreign Office telegram which said that the French were convinced that Lawrence was on his way to Damascus to aid Feisal in a revolt against them.' Wavell was given the task of intercepting Lawrence and ensuring that he was 'on no account to be allowed to proceed to Syria'.[14]

The truth behind Lawrence's trip to Cairo, therefore, can be said to lie somewhere between French suspicions of his plans to encourage Feisal and any intention Lawrence might have had to be present at the battle on the border of the Hejaz between the forces of Hussein and Ibn Saud. But

Lawrence had not reckoned with the inordinate delays which would befall him on the way.

In the event, Hussein's men were led into a disastrous defeat by Abdullah, Hussein's second son, who had his army decimated by Ibn Saud and barely escaped with his life. For Lawrence and other backers of the Hashemites, this was a mighty blow. He had told the Eastern Committee in London that Ibn Saud was of no consequence and would be soundly thrashed in any engagement with the Hashemites. He was wrong, and his other advice, therefore, became suspect. Consequently, Feisal's position was damaged even further.

Hearing of Abdullah's defeat, Lawrence collected his papers from the Arab Bureau in Cairo and, within a few days, started back for Paris to have one more attempt at reaching a settlement in what he saw as the British interest. He made no attempt to go to Syria, and Wavell noted in his memoirs that T.E. was 'rather ruffled' when he saw him in Shepheard's Hotel in Cairo in a characteristically misranked uniform.[15] Two other snippets of information are worth mentioning. During the flight to Cairo, Lawrence had mentioned to Captain Henderson the possibility of joining the Air Force and also, when he arrived in Cairo, he sent £10 to the man who had 'dug him out' from the crashed bomber in Rome.

Lawrence did the most sensible thing he could under the circumstances by returning to Paris in a final attempt to restore Feisal's dwindling prestige. On 15 July, having assessed the situation as gloomy, he sent a telegram to Feisal urging him to remain in Syria as nothing relevant was going to happen in Paris until September.

Meinertzhagen's *Middle East Diary* reveals that he and Lawrence were staying in the same hotel again, Lawrence's room being immediately above his own. They communicated to each other by banging their respective floor and ceiling. Meinertzhagen wrote: 'This evening he bumped the floor and let down on a string the manuscript of the book he is writing,' and the next day's entry added:

> I had been considering what he had said about me in his book and begged him to expunge it as the first part was not true and put me in a false light. Then he started. He surprised me by saying little of the book was strict truth, though most of it was based on fact; he had intended giving me a copy of his book; I begged him not to as I loathe fakes: he then told me that was precisely his trouble: he also hated fakes but had been involved in a huge lie – 'imprisoned in a lie' was his expression – and that his friends and admirers intended to keep him there. He was now fighting between limelight and utter darkness. It was slowly corroding his soul.

Lawrence went on to confess to Meinertzhagen his illegitimacy. He also said that his account of the Deraa incident was false but he was too embarrassed to write the truth, which was that he had been raped by the Governor and his servants. Lawrence's room in Paris had no bath and he asked if he could use Meinertzhagen's; the latter agreed and Lawrence stripped:* 'I was shocked to see red weals on his ribs, standing out like tattoo marks.' Lawrence palmed them off as the result of being dragged over barbed wire at Azraq. Meinertzhagen also noted that 'there was no sign of the many bullet and other wounds he claims to have suffered'. Despite the dubious chronological veracity of Meinertzhagen's diary, this is an important observation, especially as it was published years before Knightley and Simpson revealed Lawrence's bizarre relationship with John Bruce, the young man whom Lawrence hired to flog him after the war. One further comment of Meinertzhagen's on Lawrence is worth quoting: 'His nature shrinks from obscurity unless it would bring mystery and applause.'[16]

Lawrence returned to England in August; a man with some reputation among leading political and military figures with a special interest in Middle Eastern affairs, but virtually unknown to the general public. He was about to find himself cast in a very different role.

*As previously noted, there is a sexual undercurrent in Meinertzhagen's diary entries on the subject of Lawrence.

INTERLUDE

Interlude

It was almost overnight that Lawrence became the outstanding, most romantic and most mysterious military hero of the First World War. There can be no doubt that this reputation, which was to have such a profound effect on his life, was launched in the first place by the stage shows conceived and presented by Lowell Thomas. Both Robert Graves and Liddell Hart dismissed Thomas in a few lines, but though Lawrence's licensed biographers belittled him, and though he can be rightly criticized for his inaccuracies, it should be remembered that it was Lawrence himself who provided his eager American Boswell with a selection of marketable Arabian fairy tales in full knowledge that they would be used to sensationalize the Arabian Campaign and his part in it.

Following a successful run in New York and an extensive publicity campaign in London, Lowell Thomas's pseudo-documentary extravaganza *With Allenby In Palestine* opened at the Covent Garden Theatre on 14 August 1919. The exotic film, music and lecture presentation, retitled and otherwise adapted for a British audience, was an immediate critical and commercial success. Part of the show was devoted to 'Shereef' Lawrence and his adventurous exploits as 'The Uncrowned King of Arabia'. This section proved so popular that it was gradually expanded, and 'With Allenby in Palestine' evolved into 'With Allenby in Palestine and Lawrence in Arabia'. By the end of the summer of 1919, having been previously unknown to the British public, T. E. Lawrence was firmly established as a national hero. Lowell Thomas cashed in on various spin-offs and, with Lawrence's secret co-operation during the autumn of 1919, began writing a series of articles for American magazines which were later combined into the transatlantic best-seller *With Lawrence in Arabia*.

In most biographies of Lawrence, Lowell Thomas, if mentioned, is portrayed as a slick American journalist, a description which is partially true but misleadingly incomplete. No detailed attempt has been made to examine the motives, background and resources which led to Lowell Thomas encountering and glorifying T. E. Lawrence. In England, Thomas is now only remembered for his association with Lawrence; in the United States, he became a personality in his own right as one of America's best known and most durable radio presenters. His name was still familiar in the 1980s to millions of middle-aged Americans.

Reliable personal information about Lowell Thomas is almost as difficult to find as that about Lawrence. Thomas was once a notably unco-operative victim in a *This Is Your Life* television production. When confronted with the programme's famous opening words, he replied icily 'This is a sinister plot' and refused to answer any questions. It appears that Thomas, who was anything but shy, was keen that he, rather than a television network, should market and profit from his life-story, and he subsequently produced several entertaining autobiographies. In order to understand how Lawrence of Arabia (a phrase first used by the British tabloid press) developed, one must first look back into the unusual career of the dynamic media professional who first presented him to the American and British public.

Thomas started his working life as a reporter and editor on local newspapers, combining his journalism with studying at various universities. By his early twenties he had acquired four degrees and a job as reporter on the *Chicago Evening Journal*. He learnt the craft of popular writing surrounded by some of the best professionals in the country. One friend and colleague on the *Journal*, Ben Hecht, co-wrote the classic newspaper book *The Front Page* – basing it on exactly the sort of life that Lowell Thomas was then leading.

While working at the *Chicago Journal* in the autumn of 1913, Thomas was assigned to investigate the background of a shady character called Carlton Hudson. After prolonged inquiries, he discovered that Hudson, alias Hudson Betts, was a notorious conman already wanted by the New York police. In exchange for an exclusive story, the ambitious reporter arranged for Hudson's arrest and obtained an unexpected bonus. Hudson Betts had apparently been attempting to blackmail some of Chicago's most influential businessmen, the meat-packers. According to Thomas's account (the only one available), these worthy citizens, who might have been more prudent to have counted their blessings, quietly contacted him through a lawyer, ostensibly to pass on their thanks. Even more surprisingly, the lawyer volunteered the very information that Betts had discovered, and used as ammunition for his blackmail attempt. The businessmen had been involved in a shady oil deal and had 'inadvertently broken a federal statute'. This innocent mistake would have cost eleven million dollars had it been brought to the attention of the relevant authority. Why Thomas, a reporter, was told of this one can only guess, but the lawyer assured him that, should he ever need help in the future, he should not hesitate to ask his new fairy godfathers. Four years later, when Thomas needed extensive backing to go to Europe and the Middle East as a war correspondent, he was funded by the same businessmen.[1]

In the spring of 1914, Thomas temporarily left Chicago and his job on the *Evening Journal* to write as a freelance travel correspondent. He made extensive tours of South West America and Alaska under sponsorship from several railway companies before returning. Once back in Chicago, restlessness and his hunger for academic qualifications soon got the better of him. He applied for a scholarship to Princeton University, and in the meantime went to Alaska again, this time armed with a motion picture camera and the vague idea of making money from a film of his travels. When he came back from his trip Thomas discovered that his scholarship application had been successful, and there was more good news when he arrived at Princeton to take it up. He was offered an assistant professorship in the speech department – a noteworthy distinction for a 23-year-old. His appointment coincided with the recent election of Woodrow Wilson as President of the United States; before taking office in the White House, Wilson had been President of the university.

Characteristically, Thomas was not content just to pursue his academic career, and soon began to present the films he had taken in Alaska to paying audiences. In early 1917, he was asked by Franklin K. Lane, Secretary of the Interior, to go to Washington. Lane, originator of the catch-phrase 'See America First', was organizing a conference to promote American tourism but lacked a speaker for Alaska.

Lane offered the job to Thomas (he had been recommended by a mutual acquaintance), who readily accepted the chance to present a lecture before a prestigious audience at the Smithsonian Institution. He prepared to give the talk with what might appear as an uncharacteristic lack of confidence, and hired Dale Carnegie (who later wrote *How to Win Friends and Influence People*) to tutor his already highly developed skill as an orator. Hiring Carnegie was, however, typical of Lowell Thomas; throughout his life he readily hired the best 'professionals' available to supplement his own considerable talents.

The Alaska lecture at the Smithsonian went well and Thomas stated that because of this, Lane asked him to take over the 'See America First' campaign. These plans were interrupted on 6 April 1917 when America entered the First World War, and suddenly Lowell Thomas found a new outlet for his communication skills. President Wilson's administration was in desperate need of propagandists to defend America's entry into the war, especially as the President had been elected on a 'ticket' which promised America would not get involved in a European conflict. Germany had taken full advantage of America's apparent neutrality to swamp the country with pro-German propaganda.

According to Thomas, he was approached by Lane, who requested that he go to Europe, find material which would encourage the American people to support the war and rush back to present his story. Thomas wrote that Lane apologized to him because it was not possible for the Government to sponsor the trip, and he would therefore have to find private backers for his patriotic mission.[2] From the start, Thomas had no intention of travelling as a mere journalist; he had bigger plans, an indication of which was that he budgeted his expedition at $75,000 (perhaps the equivalent of a million dollars today). Unable to find the money in Washington, he went back to Chicago and approached the businessmen who owed him a favour, and with their support the money was quickly raised. The curious dedication in his 1924 best-seller

With Lawrence in Arabia, originated here:

TO EIGHTEEN GENTLEMEN OF CHICAGO
THIS NARRATIVE OF A MODERN
ARABIAN KNIGHT IS GRATE-
FULLY DEDICATED.

By the summer of 1917, Thomas's preparations were complete and he set off by ship for France. He took with him his wife (he had just married) and an expert cameraman, Harry Chase. They arrived in Bordeaux and went straight to Paris, which became their temporary base. It did not take Thomas long to realize there was little propaganda or entertainment value in the grim carnage of the trenches of the Western Front – he was searching for something far more romantic than mechanized slaughter. Richard Aldington, who experienced the horror at first hand, pointed out:

> For the newspaper-fed civilians of those days war was still 'romance', culminating in charges of cavalry dressed in full ceremonial uniform, our side triumphantly sweeping 'them' into defeat and surrender – in short, popular war had to be, as SEVEN PILLARS OF WISDOM announces itself, A Triumph.[3]

On 28 June 1917, General Allenby had assumed command of the Allied Army in the Middle East, taking over from a far less talented officer, General Sir Archibald Murray. Allenby was already a hero of the Boer War, but until he went to Egypt, his unconventional approach had not been appreciated by many senior colleagues in Europe. During December 1917, Lowell Thomas, by then in Italy, heard of Allenby and of the progress he was making. In *Lawrence by his Friends*, published in 1937, Thomas stated that John Buchan, then Director of Information at the Foreign Office, had first drawn his attention to Allenby's campaign.[4] Forty years later Thomas wrote that, having accidentally noticed a despatch about Allenby 'posted on a sandbag' in Rome, 'I decided that was where I wanted to be and immediately sent off a long cable to the Foreign Office in London'. Thomas continues that by chance the letter came to Buchan's attention, who did all he could to help the American propagandist.[5] Whatever the truth is, John Buchan did aid Lowell Thomas to get to Egypt, and had him officially accredited as a war correspondent to Allenby's army. Buchan realized that there was a good story in Arabia; he had friends in the Arab Bureau, and although he did not meet Lawrence until after the war, he had certainly heard of him and his secret war.

For all his credentials, Thomas was grudgingly received by General Allenby, who had a well-known antipathy towards 'gentlemen of the Press'. Despite this unforeseen setback, Thomas set Chase filming and appealed to London for help. The initial difficulties were overcome, and Thomas and Chase were invited to film in Jerusalem after Allenby's triumphant entry.

It was in Jerusalem in the spring of 1918 that Thomas was first introduced to Lawrence (although Hubert Young stated that they first met in Cairo). The story goes that having seen a mysterious blue-eyed Arab wandering in the street, he went to the headquarters of the Governor, Ronald Storrs, and asked about this strange-looking prince. Without a word, Storrs opened the door to the adjoining room where Lawrence, in spotless white, was reading a book on archaeology. Storrs then said, 'I want you to meet the Uncrowned King of Arabia', which, if it was said at all, was probably intended to have a hint of friendly sarcasm.[6]

According to Thomas, Lawrence was due to return to his Bedouins in Aqaba 'through the Turkish lines'. Obviously flattered by American interest in him, he had few objections to becoming a 'story'. In fact Thomas was granted permission to visit him in Aqaba, and it is unlikely that such permission would have been granted without Lawrence's own approval. There he became a willing model for the cameras of Harry Chase, who has never received the credit he deserved. The popular image of Lawrence dressed in flowing Arab costume is directly due to the impact of his skilful photography. For many years, Thomas pandered to the myth that Lawrence was modest by claiming that he was 'tricked' into being photographed, both in Jerusalem and later in Arabia. This is blatantly not true; an experienced photographer can instantly see that the pictures were posed, and in 1937, in *Lawrence by his Friends*, Thomas admitted that when asked by an acquaintance if Lawrence had posed for photographs, 'I gave . . . the same cock-and-bull story I had put in my book. Harry Chase and I had tricked 'Aurens' . . . Now that he is gone, no such rot is necessary'.[7] More important, he realized that the probable publicity could be politically useful.

Lawrence, Feisal and their supporters all showed hospitality to the Americans, who were understandably impressed. The question which remains unsatisfactorily answered is how long the Americans stayed in Arabia, and how much of this time was spent with Lawrence himself. Lawrence once said that 'Lowell Thomas was ten days in Arabia. He saw me for two of those and again a day in Jerusalem.'[8] Thomas states that he was with Lawrence for several weeks. Looking at the films and numerous photographs of Lawrence in different costumes and locations, it appears most unlikely that Thomas and Chase were with Lawrence himself for less than a week – an estimate which is confirmed by documents in a private collection in the United States.

The fact remains that, with Lawrence's and Feisal's co-operation, Thomas was able to collect enough material to present a good story and, having fulfilled the purpose of his visit, he left.

There is a basic inconsistency in Lowell Thomas's activities as a war correspondent. He never did rush back home to whip up the American public into a sabre-rattling frenzy. It is possible, though there is no evidence, that he contributed syndicated articles to American newspapers during the war. However, the stories he did get – Allenby, Lawrence, the American Expeditionary Force in France, various pieces on American flyers, the Italian Ski Patrol and the fall of Germany – he jealously guarded until he could successfully market them.

After the armistice, he sent Chase back to New York to process and edit the thousands of feet of film which he had taken in Europe and the Middle East.

Thomas realized that, in the post-war euphoria sweeping the country, a serious documentary would not be a sound financial proposition, and speculated on something with more popular appeal. He proposed to tell 'dramatic stories' as the film was projected, 'with appropriate music synchronised into the background', and envisaged the result as 'wholly new and spectacular'.[9] In order to raise more capital, he made a deal with the New York *Globe* at the suggestion of Harry Chase. Before the war, Chase's former employer, another travel lecturer, had been sponsored by the *Globe*, and the loyal cameraman suggested them to his new boss as a possible source of cash and free advertising.

In March 1919 Thomas's illustrated lecture opened at the Century Theatre in Central Park West – outside the main entertainment district. His opening address started: 'Come with me to lands of history, mystery and romance.'[10] This presentation was substantially different from the one which later appeared in London. At each performance, Thomas told a different story, apparently at the insistence of the editor of the *Globe*. These stories included accounts of the American Expeditionary Force in France, the Italian Front, the war in the Balkans, and the German revolution as well as the Allenby and Lawrence stories. All of them were successful. The first-night reviews were excellent, but it was clear that the public responded more enthusiastically to the romance of the desert and 'the liberation of Holy Arabia' – the latter proving particularly popular with New York's influential Jewish community. Thomas moved on to Madison Square Garden, dropped the *Globe* sponsorship, and planned a country-wide tour.

Fate brought the British impresario Percy Burton to Thomas's last night in New York. Burton, who had represented both Sarah Bernhardt and Sir Henry Irving, wanted Thomas to go to London. Myth has it that Thomas told him that he would bring his show to Britain on the condition that Burton got him Covent Garden or Drury Lane, and an invitation from the King, and that Burton managed both. In fact, Thomas arrived in England under the auspices of the English Speaking Union, among whose vice-presidents were Churchill and Northcliffe.

Thomas realized that what appealed to an American audience would not necessarily be right for an English one. He hired his old acquaintance, Dale Carnegie, to help rewrite the show, and Thomas, his wife Fran, Chase and Carnegie worked on the script and other details on board ship. By the time they docked at Southampton, he and Carnegie had rewritten 'a tight, swiftly moving show',[11] the basis of the show which opened on 14 August 1919 at Covent Garden under the title *With Allenby in Palestine*. It was an enormous success, but the rave reviews do not really give a precise indication of its format, and the films themselves, being on a nitrate base, have decayed beyond repair. Thomas kept no copy of the lecture which Carnegie rewrote – he claimed that he made it up afresh every night – but it does seem strange that there is no record, apart from press reviews, a very short sequence of film in the Imperial War Museum, and a first-night programme, of the full content of the performance. Nevertheless, from these sources it is possible to piece together something of the London première.

The *Daily Telegraph* wrote the morning after the première:

> Travelogue is the word which Mr Lowell Thomas, the well known American war correspondent, has coined for the story of his experiences 'With Allenby in Palestine', including an account of 'the capture of Jerusalem and the Liberation of Holy Arabia' . . . . The Royal Opera House, Covent Garden, where last night Mr. Thomas gave his address for the first time in England, was well filled. Mr. Thomas's 'pilgrimage' is illustrated by a continuous series of still and motion pictures taken by camera and cinematograph from earth to sky.[12]

The piece went on to describe specific high points of the show, but made no mention of Lawrence.

Burton had hired the band of the Welsh Guards to provide Thomas's musical accompaniment, and they were on stage to warm up the audience as it arrived. When the house had filled up, the Guards returned to the orchestra pit, the curtain went up and on came 'the Nile set, the moon faintly illuminating distant pyramids'[13]; then exotically dressed young ladies appeared on the stage to perform the dance of the Seven Veils. Thomas's wife, Fran, had created a musical parody of the Islamic call to prayer, and, to quote Thomas, 'a lyric tenor sent this haunting, high pitched melody sailing away to the farthest reaches of the theatre'.[14] Braziers filled with incense in the aisles increased the mystical effect.

Once the tenor had done his bit, Thomas came onto a darkened stage, and a spotlight picked him out while he gave a brief introduction explaining that the show was originally intended for an American audience: 'I had never even dreamed you British might be interested in hearing the story of your own Near Eastern campaign and the story of your heroes told through the nose of a Yankee . . . But here I am, and now come with me to lands of mystery, history and romance'.[15]

The audience was taken on an exotic odyssey split into two parts. Part I, 'With Allenby in Palestine', began with a journey 'by battleplane' from Cairo to Palestine. Having seen the Pyramids from the air, the audience was introduced to Allenby and his 'twentieth century Crusaders', and then was taken on a partially airborne tour of Palestine. The climax of the first half was 'The Fall of Jerusalem . . . The Entry of General Allenby the Deliverer.'[16]

The audience was given ten minutes to recover their nerves for Part II, The Liberation of Holy Arabia,' which began 'down the Nile into the heart of Africa' and on into 'Khartoum, the gateway of the jungle'. After they had witnessed the crossing of the Red Sea on a tramp steamer 'with a mottlier crew than ever sailed the Spanish Main', they were introduced to 'Shereef Lawrence, the uncrowned King of Arabia, and his Arabian Knights'. Then followed a sightseeing romp through Mount Sinai, Edom and Petra, a 'journey in an armoured car through the Land of Moab', and 'a battle in the air above the hills of Moab'. Next they heard an account of the 'triumphant twentieth-century Crusaders sweeping back the Turks on the Plains of Sharon where the Moslem horde of Saladin vanquished the flower of feudal chivalry'. Photographs showed Allenby and Lawrence advancing on Damascus as the Ottomans retreated, and then came a brief biographical sketch of Lawrence entitled 'Thomas Lawrence, archaeologist'. The climax of the show was the 'capture of Aleppo and the downfall of the Ottoman Empire – Mesopotamia, Syria, Arabia and the Holy Land at last freed after four hundred years of oppression'.[17]

Thomas lectured for over two hours as film and hand-coloured slides were projected on to the screen. Putting up an equally energetic performance in the projection room was Harry Chase, who might have been justly angry at the reviews which were to praise 'Mr Lowell Thomas's wonderful pictures'. Chase had developed a technique using three arc-light projectors simultaneously. He had modified the equipment and incorporated a fade and dissolve facility which was far ahead of its time. Little is known of this remarkable pioneer cinematographer, but Lowell Thomas's production would not have been possible without his mechanical and photographic skills. We will also never know to what extent Dale Carnegie's persuasive writing contributed to Thomas's success. Nevertheless, Thomas's performance on stage, six days a week with two matinées, was a tour de force.

It was not, of course, the 'darling cavalry gentleman' Allenby who became the centre of attention, but Lawrence, and Lowell Thomas received many commissions for articles about him in newspapers and periodicals. The first appeared in the American *Asia Magazine* in September 1919 under the heading 'THOMAS LAWRENCE – PRINCE OF MECCA' by Lowell Thomas, with the untruthful statement, 'photographs by the Author'. (By the next month, this had changed to 'photographs by the Author and Staff'.) The articles are probably very similar to the lectures he gave. In them, Lawrence is described as a 'young archaeologist' who, without 'a day's military experience in his life', became 'the terror of the Turks' and the 'idolised leader' of the Bedouins, with a '$500,000' price on his head, dead or alive. This 'breathless youth' had 'placed himself at the head of the Bedouin army of the King of the Hejaz', driven the Turks from Arabia and 'restored the caliphate to the descendants of the prophet', and would 'go down in history as one of the most romantic figures of the War'. Thomas also wrote of how Lawrence went to extraordinary lengths to avoid having medals pinned on him: 'Although he had been cited for nearly every decoration that the British and French Governments had to offer, he sedulously ran away from them by camel, aeroplane or any available method of swift transportation'. If anyone mentioned Lawrence's bravery to him, 'he would blush red as a schoolgirl'. Thomas continued always to give the impression that he was letting his audience in on a secret. The character of Allenby, although 'smashing', was far less exciting than that of the white Prince of Mecca who disappeared on secret expeditions and single-handedly defeated the Turks in Arabia.

Lawrence co-operated with Lowell Thomas in creating this image of a hero whose chief characteristics were courage, mystery and modesty. After the first night at Covent Garden he left a note for Thomas saying, 'Saw the show last night and thank God the lights were out,' but he became a frequent visitor to it.

He gave Thomas help with his articles in *Asia Magazine* which later evolved into the book *With Lawrence in Arabia*, and he even accepted the suggestion that he should contribute to American magazines himself. (Chapters from an early version of the *Seven Pillars of Wisdom* were to appear in the *World's Work* magazine.)

The English Press quickly picked up Lawrence's story. Nine days after the opening of *With Allenby in Palestine*, the illustrated weekly *The Sphere* devoted a page to Lowell Thomas's travelogue, and at least half of that to 'the strange story of Colonel Thomas Lawrence, the leader of the Arab army'.[18] There were two photographs of Lawrence in Arab dress, one accompanied by Lowell Thomas. Thomas had this photograph turned into a postcard and used it as an advertising gimmick for his lectures.

Following the success at Covent Garden, Thomas moved his entourage to the Albert Hall. There, battling against fog (which sometimes seeped into the auditorium) and the poor acoustics, they played for an unprecedented two months. In the new year (1920), the show moved again to Queen's Hall, where a Royal Command performance was presented.

Lowell Thomas had become a star in his own right. He was guest of honour at a banquet given by Fleet Street, at which Northcliffe, Rothermere, Beaverbrooke and John Astor were all present. He was in contact with Lawrence throughout this period, and the latter used to visit him in Wimbledon, where he had rented a house, to discuss plans for a biography.

After the successful run in London, Thomas briefly returned to the United States, where he presented 'With Allenby in Palestine and Lawrence in Arabia' in Washington and Philadelphia. He was forced to do this because of his contractual obligation, but he returned to Britain and went on a nationwide tour. In April 1920, he took the show to Australia and New Zealand, and after another record-breaking season, toured South East Asia and India with equal success.

Eventually, he returned to the United States for a remarkably successful coast-to-coast tour ending in Canada. Since its opening in 1919, it is estimated that four million people went to see the show.

It soon became clear, however, that Lawrence did not appreciate all the benefits of stardom. Sometimes, though not always, he wanted to destroy the Frankenstein monster he had helped to create – for that reason, he rejected Lowell Thomas and any association with him. He instructed Robert Graves to write in his potboiler *Lawrence and the Arabs*: 'The advertising of his Arabian adventure, both by the Press and Mr. Lowell Thomas's cinema lecture-tour, proved most unwelcome to him.'[19]

Richard Aldington maintained that Lawrence dropped Thomas when he ceased to be of any use to him. 'Lawrence was always careful to foster the illusion', he wrote, 'that he was frantically avoiding publicity, which naturally created the illusion that he had something of great public interest to conceal.' He went on to quote Bernard Shaw on Lawrence: 'When he was in the middle of the stage, with ten limelights blazing on him, everybody pointed to him and said: "See! He is hiding. He hates publicity."'

But Lawrence's attitude to his fame was not consistent. Initially he helped Lowell Thomas because since his childhood his ambition had been to become an imperial hero. On a more mature level, Lawrence realized that his public reputation could supplement his political influence. But if it could sometimes be useful, it was also a great burden. As he matured, so did his attitude to fame and he began genuinely to reject the adulation – which had been artificially created – as worthless. This rejection was never total, although a part of him would have liked it to be.

PART TWO

14 Politics and Literature

For the best part of three years – from the autumn of 1919 to the summer of 1922 – Lawrence divided his time between the political troubles in the Middle East and work on *The Seven Pillars of Wisdom*. So far as the former was concerned, he complained to his friends that he wanted to rest and forget Arabia and all that went with it. Nevertheless, his newly acquired fame had a political potential which might yet enable him to influence the final settlement in the Middle East.

After several incognito visits to Lowell Thomas's travelogue in London, he went home to Oxford to take up a fellowship at All Souls. Geoffrey Dawson, ex-editor of *The Times* and a prominent member of The Round Table, had recommended Lawrence for the fellowship, which carried with it an income of £200 per annum for three years. There were few conditions, but Lawrence was expected to pursue research connected with the Near East. Although this was hardly calculated to take his mind off Arabia, he hoped it would enable him to concentrate on completing *The Seven Pillars of Wisdom*. He found it impossible, however, to withdraw from politics, and the rapidly deteriorating situation in Syria and Mesopotamia ensured his continued involvement.

Throughout 1919, Feisal had tried to hold together a provisional Arab Government, based in Damascus, but all his efforts to establish a successful regime with long-term independence from France (or Britain) were doomed to failure. The French made it abundantly clear that they were not willing to renounce their claim in Syria, and continued to insist that the whole country should come under their overall protection once British troops were withdrawn. Even if Feisal accepted the necessity of making a compromise (and there is considerable evidence to suggest that he did), his staff, many of whom were Mesopotamians firmly committed to Arab nationalism, demanded that their leader should accept nothing less than complete autonomy in Syria.

Lawrence had hoped that the United States might intervene, declare the Sykes–Picot Treaty void and insist that the people of Syria be allowed the right of self-determination under the protection of an American mandate. President Wilson had given his approval in Paris to allowing the King–Crane Commission to visit Syria in order to ascertain the desires of the native population. However, when the Commission reported in August 1919 recommending an American mandate for the country, the suggestion was rejected out of hand.

For its part, the British Government wanted to avoid further confrontation with France. Under the terms of Sykes–Picot the French still had a hold over the largely unexploited Mosul oil-fields of Northern Mesopotamia, although the rest of Mesopotamia was clearly within the British sphere of influence. The Mosul Vilayet had been incorporated into the French sphere as part of an artificially enlarged Syria. Lloyd George was determined that this mistake should be rectified, but he realized that it would be necessary to give up something to France in exchange. He sought a compromise with Clemenceau, and in so doing abandoned Feisal.

This was a major, if not unexpected, disappointment for Lawrence. He brooded over what he regarded as his personal failure – a failure which went far beyond the Syrian question. He expressed dissatisfaction with his life, and was afflicted with frequent bouts of depression. His reaction to the horrors of war had to some extent been blocked by his busy political schedule; in Oxford, with more time to reflect, it descended on him in full. Mrs Lawrence told David Garnett that during the autumn of 1919 her son had sat for many hours motionless, silent, engrossed in his thoughts and evidently distressed. He displayed similar symptoms of withdrawal at the University, although at times his depression contrasted with unnaturally high spirits and adolescent practical joking. His unpredictable behaviour caused some acquaintances to think he had gone mad.

Lawrence was soon longing for a more complete retreat than was available at Oxford. On 1 September 1919, the day he was officially discharged from the Army, he wrote to his old friend Vyvyan Richards to say that he had just bought a five-acre plot of land at Pole Hill, Chingford, where the two of them might build their William Morris dream-house and retire from public life to produce small editions of their favourite books on a private printing press. This idealistic plan, which they had long nurtured, never materialized. Seven days later, Lawrence felt compelled to write a letter to *The Times* in reply to a piece about Syria; it appeared on 11 September. 'Your Syrian correspondent', he wrote, 'has just referred to British promises to the French and the Arabs. When on Feisal's staff I had access to the documents in question, and as possibly the only informed freelance European, I may help to clear them up.'[1]

He went on to list and give his interpretation of the documents in question, and commented: 'I can see no inconsistencies or incompatibilities . . . and know of nobody who does.' He did state, however, that Sykes–Picot was 'unworkable', but he stressed that its 'necessary revision' was a delicate matter and could not be done 'without giving weight and expression also to the opinion of the third interest – the Arabs.'

A mere two days after the publication of the letter, Lloyd George and Clemenceau concluded a provisional agreement in Paris which accepted eventual French control of Syria and specified the withdrawal of British troops by

November, 1919; the French, in return, would agree to British control of the Mosul and its oil-fields, though retaining an interest in their production. This arrangement was publicly endorsed by the Supreme Allied Council in Paris on 15 September.

The Foreign Office was embarrassed by one of its associates making public secret documents while sensitive negotiations were in progress, and the letter was circulated for comment. Lawrence's former understudy, Major Hubert Young, minuted as follows:

> Colonel Lawrence's letter is a carefully calculated indiscretion, written with the object of presenting the Arab case, and of guarding against the risk of the whole subject being discussed from the Franco–British point-of-view. He hits us as hard as the French, and if the letter had been written by an Arab, no possible exception could be taken to it. It is quite clear that . . . his motive is solely to justify himself in the eyes of the people who helped to overthrow the Turks through his influence, and, as a result of the confidence placed in him personally; and his attitude is quite understandable. But it is perhaps open to question whether, as an employee of the F.O. his action is justifiable.[2]

Another less forgiving Foreign Office official, whose signature is unfortunately indecipherable, wrote:

> From the official point of view Col. Lawrence's publication of his letter is quite unpardonable. His claim to be freelance is definitely disposed by Mr. Balfour's insistence that he is an official member of the Delegation in Paris.
>
> But from the practical point-of-view I believe his 'indiscretion' may be productive of good. It remains to be seen how the French Government and the French Press take it. If they accept Col. Lawrence's statement that he is a freelance and his access to these documents 'through' Faisal all may be well, but if they realise his official position and imagine that he has been put up to publishing his letter by H.M.G., there may be a row.[3]

A short comment from the Foreign Secretary, Curzon, ended the matter:

> I really don't see that any harm is done, but then pace Mr. Balfour I have never regarded Colonel L. as a member of the British Delegation.

On 15 September, Lawrence sent a 'memorandum' direct to the Foreign Office, presenting his views on Middle Eastern policy in considerable detail and setting out a somewhat unrealistic plan for a compromise between Feisal and the French in the light of the new Lloyd George–Clemenceau understanding. He urged that an outbreak of violence between the French and the Arabs should be avoided at all costs because it might 'unite all Moslem Syria against the French in arms', would damage the British position in Palestine and Mesopotamia, and might promote an alliance between Feisal and Mustapha Kemal. Lawrence also warned of a 'Wahabi-like Moslem form of Bolshevism' evolving in Mesopotamia,[4] where he predicted an outbreak of violence by 'about March 1920' unless policy was radically altered. He was not far out: a major insurrection occurred in the early summer.

Shortly after the Foreign Office received Lawrence's memorandum, Feisal arrived in England and immediately protested to Lloyd George over the new Anglo–French agreement, which was even less favourable to his position than Sykes–Picot had been. The War Office and the Foreign Office had instructed Lawrence to stay away from Feisal during the month he spent in London as a guest of the British Government; there is no record of their meeting, but it seems unlikely that they did not communicate in any way. On 25 September, Lawrence wrote a second memorandum to the Foreign Office, this time in the form of a long letter to Lord Curzon. Again, he detailed his proposals for Mesopotamia and Syria, and hinted that if these suggestions were followed, he might be able to make Feisal accept the Lloyd George–Clemenceau Agreement 'reasonably'. Despite his recent contribution to *The Times*, it appears that the Foreign Office was still willing to accept him as a mediator with Feisal.

Lawrence's letter to Curzon began with a series of recommendations about Mesopotamia, where a major crisis was developing, largely due to lack of co-operation and communication between the Foreign Office, the War Office and the India Office, which jointly bore the responsibility of administration. Lawrence wanted Sir Percy Cox (who had been temporarily appointed British Ambassador to Tehran) to return to Mesopotamia as Civil Commissioner to help sort out the mess, and he bluntly suggested that the acting Civil Commissioner Colonel A.T. Wilson should be 'employed outside the province'. Cox, Lawrence declared, should set up a Government of visibly 'Arab character... What is needed is not a change of fact but of spirit' – in effect, the illusion of self-government.

> My own ambition is that the Arabs should be our first brown dominion, and not our last brown colony. Arabs react against you if you try to drive them, and they are as tenacious as Jews; but you can lead them without force anywhere, if nominally arm in arm. The future of Mesopotamia is so immense that if it is cordially ours we can swing the whole Middle East with it.[5]

That was the key to Lawrence's plan. He conceded that a limited French presence might be necessary in Syria, especially as it would save British money in a country which had little to offer in terms of natural resources, and outlined a complex Anglo–French settlement, roughly based on Sykes–Picot, which would accept the French occupation of the Syrian coastline. The four great towns of Syria (Damascus, Homs, Hama and Aleppo) would be handed over to Arab control and form a single state with French and British advisers. To avoid the unviability of a land-locked Arab state, Lawrence suggested that both the French and the British should concede a port to Feisal: Alexandretta or Tripoli in the case of the French, and Haifa in the case of Britain. If the French refused to co-operate, Lawrence proposed that Feisal and his Government should be removed from Damascus to Deraa, where they would continue to operate under British protection. 'I think Feisal will accept these terms, if I explain them to him,' he wrote, and he concluded that the key to British control in the Middle East was always to appear more benevolent and less restrictive than the French: 'So long as we are more liberal ('left' in the Parliamentary sense) we call the tune.'[6]

Curzon circulated Lawrence's letter (at Lawrence's suggestion), and a copy arrived on the desk of Sir Arthur Hirtzel of the India Office. On 4 October Hirtzel wrote to Edwin Montagu, Secretary of State for India, who in turn sent a copy of Hirtzel's letter to Curzon. In it, Hirtzel said:

> I am too ignorant of what is and has been going on since September 19th to be able to offer any valuable comment. I mistrust Lawrence profoundly and do not accept the starting point of his policy. But subject to that, I do not see much to take exception to in these particular proposals. There are, however, some points to be noted.
>
> Lawrence is a politician: he admittedly neither knows nor cares anything about administration. To him these peoples and places are pawns in a political game. But behind his political game lies an assumption – that of the 'immense future of Mesopotamia'. Now Mesopotamia has no future at all unless it is properly administered, and a sound administration there must accordingly be the foundation of our position in the Middle East. We must take full account of political considerations, but we must not, to begin with, postpone good administration to them. I think we are bound to have an 'Arab Government' in Mesopotamia, (I) because we have promised it, (II) because it is required by the principles we have professed at the Peace Conference and by the best political thought of the day, (III) because Arab nationalism will, sooner rather than later, make anything else impossible. But we have got to get the country on its legs – no Arab Government can do that, and it must be a camouflaged British Government at first. I think that is generally admitted: Lawrence suggests that there need be few changes in fact, but a change in spirit, and I entirely agree. But what I am intensely anxious about is lest Mesopotamia should not be dealt with on its merits, but subordinate to political considerations elsewhere. . . .
>
> . . . I submit that we cannot for a moment allow Feisal or Lawrence to dictate to us who we shall and shall not employ. As regards Cox, we are fortunately able to say that his return has already been arranged for, but it should be made quite clear to Feisal that his wishes had nothing to do with it. As regards A.T. Wilson – Lawrence told me months ago (the first time I ever met him, in fact) that he hates Wilson, and he practically admitted that his attitude towards Mesopotamian questions is coloured by his personal feeling. . . . I submit that we cannot undertake that Wilson 'should be employed outside the province': but I think that it should be good both for him and for Mesopotamia that he be so employed; and I would propose that he should take long leave (he has had none for 5 years) when Cox has been back a month or two. If in the meantime a new office has been created in London, he might well be employed in it for a year or two before returning to Mesopotamia . . . .[7]

As emerges from his letter, published here for the first time, Hirtzel disliked Lawrence intensely, but in judging whether his accusations were justified, it is fair to say that many of Lawrence's suggestions to Curzon were valid, and also that both Hirtzel and Montagu bore personal and professional grudges against him for his attacks on the India Office.

All the same, in assessing the situation in the Middle East, Lawrence had made some important mistakes. He professed expertise on Mesopotamia, a country of which he had only the briefest first-hand experience. He underestimated both France's military power and her determination to colonize Syria and the Lebanon. Above all – perhaps his most serious mistake – he underestimated French national pride. The Feisal–Weizmann proposals he had helped to arrange (and may well have believed in) were at best unrealistic, and frightened powerful elements within the Foreign and India Offices. Nevertheless, he believed that if his schemes were put into action, the French would 'hold an uneasy position for a few years on the Syrian coast',[8] but would quickly be forced to abandon the region.

Lawrence was unsuccessful in lobbying British support for Feisal in Syria. On 19 October 1919, Feisal left London for Paris, where he was forced to make a compromise with the French Government. By the end of November, all British troops had been evacuated from Syria, and Lawrence, angry but relatively powerless, temporarily redirected his energy into his book and life at Oxford.

His progress there was as erratic as his mood. Seeking distraction, he made a vain attempt to join in college life with the undergraduates, but he realized that he did not really belong, any more than he belonged when mixing with the Arabs. One or two facts emerge about this period of his life. Learning that Charles Doughty, one of the few men he revered and had consistently praised all his adult life, was crippled both by age and by financial difficulty, he went to endless trouble to bring the poet-explorer's undeservedly obscure work, *Arabia Deserta*, to a wider audience. Eventually, the Medici Society agreed to bring out a de luxe edition in conjunction with Jonathan Cape, on condition that Lawrence wrote an introduction. This he did; the new *Arabia Deserta* appeared in January 1921 and quickly sold out, and in the reprint Lawrence withdrew his introduction, feeling that the book should now stand on its own merits.

It was this project that launched Jonathan Cape as a publisher, and he was, of course, later to publish *The Seven Pillars of Wisdom* and its abridgement *Revolt in the Desert*. Lawrence assisted Doughty on two further occasions, arranging for the British Museum to acquire the manuscript of his poem *The Dawn in Britain* – indeed, there is some evidence that Lawrence contributed £400 to the cost himself – and successfully lobbying, in 1927, for the award of a Civil List pension to Doughty.

His feelings towards his own work were less enthusiastic. He was dissatisfied with the first draft of *The Seven Pillars of Wisdom*, which he completed in November 1919 and promptly lost. Needless to say, he gave conflicting reports of the incident, telling Doughty that 'it was stolen from me in the train'[9] and Liddell Hart that the book, apart from the first nine chapters, had disappeared from the refreshment room at Reading Station.[10] D.G. Hogarth suspected that the theft had been encouraged through deliberate carelessness, and urged Lawrence to pull himself together and write the book again. But

Lawrence was under an intolerable strain as he relived and rewrote his Arabian experiences. His bitterness and self-deprecation are revealed in a letter he wrote to S.F. Newcombe in February 1920:

> In the History of the World (cheap edition) I'm a sublimated Aladdin, the thousand and second Knight, a Strand-Magazine strummer. In the eyes of 'those who know' I failed badly in attempting a piece of work which a little more resolution would have pushed through, or left un-touched.[11]

It was in this letter that Lawrence mentioned for the first time that he was going to change his name 'to be more quiet'. His search for privacy is also connected with a series of visits to, and temporary residence in, a room in Barton Street, Westminster. Lawrence had repeatedly complained to friends that he could find nowhere to work on his book in peace. In response, Herbert Baker (a young architect he had met in Oxford) offered him the use of a vacant room above his London office, which Lawrence gratefully accepted. Baker was somewhat surprised when his eccentric new tenant 'refused all service and comfort, food, fire or hot water', frequently forgot to go out for a meal, but kept a stock of chocolate as 'it required no cleaning up'. He worked many hours without rest 'until he became delirious'.[12]

Lawrence seemed to believe that pain, even if self-induced, would improve his prose: '[I] excited myself with hunger and cold and sleeplessness more than did de Quincy with his opium'.[13] A large part of the *Seven Pillars* was completed in the room above Baker's office. Lawrence appears to have grown attached to his spartan *pied-à-terre*, describing it as 'the best-and-freest-place I ever lived in.'[14]

It was not in Westminster but at All Souls that Lawrence met his future biographer, Robert Graves, for the first time at a dinner in March 1920. An intense relationship grew between the two men. They shared a love of literature. Both had been scarred by their experiences during the War; both shared a contempt for conventional morality, paradoxically combined with sexual puritanism. They later corresponded about their respective sexual problems. Martin Seymour-Smith, Robert Graves's biographer, noted that Graves was one of the very few of Lawrence's friends 'to whom he gave detailed information about his irresistible compulsion to be punished'.[15]

Some of their letters have been published in an abridged form, but they are full of riddles – both men were fond of the rituals of secrecy, and enjoyed teasing one another. Graves advised Lawrence on his writing and later rewrote the deliberately obscure dedicatory poem 'To S.A.' at the beginning of *The Seven Pillars of Wisdom*. Graves later claimed that 'S.A.' was a woman, but his argument is not convincing.[16]

The close relationship between Lawrence and Graves persisted throughout 1920 and 1921. They introduced each other to poets and writers (through Graves Lawrence met Siegfried Sassoon and, somewhat later, Thomas Hardy). Lawrence assisted Graves through serious financial difficulty. The initial intimacy only began to falter when in 1923 Lawrence joined the Air

Force, and their friendship can be said to have ended when Graves published *I, Claudius*, a book which Lawrence found 'sickening'.

The date on which Lawrence completed the second draft of *The Seven Pillars of Wisdom* cannot be determined, as he gave different information to different correspondents. In the manuscript in the Bodleian Library, he wrote that the second version was completed on 11 May 1920, but corrected and slowly added to during the next two years. This would seem quite possible, for there is every reason to believe that he would have had to stop work on it in May 1920. However much he may have wished to escape anonymously into the Oxford literary world, his Arabian connections would not permit it. By now a major crisis was developing in Mesopotamia.

15 Farewell to Politics

The situation in both Mesopotamia and Syria was extremely complicated and dangerous at the beginning of 1920, and grew more so as the year continued. Feisal was elected King of Syria at the Syrian National Congress held in Damascus on 8 March. The Congress consisted largely of his own staff officers and the 'election' meant little, but in the current mood of nationalist fervour Feisal had little option but to accept the title or be swept away by the mob.

The British Government under Lloyd George was irritated by the news, but Feisal's sovereignty had little hope of success without recognition. As Ernest Main wrote: 'This effort to present the Allies with a fait accompli was doomed to failure because there was nothing behind it. The Arab Government in Damascus was but a façade, which was bound to collapse as soon as British support was withdrawn.'[1]

At the end of April, an Inter-Allied Conference convened at San Remo to discuss the terms of a Treaty with Turkey and to allocate mandates. Syria (as it then was) was officially split into Syria (as it is to-day), Palestine and the Lebanon. France was officially appointed as the mandatory power responsible for Syria and Lebanon. Great Britain was allocated Iraq (Mesopotamia) and Palestine. The final rubber-stamping took place at Sèvres, where the decisions taken at San Remo were ratified by the Supreme Allied Council.

Shortly afterwards, French troops entered Syria and, amid considerable bloodshed, ejected Feisal from the country.

Meanwhile, the situation in Mesopotamia had also been deteriorating. The inflexible Anglo-Indian administration had failed, internal resistance to British rule was growing, and keeping it in check was proving extremely costly. Churchill, the Secretary of State for War, had asked Trenchard, Chief of Air Staff, if the RAF could take over the policing of the country from the Army by means of air patrols and selective bombing at a reduced cost to the Exchequer. Trenchard's reply was favourable, and Churchill asked him to draw up a plan.

Through his elaborate network of information, Lawrence heard of these preliminary and highly secret discussions, and offered his services to Trenchard as an unofficial adviser. He wrote to Lord Winterton on 14 April that he had seen Trenchard and 'now I think he is right in all points . . . I feel inclined to back his scheme.'[2] It is, perhaps, in character that he should state to Liddell Hart in 1933 that it was he who had originated the idea of putting the RAF into Mesopotamia:

> . . . the war showed me that a combination of armoured cars and aircraft could rule the desert: but they must be under non-army control, and without infantry support. You rightly trace the origin of the RAF control in Irak, Aden & Palestine to this experience. As soon as I was able to have my own way in the Middle East I approached Trenchard on the point, converted Winston easily, persuaded the Cabinet swiftly into approving (against the wiles of Henry Wilson) [Field Marshal Sir Henry Wilson, CIGS] and it has worked very well.[3]

It is also interesting to contrast two letters located by John Mack. On 14 May 1920 Lawrence wrote to Frederic Stern, to say that he had 'dropped politics' the previous year and was 'out of them for good'.[4] Only a week later, he was writing to Harry St John Philby, asking for support in a petition to the Prime Minister to remove responsibility for Mesopotamia from the joint hands of the India and Foreign Offices, and give it to a newly proposed Middle Eastern Department. Lawrence asked Philby if he would add his name to those of Hogarth, Lionel Curtis and Arnold Toynbee, who had all agreed to sign.[5]

He now began an intensive press campaign attacking Britain's confused policy in the Middle East. Two articles in the *Daily Express* (28 and 29 May 1920) were mainly directed against old men in politics who failed to notice the changes in Asia or the dangers of the spread of Bolshevism, and an article in *The Sunday Times* (30 May 1920) concluded with a tribute to Feisal, noting the attempts being made by the Allies to deceive him: 'It was not for such politics I fought.'

Less than a month later, a widespread insurrection broke out in Iraq. Such a disturbance had been forecast by others before Lawrence, but he received all the credit for the prediction. The rebellion was suppressed (at a great cost) by the end of the year, but damage to British prestige was immense.

Gertrude Bell was active as a political officer in the British Government of Iraq, and she wrote to Lawrence in July: 'Beloved boy – I've been reading with amusement your articles in the papers; what curious organs you choose for self expression!'[6] She enclosed a copy of a report she had drawn up to brief Sir Percy Cox, who arrived in Mesopotamia to assess the situation after the Government had announced its intention to set up a provisional Arab government under his guidance. Lawrence was told by Gertrude Bell that he could show the report to Hogarth but to no one else, 'it was only for Sir Percy's eyes'.[7] She found it difficult, she wrote, 'to maintain a dispassionate calm when I reflect on the number of blunders we've made'.[8]

Few other political officers had a better grasp of the Mesopotamian crisis than Gertrude Bell. She had devoted a considerable portion of her life to studying the country and its people, and she realized the inevitability of violence, but hoped that Cox's sagacity and reputation might yet prevent an uncontrollable explosion. Sadly, his stay was a short one, but it is unlikely that he would have been able to prevent the insurrection even if he had remained in Mesopotamia.

Lawrence continued his press campaign during July and August with a letter and two anonymous articles in *The Times*,[9] and two signed articles in *The Observer*[10] and *The Sunday Times*.[11] The Arabs, he wrote in stirring terms, 'did not risk their lives in battle to change master, to become British subjects or French citizens, but to win a show of their own . . . Whether they are fit for independence or not remains to be seen. Merit is no qualification for freedom.'[12]

Some of his proposals, such as raising two divisions of Arab volunteers to police the country, were not so persuasive.

In the first week of September 1920 Gertrude Bell wrote in her diary: 'The thing isn't made any easier by the tosh T. E. Lawrence is writing in the papers. To talk of raising an Arab army of two divisions is pure nonsense. Except for officers, we haven't got the materials . . . I can't think why the India Office lets the rot that's written pass uncontradicted.' Two weeks later, she was even more scathing.

> The fact that we are really guilty of an initial mistake makes it difficult to answer letters like those of T. E. Lawrence. I believe them to be wholly misleading, but to know why they're misleading requires such an accurate acquaintance not only with the history of the last two years but also with the country and the people, apart from our dealings with them, that I almost despair of putting public opinion in England right. I can't believe that T.E.L. is in ignorance and I therefore hold him to be guilty of the unpardonable sin of wilfully darkening counsel. We have a difficult enough task before us in this country; he is making it more difficult by leading people to think it's easy.[13]

In spite of his journalistic outpourings Lawrence continued to finish the second draft of *The Seven Pillars of Wisdom* by the end of September, and by the end of the year he was once again playing a major role in Middle Eastern affairs. In December, Feisal made a visit to Britain, theoretically as his father's Ambassador, and during his stay was discreetly asked how he would react if offered the throne of Iraq. Six months earlier the same proposal had been rejected by the British Government because they believed that any support for Feisal in Mesopotamia would be regarded by the French as a hostile act. But by now the Government were becoming frantic in their search for a solution to the Mesopotamian issue – the cost of the insurrection in the summer had been £100 million – and when Feisal cautiously refused the suggestion, Lawrence was brought in to make him change his mind, although as yet nothing firm had been proposed. At a protracted meeting at the house of Lord Winterton (in Sussex) Feisal agreed that if he were offered the throne of Mesopotamia he would accept, but only on the condition that he was allowed real freedom to govern and that his brother Abdullah agreed to renounce his claim.

The formation of a stable government was the first consideration, and a degree of autonomy could be tolerated by the British as long as the supply of Mesopotamian oil and the security of the Persian Gulf remained certain.

It was evident that, before any real stability could be achieved, the formulation of policy for the whole of the Middle East would have to be centralized. Churchill persuaded Lloyd George of this necessity, and the Cabinet finally scrapped the absurd system which brought so many Government agencies into conflict. In future the Colonial Office would have overall responsibility for the Middle East, and a special Committee was formed to oversee the handover. Lord Milner turned down the job of Chairman, but Churchill agreed to take it on. 'I must feel my hand and feel sure of my way,' he wrote to Lloyd George. 'I have seen Lawrence and am making certain enquiries.'[14] A small department (fourteen strong) was formed within the Colonial Office devoted exclusively to the Middle East – exactly as Lawrence had suggested to Philby in May. Churchill asked Lawrence to join as 'special advisor on Arab affairs'. Lawrence had sworn to himself and friends that he would never again take an active role in politics, but the opportunity was too good to miss, and he accepted.

Apart from other considerations, the post made him financially solvent – it carried a salary of £1,200 per annum. The extent of Lawrence's financial difficulties after the first war have never been fully brought to light. Whatever money his father left him did not last long, and he became increasingly dependent on the small income from his fellowship. He could have survived had it not been for his ambitious plans for *The Seven Pillars of Wisdom*. He had conceived this idea of publishing it himself in a super de luxe edition incorporating his ideals of book-production as to typography, illustration and binding. The pursuit of this project bankrupted him, and only through the intervention of friends was a scandal avoided.

The official war artist Eric Kennington told a revealing story. Lawrence had bought two of his portraits of soldiers and invited him to visit All Souls. Kennington was flattered, especially when Lawrence explained that he wanted him to make portraits from photographs of Arabs as illustrations for a book. Kennington explained that adequate results could not be achieved from photographs, and asked if Lawrence would like him 'to go out and draw them. He giggled: "You cannot have any conception of the difficulties. I should have to be your guide, and it would be expensive. I have no money."'[15] When it came to the point, Kennington offered to raise £600 for both of them to go to Arabia, but the plan fell through and Kennington went alone after being fully briefed by Lawrence.

But it would be wrong to suggest that financial considerations were the only or even the main reason for his accepting the post offered him by Churchill. He still felt bitter over his failure in Paris, and now he had another chance. This time he would fight from a position of real political power, able to take an active part in policy-formation.

Churchill's outline plan for Mesopotamia had two basic objectives: a) to replace the Army with the cheaper RAF option, and b) to put Feisal on the throne. At the beginning of February, Churchill announced that an Imperial Conference would take place the following month in Cairo to consider Britain's future policy in the Middle East, and in particular the Mesopotamian question. Aided by Lawrence, he drew up an agenda which led T.E. with characteristic exaggeration to claim later: 'The decisions of the Cairo Conference were prepared by us in London, over dinner tables at the Ship Restaurant in Whitehall.'[16]

The Conference had a real contribution to make, not least bringing together many experts too often separated by telegraph wires and code books. Lawrence was to play a crucial role, yet a month before the Conference started, and a few days before his appointment was announced in *The Times*, he wrote to Lady Scott (a sculptress making a statuette of him): 'I'm tired of the limelight, & am really not stagy at all, & not ever going to be a public figure again.'[17]

The main item on the agenda of the Cairo Conference, which opened on 12 March 1921, was Iraq (a term gradually replacing the more ambiguous 'Mesopotamia'), although policy in other regions, notably Palestine and Trans-Jordania, was also reviewed. To take part in these deliberations, Churchill had arranged for forty of the most able political, military and economic experts to gather in the Egyptian capital. Winston's 'forty thieves' (a remark attributed to Churchill himself) included three High Commissioners – Cox (Iraq), Allenby (Egypt), Samuel (Palestine) – and half a dozen generals, not to mention Trenchard and Sir Geoffrey Salmond, the Air Officer in Charge of the Middle East. Also present were Lawrence, Hubert Young, Gilbert Clayton, Kinahan Cornwallis, Gertrude Bell, Jaafar Pasha (the former commander of Feisal's regular army, who had recently been invited by Cox to become the Minister of Defence in the provisional Government of Iraq) and A. T. Wilson (attending as representative for his new employers, the Anglo-Persian Oil Company (the ancestor of BP). The conference provided an opportunity for many old friends, and few old enemies, to see each other again; its atmosphere was intimate, the prevailing attitude pragmatic. The only significant absentees were delegates from India. The new management at the Colonial Office, maintaining the traditions of the Arab Bureau, were trying to keep Delhi out of the decision-making process.

Lawrence, hopeful that things were at last going the way he desired, arrived in Cairo on 3 March to find a room booked in his name at the Semiramis Hotel – a marble and bronze edifice which offended the ascetic in him and prompted him to write home: 'horrible place: makes me Bolshevik'.[18] Dressed in dull and ill-fitting clothes, he made a curious impression on those who did not already know him. Captain Maxwell Coote, who was acting as Churchill's Orderly Officer, assumed at first glance that the odd little man in the drab grey suit was a 'junior secretary to some lesser light' rather than the famous Arabian Knight.[19]

A senior adviser to Churchill, Lawrence was in an undeniably influential position – though later he rather exaggerated the degree of control he exerted over the conference. Churchill was determined to construct workable and cost-effective policies, but his knowledge of the Middle East was limited, and although he never lost control, he needed and asked for advice. Lawrence admired his new Chief's energy and natural authority, much in the same way as he respected Allenby, and for his part Churchill found Lawrence both intriguing and entertaining.

Even as the conference opened, disquieting news was received from Trans-Jordania, where Feisal's brother Abdullah was raising an army. Apparently King Hussein had given orders to march on Syria, eject the French and restore Feisal to power. It is doubtful that Abdullah would ever have undertaken to lead such a suicidal mission, but his wartime reputation, his father's authority, and a general mood of dissatisfaction had helped him to recruit an army rumoured to be two thousand strong. The last thing Lawrence wanted now was a return to the violence of 1920 – if trouble erupted in Syria, it would certainly spread. Abdullah presented a second problem as another candidate for the Iraqi throne. In an attempt to improve family relations, Feisal had announced that he would not accept any position in Iraq unless his brother agreed to withdraw his claims to that country. (Ironically, Lawrence had been one of those chiefly responsible for encouraging Abdullah's ambitions, and Abdullah had been declared Emir of Iraq at the Congress held in Damascus in the spring of 1920.) Clearly if Feisal was to secure the throne of Iraq rather than any other pretender, decisions would have to be made quickly, and could not exclude consideration of Abdullah and King Hussein.

At the centre of events in Cairo was an exclusive group known as the Political Committee, its principal members being Churchill, Cox, Lawrence, Gertrude Bell and Young. One of their first tasks was to consider in what manner the institution of monarchy, with Feisal as first king, could be introduced into the new nation of Iraq without giving the impression to both the Iraqis and to the outside world that it was a put-up job. Cox, who had been building a new administration in Baghdad, explained to the Committee that in just over a month elections were due to take place for a National Assembly. He predicted that this pseudo-European legislature would in its turn be willing to elect Feisal as King, but Churchill was opposed to this plan. It was possible that, for reasons unforeseen, the Assembly might not elect Feisal by a clear majority, or, worse still, elect another candidate.

An elaborate intelligence network existed in Iraq which had been extensively developed by Gertrude Bell. It would be possible to be informed of, and have the chance to thwart, opposition to Feisal as and when it developed – similarly, support for him could be subtly engendered. Politically, Iraq was a fractured entity with little real cohesion; any elections would be under British supervision, and if a situation arose where it was determined 'necessary' to rig election returns, this should present few problems. It would have been harder to coerce a hostile National Assembly.

The Committee accordingly decided to present Feisal direct to the people, and a plan for his progress towards the throne was rapidly drawn up. The first stage was to inform him officially that HMG would not oppose his candidature. He could then telegraph his supporters in Baghdad that he had been accepted by the British (though this would have to be done in such a way as to play down British involvement), and that he intended to come to Iraq at the first opportunity.

Churchill telegraphed these proposals to Lloyd George, who replied cautiously that Feisal was acceptable, but for the sake of Anglo-French relations it was imperative that any initiative was seen to come from within Iraq. On 22 March the Cabinet met and approved the recommendations made by the Political Committee in Cairo on the condition that Feisal make an undertaking not to use his new position in Iraq to undermine the French position in Syria. Lawrence received this news gratefully, and with Churchill's consent sent a telegram to Feisal in London via the Foreign Office:

> THINGS HAVE GONE EXACTLY AS HOPED. PLEASE START FOR MECCA AT ONCE . . . I WILL MEET YOU ON WAY AND EXPLAIN DETAILS. SAY ONLY THAT YOU ARE GOING TO SEE YOUR FATHER AND ON NO ACCOUNT PUT ANYTHING IN PRESS.[20]

Curzon was anxious lest the French should discover that Lawrence was meeting Feisal. Nevertheless, a secret meeting between the two did take place later at Port Said.

Apart from the French and the population of Iraq, the only major remaining obstacle to Feisal's kingship was his brother. Abdullah would have to be bought off in some way. One solution might be to help him create a state of his own in Trans-Jordania, and Churchill adjourned the Conference, announcing that talks would reconvene in Jerusalem. Three days later, a party including Churchill, his bodyguard Inspector Walter Thompson of Scotland Yard, Lawrence and Captain Coote set out by train from Cairo.

They stopped in Gaza, where a large crowd had gathered, and Lawrence, tempted back into his desert robes, translated Churchill's speech to an appreciative audience. According to Inspector Thompson, Lawrence's presence had an electrifying effect on the Arabs who had gathered in Gaza. He wrote in his autobiography *Assignment Churchill* that Lawrence 'could have established his own Empire from Alexandretta to the Indus'.[21]

From Jerusalem, Lawrence and an RAF officer (probably Coote) were despatched to fetch Abdullah from his camp at Salt – a six-hour drive. When their car reached Jerusalem it was mobbed by a jubilant crowd which had turned out to greet the Arab prince, and it was only with some difficulty that they reached Government House on Mount Olivet, where a Guard of Honour and an official banquet had been arranged. The following day, Churchill explained the British position to Abdullah and attempted to persuade him that he should accept the results of the Cairo Conference and support Feisal's candidacy for the throne of Iraq.

As Colonial Secretary he promised that if Abdullah backed British policy, he could expect rewards commensurate with his loyalty, the tangible proof of which would be the chance to establish his own state in Trans-Jordania. Abdullah replied that he could make no final decisions without consulting his father, but after some further bargaining he accepted Churchill's offer of Trans-Jordania, subject to his father's approval and an assurance that the idea of an Arab Government in Damascus had not been forgotten. Abdullah needed the latter both to save his own pride and as a sop to the followers to whom he had declared himself as an apostle of Arab nationalism, and who might now turn on him and call him the lackey of the British.

The next few weeks were busy ones for Lawrence. He was constantly on the move between Egypt, Palestine and Trans-Jordania. In the second week of May, he sailed for England. Although official policy was at last moving in the direction he wanted, his recent activities had further reduced what few emotional and physical resources he still retained. Briefly 'Lawrence of Arabia' had been in the ascendant. Now T. E. Lawrence had to fight his intense depression.

Churchill had returned to London shortly after the talks with Abdullah in Jerusalem, and on 14 June he announced in the House of Commons that HMG had decided to back Feisal as 'the most suitable candidate in the field'. It is of little surprise that no mention was made of the considerable opposition which existed in Iraq to Feisal's candidature, or the fact that it had been arranged for Sayid Talib, the most prominent opposition candidate, to be kidnapped by British soldiers as he left a tea party given by Sir Percy Cox, and sent on an enforced 'holiday' to Ceylon. Churchill declared authoritatively that he believed Feisal would 'secure the support of the majority of the people of Iraq'. When elections were held in August (Feisal had arrived on 23 June) he won by the (literally) incredible majority of 96 per cent.

The agreements made with Feisal and Abdullah were provisional, and their father had not yet been directly consulted. Apart from the fact that important negotiations on his subsidy and the pilgrimage to Mecca were outstanding, the old King was also in a position to make embarrassing claims on Syria and Palestine following various pledges made to him over the years by successive representatives of the British Government. If King Hussein could be persuaded to sign a treaty accepting the new status quo, and agreeing to forget the promises made to him in the past, five years of confusion would be brought to a tidy conclusion. In return HMG could offer him protection against his ambitious neighbour, Ibn Saud, and a comfortable annual income to supplement his local revenues.

Hussein was a notoriously difficult man to deal with, and Lawrence was temporarily attached to the Foreign Office and selected to go to Jeddah to open negotiations. He was an odd choice, as he had never got on well with the King. Nevertheless, detailed preparations were made and a draft treaty drawn up in London. To convince Hussein that this time there would be no misunderstandings, Lawrence was awarded full plenipotentiary powers and took with him to Jeddah an impressive document carrying the Great Seal of England, describing the bearer as: 'Our most trusty and well beloved Thomas

Edward Lawrence Esquire, Lieutenant Colonel in our Army, Companion of our Most Honourable Order of the Bath, Companion of our Distinguished Service Order.'[22] This was strange considering Lawrence's conversation with the King in October 1918 about his decorations. (Even stranger is the fact that the following year, when Lawrence joined up in the ranks of the RAF under an assumed name, he took this document with him to Uxbridge Camp and allowed it to fall to the floor of the recruits' hut.)

Lawrence's mission was announced in *The Times*, which reported that he was due to discuss with the King of the Hejaz 'certain matters pending between the British Government and the Court of Mecca, the most important of which is the regulation of the Haj or Moslem pilgrimage to the Holy Cities of Islam which are in the Hejaz'.[23]

Before his departure, Lawrence received a telephone call from Kennington, who had recently returned to England. The two men had met twice during Lawrence's recent travels, once in Cairo and once in Jerusalem. Between these meetings, Kennington had been on a motoring tour of Syria and Palestine at Lawrence's suggestion, and in Cairo the artist had sketched Lawrence, Allenby and General Ironside, whom Lawrence described as 'Six feet four and sixteen stone. Brains too.'[24] Now the portraits from Arabia were complete, and the artist invited Lawrence to see them. Lawrence was delighted with the results and offered Kennington £720 for eighteen of the pictures. Although this was accepted, it appears that Lawrence's cheque was never cashed. Late in the year he was to write a foreword for the catalogue of Kennington's Arab portraits which were exhibited at the Leicester Galleries in London.

Lawrence left for Jeddah on 8 July, and the talks with King Hussein, which opened on 30 July, deserve a unique place in the annals of diplomacy. At first the King's main concern related to the purchase of a yacht at a discount price (apparently an incentive held out in previous negotiations) and the talks became progressively more difficult. Lawrence's first extended report to London included an assessment of Hussein's lack of military strength:

> Jeddah 40 men, Mecca 50 men, Taif 500 men, 30 automatics, some German Maxims, 60 mounted infantry. Troops are regularly paid but underfed and not satisfied . . . It appears certain that any expedition of one thousand armed Wahabis could take Taif and Mecca . . .

Of the King himself, Lawrence noted:

> [He] has not referred to the draft treaty since he saw it . . . He has announced his abandonment of position founded on McMahon letters, but raises absurd new ideas daily. Old man is conceited to a degree, greedy, and stupid, but very friendly, and protests devotion to our interests. . .[25]

Hussein meanwhile tried to contact his son Feisal for advice on how to proceed but Lawrence, who had all the resources of the Foreign Office and Military Intelligence services at his command, cabled Baghdad:

> King Hussein has wired to Feisal in cypher tonight. I hope you will suppress it, and deliver him the following begins: 'Negotiations with Lawrence are going well and conclusions will be submitted to you. Zeid.'[26]

Zeid was, of course, the King's third son. In fact negotiations were going anything but well, as Lawrence's report to London on 4 August indicated:

> Have had more conversations with the King. He was only playing with me so I have changed tactics and forced him to make exact statement. After some questions he made clear that he refused absolutely all notion of making a treaty but expected acknowledgement of his Kingship in Mesopotamia and Palestine, priority over all rulers in Arabia who were confined to their pre-war boundaries, and cession to himself [the districts of] Asir and Holeida. His ambitions are as large as his conceit, and he showed unpleasant jealousy of his sons.
>
> I gave him my candid opinion of his character and capacity. There was a scene, remarkable to me in that not only the Foreign Secretary but the King also burst into tears. I walked out with parting remarks which brought Zeid to me last night with a rough draft of a treaty based on ours for my consideration.
>
> The King is weaker than I thought, and could, I think, be bullied into nearly complete surrender. Reason is entirely wasted on him since he believes himself all-wise and all-competent, and is flattered by his entourage in every idiotic thing he does. The difficulties of using force are short time, and the fear that if I hurt him too much he will sulk in Mecca. I will not be able to finish anything before the pilgrimage [the King was due to leave for Mecca to supervise the pilgrimage], but his draft, if he submits it formally today, will give me grounds for returning here at the end of the month.[27]

Lawrence's tactics were unsuccessful. The draft was not submitted, and he reported on 7 August:

> On my next visit King Hussein went back on his previous suggestions and disclaimed any idea of considering a treaty. I got up and walked out, this flustered them, King saying he thought no one could treat royalty so. His titles have turned his head and made him absurd.
>
> Marshall [a British officer stationed at Jeddah] saw him the next day after messengers had come to us, and explained how regrettably the breaking off of negotiations would affect the prosperity of the Hejaz. King thereupon yielded and sent last night alternative draft and comments on a treaty which he is today anxious to make with us. It contains too much rubbish to wire to you, but in final interview I hope to throw out some of this and will then refer it, but as the old man forgets yesterday tomorrow the issue is still uncertain. The need is not so much to secure his signature as to break down his convictions that we are dependent on him for our prestige in the East, and will pay any price and swallow any vexation to keep his friendship. If he is beaten over this business he will soon come easier next time.[28]

Lawrence's predictions proved incorrect. However, during the final interview there was an unexpected breakthrough in the bargaining, but it proved to be artificial. Apparently unknown to Lawrence, the King had bought six aeroplanes from the Italian Government after an export licence for British machines had been refused. In desperate need of cash to pay this and other debts, the King suddenly agreed on an outline treaty, relieved Lawrence of 80,000 rupees (£5,000) and departed to Mecca.

A Royal Navy ship took Lawrence to Aden, where he stayed for the rest of the month as the guest of the British Resident, General Scott, but on the 29th he was back in Jeddah, still not fully recovered from the strain of his last visit. He reported to London after his first meeting:

> On my return the King went back on his decision and demanded
>
> 1 Return of all states in Arabia except his to their pre-war boundaries.
> 2 Cession to him of all areas so vacated.
> 3 Right to appoint all Cadis and Muftis in Arabia, Mesopotamia, Palestine.
> 4 Recognition of his supremacy over all Arab rulers everywhere.
>
> My reply made him send for his dagger and swear to abdicate and kill himself. I said we would continue negotiations with his successor.[29]

Lawrence was later to tell Kennington that this incident never took place. The Foreign Office in the meantime learnt about the purchase of the Italian aircraft and immediately telegraphed Lawrence to ask him to do all in his power to prevent them being used against Ibn Saud. Lawrence refused to take the matter seriously, reporting that only one of the machines had been assembled, that it was not capable of sustained flight, and that the pilot was 'leaving the country' in order to avoid the King's wrath.

The talks dragged on. Meanwhile a crisis had developed in Trans-Jordania: Abdullah was proving incapable of firm leadership, and had even asked to be allowed to retire to London. Lawrence was asked to wind up his negotiations as soon as possible and to proceed to Amman to assess the situation there. In his final reports from Jeddah to the Foreign Office, Lawrence claimed that the King had gone mad. It seems more likely that Lawrence could no longer cope. Three years later Ibn Saud occupied Mecca. His success was a direct consequence of Lawrence's failure to reach an agreement with Hussein.

On 22 September, Lawrence sailed for Egypt, en route for Trans-Jordania. He described himself as 'bored stiff', 'very tired' and 'a little ill'.[30] Nevertheless, after a brief stay in Cairo, he took the train to Jerusalem for talks with Herbert Samuel. Lawrence had also arranged to meet his mother and brothers in order that they might accompany him when he moved on to visit Abdullah in Trans-Jordania. An odd occasion for a family reunion; there is no record of how long they stayed.

Intelligence reports had led Lawrence to believe that the situation in Trans-Jordania held scant hope for Abdullah's continued leadership. However, upon his arrival in Amman he found the situation better than he had expected, and reported that, if properly supported, Abdullah's regime could be held together. He maintained that the problem had arisen because of (1) a failure to recognize, and compensate for the weaknesses of Abdullah as a leader; (2) local suspicions about British policy towards Zionists; (3) agitation on the part of the French; (4) failure to supply 'the Arab Reserve Force' – a locally recruited militia set up by the British and commanded by F. G. Peake, who had seen action with Lawrence in the closing days of the war – with weapons; (5) the appalling state of the small British force in the country.

Lawrence sent a long despatch to the Colonial Office emphasizing several of these points, and a small British armoured car unit in Amman did not escape his scathing humour:

> There were two drivers and two gunners – not enough to man the cars or fight the guns, though in this case it was no matter since there were no gun belts, no ammunition, no gun spares. Of the two drivers, one was a 'second driver', intended to take over in an emergency. How good he is I do not know. The first driver who is supposed to be qualified, can drive the car forward but is not good at reversing.[31]

Lawrence worked frantically during October and early November. Using similar techniques to those he had developed during the war, including liberal dispensation of cash, he succeeded in re-establishing Abdullah's Government in six weeks and at the relatively small cost of £100,000. He had transformed a situation which had looked hopeless. It was a triumph of pure will, and just as his failure to resolve the situation in the Hejaz was to have lasting results, so did his success in Trans-Jordania make a permanent contribution to the history of the Middle East. Abdullah was to remain in control through the many vicissitudes of his country, becoming the first King of Jordan after the Second World War. Though he was assassinated in 1951 by a follower of the former Mufti of Jerusalem, Amin el Husseini – who had accused Abdullah of deceiving his own people and being a British puppet – he was succeeded by his son and subsequently his grandson, the present King Hussein of Jordan, who as a small boy had been accompanying his grandfather when he was shot down.

In spite of his success, Lawrence was ill and extremely depressed. Realizing that he could not go on for much longer, he arranged for his replacement by Harry St John Philby who, ironically, had been acting as British Adviser to Ibn Saud.

There was a brief hand-over period. Philby, who was impressed by Lawrence's 'intensely practical, yet unbusinesslike methods', noted in his diary that all Lawrence handed over to him was 'a few documents [he had destroyed most of the embarrassing material] . . . and a small sheet of paper containing his accounts for the expenditure of about £100,000 during his short term of office. One item of £10,000 was simply written off as "lost or mislaid".'[32]

Lawrence had one final commission in Arabia. Having persuaded Abdullah to sign a treaty recognizing (among other things) Jewish colonization of Palestine, Lawrence returned to Jeddah to make a show of asking Hussein to endorse it. It must have come as little surprise that the King refused to co-operate. Lawrence did not labour the point, and started his journey home to England, arriving by early December.

But he still could not rest. Dissatisfied with the second draft of *The Seven Pillars of Wisdom*, he spent the winter working on the third version. As it neared completion, he arranged with *The Oxford Times* to have eight copies printed, five of which still exist, one in the Bodleian Library.

Lawrence had wanted to leave his job at the Colonial Office but Churchill persuaded him to stay on until July 1922. His parting remark was that he was quit of the Arabian affair 'with clean hands'. By now, it was obvious to his closest friends that his mental health had finally broken down. But the cure that he had devised for himself appeared as yet another self-inflicted ordeal. He joined the ranks of the RAF.

16 Aircraftman Ross and Trooper Shaw

It would be difficult to conceive of anything that could have better confirmed, or was more likely to draw attention to Lawrence's reputation as a mysterious eccentric, than his decision to subjugate himself to the coarseness and petty discipline of the RAF barrack room. Although, as his friends have noted, he was adept at concealing the full extent of his psychological problems, he realized he could no longer disguise his inner turmoil and that he was losing control. He hoped that the radical change to his life-style might bring to an end his agonizing confusion. He was still in search of an identity, he desperately wanted to belong, and he had been attracted for some time to the idea of service in the ranks. It was, as he himself noted, the modern alternative to a monastery. It offered a means of escape – escape from responsibility, from women and from the Frankenstein monster of his own fame. He looked forward to the discipline, the tightness of the life, as a means to rest his mind and to regenerate himself. He told Robert Graves that he wanted to become ordinary, to put himself on a common level with other men. The RAF would offer him a chance of a 'brain-sleep'. He predicted he would come out less 'odd' than when he went in.[1]

His choice of the RAF rather than any other Service presents no mystery. He had long been excited by the idea of manned flight and the speed and freedom which it offered. During the war he had clocked up as many flying hours as possible, although he never qualified as a pilot. At the Cairo Conference of 1921, Lawrence had mentioned his idea of joining the Royal Air Force to his fellow-delegate Trenchard, but added, apparently in jest, that he would not be interested in a career as an officer.

In January 1922, when Lawrence was still working at the Colonial Office, he wrote to Trenchard specifically asking to enlist in the ranks, explaining that his main reason was to find material for a book. The Chief of Air Staff was surprised at the request (he appears to have forgotten the conversation in Cairo). Although he disapproved of the idea, he felt an obligation towards Lawrence and agreed to help on condition that Churchill also gave his approval. But Winston also disapproved. He thought the idea a terrible waste and refused Lawrence's initial application to resign, but faced with his friend's determination, he eventually gave the necessary sanction on the understanding that Lawrence would stay on at the Colonial Office until July. It says much for Lawrence's powers of persuasion that he managed to secure the help of both Trenchard and Churchill in making the strange metamorphosis from Colonel to Aircraftman.

On 16 August 1922, Trenchard sent a memo to Air Vice-Marshal Oliver Swann, his senior personnel officer, who was a reluctant conspirator in Lawrence's secret enlistment in the RAF:

> It is hereby approved that Colonel T. E. Lawrence be permitted to join the Royal Air Force as an Aircraft Hand under the alias of
>
> John Hume Ross
> AC 2 No. 352087.
>
> He is taking this step to learn what is the life of an airman. On receipt of any communication from him through any channel, asking for his release, orders are to be issued for his discharge forthwith without formality.[2]

Two weeks later, Lawrence arrived at the RAF recruiting office in Henrietta Street, Covent Garden. He was expecting his enlistment to be a mere formality, and he had been told to seek out a Flight Lieutenant Dexter who had been briefed to admit 'J. H. Ross' without fuss. However, things went drastically wrong. Suffering from an acute attack of nerves, Lawrence was brought before another officer, Captain* W. E. Johns (later to become famous as author of the Biggles Books). Captain Johns asked to see both references and birth certificate. Lawrence was flustered but left to fetch, or rather to forge, them. In the meantime Johns, whose suspicions had been aroused, checked with Somerset House and found out that no J. H. Ross existed. When Lawrence returned he was confronted with this information and told to leave the building. He made his way to the Air Ministry, and returned to Henrietta Street with an official messenger carrying specific orders to enlist J. H. Ross without further delay.

Things still went wrong. Lawrence's mental and physical health were at their lowest ebb, and the RAF refused to pass him fit, although he does not make this clear in the account of his 'medical' in *The Mint*. He does, however, describe how one of the doctors commented that 'Ross' had 'Nerves like a rabbit',[3] ordered him to turn around and bend over, and then noticed scars on his back which looked as if they were the result of a whipping.

'Hullo, what the hell's those marks? Punishment?' Lawrence replied: 'No, Sir, more like persuasion, Sir, I think.'[4]

In *The Mint*, Lawrence claimed that the doctors were willing to overlook this (although he admits flushing, apparently with embarrassment). Having drawn the reader's attention to the unusual marks, Lawrence does not confirm that they were caused by a flogging. Captain Johns, who also saw

*For some years after the creation of the Royal Air Force in April 1918 (by the amalgamation of the old Royal Flying Corps and Royal Naval Air Service) many officers and NCOs in the new Force retained their former military ranks.

them, later wrote that they were in his opinion the scars of punishment, but the real question is whether they were in fact inflicted at Deraa or during a more recent incident.

Lawrence was also suffering from malnutrition, and was only enlisted when Captain Johns called in an outside doctor to sign the necessary forms. Johns now knew Ross's true identity and had been threatened that he would get his 'bowler hat' if he failed to get Lawrence accepted.[5]

Lawrence was posted to the RAF depot at Uxbridge where he spent two months undergoing a normal recruit's basic training – the actual course was considerably longer, and it appears that he pulled strings to gain an early transfer. Lawrence left a graphic though not entirely accurate account of his experiences at Uxbridge in *The Mint*. He described the period at the depot as both humiliating and brutal, and it is clear that, physically, he found it hard going. Although he claims to have been – and indeed sometimes tried to be – just another recruit, he seems to have been unable to resist the temptation to use his extraordinary and supposedly secret status to get special treatment. According to his squadron commander, G. F. 'Stiffy' Breeze, within days of arriving at Uxbridge, Lawrence requested an interview. At this point, Breeze was unaware of Aircraftman Ross's true identity, although he claims that he had been warned by the Sergeant Major that he was 'a real troublemaker'. Breeze described their first meeting thus: 'Ross twisted and turned like a ballet dancer, kept looking at me shyly and with a broad grin and then said (looking at the floor), "I suppose you know who I am?"'[6]

Breeze did not, to which Lawrence replied, 'I think they should have told you who I really am.' Without revealing his true identity, he went on to demand a room away from the other recruits that he could use for writing. Breeze explained that he had 1,100 recruits on the square and that it was not possible to grant a request of that sort. He said Ross could go to the NAAFI where there was an excellent writing room.[7]

Breeze said that Lawrence was soon back before him to face a series of minor disciplinary charges, becoming so persistent an offender that he was recommended for discharge. Breeze later wrote to Richard Aldington:

> I had the perisher under his assumed name, under my direct command. I tried to get him out three times until I was ordered to Headquarters and partially told the reasons for his recruitment. For years I had been trying to debunk him but was held down.[8]

The Mint, which was not published until after Breeze's death, paints a gruesome and degrading picture of the RAF depot at Uxbridge and, despite its omissions, is an effective condemnation of the military method which seeks to break all men to a lowest common denominator. Lawrence's attitude towards his fellow-recruits is ambiguous. He was both attracted to, and repelled by, their animality. He drew special attention to the sadism of NCOs and officers, and described in particular the malevolent personality of a corporal with a VC. Lawrence contrasted the sexual naïveté of his barrack-mates with their vulgarity. He also drew attention to the sexual undertones of discipline:

> I have been before at depots, and have seen or overseen the training of many men: but this our treatment is rank cruelty . . . There is a glitter in their faces when we sob for breath; and evident through their clothes is that tautening of the muscles (and once the actual rise of sexual excitement) which betrays that we are being hurt not for our good, but to gratify a passion. I do not know if all see this: our hut is full of innocents, who have not been sharpened by my penalty of witnessing:— who have not laid their wreath of agony to induce:— the orgasm of man's vice.[9]

The sexual theme runs throughout *The Mint*. At one point Lawrence implies that he is a virgin and that 'six out of ten enlisted men share my ignorance despite their flaming talk', adding:

> . . . if the perfect partnership, indulgence with a living body, is as brief as the solitary act, then the climax is indeed no more than a convulsion, a razor-edge of time, which palls so on return that the temptation flickers out into the indifference of tired disgust once a blue moon, when nature compels it.[10]

The main theme of the book, which the sexual references reinforce, is degradation. One chapter, entitled the Shit Cart, describes in detail the clearing out of slops from the cook-house[11]. Like the *Seven Pillars*, *The Mint* appears obsessed with the putrefaction of organic matter; but it has its comic interludes. During a kit inspection, an officer noticed a book in Danish among Lawrence's possessions: 'Oh, you read Danish: why did you join the Air Force?' Ross replied, 'I think I had a mental break-down, sir.' On another occasion, the following exchange took place with an aggressive NCO. 'Short-arse, you there, Ross, what's your bleedin' monaker:— what d'you know?' Lawrence sprang to attention, saying, 'Sergeant.' 'I arst you a question, you little cunt.' Lawrence replied, 'Well, Sergeant, specifically of course we can know nothing – unqualified – but like the rest of us, I've fenced my life with a scaffolding of more or less speculative hypothesis.' He was not called out again for public sport.

Lawrence may have over-emphasized his hardships at Uxbridge. As one recruit who was there at the same time put it:

> The drill and discipline were easy compared with life at many boarding schools, child's play by Army standards and baby's stuff compared with Commando training in the Second World War. Ex-Colonel Lawrence couldn't take it . . . Lawrence's great achievement was to be an officer and a ranker at the same time. He over-awed his comrades, frightened sergeants, made squadron leaders feel uncomfortable and patronised the Air Council.[12]

In November 1922, Lawrence was suddenly posted to the RAF school of photography at Farnborough, possibly at his own request, as he later wrote to Air Vice-Marshal Swann to thank him for the transfer. But his stay at Farnborough was to be a short one. His identity had become an open secret, and the Station Commander found the whole situation prejudicial to good discipline. Nevertheless, the Secretary of State for Air, acting apparently on Trenchard's advice, approved Lawrence's continued service, but when the story finally broke to the Press, his position became intolerable. Lawrence claimed that a 'beastly' officer had leaked his identity to the *Daily Express* for £30. Whether or not that was true, the newspaper broke the story on 27 December 1922, in a succession of headlines as was the fashion of the day:

'UNCROWNED KING' AS PRIVATE SOLDIER
LAWRENCE OF ARABIA

FAMOUS WAR HERO BECOMES A PRIVATE

SEEKING PEACE

OPPORTUNITY TO WRITE BOOK

Three weeks later, Lawrence was discharged from the Air Force, but – astonishingly – this did not end his career in the ranks. Within six weeks of leaving Farnborough he had enlisted as a private in the Tank Corps.

His service in the Air Force had not interfered with his literary and other activities. He acquired a motor-cycle on which he made frequent (and probably illegal) excursions to London, kept up his diary and worked on an abridgement of the *Seven Pillars*, which was to be published by Jonathan Cape. In the meantime, Lawrence had received eight copies of the full text printed by *The Oxford Times* in newspaper style, but he was still dissatisfied. He made constant alterations and sought criticism from his friends – although it was really encouragement that he needed. Earlier that year, in March, he had been introduced to George Bernard Shaw by Sidney Cockerell, and this led to Lawrence's deep and lasting friendship not only with the playwright but also with his wife Charlotte. They came to love him like a son. Lawrence shared many of his most personal secrets with Charlotte in a long and intimate correspondence which began in 1922 (Charlotte herself evidently had sexually related problems, remaining a virgin for the forty years she lived with her husband). George Bernard Shaw also had more in common with Lawrence than might be noticed at first glance. He was a rebel. He was a writer. He was a proud Irishman, a lover of speed, who had been both a pedal and motor-cycling enthusiast. Like Lawrence, he was a vegetarian, and they shared not only a hatred of the unnecessary waste of life in both war and blood sports, but also a paradoxical fascination with the military. They had a common attitude towards sex, which was, to quote Anthony West, 'a dissipation of vital forces', they were both brilliant, wilful men whose natures tended towards the ascetic, and they were both born actors and accomplished self-publicists.

In August Lawrence had sent one of the copies of *Seven Pillars* to Shaw with a characteristically self-deprecating letter.

> My real wish is to ask if you will read, or try to read, a book which I have written . . . I have very little money and do not wish to publish it . . . To my astonishment, after peace came I found I was myself the sole person who knew what had happened in Arabia during the war: and the only literate person in the Arab Army. So it

> became a professional duty to record what happened . . . In my case, I have, I believe, taken refuge in second-hand words: I mean, I think I've borrowed expressions and adjectives and ideas from everybody I have ever read, . . . it's long-winded, and pretentious, and dull to the point where I can no longer bear to look at it myself. I chose that moment to have it printed!
>
> You'll wonder, why if all this is true (and I think it is) I want any decent person . . . to read it. Well, it's because it is history, and I'm shamed for ever if I am the sole chronicler of an event, and fail to chronicle it: and yet unless what I've written can be made better I'll burn it. My own disgust with it is so great that I no longer believe it worth trying to improve (or possible to improve). If you read it or part of it and came to the same conclusion, you would give me courage to strike the match: whereas now I distrust my own judgement, and it seems cruel to destroy a thing on which I have worked my hardest for three years.[13]

He had not received Shaw's judgment by the time he joined the Tank Corps. Once again he changed his name, but this time, evidently influenced by his friendship with G.B.S. and Charlotte, he adopted their name. He made the change official by deed-poll, and Aircraftman Ross became Trooper Shaw, T.E., No. 7875698.

Trooper Shaw was posted to the Royal Tank Corps Depot, Bovington, Dorset on 12 March 1923. The peace-time ranks of the Army struck him, at least initially, as utterly base, populated by society's rejects, desperate men devoid of hope and full of aggression. Ever in conflict with himself, Lawrence was unable to accept the status of a normal recruit, even had he wished to; his age (thirty-three), his height, and his accent set him apart. He would always be, as George Bernard Shaw noted, 'a most embarrassingly uncommon soldier'.

Lawrence had not arrived at Bovington Camp alone. He had taken with him a large and expensive motor-bike and a young (eighteen years old) Scot – John Bruce. The evidence is not complete (a concerted effort has been made for many years to suppress it), but it appears that he had hired Bruce as some sort of part-time general factotum in 1921 or 1922, putting him on a small retainer on the understanding that he should be available when required. Bruce stated to *The Sunday Times* that at one of his first meetings with Lawrence he was told by his future employer: 'What I'm looking for . . . is someone like you, young, strong and alert who can be trusted with highly confidential personal matters, and to do what he is told without question. He should be able to look after himself, probably others too.'[14]

Having accepted the job, Bruce was initially asked to do little more than post a few letters. No greater demands were made of him until after Lawrence's expulsion from the RAF, and his decision to join the ranks of the Army. In order to encourage Bruce to enlist with him, Lawrence now expanded a fantasy, the seeds of which had been sown some time before. Lawrence told the young Scot that he had not willingly chosen to abase himself in the ranks; rather, it had been forced upon him by a distant but sinisterly powerful relation to whom he owed money, and to whom he referred as the 'Old Man'; if he did not comply with the Old Man's demands, he would be ruined. All this was complete fiction, but Bruce claimed he accepted the story and, at a meeting in London, agreed to join the Army too. He made one condition – should he seek discharge at any time, it must be available without fuss. This was agreed, and Bruce went up to Aberdeen to organize his own affairs. By arrangement with Lawrence, he was officially inducted into the Army at a recruiting office in Scotland, and then returned to the south to meet up with Lawrence so that they could proceed together to Bovington. Bruce wrote of their arrival that they 'entered the guard room together at the Royal Tank Corps depot . . . and were put into Hut 12 in "B" Company, there were already nine chaps there and a tough looking bunch they were too.' Bruce was soon called upon to act as Lawrence's bodyguard:

> It was the bad ones I had to keep my eyes on, especially the drinkers, who were constantly touching for money, it's strange how easy they can pick their mark, but I had already told Lawrence to refuse all borrowers money, this led to trouble . . . I came into the hut and heard a fellow giving Lawrence a mouth full of filth because he refused to give him a pound. I jumped him there and then and one hell of a fight took place . . .[15]

Lawrence's motive for asking Bruce to enlist with him turned out to be more than a simple need for support or protection. Later, as we shall see, Bruce was persuaded to administer a series of ritualized floggings. A few weeks after arriving at Bovington, Lawrence wrote to Edward Garnett: 'The Army is unspeakable: more solidly animal than I believed Englishmen could be. I hate them, and the life here: and am sure that it's good medicine for me.'[16]

Good medicine or not, the basic course of training at Bovington lasted sixteen weeks, and Lawrence found it hard going. Bruce helped him but endeavoured to stay in the background as much as possible. Lawrence did manage to make a few new friends, in particular a Corporal Alex Dixon, who shared his love of literature. It did not take long for Trooper Shaw's real identity to become known, but Lawrence gradually overcame the initial suspicions of the other soldiers, and became accepted as 'Broughie Shaw', a nickname derived from his much-admired (and no doubt envied) Brough Superior motorbike. After completing the recruits' course, Lawrence was assigned to a relatively soft job in the Quartermaster's Stores. By now the British and American Press had discovered his new hiding-place, but this time there were few important consequences. When reporters made inquiries around Bovington Camp, they got little information from the soldiers who rallied to protect 'one of their own'.

Like Churchill, George Bernard Shaw was irritated by the waste of having Lawrence serving as a private soldier. Many of Lawrence's friends, including Shaw, had been told by T.E. that one of his primary motives for entering the ranks was financial. Although we have already seen that there were other more important reasons, money was a very real problem, especially when one considers the cost of his obsession with *Seven Pillars*, the upkeep of his motor-bike, and his undeniable generosity. G.B.S. established from Lawrence that £300 per year would keep him comfortably, and mounted a campaign on his behalf (though without his knowledge) to get him a State pension or some sort of acceptable employment. The distinguished playwright prepared a letter to the new Prime Minister, Baldwin, but before sending it, asked D. G. Hogarth to comment on its contents. As Stanley Weintraub has quoted, Hogarth replied:

> The fact is that money weighs much less with him than his mode of life. I cannot conceive any Government post, such as the P.M. could offer, which L. would accept, or if accepted, retain. He begins at once to talk of 'moral prostitution' and quits . . . Lawrence is not normal in many ways and it is extraordinally difficult to do anything for him! In some measure the life of letters is best suited to him. He will not work in any sort of harness unless this is padlocked onto him. He enlisted in order to have the padlocks rivetted on.[17]

Undeterred, Bernard Shaw made his appeal to Baldwin at the beginning of the summer of 1923:

> The fact remains that he is serving as a private soldier for his daily bread: and however much his extraordinary character may be accountable for this, it strikes all who know about it as a scandal that should be put an end to by some means. They feel that the private soldier business is a shocking tomfoolery and are amazed to find that Lawrence is not in a position of a pensioned commanding officer in dignified private circumstances.[18]

Nothing came of this but Lawrence did later find out about the appeal and told Hogarth, surprisingly, that he might well have accepted the pension had it come through. He had been touched by Bernard Shaw's efforts on his behalf and did not criticize him for his intervention, though later he dissuaded his friend from embarking on a second attempt.

The Shaws played an important role in the development of Lawrence's career as an author. Their influence ensured that the typeset manuscript of *Seven Pillars* evolved into a more widely available book. Before G.B.S. found time to finish reading it, he sent encouraging notes to Lawrence, who was eager for an opinion, but told him to be patient. Charlotte, who read the 300,000 words before her husband, showered Lawrence with praise and insisted that he must publish a general edition. This advice was soon repeated by G.B.S. who eventually helped to edit the book – the form of the so-called 'subscriber's edition of 1926' was much influenced by him. Bernard Shaw's main project for 1923 and 1924, the play *Saint Joan*, seems to have been influenced by his simultaneous work on Lawrence's *Seven Pillars* – several authorities have noted that aspects of Lawrence's character were shared by Shaw's martyred heroine – and he would write a play specifically based on Lawrence, *Too True to be Good*.

Under pressure from the Shaws and other friends, including Hogarth,

Lawrence finally decided to go ahead with a limited private edition of *Seven Pillars*. He searched for a retreat where he might write undisturbed. One mile north of the camp, surrounded by clumps of rhododendrons, was a small disused cottage known as Cloud's Hill. It was owned by a distant relation on his father's side. It has never been made clear whether this was only coincidence. Nevertheless, he was able to rent Cloud's Hill for a nominal sum, and rebuilt it with the aid of pioneer Sergeant Knowles, who had become a friend and who lived conveniently opposite the cottage. Cloud's Hill was redesigned to need a minimum of upkeep. Apart from a mass of books, a gramophone and a large collection of records, there was little furniture. Lawrence slept in a sleeping-bag to avoid using sheets (he required two sleeping-bags, one marked 'meum', the other 'teum'). He never built a kitchen but water could be boiled and bread toasted over the cottage's open fire; his preferred foods involved no preparation; he would often eat directly from the cans because the containers could be thrown away after use. Sometimes he would have his meals across the road with the Knowleses.

Whenever there was an opportunity, he would jump on his Brough at Bovington and drive the mile to Cloud's Hill. He would entertain his fellow-soldiers at his new home, sometimes with friends from his other life. Both Bernard Shaw and E. M. Forster shared tea with the troopers and were pleasantly surprised. G.B.S. commented on his visit with friendly sarcasm that Private Shaw, amid his comrades, still 'looked very like Colonel Lawrence with several aides-de-camp'.[19] Having entered the Army in a trough of despair, Lawrence gradually came to terms with the existence, though he could never rid himself of his attacks of depression which, on more than one occasion, led him to contemplate suicide.

As well as giving him somewhere to write, the cottage provided the privacy Lawrence required to play out his flagellation fantasies. This is a complex area and the evidence still has many gaps. It appears (and this is the view confirmed by Lawrence's brother) that he felt the need for punishment as a means to purge his soul of carnal desire. It also seems possible that Lawrence may have felt guilty because he was again beginning to enjoy life. Whatever the motive, Lawrence began writing letters to John Bruce, purporting to come from the 'Old Man', containing instructions that 'Ted' should be beaten by Bruce, who was then to report back in writing, using Lawrence as the postbox, on his victim's conduct during the sessions. Bruce complied, subtly encouraged by his older friend, who again professed fear of not following the Old Man's orders. John Bruce writes of the floggings: 'There were nine during [the period] 1923 and 1935 . . . The first was in 1923 in his cottage Cloud's Hill. A birch was used, and he got twelve over his trousers.'[20]

Bruce sent a report via Lawrence to the Old Man, who was not satisfied and gave orders that the punishment should be repeated on the bare skin. This took place a week later. There is evidence, independent of Bruce, that the floggings continued periodically (with gaps because of service abroad) until Lawrence's death. Lawrence kept a sketchy diary recording the number of strokes he received on each occasion. Dr John Mack has obtained documentary evidence that during three of the beatings by Bruce, another 'service companion' of Lawrence's was present who noted that they followed an exact ritual and were 'severe enough to produce a seminal emission'.[21] There is further evidence that Lawrence may have involved other young men in his rituals of self-punishment. During 1924, Bruce exercised his option to leave the Army and, though in good health, obtained a discharge on medical grounds with Lawrence's assistance. He did not abandon Lawrence entirely but took a job in a garage in near-by Bournemouth.

Any further consideration of these episodes can only lie in the field of conjecture, where the reader's interpretation of the facts that have been presented is likely to be as reliable as anybody else's. Bruce's testimony cannot be relied upon entirely. However, it is important to note that A. W. Lawrence, while rejecting some ot Bruce's claims, admits the essential fact that his brother invented the myth of the Old Man and persuaded Bruce to beat him.

In November 1923, Lawrence wrote to Eric Kennington saying, 'The Army is muck, stink, and a desolate abomination',[23] yet it is clear that his attitude towards his comrades and Bovington itself was gradually changing. Six weeks after writing to Kennington, he could write to Bernard Shaw:

> People come into the Army often, not because it is brutal and licentious, but because they haven't done very well in the fight of daily living, and want to be spared the responsibility of ordering for themselves their homes and food and clothes and work – or even the intensity of their work. Regard it as an asylum for the little-spirited.[24]

Another literary connection which played an important role from early 1923 was his friendship with Thomas Hardy and his wife. This was a very different relationship from the one with Bernard and Charlotte Shaw. The Hardys, to whom Lawrence had been given an introduction by Robert Graves, were very elderly. Hardy himself was over eighty, and Lawrence approached him from the start with reverence. He found complete peace at their home, Max Gate, a villa designed by Hardy himself on the outskirts of Dorchester. Indeed, he enjoyed his visits so much that he denied himself the pleasure of returning as often as he would have liked. When invited to spend the Christmas of 1923 at Max Gate, he refused, explaining to a friend that 'It's not good to be too happy often'.[25]

In March 1924, Lawrence wrote to Trenchard, enquiring optimistically about the possibility of returning to the Air Force: 'I've served exactly a year in the Army now, and been found amenable to discipline.'[26]

Trenchard tried to persuade the new Labour Secretary of State for Air (the first Labour Government had just come into office) to consider Lawrence's reentry, but without success. As an alternative, the Chief of Air Staff offered Lawrence the opportunity to complete the Official War History of the Air Force as the author of the first volume, *The War in the Air*, Sir Walter Raleigh (a descendant of the famous author/explorer, and thus distantly related to

Lawrence) had just died. Lawrence did not accept. His major concern throughout 1924 was *The Seven Pillars of Wisdom*.

He decided to offer the book to a hundred odd subscribers at thirty guineas a copy, but it soon became clear that the money so acquired would not even cover the production costs. Lawrence wanted the book to be the acme both of literature and of the bookmaker's craft. The original estimated cost of production, £3000, turned out to be £10,000 short. To meet the cost, he arranged that a banker and former wartime comrade, Robin Buxton, would finance the book's manufacture, and Lawrence put up the royalties from the still unpublished abridgement, *Revolt in the Desert*, as security.

In October, Bernard Shaw sent back the *Oxford Times* version of *Seven Pillars* to Lawrence, completely re-punctuated and with many detailed criticisms. 'Confound you and your book,' he wrote. 'You are no more to be trusted with a pen than a child with a torpedo.'[27]

Lawrence was not content just to work on *Seven Pillars*. He would dash to London on his motorbike. Sometimes, dressed in khaki, he would attend dinner parties with the most influential political and literary figures of the day. Despite his attempt to reject it, Lawrence remained attracted to power. He somehow also found time during 1924 to translate, from the French, *The Forest Giant*, and this was published later in the year. With his many literary commitments, Lawrence engaged a professional agent, Raymond Savage, who remained his representative until Lawrence's death.

Lawrence's ambiguous attitude to his own fame is emphasized by the fact that only a few months after engaging Savage, he allowed him to publish an article in an American periodical, headlined 'LAWRENCE OF ARABIA IN NEW DISGUISE'; the subtitle ran: 'Adventurous Archaeologist who rallied the Desert Tribes for the Allies in the World War Serves now as a Private in the British Tank Corps, having refused High Appointments.' The article publicly admitted that Lawrence had been caught and flogged by the Turks.[28]

In 1925, Lawrence began to renew his appeals to re-enter the Air Force with desperate urgency. He asked his well-placed friends for their help. Finally, in June, following the latest rejection by the RAF, he threatened suicide. These histrionics won the day. Bernard Shaw wrote in a memo, which arrived on the Prime Minister's desk, 'There is a possibility of an appalling scandal, especially after Lowell Thomas's book,'[29] which had just been released in England. Through a concerted effort by John Buchan, George Bernard Shaw and Trenchard, Lawrence's transfer back to the RAF was finally approved, despite the opposition of the Minister for Air. Lawrence had manipulated the system yet again. Exit Trooper Shaw, enter Aircraftman Shaw.

NEWS CHRONICLE, Friday, May 11, 1934

News Chronicle

WEATHER: Fair and warm in most districts. RADIO: Page Nineteen

No. 27,472 LONDON FRIDAY, MAY 11, 1934 MANCHESTER ONE PENNY

LAWRENCE OF ARABIA TALKS (*Exclusive*)

Bitter Cry: "I Want to be Left Alone"

No Interest in the Desert War

Banned from Every Country Because of Espionage Suspicion

Aircraftman Shaw's Confessions to the "News Chronicle"

Lawrence of Arabia—half a dozen years ago.

By Our Special Correspondent
J. M. PUGHE

SOUTHAMPTON, Thursday.

TO-NIGHT I interviewed the ghost of Lawrence of Arabia.

A fair-haired, grim-jawed man, Aircraftman Shaw, living near here in modest lodgings, told me in 50 minutes of his bitter disillusionment and his resolve that Lawrence of Arabia is dead and that his memory shall, so far as he is able, never be resurrected.

This quiet, cultured man sat on his bed and told me that the spectre of Lawrence of Arabia has haunted him, followed him relentlessly for 15 years, made him a pariah of the nations of the world.

"No country will have me," he said. "France, Germany, Turkey, all of them refuse me a passport visa. I have been deported from India and sacked from the Air Force because of my fame—no, call it infamy or notoriety.

"I am banned from every country in the world because I am supposed to be a secret service agent. I am nothing of the kind, and I never have been. Next year I leave the Air Force. I do not want to, but I cannot sign on for another 20 years—I am too old. The Air Force would not have me. It is still a young man's game.

"I Will Not Write"

What I am going to do after that I do not know. I do not intend to soil my hands by writing sensational stories of my alleged exploits during the war. I have only done it once and simply because there have to be official records; but apart from that one omission I think my hands are comparatively clean."

Aircraftman Shaw smiled wanly and he looked at his hands. They were soiled. They were the hands of a mechanic, greasy, dirty.

"No reputable firm," he went on, "will have me because of my reputation. I will not entertain any offer from any firm that wants to make capital out of my reputation."

I had called on Aircraftman Shaw to ask him his views on the situation in Arabia, where the two Arab Kings, the powerful Ibn Saud and the Imam of Yemen, are at war.

"I am not interested in Arabia," he said bluntly. "I do not know anything about the situation in Arabia. I am 15 years behind the times. I have not been there for 15 years, in spite of reports to the contrary.

"As a matter of fact I am in the Air Force, and I cannot even if I could or would write a line about Arabia. King's Regulations definitely forbid it. I was nine months in Arabia and I do not know anything about Arabia to-day. Though probably I know a little more than the average man who has been there only nine days or so."

"In any case what is all the bother about?"

Aden is Safe—

"What about Aden?" I asked.

Mr. Shaw bluntly replied:

"Aden is safe. When I was at the Colonial Office I put Aden in the care of cars and aeroplanes. What use would be an army? No use at all. One only has to dig it out. It is always the same.

"I know nothing of the Imam of Yemen beyond the fact that he or his family has been there for a thousand years. I do not know Ibn Saud. I hape never known him, never met him. I have no interest in Arabia to-day. I happen to be interested only in aeroplanes and in boats."

Aircraftman Shaw has been for months working at Mr. Scott Paine's British Power Boat Works at Hythe. There he has been carrying out tests on behalf of the Air Ministry. "I am in the Air Force," Aircraftman Shaw explained, "because I cannot afford an aeroplane. I don't think I will ever be able to. The Air Force provides me with the opportunity of working with machines that cost fortunes."

I asked this strange, young-old man why he had not risen from the ranks. "Because," he said, quietly, "officers only fly the machines. We in the ranks make them and run them, and I am interested in machines, not money or rank."

The Most Bitter Man

Aircraftman Shaw is the most bitter man I have ever met. He is the great unfathomable anomaly. His eyes have a strange sadness that lingers behind the cynical smile that is so often on his lips. Yet he denies that he is unhappy.

"I am not unhappy," he retorted, when I suggested that he was.

"I have a good job," he said. "I like my work on aeroplanes, power boats, machines. It is an ordinary man's job. It gives me pleasure. There is no mystery about me. I am just an ordinary man trying to earn his living in the way that he likes. The mystery

A la Garbo: the reaction of A/C Shaw.

Lawrence – or Shaw – in RAF overalls.

Lawrence and Liddell Hart at Southampton, when Lawrence was working on rescue tenders.

Cloud's Hill: a Greek inscription above the front door translates as 'Why worry?'

Lawrence on Boanerges (like James and John, son of thunder).

Charlotte Shaw in 1905.

The portrait (1919) of Lawrence by Augustus John.

Lawrence at Bridlington, 1935.

Lawrence and the last act.

The pall-bearers representing the various phases of Lawrence's life.

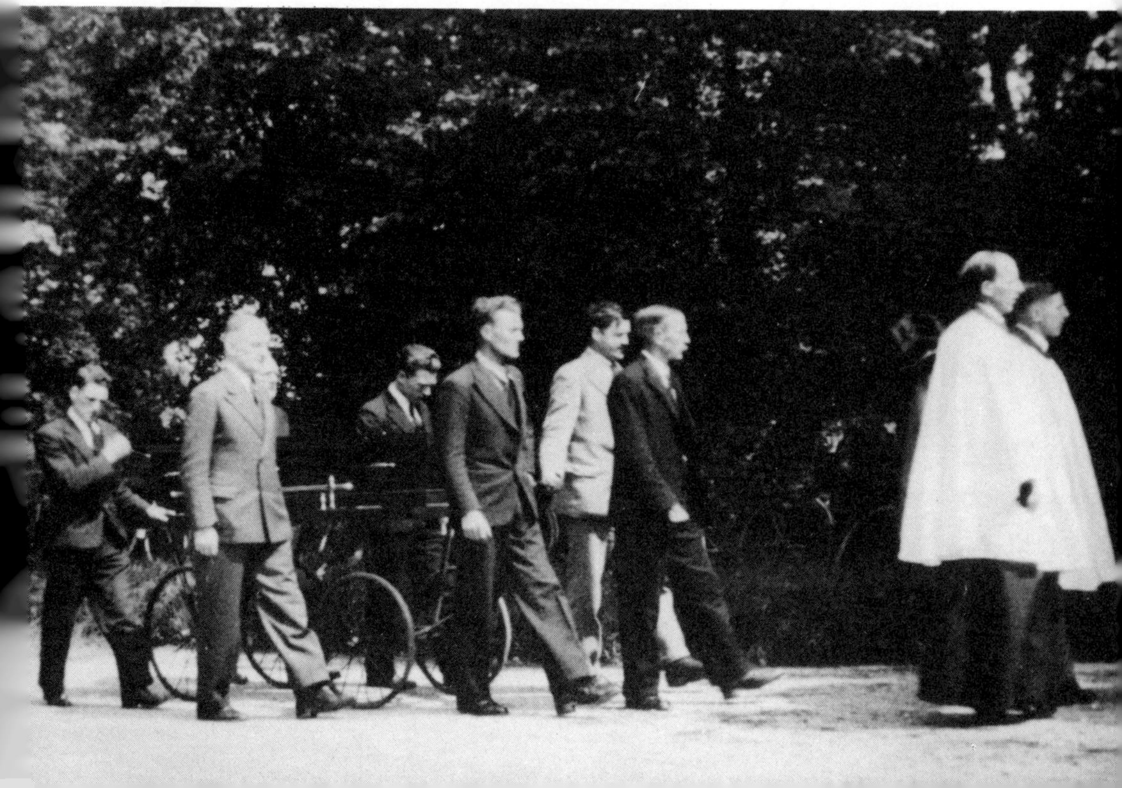

DAILY SKETCH, MONDAY MAY 20, 1935

WHAT 50 YEARS ON STAGE HAS TAUGHT ME—MARIE TEMPEST | WIRELESS: P. 20

DAILY SKETCH

THINGS I HATE BY BERNARD SHAW

No. 8,131 [Registered as a newspaper.] MONDAY, MAY 20, 1935 ONE PENNY

TOO BIG FOR WEALTH AND GLORY

Lawrence the Soldier Dies to Live for Ever

Having lingered for six days, Lawrence of Arabia (Mr T. E. Shaw) died in hospital at Bovington Camp, Dorset, yesterday from injuries received when he crashed with his powerful motor-cycle at Moreton. He was 46. In the year 1914 Lawrence was excavating Hittite ruins near Carchemish on the Euphrates. Two years later he organised and virtually commanded the Arab Army that gave such powerful help to the British campaign in Palestine. In this rôle he became famous the world over as Lawrence of Arabia (right). Scorning notoriety and wealth, he declined an offer of £10,000 to appear in a film.

20 May 1935: front-page notice of a death.

LAWRENCE: THE LAST HOURS

A Tragedy Had He Lived—His Mind Damaged

. P. Knowles, Mr. E. Shaw's batman, otographed yesterday at Wool.

Simple Village Funeral for Uncrowned King of The Desert

HIS OWN WISH

Aircraftman T. E. Shaw—Lawrence of Arabia—is dead.

To-morrow he will be buried—this Uncrowned King of the desert, o of a thousand wartime exploits, the supremely modest man of mystery whose head the Turks set a price of £10,000.

He will lie in a simple grave close to the peaceful village church of oreton, amid the Dorset hills, near the cottage in which he had been living. ere will be no mourning and no flowers—there may not even be a litary escort.

So Lawrence of Arabia will pass imply and quietly, in accordance th his own wishes.

He died at Wool Military Hospital 8 a.m. yesterday—and after his th it was revealed that his overy would have been a greater gedy than his passing.

HT AND SPEECH MAGED

's brain, that brilliant brain that had eived and carried through such tremen- exploits, had been irreparably damaged ast Monday's motor-cycle accident.

was stated last night that had he lived would have regained only partial use of speech and sight.

death, as in life, Lawrence remains a ery. Not until to-morrow, when the est is held at Bovington Camp, Wool, the facts of the tragedy be known.

e King and Queen have been informed of rence's death. His 73-year-old mother not yet know.

th another son, she is steaming down Yangtze river in China. When she reaches ghai she will find a cable awaiting

e crisis of Lawrence's illness was reached on Saturday night.

E. Farquhar Buzzard, Physician in nary to the King, and one of the greatest

G. B. S." AND LAWRENCE

Vhen Mr. Bernard Shaw was told of wrence's death he said (according to iter from Durban): "What about stminster Abbey? His country, which used to give him a small pension, es him at least a stone."

orities on neurology, Mr. H. W. B. Cairns, noted brain specialist, and Dr. Hope e, the lung specialist, dashed to the tal.

Cairns made the journey by car from ome at Arundel, over 100 miles away, in han three hours.

ygen was administered. X-ray photo- s were sent for and Captain C. P. Allen, pecialist who has had the case in hand the first, remained almost continuously s patient's bedside.

ortly before 8.30 a.m. yesterday Captain entered the little hospital waiting-room, friends and others were gathered, and simply: "It is all over now."

n was falling gently as the body, ped in a Union Jack, was borne from ospital to the little slate-roofed mortuary by.

re, in simple state, before an altar on stood a small crucifix. Lawrence of a lay.

wrence—Man of Mysteries: Page 5.)

The lonely road where the fatal accident to Mr. T. E. Shaw occurred.

Frank Fletcher, aged 14, who was cycling with Albert Hargreaves when Lawrence of Arabia came along on a motor-cycle. Both cyclists fell. Hargreaves was injured.—(*D.S.*)

A brief obituary of Lawrence. (Incidentally, Pat Knowles was not *his batman.)*

Lawrence's crashed bike is taken away under military supervision.

Lawrence's grave at Moreton Cemetery.

17 Life on the North-West Frontier

Whether arrangements had been better planned, or fate was proving kinder, the passage from Trooper back to Aircraftman was not a rough one for Lawrence. Once his re-admission had been formerly approved, his formal application for a transfer to the RAF went through without incident, and instructions arrived for Trooper Shaw to proceed to the Air Force base at West Drayton for preliminary documentation and a medical. This time the doctors accepted him without fuss and he was sent on from West Drayton to the training depot at Uxbridge to pick up a new uniform and other kit before being posted to Cranwell – the RAF's Sandhurst. He arrived at the Cadet College on 24 August 1925 and was allocated the next day to B Flight, one of several Flights responsible for servicing the planes in which student pilots were trained.

Aircraftman Shaw's arrival came as something of a shock to the Commandant at Cranwell, Air Commodore A. E. Borton, who had not been forewarned but who had, coincidentally, served in the Hejaz in the Royal Flying Corps and knew Lawrence by sight. The Air Commodore, having come upon his illustrious 'guest' by accident, received him in friendly spirit but could not prevent some of his officers believing (as had happened at Farnborough) that a spy had been put in their midst.[1]

From his first days there, Lawrence reacted favourably to the Cadet College. He made an effort to befriend those he came into contact with and was quickly accepted by his fellow-airmen. He now had the advantage of three years' experience in the ranks, and Cranwell appears to have been a far happier camp than Bovington – although it is dangerous to assume this merely from Lawrence's own writings.

A/C Shaw's duties were chiefly clerical, but whenever the chance arose, he would work on the aeroplanes maintained by other members of his Flight. Similarly, several of the instructing officers, eager to have Lawrence of Arabia as their passenger, would allow him to fly with them when machines needed checking out or when they were not busy with cadets. Lawrence loved aeroplanes. He would even sneak into the hangars to wash them down, not because they needed cleaning or because he had been ordered to, but because he enjoyed it. His genuine enthusiasm for things mechanical is well illustrated by his intimate, and ultimately fatal, relationship with his motorbike

'Boanerges'. He spoke and wrote of his powerful Brough machine as if it were a living being. The following passage is from *The Mint*, Lawrence's RAF diary which he took up again on arriving at Cranwell:

> Boanerges' first glad roar at being alive again nightly jarred the huts of the Cadet College into life. 'There he goes, the noisy bugger', someone would say enviously in every flight. It is part of an airman's profession to be knowing with engines: and a thoroughbred engine is our undying satisfaction. The camp wore the virtue of my Brough like a flower in its cap. Tonight Tug and Dusty came to the step of our hut to see me off. 'Running down to Smoke, perhaps?' jeered Dusty; hitting at my regular game of London and back for tea on fine Wednesday afternoons.
>
> Boa is a top-gear machine, as sweet in that as most single-cylinders in middle. I chug lordly past the guard-room and through the speed limit at no more than sixteen. Round the bend, past the farm, and the way straightens. Now for it. The engine's final development is fifty-two horse-power. A miracle that all this docile strength waits behind one tiny lever for the pleasure of my hand.
>
> Another bend: and I have the honour of one of England's straightest and fastest roads. The burble of my exhaust unwound like a long cord behind me [like a man about to be flogged?]. Soon my speed snapped it . . .[2]

Lawrence went on to describe how, on one occasion, he raced a Bristol fighter along the highway, delighting in his flirt with death and his power over his own machine.

Not surprisingly, Aircraftman Shaw and his motorbike aroused the interest of the civilian police at Cranwell. When one constable stopped him, Lawrence complained to the local superintendent; he was not stopped again. This sort of victory over authority, which he extended to his life in camp, achieved for him the admiration of many of the enlisted men. He appears to have had few of the problems of bullying which he had suffered at Bovington, and was happier at Cranwell than he had been for many years. Nevertheless, he was still desperately confused. John Mack has quoted a letter he wrote to Charlotte Shaw only a month after arriving at the Cadet College. Lawrence wrote that he haunted the company of his fellow-airmen as their 'noise' stopped him thinking:

> . . . Thinking drives me mad, because of the invisible ties about me which limit my moving, my wishing, my imagining. All these bonds I have tied myself, deliberately, wishing to tie myself down beyond the hope or power of movement. And the deliberation, this intention, rests. It is stronger than anything else in me, than everything else put together. So long as there is breath in my body my strength will be exerted to keep my soul in prison, since nowhere else can it exist in safety. The terror of being run away with, in the liberty of power, lies at the back of these many renunciations of my later life. I am afraid, of myself. Is this madness? The trouble tonite [sic] is the reaction against yesterday when I went mad.

Lawrence continued that he was seeking total degradation.

> I long for people to look down on me and despise me, and I am too shy to take the

> filthy steps which would publicly shame me, and put me in their contempt.* I want to dirty myself outwardly, so that my person may properly reflect the dirtiness which it conceals.[3]

Lawrence mentioned in his letters to Charlotte Shaw his conflict with his old life. He had just visited Feisal, who was staying in London as Lord Winterton's guest. Lawrence said that he felt nothing in common with these ghosts of the past. This may, or may not, have been true but he was unlikely to forget his past while he continued to work on *Seven Pillars* as he did throughout 1925 and 1926. This in itself must have proved difficult as Lawrence no longer had the benefit of the sanctuary of Cloud's Hill, although the Dorset cottage was kept up in his absence by Sergeant Knowles. By the spring of 1926, he had at last finished rewriting the book – although he still remained unsatisfied. He was now left with a myriad of problems connected with his private publishing venture. There was also another related task to be completed – the abridgement, to be known as *Revolt in the Desert*. One abridgement, edited by Edward Garnett, was already in existence, but Lawrence did not regard this as suitable and set to work in March 1926 to do the job again. His method was simple. He took a set of printed sheets of *Seven Pillars* and set about them with scissors and India ink. With remarkably little rewriting, he massacred his original text and created an uncontroversial volume some 200 pages shorter. Of the many casualties, the Deraa chapter was the most prominent.

In the summer, anticipating the publicity which would surround the publication of *Seven Pillars*, Lawrence applied (or may have been told to apply) for service abroad. 'Parts of that book of mine are to come out with Cape and Co,' he wrote to T. B. Marson, formerly Trenchard's assistant, 'and people sort of agree that I'd better dodge out of reach of the daily press before that happens.'[4] Lawrence spent the summer and autumn arranging his affairs for what he thought would be a long period of service overseas. In November, he was given a month's leave during which he saw old friends and made his final preparations. On the last day of the month, he wrote to Pat Knowles as if to blame Lowell Thomas rather than *Seven Pillars* for his voluntary exile:

> I wish Lowell T would die a natural death. He has, always quite honestly & with the best possible motives, made life nearly impossible for me. If he had never piped up I'd have been well off & happy now.
>
> I'm rushing madly about (with a crocked knee due to contact with Islington High Street – the bike is a ruin –) in the last 3 days before rejoining at Uxbridge for India. Life is *not good*[5]

Lawrence left Southampton on 7 December 1926, bound for Karachi, one of 1200 passengers aboard the overcrowded troopship *Derbyshire*. Conditions on the ship were not good as, with friendly sarcasm, he informed Edward Marsh (Churchill's private secretary):

*Again, this comment could be a reference to Bruce and the floggings, or perhaps to plans or actual incidents that remain concealed.

> Your improper department has ruled that at sea three airmen can be packed into the airspace of two sailors. Kindly meant, no doubt, to keep us warm and comfortable. But in the Red Sea and the Gulf we grew sick of each other's smell.[6]

Lawrence wrote some notes of his experiences on board the *Derbyshire* which appear to have been intended as an addition for *The Mint* (which, in its published form, ends at Cranwell). They are provisionally titled 'Leaves in the Wind', and convey in explicit terms their author's distaste for the functions of the body, and especially the female body. Here are some of his detailed observations while on guard duty outside lavatories used by the airmen's wives, and of their disgusting condition:

> Wave upon wave of the smell of stabled humanity: the furtive creeping by rushes along the alley way of the women to their latrine, fending themselves from wall to wall with the right arm, while the left held the loosened dress across their body. Belches of gas come back up my throat – hullo, I'll be sick if I stay here for ever . . .[7]

The lavatories become blocked and the smell intolerable but Lawrence volunteers to the guard Commander to do shifts because, he writes, another man has been overcome by the stench. (This excuse is not adequate – rather it is as if he was symbolically completing his degradation.) 'Tactless posting a sentry over the wives defecations,' he writes. 'Tactless and useless all our duties aboard.'[8]

When the Officer of the Guard comes past on a routine inspection, Lawrence brings to his attention that the lavatories are now blocked entirely. There are gruesome details as the officer – an 'ex-naval warrant' risen from the ranks and 'no gentleman' – removes his tunic, rolls up his shirt-sleeves, clears the offending blockage with his bare hand, rolls his sleeve back without washing, puts on his tunic, and moves off as the excrement 'gurgled contentedly' down the now unblocked drain.[9]

At Port Said, Lawrence had the chance to breathe less stagnant air as he spent a day ashore with his old friend Colonel Stewart Newcombe and his son, to whom he had become godfather six years before.

A month after leaving England, Lawrence reached Karachi to take up his posting at the RAF station at Drigh Road, seven miles outside the city, 'a dry hole, on the edge of the Sind Desert'.[10] No accommodation was immediately available and, together with the other men in his draft, he was temporarily quartered in one of several tents on the parade ground. The intake soon moved into barrack rooms, fourteen men apiece, and A/C 338171 distinguished himself by acquiring a small bookcase, a gramophone and an ingenious reading lamp which he constructed from a piece of flexible metal tubing.[11] He never left the camp and commissioned other airmen to buy records for him. He also acquired a blow-lamp and an old tin tub so that he could heat water and have a bath whenever he wanted one.

From general duties, Lawrence was posted to the engine repair shop at

Drigh Road as clerk-in-charge of records (similar work to that he had done at Cranwell). He was, somewhat naturally, extremely good at this relatively undemanding job. He was respected by his fellow-airmen, not only for his evident competence, but also for a willingness to offer advice or assistance whenever it was needed. His Arabian image, though always in the background, did not intrude on his relationship with his peers, who regarded it, or so he claimed, as a 'huge joke'[12] in the distant past. The same can not be said of the officers who were in the difficult position of having Lawrence of Arabia under their command, especially as he maintained, and was known to maintain, a close friendship with the Chief of Air Staff. Even before his identity came out, he proved to be a disruptive influence. For example, his reading light was copied by the other men in his barrack-room, all pirating power from the switch boxes for the room's fans. This did not please the Commanding Officer on his inspection, who ordered that in future no one could drain power from the official system. On his next visit, all the lamps had disappeared except Lawrence's. The CO strode menacingly towards A/C Shaw's bed but, to his fury, discovered that Lawrence's lamp was now powered by battery. What the CO did not discover was that the battery was a dummy; the lamp was still connected to the switchboxes but the wires had been cunningly camouflaged.[13]

Despite frequent attacks of depression, Lawrence claimed he was content in India. The sterility of garrison life satisfied the ascetic side of his personality; there were echoes, not always pleasant, of his time in Arabia. The countryside around Karachi, and later on the North-West Frontier, was not dissimilar to the Hejaz. The letters he wrote in this period, such as are available, reflect the dominant feature of this existence in India – the attempt to lose himself in his obsession for literature and, in particular, his craving to be accepted, if only by himself, as an artist in words. During the two years he spent in India, the distribution of the subscriber's edition of *Seven Pillars* was completed, *Revolt in the Desert* was published, *The Mint* finished, and the translation of the *Odyssey* begun. Lawrence's creative libido must have been stimulated by the fact that he had few other outlets for his energy – his beloved Boanerges he had had to leave behind. Whether Lawrence resorted to flagellation in India is not known.

In March 1927, *Revolt in the Desert*, having been part-serialized during the winter in the *Daily Telegraph*, became generally available, receiving rave reviews. The lucky owners of the subscriber's copy of *Seven Pillars* found that for their initial investment of 30 guineas, they now had a book worth £500 on the open market – a staggering sum in 1927 for a newly published book. The success of the project may well have stimulated Lawrence to begin drafting the notes he had made on his RAF experiences into a book. *The Mint*, like *Seven Pillars* before it, was completed amid an atmosphere of carefully nurtured secrecy. Lawrence had originally intended to give his Uxbridge notes to D. G. Hogarth. However, Hogarth died in November 1927 at the age of seventy-five. His death was a great blow to Lawrence, who later dedicated

The Mint (as the notes became), to Edward Garnett. Lawrence had barely recovered from Hogarth's death when he heard that Thomas Hardy had also died.

Lawrence's position at the large Karachi depot was difficult: at one stage the camp commandant thought he was being informed upon and it is unlikely that Lawrence was able entirely to eradicate the suspicions which his presence often aroused. Then, in the spring of 1928, Lawrence's progress in the ranks was the feature of an article in the *Daily Express*.[14] Lawrence was putting the finishing touches to *The Mint* at the time. He posted it to Edward Garnett in March 1928, and next day he wrote to Trenchard to explain what the book was about and to assure him that it would not be published until after the author's death. Lawrence felt obliged to give Trenchard the chance to read *The Mint* and arranged for him to be supplied with a copy.

Circumstances were gradually accumulating which made Lawrence's continued service in Karachi impossible. During the summer of 1928, he received notification of his transfer to the North-West Frontier. This would lead to a new and completely unexpected Lawrence controversy.

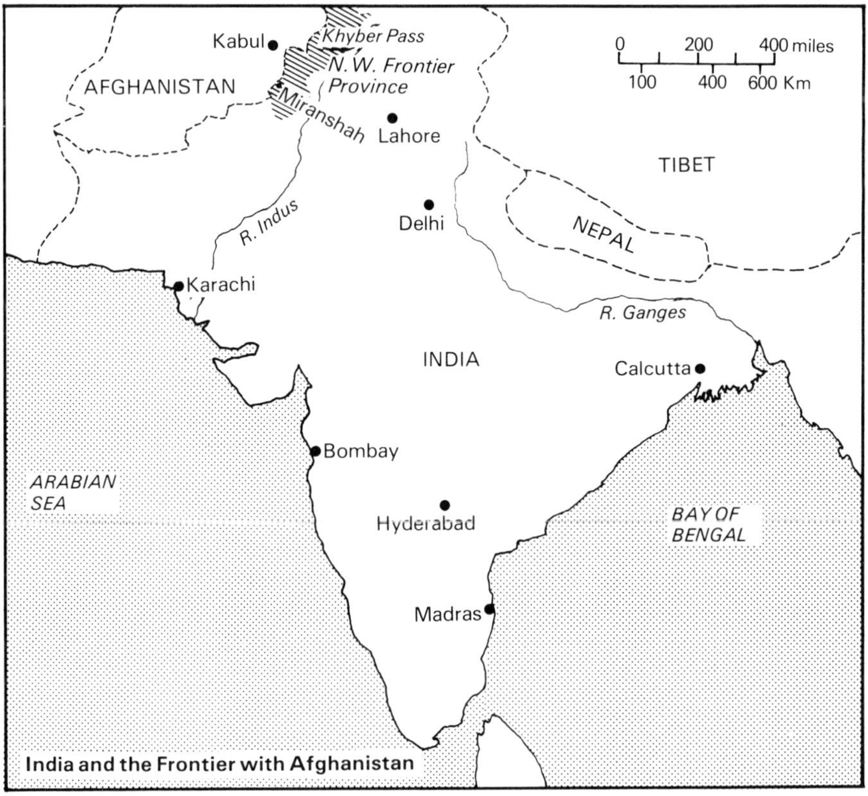

India and the Frontier with Afghanistan

He was transferred from Karachi in late May, or early June, to Miranshah Fort, Wazirstan, a bleak, remote station lying only ten miles from the Afghan border. It conformed to the popular image of the North-West Frontier – twenty-five RAF personnel and over five hundred Indian Scouts lived behind barbed wire and watch towers in a traditional brick and earth fortress deep in the hill country. The small RAF detachment, whose role was to maintain an airstrip, had little contact with the Indian Scouts. By day, the RAF men were not allowed outside the barbed wire perimeter; by night, they were confined to the fort itself. This isolated existence suited Lawrence, who took over similar though less time-consuming duties to those he had performed at Drigh Road. There was time to write and relative privacy. To a friend, H. S. Ede, an art critic working at the Tate Gallery, he wrote: 'the only temptations at Miranshah are boredom and idleness. I hope to escape the first and enjoy the second: for, between ourselves, I did a lot of work at Karachi, and am dead tired.'[15]

If he was really looking forward to a rest, Lawrence was doomed to disappointment. Before the year was out, he was to be the centre of a new and furious international press controversy, a severe embarrassment to the British Government, and the subject of enough invented stories to confirm that his persecution mania was justified. And all the time he was innocently serving at Miranshah, seeking reactions to *The Mint* from a carefully selected group of friends and enjoying his collection of gramophone records and books. He had even rigged up a bath, as he had done at Drigh Road, which enabled him to indulge in one of his few sensual pleasures – immersing his body in hot water.

Among the many books arriving at the fort was a copy of *Lawrence and the Arabs* by Robert Graves. The book was eagerly read by all the airmen, causing some embarrassment to its co-writer, who noted to Ede: 'They regard my legend as a huge joke: if it wasn't my legend, I'd do ditto.'[16]

In early July, he received a puzzled and sarcastic letter from George Bernard Shaw, who was still unable to comprehend why such a talented man had elected to enter, and remain in, the ranks. He asked Lawrence 'What is your game, really?'[17] The question was not well received and Lawrence immediately wrote back a long reply, explaining what he was doing, why he had done it and what he planned to do next. He tried to justify his lifestyle by explaining that he had no choice, being 'all smash, inside'.[18] He felt safe in the RAF; at times he was even able to pretend that he was like other men, and that just because he laughed at himself and others did not mean he was playing a game, rather he was making a determined effort to keep sane: 'It would be so easy and so restful to let sanity go and drop into the dark'.[19] Evidently, the inner conflict was as active as ever; it was only his contact with 'simple-hearted people', Lawrence maintained, which prevented him falling into the abyss of madness. Lawrence told Shaw he would leave the RAF in 1930 or 1935, and that if he could arrange for a secure income of £1 a day, he would retire to Cloud's Hill. Failing that, he had arranged, through Sir Herbert Baker, to get a job as nightwatchman at the new Bank of England (Baker was the architect in charge of the project). No doubt, this latter plan would have infuriated George Bernard Shaw even more.[20]

In June, Lawrence received a reply from Trenchard about *The Mint*. The Chief of Air Staff, who had recently been criticized in the Press for his love of the parade square, was unlikely to be overjoyed by the classic but brutal account of barrack-room life, and although Lawrence anticipated Trenchard's negative reaction, he had felt obliged to let him read the manuscript. Trenchard pretended not to be affected by the book, but in his roles, both as 'the father of the Modern Air Force' and older friend to Lawrence, it was obvious that he was:

> There are many things you have written which I do feel we know goes on and we know should not go on, though what you have written does not hurt me one bit – far from it, and yet, if I saw it in print, if I saw it being published and misunderstood by the public, I should hate it, and I should feel my particular work of trying to make this force would be irretrievably damaged and that through my own fault.*[21]

Lawrence immediately wrote back to him to say he would not publish the book until 1950, unless he was 'made to hate the Air Force which he said was most unlikely', adding impishly: 'A very subtle CAS would prolong my service indefinitely, so that he could court-martial me if I published.'[22]

This odd correspondence between a man in the ranks and the Chief of Air Staff is unique. Trenchard became another substitute father in a list which had at one time or another included Hogarth, Allenby, Churchill and George Bernard Shaw.

Lawrence also continued his exchange of letters with Charlotte Shaw. Her warmth and love complemented the solid male authority of Trenchard and the sarcastic but well-intentioned criticism of G.B.S. Lawrence confessed many of his most intimate secrets to Charlotte; he opened up with her in a way he was unable to with any other human being. This was a two-way process and, as Charlotte Shaw's biographer Janet Dunbar pointed out, Lawrence was one of the only two people Charlotte had ever confided in – the other was Axel Munthe. On his fortieth birthday in August 1928, Lawrence wrote to Charlotte summing up his life to date. He said that he was 'growing old too late' but at least, he remarked, it was comforting 'to be over half-way'. He hoped that the residue of his life would be shorter as it was 'unpleasant to feel the decay'.[23]

Meanwhile, Lawrence had sent off the first part of his translation of the *Odyssey* to an American publisher and was waiting for a favourable reply before continuing. When this came, together with the promise of £800 on completing, he spent much of his time on the project.

During the summer, Lawrence heard that Miranshah was to be closed down the following February. He had developed an agreeable routine and did not look forward to leaving. But his tour of duty came to a much more abrupt end than he had anticipated.

Rumours had been circulating that there was a political motive behind his

*Because of his agreement to Lawrence's enlistment into the RAF.

remote posting, and in a sense there had been – to keep him out of the limelight. Some correspondence between him and Trenchard on the situation in Iraq may have leaked. In July the *New York Sun* carried stories saying that he was 'straightening out Middle East muddles'.

'Disguised in Arab garb, but known to every chieftain in the desert plains and hills between the Suez Canal and the Afghanistan frontier,' ran one story, 'the former Col. Lawrence is continuing his peregrinations in the Middle East.' The article went on to say that he had drawn up a treaty with the Shah of Persia, had been sent to rap Ibn Saud on the knuckles and at the time of writing, it was alleged he was in the Yemen.[24]

While all these events were being reported, Lawrence had not left Miranshah, but as the reports persisted the Foreign Office put out a denial. Nevertheless, the *New York World* reported in September that, disguised 'as a Mohammedan spiritual guide', he was roaming about the Punjab fighting the 'Soviets' and that 'native women were bringing him their children' so that he could ward off the evil eye.[25] Then the *New York Herald Tribune* claimed that he was not in India at all but had crossed the frontier into Afghanistan 'clad in turban and flowing robes with a coffee-stained face.' There he was said to be negotiating a treaty between Great Britain and the Ameer Amanullah.[26]

Now the Indian Press began to follow suit, reporting that, disguised as a *fakir*, he had attended the funeral of the Indian Nationalist leader Lala Rajpat Rai, which gave the Soviet authorities the chance to allege that he was really spying on the Nationalists. The British Press had so far kept out of this farrago of nonsense, but in December the *Daily News* claimed that Lawrence was 'busy learning the Pushta language' prior to moving into Afghanistan,[27] while the *Empire News*, a Sunday tabloid, outdid all its rivals with a piece of fiction by someone calling himself Dr Francis Havelock, alleging that Lawrence had already been in Afghanistan for three weeks. After interviews with King Amanullah, the Chief of Police and the War Minister, he had suddenly disappeared into the wild vastnesses of Afghanistan to engage in a duel to the death with 'the notorious spy Trebitsch Lincoln, the traitor'.[28]

The *Empire News* retracted the ridiculous story after complaints from the Foreign Office, but the damage had been done. Dr Havelock's 'revelations' had been telegraphed to India, reinforcing suspicions that Lawrence was spying on the Indians. Unfortunately, the independently minded subjects of King Amanullah chose that moment to start an uprising in Afghanistan, in protest against his attempt to westernize the notoriously unstable country. On 22 December, the RAF began to fly out British and foreign nationals from the capital, Kabul. Further Foreign Office denials about Lawrence's involvement in Afghanistan had no effect. The Left in England began to attack him as the agent of reactionary imperialism, trying to thwart the progressive reforms which Amanullah was trying to instigate. The fact that the reforms were universally unpopular, and that Lawrence had not left Miranshah Fort, were quite irrelevant.

The stories gathered momentum and became a severe embarrassment, especially as the French, as well as the Russians, began to exploit them. The Afghan Government was now convinced that Lawrence was 'scheming against them in some mysterious way',[29] as the head of the British delegation in Kabul informed Delhi. After a good deal of behind-the-scenes negotiations, Lord Trenchard, the Chief of Air Staff, reluctantly decided that there was no option but to transfer Lawrence out of India. He instructed Air Vice-Marshal Sir Geoffrey Salmond to ask Lawrence if 'he would like to go to Aden, or to a small detachment in Somaliland consisting of two or three men, or to Singapore for a year or whether he would like to return to England. I want to help him as much as I can.'[30]

Even while these negotiations were proceeding the wild stories continued, including a report in the *Daily Herald* that the Afghan authorities had ordered Lawrence's arrest.[31] The situation was not helped by statements released by the India Office that they had instructed local Governments to consider prosecuting those who repeated the rumours and that it had been decided to transfer Lawrence from the North-West Frontier. Trenchard was doing his best to handle the awkward situation and was furious when a telegram from Sir Arthur Hirtzel, Permanent Under-Secretary at the India Office, to Sir Denis Bray, the Government of India's Foreign Secretary, was brought to his attention. In somewhat hysterical terms, Hirtzel suggested that Lawrence should be 'closely watched' as 'it would be very awkward if he disappeared before he could be transferred'.[32] This communication only added to the rumours circulating in official and unofficial circles.

The activities of Lawrence of Arabia, India and Afghanistan continued to be closely followed in the United States, where *Revolt in the Desert* had just become a best-seller. The *New York Times* wrote perceptively:

> LAWRENCE THE UBIQUITOUS
>
> Russia, always the victim of odious conspiracies, has discovered that someone has upset the apple cart in Afghanistan and trembles lest it be an act of Lawrence of Arabia.
>
> The tale is almost like an incident from 'Kim', reversed. Instead of the Russian agent working down from the north, the British agent is working northward into Russia's sphere. In this instance he is invested with the mystery and charm that have followed the name of Lawrence in the East, regardless of his actual whereabouts. 'If Colonel Lawrence were to write the memoirs of adventures which he had been through, he could produce a volume even more enthralling than "Revolt in the Desert"'.[33]

On the 7th of January, Lawrence was advised that he would be transferred from Miranshah to Lahore within twenty-four hours. This was fairly traumatic for him, and in the rush he was not able to pack up all his books. The next morning he was flown to Lahore where he was met by a senior RAF officer carrying a letter from Salmond. This letter was the first official explanation he had received of the need for his rapid transfer from the North-West Frontier, and offered him a choice of returning to England or being posted to another remote station out of India. Lawrence, no doubt convinced that nowhere would be remote enough, decided he would accept the option to go home to England. Salmond's representative arranged for Lawrence to be flown to Karachi that day and from there on to Bombay where he boarded the S.S. *Rajputana* mail liner.

The fact that he had left India did little to abate the international incident which was developing over his alleged activities in Afghanistan; it was even suggested that only Lawrence's double had sailed for England. On 12 January, the *Deutsche Allgemeine Zeitung* reported that 'Kabul telegraphs that Colonel Lawrence is one of the main intriguers behind the insurgents, and that an attempt to lay this unruly spirit of the Orient will be made'. The article also noted that Lawrence's next book might be titled 'Revolt in Afghanistan'. Another German newspaper made the much more creative observation that the whole story of Lawrence in Afghanistan had been invented as a 'stunt' to build up publicity for the film of *Revolt in the Desert* which, they claimed, was due to be released soon.

The German Press notably stopped making rude comments about Lawrence when RAF planes evacuated German women and children from Kabul in part of the general evacuation of foreign nationals which the RAF had volunteered to undertake.

Lawrence travelled back to England in relative comfort – he had been allotted a second-class cabin and spent most of the time working on his translation of the *Odyssey*. His ship stopped at Port Said to take on coal. Lawrence was not allowed ashore but was handed a message from Trenchard by an RAF officer:

> On your arrival the Press will, I am afraid, meet you and as much as possible will try to interview and photograph you. Endeavour as much as you can to avoid being interviewed. Disembark at Plymouth, where I am sending someone to meet you who will be in plain clothes. From Plymouth you can go off on leave, but as soon as you can, come and see me.[34]

In England, the Labour Party continued to believe and make political capital out of the rumours, and a frenzied mob even burnt an effigy of Lawrence on Tower Hill! Inevitably, the issue was raised in Parliament. *Hansard* records that on 29 January, the Labour MP Ernest Thurtle – who later became a good friend of Lawrence's – asked the Secretary of State for Air if Lawrence had carried out the normal duties of an Aircraftman in India, and if he had been granted any leave. When these questions were answered 'Yes' and 'No', respectively, Thurtle asked if it was normal practice to allow enlistment under a false name. The question was referred to the Air Minister and answered the next day by Samuel Hoare:

> Colonel Lawrence's identity was known when he transferred from the Army to the Air Force under the name of Shaw; he preferred to be known by that name and no objection was seen to his being accepted for service under it.[35]

The *Rajputana* arrived at Plymouth Sound amidst thick fog early on 2 February. Trenchard had anticipated the interest of the Press and arranged for an old acquaintance of Lawrence's, Wing Commander Sydney Smith, to meet the liner. Smith was Commanding Officer of the near-by flying-boat station of Cattewater; his orders were simple – bring Lawrence to London as quietly and quickly as possible. He carried with him a letter from Trenchard to pass on to Lawrence:

Dear Lawrence,
Wing Commander Smith will hand you this letter when he meets you. He is in mufti, and he will do anything he can to help you.

I enclose, in case you want it, although you may not, a couple of pounds. You may want something to begin with, and you can repay me when you like.

You may be caught by the Press on the way up, and if so, I am afraid I cannot help it, but Wing Commander Smith is out to help you get away from the Rajputana to the railway, and lose the Press somewhere between those two points if you wish to.

You can consider yourself officially given now a week's leave from the time you get this letter without the necessity for reporting officially to anybody except that you must report to me as early as you can and as privately as you can, either at the Air Ministry or at Dancers Hill House.

I know there are a hundred people who will put you up, but if you find any difficulty, or if you don't want to go to anybody else, you can count on me to put you up if you want to go somewhere while you look around and decide what to do. My full address is Dancers Hill House, Barnet, Herts. I am out to help you all I can.

I am prepared to post you to Cranwell, or Upper Heyford, or where you like, but that we can talk about later.

I don't want to see a lot of placards to the effect that the Air Ministry have spirited you away in fast motor boats and cars, but there is no reason why you should not lose everybody at Plymouth if you can. At the same time, if you prefer to come to London in the ship, I have told Wing Commander Smith not to prevent you doing so, but there it will be impossible to prevent whole swarms of people coming off tugs to meet you.

Wing Commander Smith has a warrant to give you to bring to London, and we can get your ticket without your appearing.

Best of luck.

Yours,[36]

Things did not go smoothly, however. Wing Commander Smith went out to the *Rajputana* aboard the naval pinnace which traditionally met all large incoming vessels at Plymouth. His plan, which he had radioed to the liner, was to spirit Lawrence away in the Navy boat, while the other passengers transferred from the liner to a large P & O tender. Initially, the scheme worked well; the pinnace pulled up alongside the *Rajputana* not far from the tender and Smith and a naval officer went aboard.

The Press had hired a number of small boats which had converged on the liner. Reporters and photographers carefully scrutinized the passengers as they walked down the gangplank into the P & O tender. The naval launch attracted little attention as it moved off into the mist towards Plymouth, without taking on passengers. However, its real destination was the opposite side of the *Rajputana* where Lawrence, Smith and the naval officer were waiting with a rope ladder hanging down from a hatchway. There were some minor problems with the ladder and by the time Lawrence, easily recognizable because of his blue RAF uniform, began to climb down it, a small boat containing an enterprising photographer from the *Daily Mirror* appeared and just had time to take two shots before Lawrence and the naval launch moved off.[37]

Wing Commander Smith suggested that it might be prudent to have a peaceful breakfast at Cattewater, rather than attempt to catch a London-bound train at Plymouth immediately. Lawrence agreed and after breakfast the two men drove to the railway station at Newton Abbot and boarded the first London train available. They were perturbed when their coach was disconnected and coupled to another train. Fate was not being kind; they had been linked to the second instalment of the boat train from Plymouth, in which many reporters had decided to return to London. The unmistakable little figure in RAF blue was quickly spotted and at Exeter, the next stop, reporters ran to the station telegraph office and wired their London offices to inform them that Lawrence had been found.[38]

At Paddington, Wing Commander Smith did his best to evade the Press but found, to his surprise, that Lawrence was rather enjoying himself. A reporter came up to Lawrence and asked: 'Is your name Shaw?' 'Certainly not', came the reply, 'my name's Smith.'[38] Soon afterwards, a slightly exasperated Wing Commander bundled his mischievous ward into a taxi; the reporters followed and the chase was on. Unable to shake off the pursuers, Smith suggested that his sister-in-law's flat in the Cromwell Road might provide temporary refuge. Lawrence agreed, but when he arrived there, he tried the Wing Commander's patience further when he 'refused to be hurried' because 'he was enjoying the joke too much'.[39] He climbed out of the taxi in a deliberately leisurely manner and was instantly surrounded by Pressmen. Even when they were in the flat, the reporters and photographers remained in the corridor and on the pavement outside. Lawrence was smuggled out after dinner and was driven to the room above Sir Herbert Baker's office in Barton Street, Westminster, the bolt-hole where so much work on the *Seven Pillars* had been done.

The following morning, a Sunday, Lawrence and Wing Commander Smith drove to Trenchard's residence to discuss what should be done next. The Chief of Air Staff made no attempt to scold or apportion blame, and readily agreed to Lawrence's suggestion that he might be posted permanently to Sydney Smith's command at Cattewater.

The same day, the *Sunday Pictorial* was able to splash the exclusive photographs taken the day before across its front page.[40]

Lawrence spent Sunday night at Barnet. The following morning, Trenchard dropped him off in London at Victoria Station, from where, unknown to the CAS, Lawrence walked to the Houses of Parliament. He wanted to confront Ernest Thurtle, the Labour MP who had been asking embarrassing questions about him. He was particularly concerned that Thurtle's questions might lead to an investigation of his change of name, and public disclosure of his illegitimacy. He spoke to Thurtle openly and told him of the family secret. Thurtle was impressed by Lawrence and agreed not to ask further questions in the House.

Although his visit to Parliament effectively silenced Labour MPs, Shapurji Saklatvala, a Parsee Communist who represented Battersea South, directed several related questions to the Foreign Secretary, Sir Austen Chamberlain, two days later. It is indicative of the worldwide interest in Lawrence that the incident was reported in the *New York Times*:

> London, Feb. 6. – Suggestions that Colonel T. E. Lawrence is still engaged in secret propaganda on the Northwest frontier of India, while some one else disguised as Aircraftman Shaw has been transfered to England, were greeted with laughter in the House of Commons this afternoon.
>
> Sir Austen Chamberlain, the Foreign Secretary, told Shapurji Saklatvala, the Parsee Communist, his insistent questioner, that if he occasionally devoted himself to laying unfounded rumours to rest rather than devoting all his energies to spreading them, he would contribute to the peace of the world.[41]

This was the last public reference to Lawrence's alleged activities in India and Afghanistan, but the story has been told at some length as it throws an interesting light on how Lawrence's reputation, by interacting with an unstable political situation, had led to the creation of the rumours in the first place. The stories were exaggerated by Britain's enemies, but were also stimulated by commercially (and sometimes politically) motivated newspapers in an endeavour to feed public curiosity. All the same, it seems rather disingenuous of the *Daily News*, having played its part in creating the rumours which forced the Government to transfer Lawrence surreptitiously from the North-West Frontier, to proceed to criticize the authorities for doing so. 'Time the Truth was known about the Arch-Spy' ran one of its headlines on the Monday after his arrival at Plymouth, and the article asked: 'Why if he is merely a humble craftsman calling himself Shaw or Smith, was he conveyed to England with such conspicuous elusiveness? And why was he landed from the liner at Plymouth in a specially ordered launch and taken to Admiralty House for lunch?'[42]

The answer should not have been difficult for the editor to discover. It was because of the fabrication of stories by his own and other newspapers.

18 The Last Years

Lawrence remained in the ranks of the RAF until February 1935. In the last six years of his service he found a degree of fulfilment in mechanical work, though he continued with his translation of the *Odyssey* (which he completed in 1931) and maintained his huge output of letters. His psychological health seems to have improved, but this is not to say that his fits of depression, and related problems, entirely disappeared. He resorted to the thought-obliterating speed of his motorbike as a means to relieve his tensions. Bernard and Charlotte Shaw had given him a brand-new Brough as a homecoming present, and whenever he felt in need of a change, Lawrence would make break-neck dashes all over England, and in particular, to London and his Dorset cottage, Cloud's Hill. On some of these trips he would secretly meet John Bruce and, by rekindling the Old Man fantasy, persuaded the Scotsman to beat him. However, Lawrence's flagellation fetish and occasional despair should not overshadow what was generally a positive, even happy period for him.

For nearly three years (1929–31), he was under the benevolent command of Wing Commander Sydney Smith at the RAF flying-boat station at Cattewater. Smith and his wife Clare offered T.E. the freedom of their home, and their support appeared to have really helped him. They provided Lawrence with the sort of non-demanding security he desperately needed, and the congenial atmosphere at Cattewater helped to heal some of his wounds. He took up a new interest in motorboats and, during the summer of 1929, enjoyed helping Sydney Smith with preparations for the Schneider Trophy Seaplane races, held at Calshot in September. The British team won the coveted trophy with one of their supermarine S6s, designed by R. J. Mitchell and Henry Royce (the S6 later evolved into the legendary Spitfire fighter).

Lawrence was present throughout the races, making no attempt to keep in the background. He was seen in conversation with, among others, Nancy Astor, then a Tory MP for Plymouth, and the Marshal of the Italian Air Force, Balbo. These tête-à-têtes with the famous came to the attention of the new Labour Government's Air Minister, Lord Thomson, who thought it inappropriate that Lawrence, as an Aircraftman, should be in direct contact with such personages. Thomson placed a restriction on A/C Shaw (via Trenchard) which stipulated that if he wished to remain in the Air Force, he should not talk to 'great men' (this might have amused Nancy Astor!), but should leave the country, or do anything other than an ordinary Aircraftman's job.[1] Thomson was killed in the crash of the R101 in October 1930 and the prohibitions died with him. Through a friend in the Air Ministry, Lawrence was now able to take up a special appointment working with and reporting on experimental power-boat designs for the RAF, though, officially, he remained an Aircraftman based at Cattewater.

As he became absorbed by his challenging new work, his name featured in a bizarre news story, arising out of one of Stalin's show trials in Moscow. According to the accused, 'Lawrence had undertaken negotiations with one industrial Party in London. The object of these meetings was to prepare a revolution against the Soviet Government in Russia, to be accompanied by armed intervention, in conjunction with the rebels, on the part of Great Britain, France and the border States. Imperialistic French circles would then receive the Caucasian oilfields.[2]

The only problem was that the prosecution alleged, and the accused confessed, that they had met Colonel Lawrence in London during 1927 and 1928, when in fact he had been in India. Lawrence was genuinely concerned and wrote to the Labour MP Ernest Thurtle:

> I am rather troubled over this Russian business . . . I know they do not much believe any English official word: but I was demonstrably in India all the time from December 1926 to February 1929. Would it be any good getting some private person they trust to tell them so? Or could anything be done? They may hang these poor creatures for all I know, else: and I would like to do something for them, if there is anything.[3]

Lawrence arranged with Thurtle for a question to be asked in Parliament, when it was officially confirmed that Aircraftman Shaw, alias Colonel Lawrence, had been serving abroad during the period the Soviets alleged he was meeting counter-revolutionary agents in London.

By February 1931, Lawrence was back in the news because of his involvement in a rescue operation after the crash into the sea of an Irish flying-boat on a practice run out of Cattewater. Lawrence raced to the scene of the accident with Wing Commander Smith in one of the launches he had been working on. Six out of twelve men were picked up. The others drowned, and the Soviet Press reported that Lawrence himself had been one of those killed. More men could have been saved had a faster boat been available. Lawrence had long realized that the RAF had inadequate rescue tenders; he used the inquest after the crash as an opportunity to urge better equipment. This became his personal crusade, and he engaged all his political, Press and Service contacts to such effect that the whole affair, and his involvement in it, became an embarrassment to the Air Ministry. In late 1932, Aircraftman Shaw, by then serving at Southampton, was taken off his special duties, but he did not suffer this situation for long. Early in the New Year, he threatened to leave the RAF if he was not allowed to continue to pursue his ideas. The news 'leaked' to the

Press, and the Air Ministry, keen to appease both Lawrence and their critics in Fleet Street, put him back to work on his chosen project. He spent his final two years in the Air Force attached to civilian boatyards (and in civilian dress) working on a new generation of high-speed launch. Similar boats went on to save many lives in the Second World War.

So ended Lawrence's career in the Air Force. He could never have been a normal ranker, as George Bernard Shaw, who had always been irritated by his service in the ranks, well understood. In a letter to Shaw from India, Lawrence had written. 'No, I am not adjutant, to this camp. Just typist, and i/c files, and duty roles. I do what I am told to do, and re-write the drafts given to me, meekly.'[4]

The last word evidently registered with the playwright, and Private Napoleon Alexander Trotsky Meek is an unmistakably Lawrence-like character in his play, *Too True to be Good*. He makes his entry astride a 'powerful and very imperfectly silenced motor bicycle' at the beginning of Act Two – the scene is a British expedition's headquarters by a 'sea-beach' in some hot and sandy corner of the globe. Private Meek has the figure of 'a boy of seventeen; but he seems to have borrowed a long head and Wellingtonian nose and chin from somebody else for the express purpose of annoying the Colonel'. The first part of the play is a dialogue between Colonel Tallboys and Meek; as might be expected, Meek always comes off better. Later in the play, the following dialogue ensues:

> TALLBOYS: . . . Quartermaster's clerk, interpreter, intelligence orderly. Any further rank of which I have not been informed?
> MEEK: No, sir.
> TALLBOYS: Quite sure you're not a field marshal, eh?
> MEEK: Quite sure, sir. I never was anything higher than a colonel.
> TALLBOYS: You a colonel? What do you mean?
> MEEK: Not a real colonel, sir. Mostly a brevet, sir, to save appearances when I had to take command.
> TALLBOYS: And how do you come to be a private now?
> MEEK: I prefer the ranks, sir. I have a freer hand. And the conversation in the officers' mess doesn't suit me. I always resign a commission and enlist again.

The day before his discharge, Lawrence wrote to Air Chief Marshal Sir Edward Ellington:

> I've been at home in the ranks . . . So if you still keep that old file about me, will you please close it with this note which says how sadly I am going?[5]

He told friends that he had considered remaining in the Service for longer but had decided that, at forty-six, he was too old and had no choice but to try to come to terms with civilian life. In any case, it is unlikely that the Air Force would have agreed to extend the special engagement of their most controversial airman, even if he had expressed a desire to do so.

Lawrence did have one debatable incentive for leaving the RAF – it would give him enough time to write another book. He once explained to Robert Graves that he had only joined the RAF and taken up mechanical work in the first place because he had failed as an artist, and as he prepared for his retirement, he realized the frustrated artist in him would feel compelled to try again to create a masterpiece.

On the same day that he wrote to the Air Chief Marshal, Lawrence wrote to John Buchan: 'Retirement without a plan is rather a daunting state, and I am a little frightened of being completely my own master.'[6]

He did not tell Buchan that he had resurrected his old dream of starting a private press, this time with the aid of his friend and neighbour at Cloud's Hill, Pat Knowles. The idea was that they would first produce a very limited edition of *The Mint* – perhaps a hundred copies. According to Knowles, the plans fell through because Lawrence was about to become involved in 'government work'. Lawrence was, however, sufficiently serious about the project to have a sketch of himself by Augustus John collotyped, and 100 copies produced as a frontispiece. Had he published even a limited edition of *The Mint* in his lifetime, as he evidently intended, he would have had to break the promise he had made to Trenchard, and probably the Official Secrets Act too. An important unanswered question is whether the Air Ministry knew of his plans. If they did, it is probable that they would have taken direct action to prevent publication as they kept a secret file, numbered S4468, the specific subject of which was 'precautions for preventing publication of *The Mint*'.[7]

On 26 February 1935, Lawrence left the Service which had been his home for twelve years. A friend took a snapshot of him in Bridlington harbour. The photograph is interesting because it shows that Lawrence, the eternal boy, had finally become middle-aged. He looks disorientated, perched on a bicycle wearing a plain suit, a muffler and trouser-clips. His hair is cut short and his face, forced into a half-smile, is no longer handsome but rough and weather-beaten. Augustus John caught a similar if more flattering likeness in several pencil sketches completed the month before.

Lawrence was still unsure of what he would do with his new-found leisure, and worried about his modest income. It was apparently because of this that he had taken to a push-bike, temporarily abandoning his Brough as too expensive to run. He told friends that he intended to cycle down to Cloud's Hill, in 'short stages'. He planned to stop in Bourne, in Lincolnshire, to see the Australian author Frederic Manning, but sadly discovered that Manning had died. This news seemed to emphasize his own mortality and he wrote to Peter Davies, Manning's publisher: 'My losing the R.A.F. numbs me, so that I haven't much feeling to spare for the while. In fact I find myself wishing all the time that my own curtain would fall. It seems as if I had finished, now.'[8]

Instead of going to Bourne, Lawrence cycled to Cambridge to see his younger brother, Arnold, who had become a reader in archaeology at the university. The two brothers had always had a close relationship but the visit was only a brief one. Lawrence felt the need of the sanctuary of his Dorset cottage and, leaving Cambridge, began the long journey towards the West Country.

He arrived at Cloud's Hill to find the old spectre of Lawrence of Arabia was back to haunt him. A mass of reporters were waiting in the hope of an interview or photograph. This was one time in Lawrence's life when there was no doubt that he genuinely desired to withdraw from the limelight. He immediately left Dorset for London, but when he attempted to return to his cottage a few days later, so did the reporters. In 1981, Pat Knowles told the writer of an incident during this period. One morning, a photographer and a reporter appeared outside Cloud's Hill, determined to confront Lawrence. When they resorted to throwing stones on to the roof of the cottage to bring him out, Lawrence lost his temper. Pat Knowles was in the cottage that day (possibly with an RAF friend of Lawrence's, Jock Chambers). Lawrence turned to him: 'Come on, Pat, let's get rid of them', and opened the door of the cottage. The Pressmen rushed up to the entrance porch and, as Knowles grabbed one, Lawrence punched the other. The two unwanted visitors retreated and Lawrence, trembling, ran up the stairs of the cottage. A few moments later, Knowles followed and found his friend distraught, looking upon a clenched fist and muttering, 'It's years since I hit a man.'[9]

Lawrence was so affected by this incident, and other similar if less violent encounters, that he determined to put a stop to the 'tripe hounds'. He went to London to see Esmond Harmsworth, Chairman of the Newspaper Proprietors Association, and asked if members could be discouraged from writing about him, or using photographs of him. He wrote to Pat Knowles that he was having meetings with the Press Association and Press photographic agencies, 'persuading all of them to leave me alone, and to refuse to buy the stolen products of the freelancers'.[10] Lawrence kept away from Cloud's Hill until interest in him had waned a little, but he was back in April, and busied himself working on the cottage. He enjoyed improving his home and wanted to build a window into the tiny upstairs bedroom. He wrote to T. B. Marson asking if he would search out a porthole in a breaker's yard which could be used instead of a normal window frame. Marson managed to acquire something suitable and sent it off. As a small gesture of thanks, Lawrence engraved Marson's initials on the rim before fitting the porthole into the wall of the cottage, where it still remains.

In the field of literature, he tried to come to the assistance of James Hanley, whose controversial novel, *Boy*, had been prosecuted for indecency. He wrote to C. J. Greenwood, the publisher, 'Most of them are afraid of the word sodomy. I wonder why.'[11] T.E.'s philosophical distaste for female-kind is a feature of his correspondence in early 1935, but it should be stated again that his attitude towards women did not prevent him from having several close female friends. However, as a rule, Lawrence preferred to be by himself or in the company of men. Thus he could write to Robert Graves that one of the advantages of being in the RAF was that it cut one off from all real communication with women. To H. S. Ede (who had just given Lawrence a cheque for £30 in order to keep up the small luxury of the Brough motorcycle), Lawrence wrote: 'I like to live alone for 80% of my days, and to be let alone by 80% of my fellow-men and all my fellow-women below 60 years of age.'[12]

Thanks to the security afforded by Ede's cheque, Lawrence felt able to forgo the economy of his push-bike and return to the speed and relaxation of his Brough 'Boanerges'. One morning in April, he went to Sandbanks near Poole, about fifteen miles from Cloud's Hill, to test the performance of his machine on the sand dunes there. Mrs Louie Dingwell, who became a well-known race-horse trainer, remembered the visit. At the time, she operated a taxi service and Lawrence appeared pushing his motorbike, which had suffered an electrical fault. Mrs Dingwell offered to transport bike and rider back to Bovington, and Lawrence helped to load the bike into her van. Mrs Dingwell was impressed by his strength and commented:

> 'You're pretty tough, aren't you?'
> 'I ought to be tough.'
> 'Why's that?' asked Mrs Dingwell. 'You don't look particularly strong.'
> 'Well,' retorted Lawrence coyly, 'I am Lawrence of Arabia.'
> 'Don't tell me such a whopper! Of course you're not.'[13]

The two of them climbed into the van and made for Cloud's Hill where Lawrence invited her in for refreshment, apologizing for only being able to offer her milk. Mrs Dingwell was struck by his modesty.

On 7 May, Lawrence wrote to E. M. Forster to arrange the latter's visit to Cloud's Hill 'any day after the 14th'.[14] The same day, he received a letter from Lady Astor which has been traced by Montgomery Hyde. She asked Lawrence to go to Cliveden to take part in a meeting of her informal but influential 'Cliveden set'. Those present would include Lord Philip Lothian, Lionel Curtis, and Stanley Baldwin (who was about to become Prime Minister, taking over from Ramsay MacDonald). Lady Astor wrote: 'I believe when the Government reorganises you will be asked to reorganise the Defence Forces,' and added, 'If you will come to Cliveden on Saturday, the last weekend in May . . . you will never regret it.' Lawrence replied:

> No: wild mares would not at present take me away from Cloud's Hill . . . Also there is something broken in the works, as I told you: my will, I think. In this mood I would not take on any job at all. So do not commit yourself to advocating me, lest I prove a non-starter.[15]

In early May, the author Henry Williamson wrote to Lawrence, asking if he could come down to Dorset. Williamson is remembered as the author of *Tarka the Otter* but he also had an intense interest in politics. His purpose in wanting to visit Lawrence was to discuss Fascism and Anglo-German relations. Williamson was a disciple of Oswald Mosley, the Blackshirt leader, and he planned to ask Lawrence if he would lend public support and hence credibility to the British Fascists.[16]

This is not the only time Lawrence had been approached by British Fascists. In June 1934, he had a conversation with Liddell Hart, who wrote that 'Fascists had been after him [Lawrence]' but that Lawrence had rejected their offer and 'wouldn't help them to power'.[17] And Stanley Weintraub has quoted the Swedish historian Erik Lonroth on the subject of Lawrence and the Fascists: 'From Germany Hitler's men sought to establish contact with him [Lawrence] and the National-Socialist foreign affairs representative Kurt von Ludecke was in touch with him in 1932, but Lawrence rejected these advances.'[18]

On Monday 13 May 1935, Lawrence left his cottage and crossed the road to the Knowles' bungalow opposite. He had decided to invite Williamson to lunch the following day, and asked Mrs Knowles (Pat's mother) if she would cook a suitable lunch for his visitor. Soon afterwards, Lawrence left on his motorcycle for Bovington Camp, just over a mile away. He arrived at the camp, parked his bike by the petrol station,[19] and walked over to the Post Office where he sent Williamson a brief telegram: 'LUNCH TUESDAY WET FINE. COTTAGE 1 MILE NORTH OF BOVINGTON CAMP'. (Williamson had written he would only come if it was a fine day.)[20]

Lawrence left the Post Office and walked back to the petrol station where the pump attendant, Walt Pitman, asked if he needed any fuel. Lawrence replied, 'I'm all right, thanks,' climbed back on to his bike, started it up and began the fateful drive back towards the cottage.

Exactly what happened next has never been satisfactorily explained. A few hundred yards before reaching Cloud's Hill (the police report stated 400 yards), Lawrence came up behind two boys on bicycles. It is usually suggested that because of the dip in the road, he did not see the two cyclists until the last moment and was forced to swerve suddenly. It is presumed that this resulted in a skid which caused him to lose control of his machine and be thrown over the handlebars, the impact with the road (or a tree) fracturing his skull. However, accounts of the crash conflict. The key witness, Corporal Catchpole of the Royal Army Ordnance Corps, an NCO at the camp, had been walking his dog by the side of the road at the time of the crash. He did not see the actual collision and was warned by his superior officers not to communicate anything else he had seen to the Press.

Having run across to Lawrence, Catchpole noticed an Army lorry coming along the road, hailed it down and helped put the injured man on to a stretcher. As well as Lawrence, one of the cyclists was injured, and he was also put onto the Army lorry. Lawrence and the boy were driven to Bovington Camp hospital where they were admitted 'between 11.30 and 11.45 a.m.'.

Lawrence was technically a civilian, yet strangely the Air Ministry was involved from the start of the events. All military personnel at Bovington were warned immediately after the crash that if they communicated any information to the Press they would be breaking the Official Secrets Act. Even before the police started their inquiries, an official statement was made by an officer from the camp stating that 'there had been no witnesses'.

An official from the Air Ministry phoned Liddell Hart at home, but could only speak to a secretary, who took a message. Hart did not return until 7.30 p.m. and immediately phoned the Ministry with the information that

Lawrence's mother and one brother were in China, and that his brother Arnold was nearest, though unfortunately also abroad on holiday in Majorca. A telephone call was put through and, remarkably, Arnold Lawrence was by T.E.'s bedside a mere twenty-four hours later – an achievement in 1935. According to the *Dorset Daily Echo*, he declined to speak to the Press when he left in a saloon car, accompanied by a motorcyclist who warned reporters to keep away.[21]

In the hospital, Lawrence was guarded by two Special Branch detectives – one by his bedside. It did not take long for the Press to suspect that information was being withheld. The day after the accident, the *Daily Express* quoted a hospital official as saying:

> All I am permitted to tell is that we have in the hospital a Mr Shaw. We have strict instructions to give no other information. No I cannot say how he is.[22]

The *Daily Sketch* reported that the credentials of all who approached were being carefully scrutinized[23] and, according to the *Daily Mirror*, the father of the injured boy had been refused permission to see him, though his condition was comfortable. Visitors were to be allowed on the day the report appeared (15 May).

'Why are such extraordinary precautions being taken in the case of Lawrence?' the newspaper asked, and put the question to Allenby, who said he had no idea.

The next day the *Mirror* reported that Cloud's Hill was being heavily guarded 'to Safeguard vital Air Ministry documents which Mr Shaw had in his possession',[24] and on 18 May the *Daily Mail* gave publicity to A. W. Lawrence's efforts to play down the mystery. The report from their 'special correspondent' at Bovington Camp is worth giving in full:

> Late tonight the condition of Mr T. E. Shaw – 'Lawrence of Arabia' – who was admitted to Wool military hospital at Bovington Camp following a motor-cycle crash on Monday, was unchanged.
>
> Mr Shaw, whose skull was fractured, has now been unconscious for more than four days. His condition remains critical.
>
> A vanished motorist who was seen at the spot where Mr Shaw crashed into two boy cyclists is being sought.
>
> 'The car was seen travelling towards Mr Shaw, who was just about to pass the cyclists on his motor cycle', I was told today. Apparently, he swerved to avoid the car, and he wrenched his machine into the banking to minimise the impact with the cyclists.
>
> SECRET WORK FINISHED
>
> Mr Shaw's brother, Mr A. W. Lawrence, who flew from Spain to England on Wednesday, said to me today:
>
> 'ALL THIS MYSTERY ABOUT MY BROTHER'S RECENT MOVEMENTS AND WORK HAS LITTLE BASIS IN FACT.
> SO FAR AS I KNOW – HE HAD NO CONNECTION WITH ANY GOVERNMENT DEPARTMENT, NOR WAS HE DOING ANY

GOVERNMENT WORK. WHATEVER SECRET SERVICE WORK HE MAY HAVE DONE IS FINISHED NOW.

The reason he is living near a military camp is that some time ago he acquired a cottage there.'

The best specialists in the country were rushed to Bovington Camp. The King telephoned to inquire of 'Mr Shaw's condition'. Lawrence managed to cling to life for six days but, early on the morning of 19 May, his heart became faint; he was given more oxygen and an injection of adrenalin but to no avail. Just after 8 a.m. he died. Arnold Lawrence and T.E.'s old friend Stuart Newcombe were at his bedside.

The official cause of death was congestion of the lungs and heart following a fracture of the skull and laceration of the brain.

19 The Legend Persists

In death as in life, mystery surrounded the name of Lawrence. Army, Air Ministry and Government were all keen that he should be buried as quickly as possible. Lawrence died on 19 May, and an inquest was scheduled for the morning of the 21st, with the funeral the same afternoon.

The inquest, which took place in a dining-room by the hospital, proved to be no more than an official rubber stamp on the accidental nature of Lawrence's death, and left many important questions unanswered. The most important witness was Corporal Catchpole, who insisted that he saw a black car travelling in the opposite direction moments before he saw the bike cart-wheeling:

> The motorcyle passed the car all right. Then I saw the motorcycle swerve across the road to avoid two pedal cyclists coming from Bovington. It swerved immediately after it had passed the car, the next thing I heard was the crash.
>
> I saw the bike twisting and turning over and over along the road. I saw nothing of the driver. I ran to the scene and found the motorcylist on the road. His face was covered with blood which I tried to wipe away with a handkerchief.[1]

The jury asked Catchpole if there had been room for Lawrence's motorbike to pass between the car and the cyclists. He replied that from his position at the time of the crash he could not be sure. Inspector Drake of the Dorset Constabulary then questioned the Corporal. Catchpole repeated that he had seen a private black saloon but could add nothing more. The Inspector told the court that although inquiries had been made, the car could not be traced, and only Corporal Catchpole had actually seen it.

The boys gave evidence next, both stating firmly that there had been no car – perhaps too firmly, considering that one had been unconscious and the other in shock immediately after the accident. Both boys were the sons of serving soldiers and had been interrogated by military authorities as well as the police.

During the inquest, one of the boys, Fletcher, referred to Lawrence as 'Mr Lawrence', not 'Mr Shaw' as he was known locally. His statements to the inquest conformed exactly to an interview which he had given to the *Dorset Echo* a few days previously*:

> We were riding single file. I was leading. I heard a motorcycle coming down from behind and then I heard a crash. Bertie's cycle hit mine and I fell off.
>
> When I looked up I saw Bertie lying in the road. The motor cycle had skidded on the other side, and the man who had gone over the handlebars had landed with his feet about 5 yards from where I fell. I got up and went to Bertie to see if he was alright. . . He seemed to go to sleep. I waited a minute or two, being afraid to go to the man, because his face was covered with blood. Then a man came up on a cycle and asked me to get an ambulance. [Who was this? It was not Catchpole] But before I could some soldiers came and he went to get it himself. A lorry came up. The men got two stretchers from the camp at the roadside and the injured man and Bertie were put on them and taken into the lorry.[2]

The boy went on to say that he had not seen a motor-car on the road. In the summing up, the Coroner, Mr L. E. N. Neville-Jones, noted that the evidence about the black car was rather unsatisfactory, and the jury returned a verdict of 'Accidental death'.

During the winter and spring of 1980–1, the present writer was stationed at Bovington and tried to see whether, even at this late date, any additional details of the crash and the circumstances surrounding it could be discovered. He spent many afternoons with Pat Knowles and his wife Joyce and was introduced by them to an elderly Dorset man who had also been present near the crash but had never been called as a witness to the inquest. This gentleman, whom I shall refer to as L.C., did not wish to become embroiled in 'the Lawrence mystery'. He had never publicized his presence near the scene of the crash, although it had been no secret to the camp authorities. L.C. spoke about what he had seen.

On 13 May, L.C., then a teenager, was working as 'mate' to a Mr O'Conner, a local lorry-driver, who had been contracted by the Army to help 'clear the gear' from an Army training camp. While L.C. and Mr O'Conner were loading the lorry, they heard the crash and ran to the spot, arriving just after Catchpole. They saw an overturned motorbike on the side of the road. This was the eastern side of the road, and therefore Lawrence was, as the boys and Catchpole later testified, on the wrong side of the road. A little way in front of the bike a man was lying in a pool of blood. L.C. recognized him and said, 'It's Lawrence.' O'Conner, noticing the blood pouring from the side of the victim's head, remarked, 'He's done for.' At this point Lawrence, who had appeared unconscious, opened his eyes and, looking directly

*Stories of espionage and an official cover-up had become so rampant that the authorities allowed Fletcher to be interviewed by a reporter from the *Dorset Echo* in an attempt to end rumours that Lawrence was the victim of foul play.

upward towards L.C., O'Conner and Catchpole, brought up his hand and held out a finger as if to indicate the number one – then he lapsed back into unconsciousness*.

Mr O'Conner had a stretcher on his lorry, and together with Corporal Catchpole put Lawrence on to it. An Army lorry came by and they loaded the stretcher, along with the injured boy cyclist, into this vehicle rather than O'Conner's.

Was there any special significance to Lawrence holding up his finger? While on a visit to Amman (Jordan) in the spring of 1982, the author mentioned this incident to Suleiman Mousa, the distinguished Arab historian (author of *T. E. Lawrence – An Arab View*). He at once said that raising a single finger could have been the dying gesture of a Moslem – one finger indicating that there is only one God. An intriguing possibility, but equally, Lawrence may have been trying to communicate something more sinister, perhaps about the car.

Predictably, there has been a great deal of speculation about the crash. Colin Graham, a Dorset journalist, has made a lengthy study of the circumstances of Lawrence's death, and after fifteen years of research, he is convinced that Lawrence was murdered (an opinion shared by the late Henry Williamson and John Bruce). It is easy to see why he has come to this conclusion.

T.E. was an expert motorcyclist. Unless a car had made Lawrence swerve, why should he have crashed into two cyclists travelling in single file on an open road? Is the explanation that they were hidden by a dip in the road really credible? Why was the black car never traced? Did anyone else see it? Who was present at the scene of the crash? The cottage was carefully guarded by the Army and the police after the accident. Why? Did the Air Ministry, or anyone else, remove sensitive documents from Cloud's Hill?

On 16 May, A. W. Lawrence had told the *Dorset Echo*:

> I am staying at my brother's cottage at present. With regard to the stories of the Air Ministry officials coming to take secret papers away from the cottage, I can only say that a special guard has been sent to the cottage. This has been done to ensure that sightseers should not bother us and to protect my brother's valuable books which are in the cottage.

But the chief question remains: was Lawrence murdered? The evidence, in

*In the summer of 1982, I tried to get back in touch with L.C. but could not. Firstly, I was told by a third party 'that the story was not entirely true' – there was no denial that L.C. had been a witness – and shortly afterwards I received an embarrassed letter from the same person stating that L.C. 'has never had any conversation with you about this' and that he was anxious lest his name be publicized. At the time (1982) I thought this might have been an attempt to conceal the information which I had stumbled across. However, now I believe that the reason for the third party's embarrassment was that they had been partially responsible for embellishing on the story (they were present at the original conversation with L.C.), to which I may have fallen victim. One thing remains certain and has been confirmed by my subsequent investigations: two important witnesses were not called to the inquest.

spite of a cover-up, suggests that the crash was a genuine accident. Rumours of a mystery were inevitably compounded because of the victim, the official cloak of secrecy which descended on personnel at Bovington Camp, the obvious guard put upon his cottage, and the rushed way in which the inquest was conducted.

At least three theories have been put forward, if the crash was not an accident:

1 That the crash was a quasi-suicide in which Lawrence, having little left to live for, made a deliberate decision to sacrifice his life to save the boys.
2 That the accident was faked so that Lawrence could retire in peace, perhaps to Morocco. The only evidence for such an extraordinary conspiracy is that none of the photographs taken of Lawrence in his coffin came out.
3 That Lawrence was murdered (and here we enter the realms of spy fiction) by either:
   a The British Intelligence Services because they were concerned that he was, once again, about to become an embarrassment, possibly because of his fringe connection with Mosley's blackshirts, or because of his intentions to make public his RAF memoirs; or
   b The Germans, to prevent Lawrence taking over the reorganization of Britain's Home Defences; or
   c The French, or their agents in revenge for Lawrence's anti-French activities; or
   d Zionists for reasons which are as confused as they are unlikely; or
   e Bolshevik Russian agents because of Lawrence's activities as 'arch spy of the world'; or
   f Agents of an Arab Government; or
   g The I.R.A. Lawrence took a keen interest in Irish Republicanism and once refused Michael Collins's offer of a brigade in the Free State army; or
   h Persons unknown because of the new secret work which Lawrence was about to, or had already, become involved in.

All the assassination theories are pure speculation and it is far more likely that the fatal crash was as it appeared. For years, Lawrence's friends had been warning him that he should be more careful on his motorbike. This is not to say that he drove without care to others but rather that Lawrence, who was a first-rate motorcyclist, used his motorbike and its speed to block momentarily his thoughts and worries. He loved the sensation of speed and found in it a freedom and relaxation to relieve psychological tension. His last motorbike was an SS 100 Brough Superior, the fastest motorbike of its day, in which the engine design had vastly exceeded the handling and brakes. Lawrence never wore a crash helmet and drove at high speed whenever the chance arose.

There are conflicting statements regarding his speed prior to the crash but the bike, when picked up by the local garage, was jammed in second gear. Pat Knowles noted that, moments before the crash, he heard Lawrence rev the bike up, something he never did normally, preferring to coast the last few hundred yards to Cloud's Hill. The machine's gears may have become jammed when Lawrence, who was undeniably cool in such circumstances, changed down to make an emergency stop and, in doing so, over-revved the engine and gear-box. George Bernard Shaw wrote that his present of the Brough motorcycle 'was like handing a pistol to a would-be suicide'.[3]

The most probable explanation is therefore that Lawrence, travelling at speed (in the past he had reached 100 miles per hour on the same stretch of road) suddenly came upon the car, negotiated this obstacle but unexpectedly came upon the two cyclists who may have previously been hidden by a dip in the road. There is a possibility that Lawrence did not see the car or the boys as soon as he might have done because of failing eyesight, or he may have misjudged the distances. In a letter written to Dr Ernest Altounyan at the end of 1934, Lawrence noted that he had recently been having serious trouble with his vision. Further, he stated that these bouts came on suddenly and were particularly bad in dull light.[4]

When Lawrence did see the boys he began to brake violently and, realizing that he could not avoid a crash, made a split-second deliberate decision to steer his bike to the right of the cyclists, thus saving their lives at the possible expense of his own. As he skidded past them he could not avoid hitting one, whose cycle went tumbling and fell on his friend. Now fully out of control, Lawrence went over the handlebars of his own machine and fractured his skull on the road.

Catchpole, L.C. and Mr O'Conner rushed to the scene of the accident, as did the unknown man 'on a bicycle' mentioned by Fletcher. Lawrence made a last effort to communicate with the faces looking down at him and raised one finger – could he have meant, 'At least there's only one casualty?' or 'Am I the only one hurt?' – and then lapsed into oblivion.

This hypothesis, if it is correct and the accident was genuine, does not explain the extraordinary security precautions which were taken. Why, for example, did the police place a detective by his bed? This is standard practice only when a statement is needed from the victim. If it was clearly an accident, why bother a dying man to try to make a statement? The police were obviously not sure of the circumstances of Lawrence's crash.

Lawrence's funeral was also handled in a strange way. Before the inquest jury had reached its verdict, a special train was already bringing the officially approved mourners from London to attend the funeral at Moreton Church, a couple of miles from Cloud's Hill. On 20 May, the day after Lawrence died, *The Times* had announced the arrangements:

> The funeral of Mr. T. E. Shaw, formerly Colonel Lawrence, will take place at Moreton Church, Dorset at 2.30 p.m. on Tuesday. The service will be a simple one, and no mourning and no flowers are requested. Apart from those especially invited the service will be confined to his particular friends and those who were associated with him in Arabia. A train leaving Waterloo at 9.30 a.m. and arriving at Moreton at 1.58 will be met by motor-cars to convey friends to the church, a distance of two miles. A train returning to London will leave Moreton at 5.5 p.m.

On the same day, the *Daily Express* reported that the family were asking the public not to attend the funeral. The inevitable result was that hundreds flocked to see T. E. Lawrence's last performance. Ronald Storrs, the chief pall-bearer, was upset, 'as we carried the coffin into and out of the little church the clicking Kodaks and the whirring of reels extracted from the dead body their last "personal" publicity'.[5] Storrs was one of six pall-bearers chosen to represent six stages of Lawrence's life (Storrs represented scholarship). The other five were Stewart Newcombe (Arabia), Pat Knowles (Cloud's Hill), Eric Kennington (Art), Private Russell (The Royal Tank Corps) and Corporal Bradbury (Royal Air Force). Absent at Moreton that day were Allenby and Trenchard, who although in England, had decided to keep away. Lawrence's mother and brother Bob were unable to attend because they were in China, and George Bernard Shaw and his wife Charlotte because they were in South Africa. Nevertheless, the list of mourners was prestigious. Amongst those present were Winston and Clementine Churchill, Lady Astor, Siegfried Sassoon, Lord Lloyd, Lord Winterton, General Wavell, Lionel Curtis and Mrs Thomas Hardy.

The service in Moreton Church was performed by Canon Kinloch, and then the coffin was carried out, not to the main cemetery, but to a piece of field just over the road which the local squire, Henry Frampton, had donated to the church. Frampton was distantly related to Lawrence through the Chapmans, and, though T.E. was always aware of this, it has never been discovered to what extent they knew each other before the crash. A copy of the subscriber's edition of *Seven Pillars* annotated by Lawrence still exists in the library of Morton Hall (the Frampton home). Its presence there indicates that Lawrence must have been on good terms with the Framptons. Some biographers have even suggested that Frampton was the Old Man of the flagellation fantasies Lawrence played out with John Bruce, but this seems most unlikely.

Lawrence's grave is extremely modest. The headstone was erected some time after the burial and would have displeased him intensely, firstly because it refers to him as T. E. Lawrence – rather than T. E. Shaw, the name he had elected to live under – and secondly because there is a biblical inscription which rings of his mother's strict brand of Christianity:

To the dear memory of
T.E. LAWRENCE
Fellow of All Souls College
Oxford

Born 16 August 1888
Died 19 May 1935

The hour is coming & now is
when the dead shall hear
The voice of the
SON OF GOD
And they that hear shall live

At the base of the grave, there is another smaller stone carved into the shape of an open book upon which is the inscription:

DOMINUS ILLUMINATIO MEA

– a quote from the 27th Psalm which is the motto of Oxford University and of the Oxford University Press. For those interested in following the Lawrence trail even further, there is an effigy of Lawrence in Arabian regalia by Kennington in St Martin's church at Wareham. There is also a memorial bust of him, again by Kennington, in the crypt of St Paul's Cathedral in London, and another identical one in the Chapel of Jesus College, Oxford.

On the subject of Lawrence's will, A. W. Lawrence made a statement to the Press:

> He has left the estate to me with certain instructions as to its disposal which I do not think will be of public interest.
>
> The estate comprises about £200 in his current account, certain investments, his cottage, Cloud's Hill, Moreton, his motorbike and books, documents, private papers and furniture in the cottage.
>
> The will is written on a small slip of paper and was drawn up by a lawyer.
>
> The will makes me and a lawyer the executors, and I have been made the literary executor. I do not think, however, that he left any works of importance.

The last sentence is odd, as A. W. Lawrence knew about *The Mint*. A great deal of Lawrence's most valuable work, however, remained tied up in the trusts created when *The Seven Pillars of Wisdom* had almost bankrupted him.

Lawrence of Arabia's death will always remain as mysterious as his life for those who wish it to. There are strange coincidences – for example, the fact that Corporal Catchpole shot himself some years after the crash. However, for those who would like to clear away the fog of confusion, and with it some of the entertainment value of the Lawrence legend, there is a logical and straightforward explanation for the official cloak of secrecy which followed the accident. The answer lies in the very newspapers in which the funeral was reported. On 23 May there was an official Government announcement that the Air Force was to be massively expanded, both in manpower and in equipment. The *Mirror* announced:

> AIR SECURITY PLANS TO BE REVEALED TODAY
> More Planes and Men for R.A.F.
> Immediate increase in Training Schools.

Speeches were made in both the House of Lords and in the Commons. In the Upper House the Minister of Air, Lord Londonderry, stated:

> Britain's home air force is to be nearly trebled. If it is insufficient we shall increase it whatever the cost . . . To the young men of the country, whatever their walk in life, I say that the time has come for them to see to it that Britain is given the Air Force she needs. Let them enrol freely so soon as the requirements of the force are made public.

In the light of these circumstances, it is not surprising that the Air Ministry were concerned about Lawrence's death and the consequent publicity. Through his many influential friends, and in particular Sir Philip Sassoon, Under Secretary of State for Air, Lawrence was aware and may have been consulted on the plans to increase the strength of the Service. It is also almost certain that his private papers contained documents relating to his vision of a modern Air Force. Lawrence had always circumvented the official chain of command when he thought it necessary. He had used politicians such as Nancy Astor and Ernest Thurtle to champion ideas for modernization. The contents of his correspondence could have proved very embarrassing had it been published. The Air Ministry was also concerned about *The Mint*. They were about to undertake a widespread recruiting drive, and the last thing they wanted was for the Press to get hold of Lawrence's brutal but perceptive account of barrack-room life.

In considering these facts, together with Lawrence's reputation, one can understand why the Air Ministry took such precautions after the accident. They failed, however, to learn the lesson of the Afghanistan fiasco: too much security is counter-productive and merely fuels speculation. Interest in Lawrence continues today because a great deal of his life was, and will remain, a secret. The gaps in his story retain enduring fascination.

AFTERMATH

The Lawrence Industry

Aftermath

Lowell Thomas was the first to commercialize the Lawrence story, as readers of this book will have seen. But to suggest that he 'created Lawrence' would be misleading. What he did was to recognize (and to stimulate) a public demand for a certain type of romantic hero, and to see that Lawrence and his desert adventures fitted the bill, needing only a little gilding for the popular audience. However much Lawrence criticized him later, it was through Lowell Thomas that he gained an international reputation. It is estimated that four million people went to see Thomas's 'travelogue', and the subsequent book *With Lawrence in Arabia* (New York, Century 1924; London, Hutchinson 1925), went into over a hundred impressions and was still available in the 1970s.

This provided an assurance of Lawrence's success as an author. Without the benefit of the aura created around him by Thomas, it is unlikely that he could have realistically considered the private printing of *The Seven Pillars of Wisdom*; the large debts incurred on the project were only paid off because of the eagerness of Jonathan Cape and Doubleday Doran to publish the abridged version, *Revolt in the Desert*, which sold extremely well. Lawrence had retained the right to withdraw it once its royalties had settled the bill for *Seven Pillars*, and *Revolt in the Desert* was declared out of print when the English print run alone had reached nearly 90,000 and demand for the book was still intense. The large number of copies more than adequately paid his debts, and the surplus was put into trust for RAF charities. (John Bruce has claimed that Lawrence did this unwillingly – and would have preferred to have kept the money himself. According to Bruce, family pressure was put on Lawrence not to profit from the book.)

Despite the exercise of his option to withdraw *Revolt in the Desert*, Lawrence encouraged Cape to commission Robert Graves to write a popular biography of him to cater for a similar market. It appeared in England in 1927 as *Lawrence and the Arabs*, and in the United States, published by Doubleday, as *Lawrence and the Arabian Adventure* in 1928. Similarly, Lawrence helped Liddell Hart in 1934 with his biography *'T. E. LAWRENCE' in Arabia and After*, which appeared in America as *Colonel Lawrence . . . the Man behind the Legend*. Both books were best-sellers on both sides of the Atlantic.

Lawrence exerted an extraordinary degree of control over books published about him, and the full extent of his machinations to prevent 'unlicensed' biographies will never be known. After his death, his brother A. W. Lawrence became his chief literary executor, inheriting the responsibility of protecting the family name and 'Ned's' reputation.

A. W. Lawrence immediately exerted his authority to prevent Cape reissuing *Revolt in the Desert* – the publishers believed that their agreement to withdraw the book applied only during T. E. Lawrence's lifetime, and immediately after his death, began preparations for a reprint. According to Michael Howard, Jonathan Cape's biographer, when A. W. Lawrence heard of this, he told Cape that his brother had not wished the book ever to reappear in an abridged form, and that if it did, 'Cape would never be allowed to publish *Seven Pillars*'.[1] An arrangement was reached whereby instead of *Revolt in the Desert*, the *Seven Pillars* (with a preface by A.W. himself) immediately went to press. It appeared on 29 July, just two and a half months after T. E. Lawrence's death – a remarkable achievement considering the size both of the book and of the first run. By Christmas 1935, over 100,000 copies of the 672-page book had been sold in England alone. It was published simultaneously by Doran and achieved a similar success in the States. The book has since been translated into many languages and continues to sell well all over the world.

While he had been overseeing the launch of *Seven Pillars*, Arnold Lawrence had also been considering what to do about *The Mint.* He was concerned lest the book be pirated and appear in the United States, and in an effort to secure the American copyright, he decided to allow *The Mint* to be 'published', making sure that the edition was so small (eight was the minimum required by U.S. law) and the few copies so expensive that no one could afford to buy it. Trenchard, the former Chief of Air Staff and new Commissioner of the Metropolitan Police, was asked to use his influence in the United States to ensure that the two books, which by statutory right would have to go to the Library of Congress, should be kept 'out of sight'. He was concerned at the proposal, having been assured by the author that the book would not be published until 1950 at the earliest, but when he realized that 'publication' was a means of limiting circulation, he gave his approval. A. W. Lawrence arranged with Doubleday Doran for the publication of fifty copies, ten of which would be for sale at half a million dollars each. This in itself became news, gaining publicity both for Doubleday and for *The Mint.* Two copies were placed in the Library of Congress as required, but there appears to have been a slip-up. Michael Howard notes that 'after one journalist had read a copy in the Library of Congress and written a review of it, the librarian booked it out on indefinite loan to himself and kept the other copy locked up'.[2]

The majority of the remaining copies had been moved, again amid much publicity, to a bank safe. A. W. Lawrence kept at least two books – one to be given to the British Museum Library on the understanding that it would be kept out of sight, while a second was sold to T.E.'s literary agent, Raymond Savage, for the nominal price of one dollar. *The Mint* was not left to be forgotten in its quasi-secret hiding places. According to the *New York Journal American* for 9 November 1937, the book was exhibited at the Boston Book Fair by Doubleday Doran:

> GUARD 'MINT'
> $500,000 LAWRENCE BOOK
> ESCORTED TO FAIR
>
> A thin leather-bound book was taken from a bank vault under armed guard, carried to a plane by Colonel Theodore Roosevelt and flown to Boston with an aerial escort to guard against hijacking.
>
> That volume, one of only 12 copies of 'The Mint', by the late Colonel T. E. Lawrence, was being exhibited today at the Boston Book Fair. Under the terms of Lawrence's will, 'The Mint' is to be held from popular publication until 1950.

In 1947 A. W. Lawrence and Jonathan Cape discussed general publication of *The Mint*, and the book was prepared and type-set in anticipation of a launch in 1950; but it was not published as planned. This was no doubt because both Lawrence's commandant at Uxbridge, who was disparagingly described, and Commander Breeze were still alive. The book, with an introductory note by A.W., eventually appeared in 1955 (Doubleday also republished it in the States). In England there were two editions – one for the general public in which the four-letter expletives were omitted with obvious blanks, and a second collector's edition, limited to two thousand copies, which was unexpurgated. Cape felt obliged to include a written warning to the book trade:

> Please note carefully that the limited edition of 'The Mint' may well be considered unsuitable for general circulation. Discretion is therefore advised in distribution of copies which have been allocated to you.[3]

Despite the atmosphere of secrecy which had been nurtured around the book for so long, it did not sell as well as had been expected.

Jonathan Cape have published a whole range of volumes by or about Lawrence – nearly a dozen titles – though their firm had no monopoly. A. W. Lawrence has edited two books about his brother for Cape and has edited and contributed to a number of books related to T. E. Lawrence for other publishers, most notably the Golden Cockerel Press. Lawrence's friends have been similarly prolific. A common feature of all these books, some of which are excellent pieces of scholarship, is that they omit vital aspects of Lawrence's personality. The members of what one journalist termed 'the Lawrence Bureau' managed to preserve an unrealistic portrait of T. E. Lawrence for nearly twenty years. Their reasons for so doing are understandable. Lawrence inspired great affection and loyalty; equally, many friends saw only one facet of this very complex man. Nevertheless, some of those closest to Lawrence have schemed to prevent publication of material which they considered 'unsuitable', and have caused great distress to those who have dared to criticize their beloved T.E.

One writer who feels that he has been a victim is Edward Robinson, a veteran of the Arab Campaign, who has written three books about T. E. Lawrence, two of which have been published. Shortly after Lawrence's death in 1935, Robinson was approached by the Oxford University Press (he states on the recommendation of A. W. Lawrence) to write a book for boys about T. E. Lawrence. There is no doubt that the project was completed with the approval of A. W. Lawrence as he contributed an introductory note, stating that the general picture seemed as accurate as could be reasonably expected.[4]

Robinson's book, entitled simply *Lawrence*, went into several editions. The author, encouraged by his success, began to write a second biography, this time for Jonathan Cape (again Robinson states that this was through A. W. Lawrence's recommendation). This manuscript was moderately critical of T.E., and A. W. Lawrence, who disputed its accuracy, fell out with Robinson over the matter. The book for Cape was never printed. In 1946, however, the firm of Lincoln-Praeger Ltd. published a third book by him, *Lawrence the Rebel*. The author noted at the beginning:

> I have written it in the hope that it will help . . . not only to understand Lawrence, but to understand the reasons for the present tangle of trouble in the Middle East. The book is an attempt to bring the mistakes of secret diplomacy into the open . . .[5]

The book makes credible, and what must have been in 1946 startling, revelations about Lawrence and the politics behind the Hejaz Campaign. Part of it takes the form of a personal diary, the accuracy of which is difficult to confirm sixty years after the events it describes; the rest of the book, though not without minor errors, is an important landmark among books on Lawrence. Robinson believes that pressure was brought to bear on newspapers not to publish reviews of his revealing and potentially embarrassing book. One of the few publications which planned a review was the *New Statesman and Nation*; they sent a review copy to David Garnett, requesting that he should return his review 'not later than June 16th [19] '46'.[6] Garnett, a close friend of the Lawrence family, seems to have ignored the request. No major review appeared, and the book, which could and should have proved a best-seller, vanished without trace.

During the early 1950s a well-known British writer based in Paris, Richard Aldington, began another independent biography of Lawrence. Aldington's researches led him to believe that a very false portrait of Lawrence had been painted, and what had originally started as a biography evolved into *T. E. Lawrence – a Biographical Enquiry*. The manuscript was accepted by Collins in 1953 against an advance of £4,500 – a large sum for the time. Aldington's book, although spiteful and pedantic, shows convincingly that Lawrence had not been truthful in his own writings and had deliberately misled his biographers. Aldington drew attention to Lawrence's illegitimacy (a fact which had not yet been publicized in England) as the key to his personality, and went on to denounce him as a mock-modest homosexual poseur, artificially made a hero by an Anglo-American conspiracy.

As might be expected, the controversy over the book began well before its publication date which had been announced as May 1954. On 15 February 1954, the American magazine *Newsweek* ran a story headlined:

LAWRENCE : LIES OF LEGEND?

Lawrence's friends were infuriated. Lawyers for the Lawrence Trust asked Collins to show them the proofs of the proposed book, suggesting it might damage the sales of the *Seven Pillars*. This request was politely refused. Some weeks later the publishers, now under considerable pressure from various influential individuals sympathetic to the Lawrence cause, agreed to allow Basil Liddell Hart to examine the proofs of Aldington's book for errors of fact. Hart was incensed at what he read and approached his own lawyer to see whether or not the publication could be prevented because of infringement of his own or Lawrence's copyrights. The lawyer stated that there were no grounds for such an action; Aldington had used no more than a 'reasonable' amount of copyright material. Robert Graves suggested that the only thing left to do was to 'publicly strike Aldington and plead the book as provocation'.

Phillip Knightley, whose careful research has brought much of this information to light, notes:

> Thwarted in their plans for stopping publication by legal methods, Lawrence's friends again started 'turning the heat on Collins'. Liddell Hart pointed out to them that it was unfortunate after publishing two books about a German national hero, Field Marshal Rommel, they should want to publish a book demolishing the reputation of Lawrence, a British national hero.[7]

Among other things, Liddell Hart claimed the book would injure Mrs Lawrence, and would be used as propaganda by the Communists.

The battle raged on, Eric Kennington, Lady Astor, Trenchard, Ronald Storrs and Sir Lewis Namier lending support. Publication was postponed in England. However, the French newspaper *Le Figaro* began a serialization in April 1954. Liddell Hart tried to enlist Churchill, then Prime Minister, into the campaign to prevent publication in England. Liddell Hart was particularly keen that Churchill should provide evidence to disprove one of Aldington's main allegations – namely, that contrary to Lawrence's claims, Churchill had never offered him the job of High Commissioner of Egypt. Churchill was not able to do this, as he had never specifically offered Lawrence the post, and was evidently anxious not to become directly involved in the increasing public controversy. A few days later, A. W. Lawrence had a meeting with Collins at which the publishers agreed that certain passages which related to Mrs Lawrence might be 'toned down'; no other excisions could be made. There were few other developments during the rest of 1954, the pro-Lawrence party deciding that they would have to wait until after publication to respond to Aldington. At the beginning of January 1955, the book was published in

France as *Lawrence L'Imposteur*. Three weeks later, it appeared in Britain amid a blaze of publicity. The rows continued in the Press, on television and on the radio, but Aldington had clearly raised some valid points, albeit in a most vindictive manner – Lawrence's reputation was never to be the same again.*

Important issues were at stake over Aldington's book. Phillip Knightley has quoted a letter written by the journalist Charles Curran to a friend of Lawrence's:

> It seems to me that it is historically important for the relevant facts about a public man to be set down to allow them to be checked against the testimony of contemporary witnesses; and that personal feelings cannot always override this consideration . . . Above all else, the suppression of any book (even only a temporary suppression) is a dangerous precedent, especially when the grounds for such an action are basically that the book presents new and unpopular (or even inaccurate) aspects of a national figure.[8]

The publicity surrounding Aldington's book, and publication of *The Mint*, may have done nothing to improve Lawrence's reputation, but interest in his life became rampant. It was only a matter of time before Lawrence became the subject of a film.

Producers had speculated on the idea since the 1920s. Valentino's epic (*The Sheik* 1921 and *Son of the Sheik* 1926), both loosely based on E. M. Hull's novel, may well have been inspired by Lowell Thomas's show and certainly capitalized on the image of Arabia which Thomas had popularized. In 1926 Lawrence wrote that a film about him was shortly to come out. It never did. Little information is available but it is known that the Irish-born director Rex Ingram (who later converted to Islam) had approached Lawrence about making a film during this period. Similarly, the producer Herbert Wilcox claims that during the mid-20s he was approached by Lawrence and his agent (presumably Raymond Savage) and was offered 'film rights'. Nothing came of it. Late in 1934 Alexander Korda, the legendary boss of London Films, bought the film rights of *Revolt in the Desert* for an estimated £30,000. Korda also bought the rights to Robert Graves's writings on Lawrence. Lawrence approached the film magnate and it was agreed, apparently without argument, that Korda would postpone his plans for a Lawrence film either until Lawrence gave his consent or until after his death. Korda seems to have been remarkably accommodating considering the amount of money he had expended on purchasing rights.

After Lawrence's death plans were set in motion to produce an epic based on *Revolt in the Desert*. Among others Leslie Howard, Laurence Olivier and Walter Hudd (who had appeared in Shaw's play *Too True to be Good*) were

*The case of the pro-Lawrence lobby was further damaged by publication of *The Mint*, a book which in the less liberated 1950s hardly reinforced the view of Lawrence's life as an example to the nation's youth. Liddell Hart expressed some irritation to Eric Kennington that A. W. Lawrence had not informed him of his plans for the RAF notes.

considered for the leading role, but the project never materialized. Korda told his nephew, Michael, in the 1950s that the reason for this was

> partly because of Palestine, and Churchill was very worried because he felt it was important to have the Turks as allies when the War came, so nothing ever came of it. Olivier would have been wonderful as Lawrence. Now I don't know, it's still difficult to do, and with the Israelis and the Arabs, I'm not sure it would work.[9]

In 1946, the London *Evening News* reported that Ortis Films Ltd were negotiating with Professor A. W. Lawrence and his executors to get the first chance of the rights to *Seven Pillars*.[10] Again, nothing seems to have come of this. Little is heard of proposed Lawrence productions until 1955 when Paramount announced their involvement in a film about Lawrence which would star Alec Guinness. Terence Rattigan, whose father had been a friend of Ronald Storrs, was to write the script, the director was named as Anthony Asquith and the producer as Anatole de Grunwald. Both Paramount and Guinness dropped out of the picture, and the project, budgeted at well over £500,000, was taken up by Rank, who announced Dirk Bogarde in the title role (though Terence Rattigan thought him unsuitable for the part). Rank began preparations in earnest and sent an advance party, including Asquith, to Iraq to scout locations – the Suez crisis had made many areas of the Middle East inaccessible. It was announced that the shooting would begin in April 1958. Costumes and props were made and precise schedules drawn up, but suddenly those involved with the project were told in March that the film was cancelled. In his autobiography, *Snakes and Ladders*, Dirk Bogarde writes:

> No one ever mentioned 'Lawrence' again. I never knew and still do not know, what stopped the plans so suddenly a few weeks before shooting. Neither if I remember did Puffin [Asquith] or anyone else connected with the production. Was it a matter of politics? Did someone object to the exposing of a very private man.[11]

Terence Rattigan still had his script. He had no wish to see two years' work wasted, so he turned it into a play – *Ross*. Once again Alec Guinness was cast in the title role. But as Rattigan put together his new production, A. W. Lawrence, encouraged by Robert Graves, made the decision to sell the film rights of *The Seven Pillars of Wisdom* to Sam Spiegel for the relatively small sum of £17,500 (Graves would later be appointed adviser on the resulting film). A. W. Lawrence was not happy about Rattigan's play. Martin Seymour-Smith writes he 'suspected Rattigan of portraying his brother as a homosexual (on the rather poor grounds that Rattigan himself was a homosexual); but as he told Graves a month later, 'I like Spiegel . . . If they make good in my eyes I'll help them actively.'[12]

Rattigan had made no attempt to conceal the text of his play, and wanted to do anything he could, within reason, to appease A. W. Lawrence. Both Robert Graves and Liddell Hart had been given the script to read. Liddell Hart saw few objections but Graves disliked the play, and wrote to Rattigan to tell him so. A. W. Lawrence refused to give his blessing to *Ross* because through the licensing system then operated by the Lord Chamberlain's office there existed the possibility that this excellent play might be banned. Rattigan told the Lord Chamberlain's office that if his play was banned he would have it done on television (which did not require A.W.'s or the Lord Chamberlain's sanction). He also wrote to Robert Graves stating that in the last resort the play could be put on in the United States. In the meantime (according to Martin Seymour-Smith) A. W. Lawrence had asked Graves to use his influence on Alec Guinness. Graves wrote to Guinness's wife Merula – her husband was out of the country – explaining his view of the situation. Sir Alec was irritated when he heard that his wife had been brought into the affair, but was also surprised to learn that A.W. was trying to stop the play, or that its contents were contentious. He assured Graves that he wanted no part in denigrating a national hero.

Anxious to calm troubled waters, Rattigan offered to amend certain passages, but his difficulties were still not over. Sam Spiegel presented a new problem. Having bought the film rights in *Seven Pillars*, it looked as if he might be able to claim that Rattigan had infringed his copyright. Rattigan overcame this with the assistance of Liddell Hart, who was also anxious that things should be brought to a reasonable conclusion. Approached by Rattigan and his lawyers, Liddell Hart allowed his 'advice' and his biography of Lawrence to be credited as official source for Rattigan's research, thus creating the curious situation of having Liddell Hart as adviser to Rattigan, and Graves as adviser to David Lean and Sam Spiegel. *Ross* finally opened in the spring of 1960 and was the success it deserved to be.

Sam Spiegel and his co-producer and director, David Lean, meanwhile failed to 'make good' in A. W. Lawrence's eyes. When it became clear how their proposed epic was to be presented, with a script by Robert Bolt and with Peter O'Toole as Lawrence (Marlon Brando had been considered at an earlier stage), A.W. withdrew his support for the production and permission to use *The Seven Pillars of Wisdom* as its title. The film which eventually emerged was made on location in Jordan, Morocco and Spain and at studios in England. It cost over £10,000,000 and took 15 months to make. Historically it is inaccurate, but like Lowell Thomas's productions, this did little to devalue its entertainment value. In its feeling for Lawrence, Peter O'Toole (despite his height) achieved a credible characterization. *Lawrence of Arabia* was a magnificent piece of film-making – and as such has been enjoyed by hundreds of millions of people.

There were few major developments in the Lawrence story until 1968. The events of that year are unusual even by the standards of the Lawrence legend. John Bruce, who had been in contact with Lawrence's solicitors since the 1930s, sold his story to *The Sunday Times*. Colin Simpson, a *Sunday Times* reporter, checked up on some of Bruce's claims, found evidence to support them, and approached A. W. Lawrence. In a state of some shock, A.W. admitted to Simpson that T.E. had been beaten by Bruce and was anxious that the background to the story should come out. Simpson, who knew that a large collection of papers relating to T. E. Lawrence had been gathered by A.W. in the Bodleian Library, Oxford, and kept secret, asked him for access. This request was granted. After a series of articles in *The Sunday Times*, Colin Simpson wrote, with Phillip Knightley, the now famous book *The Secret Lives of Lawrence of Arabia*. The book used the worldwide resources available to *The Sunday Times*, and the picture of Lawrence which emerged both personally and politically was very different from earlier versions.

Knightley and Simpson were in an awkward situation. They needed (like the present writer) A.W.'s co-operation over copyright. In the end an unusual contract was drawn up between Professor Lawrence and *The Sunday Times*, a draft of which is available in the Imperial War Museum. It is not necessary to go into all the details here, but in return for a financial consideration, A. W. Lawrence agreed that copyright material could be quoted, subject to certain conditions. These included such matters as the inclusion of certain specific phrases written by Professor Lawrence in *Lawrence and his Friends* about the cost of his brother's sexual abstinence, such as 'methods advocated by the saints', and a 'cost so terrible in waste and suffering'; an undertaking to 'slur over' matters 'that might cause distress to third parties', and other similar conditions. It is a credit to Knightley and Simpson that the integrity of their book was not damaged. It remains one of the best books on T. E. Lawrence.

One of the terms of the contract was that *The Sunday Times* would give all the John Bruce material to Dr John Mack, who was also writing a biography of Lawrence, apparently with A.W.'s approval. However, when Dr Mack published his extensive psycho-biography, *A Prince of Our Disorder*, which won him a Pulitzer Prize, A. W. Lawrence was evidently not satisfied. He has since appointed Jeremy Wilson as his brother's official biographer. In the meantime, the Lawrence Trust still tries to exert control over works of which it disapproves. In 1977, the respected Arabist, Desmond Stewart, published a radical new biography which strongly emphasizes the sado-masochistic side of Lawrence's character. Stewart also noted that he believed that Lawrence has involved others besides John Bruce in his flagellation fantasies. On the political front, Stewart stated that important secret papers concerning Britain's defence plans had been removed from Lawrence's cottage after his death.

Solicitors to the Lawrence Trust, which became aware of the contents of the book, threatened according to *The Sunday Times* (12 June 1977) that unless certain changes were made, the Trust would revoke copyright permission to quote from Lawrence's works. They later withdrew this threat but said that the 'passages should be modified if not deleted'.[13] Hamish Hamilton (Stewart's publishers) refused. Unfortunately, it has not been possible to interview Desmond Stewart because of his death in 1981.

One wonders what may happen next in the continuing saga of Lawrence of Arabia. After fifty years it shows no sign of abating. Lawrence once predicted that after his death his bones would be rattled with curiosity; in that there can be no dispute.

Notes to the text

N.B. I have endeavoured to make these Notes as complete as I can. In the case of references to PRO (Public Records Office) items I have gone back and added page numbers where possible. In most previous books on Lawrence PRO item numbers alone have been given, but as some of these documents run into several hundred pages, page numbers will obviously be useful. I apologize for several gaps in the Notes, and have pointed these out where applicable.

1 **Childhood** (pp. 19–30)

1 John Mack, a psychoanalyst, has suggested that Lawrence may have been aware of his parents' secret before he consciously discovered it.
2 Letter to Charlotte Shaw, 14 April 1927. British Museum, additional manuscript 45903. Excerpt published in *A Prince of Our Disorder*, page 31.
3 See for example *The Secret Lives of Lawrence of Arabia*, page 8.
4 *Sunday Times* papers now in the Imperial War Museum.
5 *T. E. Lawrence by his Friends*, page 25.
6 Ibid, page 44.
7 *With Lawrence in Arabia*, page 21.
8 *Lawrence and the Arabs*, pages 11–12.
9 *T. E. Lawrence* by Liddell Hart, page 13.
10 *Lawrence of Arabia – a biographical enquiry*, page 18.
11 Restricted Bodleian Collection. Lawrence to Lionel Curtis, 27 November 1927.
12 *T. E. Lawrence by his Friends*, page 25.
13 Pamphlet published in Jersey *Letters from Dr. M. R. Lawrence (eldest brother of Lawrence of Arabia) to Stanhope Landick (a Jerseyman)*. According to this document, Frank was born on 7 February 1893 at Bramerton House, Havre des Pas, Jersey.
14 *T. E. Lawrence by his Friends*, page 33.
15 Ibid, T. W. Chaundy's recollections, page 41.
16 See for example *Home Letters*, pages 6, 45, and 100.
17 *T. E. Lawrence by his Friends*, page 29.
18 Ibid, page 41.
19 Ibid, page 37.
20 *T. E. Lawrence to his biographer Liddell Hart*, page 51.
21 *A Prince of Our Disorder*, page 33.
22 *T. E. Lawrence by his Friends*, page 48.
23 Ibid, page 46.
24 Ibid, page 26.
25 Ibid.
26 Ibid, page 46.
27 Ibid, page 48.
28 Ibid, page 47.
29 Ibid, page 46.
30 Restricted Bodleian Collection, letter from Arnold Lawrence to Robert Graves, 15 June 1927.
31 Vyvyan Richards to Helen Cash, 4 March 1965.
32 *The Secret Lives of Lawrence of Arabia*, page 11.
33 *T. E. Lawrence by his Friends*, page 27.

34 Ibid, page 26.
35 Letter to Charlotte Shaw, 8 May 1928. British Museum, additional manuscript 45904. Excerpt published in *A Prince of Our Disorder*, page 420.
36 Ibid, 18 August 1928.
37 Letter to Mrs Rieder, *Letters of T. E. Lawrence*, page 148.
38 *T. E. Lawrence by his Friends*, page 41.
39 Ibid, page 53.
40 Ibid, page 57.
41 *A Prince of Our Disorder*, page 45.
42 *T. E. Lawrence by his Friends*, page 67.
43 Since completing this book, I have discovered that Lawrence had also discussed a similar fantasy with C. F. C. Beeson. See *T. E. Lawrence by his Friends*, page 53.
44 Letter from Colin Simpson to Leonard Russell, *Sunday Times* material, Imperial War Museum.
45 Interview between John Mack and C. F. C. Beeson, 22 March 1965. See *A Prince of Our Disorder*, page 25.
46 *T. E. Lawrence by his Friends*, page 46.
47 *Middle East Diary 1917–1956* by R. Meinertzhagen, page 30.
48 *Lawrence to his biographer Liddell Hart*, page 51. Since completing *Backing into the Limelight* I have acquired David Garnett's copy of *Lawrence to his biographer Liddell Hart*. Next to the passage referring to the enlistment in the Artillery, Garnett has pencilled 'Leonard Green says there is no truth in this story. See his letter to me.' I have been unable to trace the letter.
49 Letter from Jane to Robert Graves, 1927. Restricted Bodleian Collection. The letter was first published in part in Graves's *Lawrence and the Arabs*, pages 16–17, and then published in full by John Mack in *A Prince of Our Disorder*, page 63.
50 *The Home Letters of T. E. Lawrence and his Brothers*, page 8.
51 Ibid, page 26.
52 *T. E. Lawrence by his Friends*, page 49.
53 *Oxford High School Magazine*, March 1907. Also published in *The Young Lawrence of Arabia* by Paul J. Marriott.

2 **Oxford** (pp. 31–40)

1 *T. E. Lawrence by his Friends*, page 67.
2 *Portrait of T. E. Lawrence*, page 22.
3 Ibid.
4 *The Secret Lives of Lawrence of Arabia*, page 29.
5 Ibid.
6 *Portrait of T. E. Lawrence*, page 24.
7 'T. E. Lawrence' by Vyvyan Richards (*Great Lives*, No. 84), page 14.
8 Ibid.
9 Ibid.
10 *Sunday Times* papers now in the Imperial War Museum.
11 *T. E. Lawrence by his Friends*, page 62.
12 Ibid, page 63.
13 Ibid, page 64.
14 *The Young Lawrence of Arabia*, page 54.
15 John Mack's interview with W.O. Ault, 22 September 1972. Excerpt published in *A Prince of Our Disorder*, page 62.
16 *T. E. Lawrence by his Friends*, page 65.
17 *The Secret Lives of Lawrence of Arabia*, page 20. From a letter to Charlotte Shaw.
18 *T. E. Lawrence by his Friends*, page 384.

19 John Mack's interview with Janet Laurie Hallsmith. Excerpts published in *A Prince of Our Disorder*, pages 64–5.
20 Letter to Charlotte Shaw, 14 April 1927. British Museum, additional manuscript 45903.
21 *Lawrence to his biographer Liddell Hart*, page 82.
22 *The Home Letters of T. E. Lawrence and his Brothers*, page 107.
23 Ibid, page 99.
24 *T. E. Lawrence by his Friends*, page 77.
25 *T. E. Lawrence in Arabia and After*, page 21.
26 *Lawrence and the Arabs*, page 19.
27 *The Home Letters of T. E. Lawrence and his Brothers*, page 108.
28 *The Letters of T. E. Lawrence*, page 81.
29 *The Wounded Spirit*, page 55.
30 *T. E. Lawrence by his Friends*, page 35.
31 *The Home Letters of T. E. Lawrence and his Brothers*, page 604.
32 Ibid, page 401.

3 **Carchemish** (pp. 41–55)

1 *Carchemish: Report on the Excavations at Djerabis, Volume I 1914*.
2 *The Letters of T. E. Lawrence*, page 91.
3 *The Home Letters of T. E. Lawrence and his Brothers*, page 123.
4 Ibid., page 129.
5 Reference lost. Possibly Home Letters?
6 *Accidents of an Antiquary's Life* by D. G. Hogarth, Macmillan and Co Ltd, London 1910.
7 *T. E. Lawrence by his Friends*, page 81.
8 Accounts files of the British Museum relating to Carchemish.
9 *The Letters of Gertrude Bell*, page 152.
10 *The Home Letters of T. E. Lawrence and his Brothers*, page 175.
11 Accounts files of the British Museum.
12 Ibid.
13 Letter by R. D. Barnett, Keeper of Western Antiquities at the British Museum, to *The Times Literary Supplement* commenting on *The Secret Lives of Lawrence of Arabia* by Knightley and Simpson.
14 *Dead Towns and Living Men*, page 156.
15 Restricted Bodleian Collection. Letter to Leeds, April 1912. Published in *A Prince of Our Disorder*, page 81. Manuscript No. d57.
16 Accounts files of the British Museum.
17 *The Home Letters of T. E. Lawrence and his Brothers*, page 197. 20 March 1912.
18 *T. E. Lawrence by his Friends*, page 92.
19 Ibid, page 89.
20 Ibid.
21 Ibid.
22 Ibid, page 92.
23 Ibid.
24 Ibid, page 92.
25 Ibid, page 93.
26 Ibid, page 91.
27 *National Geographical Magazine*, November 1919, 'The Land Link of History's Chain' by Maynard Owen Williams, page 437.
28 Prologue by Luther R. Fowle in *Asia Magazine* to article by Lowell Thomas, April 1920, page 257.

29 *T. E. Lawrence by his Friends*, page 91.
30 Restricted Bodleian Collection, Manuscript No. d57, end of February 1913. Published by Mack, page 103.
31 *The Independent Arab*, page 16.
32 Undated letter in the Ashmolean, Oxford, partially published by Knightley and Simpson in *The Secret Lives of Lawrence of Arabia*, page 39.
33 Restricted Bodleian Collection, C 13. Letter to his family, 22 February 1913.
34 Anon.
35 *The Home Letters of T. E. Lawrence and his Brothers*, page 442.
36 *The Independent Arab* by Major Sir Hubert Young.
37 Ibid, page 19.
38 Ibid, page 19.
39 Ibid, page 20.
40 Ibid.
41 *My Diaries* by W. Blunt. 1932 single-volume edition, page 547.
42 *The Home Letters of T. E. Lawrence and his Brothers*, page 280.
43 *T. E. Lawrence by his Friends*, page 105.
44 Restricted Bodleian Collection. Letter to Leeds, 24 January 1914. Published in Mack.
45 *A Prince of Our Disorder*, page 105.
46 Ibid.
47 British Museum Accounts files relating to Carchemish.
48 *The Home Letters of T. E. Lawrence and his Brothers*, page 295.
49 *As I Seem to Remember* by Leonard Woolley. Allen and Unwin, London 1962, pages 88–91.
50 *The Letters of T. E. Lawrence*, page 170.
51 Typescript of *T. E. Lawrence in Arabia and After*.
52 Anon.

4 **The War Begins** (pp. 56–68)

1 *T. E. Lawrence by his Friends*, page 225.
2 Letter from Lawrence to John Buchan, 20 June 1927. Restricted Bodleian Collection, manuscript No. B55.
3 *T. E. Lawrence to his biographer Liddell Hart*, page 90.
4 Ibid.
5 Ibid, page 194.
6 For example, *T. E. Lawrence in Arabia and After*, pages 95–6.
7 *The Letters of T. E. Lawrence*, page 185.
8 Ibid, pages 185–6.
9 Ibid, page 186.
10 Ibid, pages 187–8.
11 PRO FO 371/4183, page 240 or 596.
12 PRO FO 882/13, page 222, telegram No. 303, 31 October 1914.
13 PRO FO 882/13, unnumbered page between 222 and 223.
14 PRO FO 882/13, page 223.
15 *The Letters of T. E. Lawrence*, page 189.
16 Ibid, page 190.
17 Ibid, page 192.
18 Ibid, page 193.
19 Ibid, pages 193–4.
20 *T. E. Lawrence to his biographer Liddell Hart*, page 17.
21 *The Letters of T. E. Lawrence*, pages 195–6.

22 PRO FO 882/12, page 6.
23 Restricted Bodleian Collection. Quote by John Mack, *A Prince of Our Disorder*, page 136.
24 King's College, London. Typescript of BBC broadcast, 14 July 1941.
25 *Orientations*, page 219.
26 *T. E. Lawrence by his Friends*, page 142.
27 Ibid, page 134.
28 Ibid, page 133.
29 Ibid, pages 131–44.
30 *Documenti per la Storia della Pace Orientale 1915–1932* by Amedia Giannini, translated here by Edward Robinson.
31 *Sunday Times* papers now in the Imperial War Museum.
32 *Francis Yeats-Brown* by Evelyn Wrench, pages 52–3.
33 *The Letters of T. E. Lawrence*, page 198.
34 Ibid, page 200. The letter Garnett refers to is in the restricted Bodleian Collection, Lawrence to Leeds, 16 November 1915.

5 **Cairo and Kut** (pp. 69–78)

1 *Orientations*, page 179.
2 PRO FO 371/2771, pages 151–6 (See also *The Conquest of Syria: if complete* PRO FO/882/16).
3 Ibid.
4 Introduction to *The Seven Pillars of Wisdom*, page 24.
5 PRO FO 141/461/1198, page 189 (Translation).
6 'Al Colonel Lawrence' al-Muqtataf, March 1931. First quoted in John Mack's *A Prince of Our Disorder*, pages 131–2.
7 PRO FO 882/2, page 46.
8 PRO FO 371/2771, page 336.
9 PRO FO 371/2771, page 340.
10 PRO FO 371/2771, page 358.
11 PRO FO 371/2771, page 370 and PRO 141/461/1198.
12 Private Collection.
13 PRO FO.
14 PRO FO 882/13.
15 Quoted from *Lawrence the Rebel*, page 29.
16 *T. E. Lawrence by his Friends*, page 123.
17 Despatch to 'Foreign, Simla (India)', Houghton Library, Harvard. Published by John Mack in *A Prince of Our Disorder*.
18 PRO FO 882/15.
19 PRO FO 882/15, page 19 and FO 141/461/1198, page 247.

6 **Intelligence Analyst** (pp. 79–86)

1 *Orientations*, page 180.
2 *Arab Bulletin*, 9 July 1916.
3 Ibid.
4 Ibid.
5 PRO FO.
6 PRO FO 371/2771, page 412.
7 *The Home Letters of T. E. Lawrence and his Brothers*, page 327.
8 *The Seven Pillars of Wisdom* (Penguin) Chapter 7, page 62.

9 *Orientations*, page 199.
10 *The Seven Pillars of Wisdom*, page 64.
11 *Orientations*, page 200.
12 Ibid, page 201.
13 Ibid, page 203.
14 Ibid, page 221.
15 Ibid, page 221.
16 Ibid.
17 *The Seven Pillars of Wisdom*, Chapter 12, page 92.
18 *Arab Bulletin*, 26 November 1916.
19 *The Seven Pillars of Wisdom*, page 92.
20 PRO FO.
21 Wingate papers, Sudan Archive, School of Oriental Studies, Durham University. Wingate to Colonel C. E. Wilson, 23 November 1916.
22 PRO FO.
23 *The Seven Pillars of Wisdom*, page 114.
24 Ibid, page 64.
25 Ibid, page 116.
26 *Orientations*, page 199.

7 **Field Officer** (pp. 87–99)

1 *T. E. Lawrence by his Friends*, page 139.
2 *The Seven Pillars of Wisdom*, page 21.
3 Ibid, page 118.
4 *T. E. Lawrence to his biographer Liddell Hart*.
5 *Arab Bulletin*, 26 December 1916.
6 *The Seven Pillars of Wisdom*, page 129.
7 *Independent Arab*.
8 *Arab Bulletin*, 6 February 1917.
9 Ibid.
10 *The Home Letters of T. E. Lawrence and his Brothers*, page 332.
11 Lawrence's report to Wilson, 8 January 1917.
12 *The Seven Pillars of Wisdom*, page 168.
13 Ibid, page 187.
14 Ibid.
15 *The Home Letters of T. E. Lawrence and his Brothers*, page 713.
16 Liddell Hart papers, King's College.
17 *T. E. Lawrence by his Friends*, page 157.
18 *The Seven Pillars of Wisdom*, page 193.
19 *Arab Bulletin*, 13 May 1917.

8 **An Irregular War** (pp. 100–108)

1 *Arab Bulletin*, 24 July 1917.
2 *The Seven Pillars of Wisdom*, page 234.
3 Ibid, page 233.
4 Ibid.
5 Wingate Papers.
6 *The Seven Pillars of Wisdom*, page 311.
7 Ibid, page 315.
8 Ibid, page 327.

9 Ibid, page 330.
10 Ibid.
11 PRO FO 882/12 page 262.
12 PRO FO.
13 *Arab Bulletin*, 20 August 1917.
14 *The Home Letters of T. E. Lawrence and his Brothers*, page 338.
15 *Steel Chariots in the Desert*, page 151.
16 Ibid, page 155.
17 *T. E. Lawrence by his Friends*, page 167.

9 The Strain Shows (pp. 109–113)

1 *The Home Letters of T. E. Lawrence and his Brothers*, page 340.
2 Ibid, page 341.
3 Lawrence to Leeds. Restricted Bodleian collection. 24 September 1917.
4 Hogarth papers, St. Antony's College, Oxford.
5 Ibid.
6 Humanities Research Center, Texas, USA.
7 *The Seven Pillars of Wisdom*, Chapter LXXX.
8 *Middle East Diary 1917–56*, page 32.
9 British Museum, additional manuscript 45903, first published by John Mack.
10 *T. E. Lawrence to his biographer Liddell Hart*, page 154.
11 *'Oxford' Seven Pillars of Wisdom*, Bodleian Library, Oxford.
12 Draft copy of contract among *Sunday Times* papers, Imperial War Museum.

10 Convention (pp. 114–120)

1 *T. E. Lawrence* by Jean Berand Villars, page 174.
2 *The Home Letters of T. E. Lawrence and his Brothers*, page 345.
3 PRO FO 882/7.
4 *Middle East Diary 1917–56*, pages 28–9.
5 Ibid, page 30.
6 Hogarth papers, St Antony's College, Oxford.
7 *The Seven Pillars of Wisdom*, Chapter LXXXVI.
8 *The Home Letters of T. E. Lawrence and his Brothers*, page 348.
9 *The Seven Pillars of Wisdom*, page 492.
10 Ibid, page 538.
11 *The Independent Arab*, pages 141–2.
12 Ibid, page 155.
13 Ibid, page 157.
14 Ibid, page 198.
15 Ibid, page 157.

11 The Battle for Damascus (pp. 121–128)

1 *The Arab Awakening* by Antonious, pages 433–4.
2 *T. E. Lawrence to his biographer Liddell Hart*, page 25.
3 PRO FO 882/13, p. 121.
4 Ibid.
5 *An Awakening* by Alex Kirkbride, page 72.
6 *Arab Bulletin*, 22 October 1918.

7 *The Seven Pillars of Wisdom*, pages 652–654.
8 *All in a Lifetime*, page 136.
9 *L'Echo*, 24 September 1918.
10 *The Advance of the Egyptian Expeditionary Force*, entry for 26/27 September 1918.
11 *An Awakening*, page 83, by Kirkbride.
12 Ibid, page 91.
13 *Crackle of Thorns* by Kirkbride, page 9.
14 *The Secret Lives of Lawrence of Arabia*, page 89.
15 *The Seven Pillars of Wisdom*, page 677.
16 *The Secret Lives of Lawrence of Arabia*, page 96.
17 Ibid.
18 Ibid.
19 *The Seven Pillars of Wisdom*, page 683.

12 **In Support of Feisal** (pp. 129–136)

1 *T. E. Lawrence to his biographer Liddell Hart*, page 165.
2 PRO FO 882/13, page 312.
3 *Sunday Times* papers now in the Imperial War Museum.
4 *T. E. Lawrence* by J. B. Villars, page 262.
5 PRO FO 882/13, page 164.
6 PRO FO 882/13, page 167.
7 *T. E. Lawrence* by J. B. Villars, page 255.
8 Ibid, page 256.
9 PRO CAB 27/37.
10 PRO CAB 37/34.
11 *Le Hedjaz dans la Guerre Mondiale* by S. Brémond, pages 310–17.
12 *The Letters of T. E. Lawrence*, page 271.
13 *La Hedjaz dans la Guerre Mondiale* by S. Brémond, pages 310–17.
14 *The Secret Lives of Lawrence of Arabia*, pages 168–19.
15 PRO FO.
16 *The Letters of T. E. Lawrence*, page 272.
17 Ibid.

13 **The Peace Conference** (pp 137–145)

1 *Letters of T. E. Lawrence*, page 739. Note also page 791 where Lawrence appears to have forgotten he had ever made the remark about Foch.
2 *At the Peace Conference* by James T. Shotwell (published diary) – entry for 20 Jan 1919. Also quoted by John Mack in *A Prince of Our Disorder*, page 265.
3 *T. E. Lawrence by his Friends*, page 193.
4 *Sunday Times* papers now in the Imperial War Museum.
5 *The Letters of Gertrude Bell*, page 381.
6 *The Letters of T. E. Lawrence*, page 275.
7 Translation in author's collection.
8 *Middle East Diary*, pages 30–31.
9 *The Letters of T. E. Lawrence*, pages 276–277.
10 *A Prince of our Disorder*, pages 270–71.
11 *Forty Years in the Wilderness* by H. St. John Philby, page 88.
12 *Lawrence of Arabia – A Biographical Enquiry*, page 274.
13 *Acquaintances* by A. Toynbee, page 184.
14 *T. E. Lawrence by his Friends*, page 147.

15 Ibid, page 148.
16 *Middle East Diary*, pages 31–3.

Interlude (pp. 149–158)

1 *Good Evening Everybody*, page 86.
2 Ibid, page 112.
3 *Lawrence of Arabia – A Biographical Enquiry*, page 280.
4 *T. E. Lawrence by his Friends*, page 200.
5 *Good Evening Everybody*, pages 122–3.
6 Ibid, page 131.
7 *T. E. Lawrence by his Friends*, page 208.
8 Source lost – probably *T. E. Lawrence to his biographer Liddell Hart*.
9 *Good Evening Everybody*, page 194.
10 Ibid, page 195.
11 Ibid, page 200.
12 *Daily Telegraph*, 15 August 1919.
13 *Good Evening Everybody*, page 201.
14 Ibid.
15 Ibid.
16 Programme of show, *Enthoven* Collection, Victoria and Albert Museum.
17 Ibid.
18 *The Sphere*, 23 August 1919.
19 *Lawrence and the Arabs* by Robert Graves, page 403.

14 **Politics and Literature** (pp. 161–168)

1 *The Times*, 11 September 1919.
2 PRO FO 371/4182.
3 Ibid.
4 FO memorandum 129405, 15 September 1919, quoted in *The Letters of T. E. Lawrence*, pages 288–91.
5 PRO FO 271/4183.
6 Ibid.
7 Ibid.
8 Ibid.
9 *The Letters of T. E. Lawrence*, page 296.
10 *T. E. Lawrence to his biographer Liddell Hart*, page 145.
11 *The Letters of T. E. Lawrence*, pages 298–9.
12 *T. E. Lawrence by his Friends*, page 249.
13 *The Letters of T. E. Lawrence*, page 360.
14 *T. E. Lawrence by his Friends*, page 249.
15 *Robert Graves – His Life and Work* by Martin Seymour-Smith, page 85.
16 An understanding of Masonic or Freemasonic vocabulary may provide important clues to decyphering the cryptic poem 'To S.A'. I have not wasted time speculating on the S.A. poem as I believe the quest is a futile one.

15 **Farewell to Politics** (pp. 169–189)

1 *Iraq* by Ernest Main, page 71.
2 *The Letters of T. E. Lawrence*, page 302.

3 *T. E. Lawrence to his biographer Liddell Hart*, page 112.
4 Californian private collection quoted by J. Mack in *A Prince of Our Disorder*, pages 287–8.
5 Ibid.
6 *Letters to T. E. Lawrence*, page 12.
7 Ibid.
8 Ibid.
9 *The Times*, 22 July 1920; Article, part 1, *The Times*, 7 August 1920; part 2, *The Times*, 11 August 1920.
10 *The Sunday Times*, 22 August 1920.
11 *The Observer*, 8 August 1920.
12 *The Times*, 22 July 1920.
13 Gertrude Bell's diary entry, 19 September 1920.
14 *Sunday Times* papers now in the Imperial War Museum.
15 *T. E. Lawrence by his Friends*, page 263.
16 Ibid, page 230.
17 *The Letters of T. E. Lawrence*, page 325.
18 *The Home Letters of T. E. Lawrence and his Brothers*, page 352.
19 *T. E. Lawrence by his Friends*, page 233.
20 PRO FO 686/85.
21 *Assignment Churchill* by W. Thompson, page 31.
22 *Sunday Times* papers now in the Imperial War Museum.
23 *The Times*, 29 July.
24 ?
25 PRO FO 686/93.
26 Ibid.
27 Ibid.
28 Ibid.
29 Ibid.
30 *The Letters of T. E. Lawrence*, page 334.
31 Colonel Lawrence's report of Trans-Jordan, 24 October 1921. Imperial War Museum.
32 *Forty Years in the Wilderness*, by Harry St J. Philby, page 108.

16 Aircraftman Ross and Trooper Shaw (pp. 182–192)

1 *T. E. Lawrence to his biographer Robert Graves*, page 23.
2 Imperial War Museum.
3 *The Mint*, Part I, Chapter I.
4 Ibid.
5 *The Secret Lives of Lawrence of Arabia*, page 180; interview with the *Sunday Times*.
6 Postscript to *Lawrence of Arabia – A Biographical Enquiry*.
7 Ibid.
8 Ibid.
9 *The Mint*, Part II, Chapter 1.
10 *The Mint*, Part II, Chapter 2.
11 *The Mint*, Part I, Chapter 19.
12 Letter from W. B. Tawse to *Evening Standard*, 2 March 1973.
13 *The Letters of T. E. Lawrence*, pages 355–6.
14 Sworn statement by John Bruce, *Sunday Times* papers now in the Imperial War Museum.
15 Ibid.
16 *The Letters of T. E. Lawrence*, page 409.

17 Hogarth to George Bernard Shaw, quoted in Weintraub, pages 60–1, and in *The Letters of T. E. Lawrence*, pages 351–2.
18 George Bernard Shaw to Stanley Baldwin, 31 May 1923, quoted in Weintraub, page 61 and *The Letters of T. E. Lawrence*, page 446.
19 *T. E. Lawrence by his Friends*, page 244.
20 Statement by John Bruce to *The Sunday Times* now in the Imperial War Museum.
21 *A Prince of Our Disorder*, page 433.
22 Author's interviews with Phillip Knightley, 14 February 1985.
23 *The Letters of T. E. Lawrence*, page 439.
24 Ibid.
25 T. E. Lawrence to Golden Cockerel Press, Californian private collection quoted by Mack, page 349. (Letter dated 25 December 1923.)
26 Cited in *The Letters of T. E. Lawrence*, page 458, and quoted in *Solitary in the Ranks* by Montgomery Hyde, page 99.
27 George Bernard Shaw to Lawrence, 7 October 1924, quoted by John Mack, page 352, based on copy provided by Jeremy Wilson.
28 Clipping in Humanities Research Center.
29 George Bernard Shaw to Garnett, 18 June 1925. Quoted in *Private Shaw and Public Shaw* by Weintraub, page 96. Humanities Research Center, Austin, Texas.

17 Life on the North-West Frontier (pp. 193–206)

1 *Solitary in the Ranks* by H. Montgomery Hyde, page 111.
2 *The Mint*, Part III, Chapter 16.
3 Lawrence to Charlotte Shaw, 28 September 1925, British Museum Additional Manuscript No. 45903, quoted on page 357 in Mack.
4 Lawrence to T. B. Marson, 26 October 1926. Restricted Bodleian Collection, quoted by Montgomery Hyde in *Solitary in the Ranks*, page 131.
5 Lawrence to Pat Knowles, 30 November 1926. Mrs Joyce Knowles Collection.
6 *The Letters of T. E. Lawrence*, page 505.
7 Ibid, page 502.
8 Ibid.
9 Ibid.
10 *The Letters of T. E. Lawrence*, page 505.
11 *T. E. Lawrence by his Friends*, page 412.
12 *The Letters of T. E. Lawrence*, page 615.
13 *T. E. Lawrence by his Friends*, page 413.
14 *The Letters of T. E. Lawrence*, pages 572–4.
15 Ibid, page 614.
16 Ibid, page 615.
17 GBS to TEL, 23 June 1928, quoted on page 157 in *Private Shaw and Public Shaw*.
18 *The Letters of T. E. Lawrence*, page 618.
19 Ibid.
20 Ibid, page 616.
21 *Letters to T. E. Lawrence*, pages 202–5. Trenchard to T.E.L., 5 August 1928.
22 Trenchard papers.
23 T.E.L. to Charlotte Shaw, British Museum Additional Manuscript No. 45904. 15 August 1928.
24 Undated clipping from *New York Sun* 1928.
25 *New York World*, 27 September 1928.
26 *New York Herald Tribune*, 1 October 1928.
27 *Daily News* and *Westminster Gazette*, 5 December 1928.
28 *Empire News*, 16 December 1928.

29 National Archives of India, New Delhi.
30 *Sunday Times* papers now in the Imperial War Museum.
31 *Daily Herald*, 5 January 1929.
32 Copies of Foreign Office documents, *Sunday Times* papers now in the Imperial War Museum.
33 *New York Times*, 11 December 1928.
34 *Sunday Times* papers now in the Imperial War Museum.
35 *Hansard*, 29 January 1928.
36 *Sunday Times* papers now in the Imperial War Museum.
37 *The Golden Reign*, pages 23 and 26.
38 Ibid, page 26.
39 Ibid, page 28.
40 *Sunday Pictorial* (forerunner of *Sunday Mirror*) 3 February 1929.
41 *New York Times*, 7 February 1929.
42 *Daily News*, 4 February 1929.

18 **The Last Years** (pp. 207–215)

1 *Solitary in the Ranks*, page 199.
2 *Sunday Times* papers now in the Imperial War Museum.
3 *The Letters of T. E. Lawrence*, page 707.
4 Ibid, page 615.
5 Ibid, page 859.
6 Ibid, page 858.
7 *Sunday Times* papers now in the Imperial War Museum.
8 *The Letters of T. E. Lawrence*, page 859.
9 Author's interview with Pat Knowles, spring 1981.
10 *The Letters of T. E. Lawrence*, page 862.
11 Ibid, page 864.
12 *The Letters of T. E. Lawrence*, page 866.
13 *Horsewoman*, page 51.
14 *The Letters of T. E. Lawrence*, page 871.
15 Ibid, page 872.
16 *Genius of Friendship* by Henry Williamson.
17 *T. E. Lawrence to his biographer Liddell Hart*, page 222.
18 *Private Shaw and Public Shaw*, page 254.
19 Author's interview with Walt Pitman, spring 1981.
20 *Genius of Friendship*,
21 *Dorset Daily Echo*
22 *Daily Express*, 14 May 1935.
23 *Daily Sketch*, 15 May 1935.
24 *Daily Mirror*, 15 May 1935.

19 **The Legend Persists** (pp 216–223)

1 *Dorset Daily Echo*.
2 Ibid.
3 Stephen Winsten, *Shaw's Corner*, page 82.
4 *The Letters of T. E. Lawrence*, page 832.
5 *Orientations*, page 531.

Aftermath (pp. 227–235)

1 *Jonathan Cape, Publisher*, page 154.
2 Ibid, page 213.
3 Publisher's slip contained in Cape's limited 'deluxe' edition of *The Mint*.
4 *Lawrence* by Edward Robinson, Oxford 1935. A. W. Lawrence's 'introductory note' dated 'July 1935'.
5 *Lawrence the Rebel*, page 3.
6 Author's collection.
7 From an article by Phillip Knightley in *Texas Quarterly*, Winter 1973, Vol. XVI, No. 4.
8 Ibid.
9 *Charmed Lives* by M. Korda, page 340 (paperback).
10 *Evening Standard*.
11 *Snakes and Ladders*, page 208 (paperback).
12 *Robert Graves* by Martin Seymour-Smith, page 496.
13 *Sunday Times* papers now in the Imperial War Museum.

Bibliography

1 I have not included in the bibliography the many hundreds of newspaper articles which I have waded through. The most important of them are mentioned in the text or notes.

2 I would draw readers' attention to the following sources:

School of Oriental Studies, Durham University. Wingate papers
King's College Library, London. Liddell Hart papers and Colonel Joyce's papers
The Public Records Office, London
The Imperial War Museum, London. (Department of Photographs, Department of Film and Library)
The British Museum, London. Accounts Archives (Carchemish) Department of Western Manuscripts (T.E.L's correspondence with Charlotte Shaw)
St. Anthony's College, Oxford. Hogarth material.
The Bodleian Library, Oxford
The Humanities Research Center University of Texas in Austin
The private library of Edwards H. Metcalf, Monrovia, Cal. USA
British Library, Newspaper Division Colindale.
The Tank Museum, Bovington
The RAF Museum, Hendon
Academy of Motion Picture Arts and Sciences Los Angeles, Cal. USA
British Film Institute, London

ABDULLAH (King of Trans-Jordan): *Memoirs.* (Cape, 1950).
ADELSON, ROGER: *Mark Sykes. Portrait of an amateur* (Cape, 1975).
ALDINGTON, RICHARD: *Lawrence of Arabia—a biographical enquiry* (Collins, 1955, 1969)
—: *Portrait of a genius, but . . . The Life of D. H. Lawrence 1885–1930* (Heinemann, 1950)
ALTOUNYAN, E. U. R.: *Ornament of Honour* (Cambridge University Press, 1937).
—: *George Antonius* (Hamish Hamilton, 1938).
ARMITAGE, FLORA: *The Desert and the Stars* (Faber, 1956).
AYOOB, MOHAMMED: *The Middle East in World Politics* (Croom Helm, 1981).

BARKER, RALPH: *The Schneider Trophy Races* (Airlife Publishing 1981)
BELL, LADY: *The Letters of Gertrude Bell* (Benn, 1947, 12th printing).
BENNETT, ALAN R.: *Horsewoman – The Extraordinary Mrs. D.* (Dorset Publishing Company, 1979).
BENOIST-MÉCHIN: *Lawrence d'Arabia ou le rêve fracassé* (Clairefontaine, Lausanne, 1961).
BLUMENFELD, R. D.: *All in a Lifetime* (Benn, 1931).
BLUNT, LADY ANNE: *The Bedouin Tribes of the Euphrates* (Best Publishing Co., Colorado, 1960).

BOGARDE, DIRK: *Snakes and Ladders* (Triad/Granada 1982, paperback).
BOULANGER, ROBERT: *The Middle East – Lebanon, Syria, Jordan, Iraq, Iran* (Hachette, Paris, 1966)
BRÉMOND, EDOUARD: *Le Hedjaz dans la Guerre Mondiale* (Payot, Paris, 1931)
BRENT, PETER: *T. E. Lawrence* (Book Club Associates London, 1975).
BROUGHTON, HARRY: *Lawrence of Arabia. The Facts without the Fiction* (Author's edition, 1972)
BROWN, OLIVER: *Exhibition* (memoirs) (London, Evelyn, Adams & Mackay, 1968).
BROWNLOW, KEVIN: *The War, the West and the Wilderness* (London, Hodder & Stoughton 1944).
BUCHAN, JOHN: *Memory hold-the-door* (Hodder & Stoughton, 1944).
—: *Greenmantle* (Penguin, 1981).
—: *A Prince of the Captivity* (Hamlyn Paperbacks, 1981).
BUCHAN, WILLIAM: *John Buchan – a memoir* (Buchan and Enright, 1982).
BURBIDGE, W. F.: *The Mysterious A.C.2: A Biographical Sketch of Lawrence of Arabia* (John Crowther).
BURGOYNE, ELIZABETH: *Gertrude Bell – from her personal papers*. (2 Vols. 1889–1914 and 1914–1926) (Benn, 1961).
BURTON, ANTHONY: *Revolutionary Violence* (Leo Cooper, 1977).
BUSCH, BRITON COOPER: *Britain, India and the Arabs* (University of California Press, 1971).

CHANT, ROY HEMAN: *The Motor Cycle that killed Lawrence of Arabia* (Dorset and West Magazine, March 1981).
CLAYTON, SIR GILBERT: *An Arabian Diary* (University of California Press, 1969).
CLEMENTS, FRANK: *T. E. Lawrence – a reader's guide* (David and Charles, 1972).
LE CORBEAU, ADRIEN: *The Forest Giant*. Translated by J. H. Ross (T. E. Lawrence) (Cape, 1924).
CURTIS, LIONEL: *Civitas Dei* (Macmillan, 1934).

DARLOW, MICHAEL, and HODSON, GILLIAN: *Terence Rattigan – the man and his work* (Quartet Books, 1979).
DINNING, HECTOR: *Nile to Aleppo* (Allen and Unwin, 1920).
DOUGHTY, C. M.: *Arabia Deserta* (Vol 1 and 2) and introduction by T. E. Lawrence (Cape, 1936).
DUNBAR, JANET: *Mrs G.B.S. A Portrait* (Harper and Row; Harrap, 1963).
DUVAL, ELIZABETH W.: *T. E. Lawrence – a bibliography* (Haskell, 1972).

EDEN, MATTHEW: *The Murder of Lawrence of Arabia* (New English Library, 1980).
EDMONDS, CHARLES: *T. E. Lawrence* (Peter Davies, 1935).
EL-EDROOS, BRIGADIER S. A.: *The Hashemite Arab Army 1908–1979* (The Publishing Committee, Amman, 1980).
ENGLE, ANITA: *The Nili Spies* (Hogarth Press, 1959).

FEDDEN, ROBIN: *Crusader Castles* (Art and Technics, 1950).
—: *Syria* (Hale, 1956).
FIELDS, MATHILDE: *Lawrence de Arabia* (Siglo XX, Editorial Tesoro, Madrid)
FITZHERBERT, MARGARET: *The Man who was Greenmantle: A biography of Aubrey Herbert* (John Murray, 1983).
FLECKER, HELLÉ: *Some letters from Abroad by James Elroy Flecker* (Heinemann, 1930).
FLETCHER, C. R. L.: *D. G. Hogarth* (*Geographical Journal*, Vol. 71 page 321)

GARNETT, DAVID: *The Letters of T. E. Lawrence* (Cape, 1938): ed. cited here.
—: *Selected Letters of T. E. Lawrence* (The Reprint Society, 1941).
—: *The Essential T. E. Lawrence* (Cape, 1951).
—: *The Familiar Faces* (Chatto, 1962).
—: *Great Friends* (Macmillan, 1979).
GARNETT, RICHARD: *Twilight of the Gods*, introduction by T. E. Lawrence (Bodley Head, 1924).
GAWSWORTHY, JOHN ("G"): *Annotations on some minor writings of "T. E. Lawrence"*. (Eric Partridge, 1935).
GERMAN-REED, T.: *Bibliographical Notes on T. E. Lawrence's 'Seven Pillars of Wisdom'* and *'Revolt in the Desert'* (W & G Foyle, 1928).
GLEN, DOUGLAS: *In the Steps of Lawrence of Arabia* (Rich and Cowan, 1939).
GLUBB, J. B.: *Britain and the Arabs* (Hodder and Stoughton, 1959).
GRAFFTEY-SMITH, LAURENCE: *Bright Levant* (John Murray, 1970).
GRAHAM, COLIN: *The Crash which killed Lawrence of Arabia* (Dorset – the county magazine, Summer 1968).
GRAVES, RICHARD PERCEVAL: *Lawrence of Arabia and his world* (Thames and Hudson, 1976).
GRAVES, ROBERT: *Lawrence and the Arabs* (London, Cape, 1927).
—: *Good-bye to all that* (Cape, 1929).
—: *T. E. Lawrence to his biographer* (Faber, 1938).

HALDANE, LT-GENERAL SIR AYLMER: *The Insurrection in Mesopotamia 1920* (Blackwood, 1922).
HART, LIDDELL B. H.: *T. E. Lawrence, Aldington and the Truth* (Reprinted from the London Magazine, April 1955).
—: *'T. E. Lawrence' in Arabia and After* (Cape, 1934).
—: *History of the First World War* (Pan, 1979).
—: *The War in Outline* (Faber, 1936).
—: *T. E. Lawrence to his biographer* (Faber, 1938).
—: *Memoirs* (Vol I and II) (Cassell, 1965).
HERBERT, AUBREY: *Mons, Anzac and Kut* (Hutchinson).
HOGARTH, DAVID GEORGE: *The Penetration of Arabia – a record of the development of Western knowledge concerning the Arabian Peninsula* (Lawrence and Bullend, 1904).
—: *Accidents of an Antiquary's Life* (Macmillan, 1910).
—: *The Life of Charles Doughty* (Oxford University Press, 1928).
HOURANI, ALBERT: *Middle East Affairs* (No. 4) (Oxford University Press, 1965).
HOWARD, MICHAEL S.: *Jonathan Cape, Publisher* (Cape, 1971).
HULL, E. M.: *The Sheik – a novel* (Eveleigh Nash and Grayson)
HYDE, H. MONTGOMERY: *Solitary in the Ranks: Lawrence of Arabia as Airman and Private Soldier* (Constable, 1977).

INGRAMS, HAROLD: *Arabia and the Isles* (John Murray, 1966).

JARCHÉ, JAMES: *People I have shot* (Methuen, 1934).

KEDOURIE, ELIE: *England and the Middle East. The Vital Years 1914–1921* (Bowes and Bowes, 1955).
—: *The Chatham House Version and other Middle-Eastern Studies* (Weidenfeld and Nicolson, 1970).
KIERNAN, R. H.: *Lawrence of Arabia* (Harrap, 1937).
KIRKBRIDE, SIR ALEC SEITH: *A Crackle of Thorns – Experiences in the Middle East* (John Murray, 1956).
—: *An Awakening: The Arab Campaign 1917–1918* (University Press of Arabia, 1971).

KNIGHTLEY, PHILLIP: *Aldington's Enquiry Concerning T. E. Lawrence* (Texas Quarterly, Winter 1973).

—: *Lawrence of Arabia* (Sidgwick and Jackson, 1976).

KNIGHTLEY, PHILLIP and SIMPSON, COLIN: *The Secret Lives of Lawrence of Arabia* (Nelson, 1969).

KORDA, MICHAEL: *Charmed Lives* (Penguin, 1980, paperback).

LARÈS, MAURICE: *T. E. Lawrence, la France et les Français* (Publications de la Sorbonne, Paris, 1980).

LAWRENCE, A. W. (Editor): *Letters to T. E. Lawrence* (Cape, 1962).

—: *T. E. Lawrence by his Friends* (Cape, 1937).

LAWRENCE, M. R. (Editor): *The Home Letters of T. E. Lawrence and his brothers.* (Oxford, Blackwell, 1954).

LAWRENCE, T. E.: *Catalogue of an exhibition of Paintings, Pastels, Drawings and Woodcuts – illustrating Col. T. E. Lawrence's book "Seven Pillars of Wisdom"* Preface written by G. B. Shaw (Ernest Brown and Philips, The Leicester Galleries. Feb 5–12, 1927).

—: *Carchemish: Report on the Excavations at Djerabis.* Vol I Co-writers L. Woolley, D. G. Hogarth and P. L. Guy (British Museum, 1914).

—: *Crusader Castles* Vol I: The Thesis, Vol II: The Letters. Foreword by A. W. Lawrence (The Golden Cockerel Press, 1936).

—: *The Diary of T. E. Lawrence* MCMXI (1921) (Corvinus Press, 1937).

—: *Essay on Flecker* (Doubleday Doran, New York, 1937).

—: *Evolution of a Revolt: Early post-war writings of T. E. Lawrence.* Edited by and with an introduction by Stanley and Rodelle Weintraub (Pennsylvania State University Press, 1968).

—: *Fifty Letters 1920–1935* (Humanities Research Center, 1962).

—: (as T. E. Shaw); *Letters from T. E. Shaw to Bruce Rogers* (Bruce Rogers, 1933).

—: *Men in Print*, introduction by A. W. Lawrence (The Golden Cockerel Press).

—: *Minorities* (edited by J. M. Wilson) (London, Jonathan Cape, 1971).

—: *The Mint* 352087 A/c Ross – with introductory note by A. W. Lawrence (London, Jonathan Cape, 1955)

—: *Mønten* (The Mint) (Det Schønbergske Forlag, Copenhagan, 1956).

—: (T. E. Shaw) *More Letters from T. E. Shaw to Bruce Roger* (Bruce Rogers, 1936).

—: *The Odyssey of Homer* (Translated by T. E. Shaw) (Oxford University Press, 1935).

—: *Oriental Assembly* – edited by A. W. Lawrence. (Williams and Norgate, 1939).

LAWRENCE, T. E. (With Leonard Woolley): *Palestine Exploration Fund 1914 The Wilderness of Zin* (Archaeological Report) (Offices of the Palestine Exploration Fund; Annual 1914–1915 Double Vol.).

LAWRENCE, T. E.: *Revolt in the Desert* (Cape, 1927; Limited Edition No. 212).

—: (article) *The Royal Engineers Journal.* Vol XXIX. No. 1 January 1919 (Pages 6–10. DEMOLITIONS UNDER FIRE). (W. & J. Mackay, 1919).

—: *Secret Despatches from Arabia* Foreword by A. W. Lawrence (The Golden Cockerel Press).

—: (T. E. Shaw) *Shaw-Ede Letters: T. E. Lawrence's letters to H. S. Ede* (The Golden Cockerel Press, 1942).

—: *Seven Pillars of Wisdom*, (T. E. Lawrence, 1922). 'Oxford Edition' (One copy kept in the Bodleian Library, Oxford).

—: *Seven Pillars of Wisdom*, Subscriber's Copy (T. E. Lawrence, 1926).

—: *The Seven Pillars of Wisdom – a triumph* (Privately printed 1926 'complete and unabridged') (London, Cape, 1935 (published for general circulation).

—: *Les Sept Piliers de la Sagesse – un triomphe* – translated by Charles Mauron (Payot, Paris, 1949).

—: *Seven Pillars of Wisdom* (this edition referred to in the text) (Penguin (paperback), 1983).
LESLIE, SHANE: *Mark Sykes: His Life and Letters*. Introduction by the Rt Hon Winston Churchill (Cassell, 1923).
LORD, JOHN: *Duty, Honor, Empire: The Life and Times of Colonel Richard Meinertzhagen* (Random House, New York, 1970).
LYTTON, EARL OF: *Wilfrid Scawen Blunt: A Memoir by his Grandson*. (Macdonald, 1961).

MACK, JOHN E.: *A Prince of Our Disorder: The Life of T. E. Lawrence* (Weidenfeld and Nicolson, 1976).
MACPHAIL, SIR ANDREW: *Three Persons* (John Murray, 1929).
MAIN, ERNEST: *Iraq from Mandate to Independence* (Allen and Unwin, 1935).
MARRIOTT, PAUL J.: *The Young Lawrence of Arabia 1888–1910* (Author's edition).
MAY, ANNABELLE and ROWAN, KATHRYN: *Inside Information: British Government and the Media* (Constable, 1982).
MEINERTZHAGEN, R.: *Middle East Diary 1917–1956* (The Cresset Press, 1959).
MEYERS, JEFFREY: *The Wounded Spirit* (Martin Brian & O'Keeffe, 1973).
MEYNELL, VIOLA: *Friends of a Lifetime* (Cape, 1940).
—: *The Best of Friends* (Hart-Davies, 1956).
MILLAR, RONALD: *KUT the death of an Army* (Secker and Warburg, 1969).
MONROE, ELIZABETH: *Britain's Moment in the Middle East 1914–1971* (Chatto, 1981).
MOUSA, SULEIMAN: *T. E. Lawrence – an Arab View* (Oxford University Press, 1966).
MUGGERIDGE, MALCOLM: *Royal Soap Opera* (*Statesman and Nation*, 22.10.1955).

NATIONAL TRUST: *Clouds Hill* (The Curwen Press for the National Trust, 1980).
—: *Clouds Hill* (County Life Ltd for the National Trust, 1946).
NUTTING, ANTHONY: *Lawrence of Arabia. The Man – and the Motive* (Hollis and Carter, 1961).

OCAMPO, VICTORIA: *338171, T. E. Lawrence of Arabia* with introduction by A. W. Lawrence (Gollancz, 1963).
O'DONNELL, THOMAS J.: *The Confessions of T. E. Lawrence* (Ohio University Press, 1979).

PHILBY, H. ST. JOHN: *Arabian Days* (London, Robert Hale, 1957).
—: *Forty Years in the Wilderness* (London, Robert Hale, 1957).
PIRIE-GORDON, H.: *The Advance of the Egyptian Expeditionary Force* (July 1917–Oct 1918) (Government Press & Survey of Egypt, 1919).
POUND, REGINALD and HARMSWORTH, G.: *Northcliffe* (Cassell, 1959).

RATTIGAN, TERENCE: *Ross* (Hamish Hamilton, 1960).
RICHARDS, VYVYAN: *Portrait of T. E. Lawrence* (London, Jonathan Cape, 1936).
—: *T. E. Lawrence* (Great Lives) (London, Duckworth, 1954).
ROBINSON, EDWARD: *Lawrence the Rebel* (Lincoln-Prager Ltd, 1946).
—: *Lawrence – the story of his life* (with an introductory note by A. W. Lawrence) (Oxford University Press, 1935).
ROLLS, S. C.: *Steel Chariots in the Desert* (Cape, 1937).
ROTHENSTEIN, WILLIAM, (contributor to): *Twenty Four Portraits* (Edward Arnold, 1925).

SEYMOUR-SMITH, MARTIN: *Robert Graves – his life and work* (Hutchinson, 1982).
SHAW, GEORGE BERNARD: *Plays* and *Prefaces* (2 Vols) (Paul Hamlyn, 1965).

SHERWOOD, JANE: *Post-mortem Journal: Communications from T. E. Lawrence* (Neville Spearman, 1964).
SHOTWELL, JAMES T.: *At the Peace Conference* (Macmillan, 1937).
SLADE, GURNEY: *In Lawrence's bodyguard* (Frederick A. Stokes, 1930).
SMITH, CLARE SYDNEY: *The Golden Reign* (with a foreword by Mrs. S. Lawrence) (Cassell, 1940).
SMITH, JANET ADAM: *John Buchan* (Hart-Davis, 1965).
—: *John Buchan and his world* (Thames and Hudson, 1979).
SPERBER, MANES: *The Achilles Heel* (André Deutsch, 1959).
STEWART, DESMOND: *T. E. Lawrence* (Hamish Hamilton, 1977).
STORRS, RONALD: *Lawrence of Arabia, Zionism and Palestine* (Penguin, 1941).
—: *Orientations* (Ivor Nicholson & Watson, 1937).

TAYLOR, A. J. P.: *Beaverbrook* (Hamish Hamilton, 1972).
THOMAS, BERTRAM: *Arabia Felix: Across the 'Empty Quarter' of Arabia* (and introduction by Col. T. E. Lawrence) (Scribner, 1932).
THOMAS, JOHN: *The True Book About Lawrence of Arabia* (Muller, n. d.).
THOMAS, LOWELL: *Good Evening Everybody* (William Morrow, 1976).
—: *With Lawrence in Arabia* (Hutchinson, 1925).
THOMPSON, WALTER: *Assignment Churchill*
TOYNBEE, ARNOLD: *Acquaintances* (London, Oxford University Press, 1967).

VILLARS, JEAN BERAUD: *T. E. Lawrence or The Search for the Absolute* (originally published in French as *Le Colonel Lawrence ou le Recherche de l'Absolu* – 1955) (Sidgwick and Jackson, 1958).

WAPSHOTT, NICHOLAS: *Peter O'Toole* (New English Library, 1983).
WAVELL, COLONEL A. P.: *The Palestinian Campaigns* (Constable, 1928).
WEBER, FRANK G.: *Eagles on the Crescent: Germany, Austria and the Diplomacy of the Turkish Alliance, 1914–1918* (Cornell University Press, 1970).
WEINTRAUB, STANLEY: *Private Shaw and Public Shaw* (George Brasiller, 1963).
WEINTRAUB, STANLEY and RODELLE: *Evolution of a Revolt* – see under T. E. Lawrence.
WEST, NIGEL: *MI6 British Secret Intelligence Service Operations 1909–1945* (Weidenfeld and Nicolson, 1983).
WILLIAMSON, HENRY: *Genius of Friendship: 'T. E. Lawrence'* (Faber, November 1941).
WILSON, J. M.: *T. E. Lawrence 'Lawrence of Arabia'*. Set of 6 slides with commentary by J. M. W. (The Ashmolean Museum, 1976).
—: *Minorities* see under T. E. Lawrence.
WINSTONE, H. V. F.: *Captain Shakespear* (Cape, 1976).
—: *Gertrude Bell* (Cape, 1978).
—: *The Illicit Adventure* (Cape, 1982).
WOOLLEY, C. LEONARD (Co-author of T.E.L.): *The Wilderness of Zin* see under T. E. Lawrence.
—: *Dead Towns and Living Men* (Re-issued in 'The Life and Letters Series' with 2 additional chapters in 1932) (Cape, 1932).
WRENCH, EVELYN: *Francis Yeats-Brown 1880–1944* (Eyre and Spottiswoode, 1948).

YARDLEY, MICHAEL: *Clouds Hill and the Lawrence Legend* (Dorset the county Magazine, issue no 96, 1981)
YEATS-BROWN, FRANCIS: *Caught by the Turks* (Edward Arnold, 1919).
—: *Bengal Lancer* (London, Victor Gollancz Ltd, 1930).
YOUNG, MAJOR SIR HUBERT: *The Independent Arab* (John Murray, 1933).

MISCELLANEOUS

Catalogue of Sale, Valuable Historical Manuscripts, (Feisal's Diary is one of the lots) (London, Sotheby's Book and Manuscript Department, March 1983).

David Garnett CBE, A Writer's Library, Catalogue of Sale (Michael Hosking Bookseller Deal. The Golden Hind, June 1983).

Letters from M. R. Lawrence (eldest brother of Lawrence of Arabia) to Stanhope Landick (a Jerseyman) (Pamphlet).

Operations of Indian Expeditionary Force 'D' 1914–1917 (General Headquarters I.E.F. 'D'. June 1917).

Military Handbook on Palestine. Third Provisional Edition, June 30, 1917 (Government Press, Cairo, 1917).

Short History of SAINT NICHOLAS CHURCH, MORETON (Henry King Ltd, The Dorset Press, n. d.).

Form of Service Used At The Unveiling of The Memorial To Thomas Edward Lawrence. Lawrence of Arabia (– held at St Paul's Cathedral) (Printers) R. E. Thomas and Newman Ltd).

Lawrence of Arabia (Presentation programme for the David Lean film) (Columbia Pictures Corp., 1962).

MAJOR BROADCASTS

T. E. LAWRENCE 1888–1935 (produced by Malcolm Brown):
BBC 27.11.62 (first transmission).

LAWRENCE OF ENGLAND

BBC WEST	Part I	12–1–79
	Part II	19–1–79

Index